The Ear of the Heart

Mother Dolores Hart, OSB
and
Richard DeNeut

The Ear of the Heart

*An Actress' Journey
from Hollywood to Holy Vows*

IGNATIUS PRESS   SAN FRANCISCO

Cover photos
Dolores Hart and Elvis Presley, NBC Universal, Digital Media Distribution Group
Dolores Hart at Her Consecration, Valerie Imbleau
Other cover photos from Dolores Hart Collection

Cover design by John Herreid

Paperback edition published 2018 by Ignatius Press, San Francisco
ISBN 978-1-62164-249-7
Library of Congress Control Number 2012933885
Printed in the United States of America ∞

For the continual renewal of religious life in the Church

—Mother Dolores Hart, OSB

Contents

Preface

What can be sweeter to us, dearest brethren, than this voice of our Lord inviting us? Behold, in his loving mercy the Lord showeth the way of life.

—Rule of Saint Benedict

The Rule of Saint Benedict, *composed in the year 530, is justly celebrated as an unerring guide for those seeking to dedicate their lives to God. The Rule is followed by the women in the Community of the Abbey of Regina Laudis in Bethlehem, Connecticut, which has been my home and my life for five decades.*

Regina Laudis was elevated to the status of an abbey in 1976, but when I entered in 1963, it was a small, enclosed monastery. There was a considerable fuss made in the press at the time of my entrance because I had enjoyed some success as an actress in the movies and on the New York stage. From time to time over the years, there were invitations to write a memoir, and I gave the undertaking some small consideration. I had ample material to draw upon—I had kept journals from an early age and was an entrenched saver of letters and articles concerning my life—and I had no problem seeing myself in the driver's seat.

On a Sunday morning in 1997, however, my life changed dramatically. When I awoke and put my feet on the floor, I was unable to walk. Subsequently and belatedly, I was diagnosed with peripheral sensory neuropathy, a neurological disease affecting the peripheral nerves and causing severe chronic pain. For the next several years I experienced a dark night of the soul, unable to find any real relief from the pain or any understanding of the cause of the disease. During this time my Community suggested again that I write the story of my life, which now seemed a total absurdity since I had no command of my arms, hands or feet and my mind was blistered with pain and anger. It was, I thought, impossible.

In 1982, Dick DeNeut had come to my aid as I was wrestling with the prospect of helping Patricia Neal with twelve hundred pages of unmanageable notes for her autobiography, As I Am, *which with Dick's collaboration was published in 1988.*

Dick is a close friend and a trusted confidant. In his childhood, he had been one of the darlings of the Our Gang *comedies, and when we met in 1957 he still had boyish good looks and the most infectious Maurice Chevalier smile. He shared his knowledge about films and theater, which educated and enlightened me, and I was constantly astounded to see what I considered the best in the business fall by the sword of his unyielding standards and acerbic wit. Early in my acting career, Dick and I had a romantic relationship, but my religious vocation has allowed Dick and me to reconnect and to find a way to be committed in love through a greater body, that of Regina Laudis.*

In 1970, when I pronounced my perpetual vows and was consecrated as a cloistered Benedictine nun, I invited Dick to hold my veil during the ceremony. I understood the extraordinary way in which he had "veiled" me throughout my professional life, making certain that my image was appropriately received by the press through his company, Globe Photos. In every professional context, he was there to inform and address the world at large that my person was to be kept within a virginal integrity, and he maintained that demand fiercely. Catholic or not, he is for me a Saint Joseph person.

So when the Community asked me to write my story, I knew I needed Dick's help to do it. Our work began within unusual and challenging limits. He lives in Los Angeles, California; I in a cloistered abbey in Bethlehem, Connecticut. When Dick traveled to Regina Laudis, our meetings had to be conducted within the confines of the enclosure and during the few hours each day I had free from my duties as prioress and dean of education. This book represents a partnership that demanded not only honesty, integrity and trust, but professionalism of a high degree.

At the beginning of The Song of Bernadette, *a film I saw as a child and still love, are these words from the author Franz Werfel: "For those who believe, no explanation is necessary; for those who do not, no explanation is possible." Nevertheless, I have presented in these pages the details of my life so far as a response to the question I have been asked countless times: How could I throw away a promising acting career for the monastic life of a cloistered nun?*

I left the world I knew in order to reenter it on a more profound level. Many people don't understand the difference between a vocation and your own idea about something. A vocation is a call—one you don't necessarily want. The only thing I ever wanted to be was an actress. But I was called by God.

Mother Dolores Hart, OSB

Introduction

"Do you think I have a responsibility to write my story?"

That is the question that Mother Dolores Hart, the new prioress of the cloistered Benedictine Abbey of Regina Laudis, asked me on a warm Connecticut afternoon in May of 2001. We were walking with the newly installed abbess, Reverend Mother David Serna, now called Mother Abbess. It was the day after her abbatial blessing, confirming her status as the second abbess of the Community founded by Reverend Mother Benedict Duss in 1948.

Mother Dolores and I had spoken of the possibility of her writing and my editing her autobiography several times over the past two decades, during and after our collaboration with Patricia Neal on her memoir, which was written at the abbey. Mother Dolores had been the subject of newspaper, television and magazine attention when, as young film and Broadway actress Dolores Hart, she abandoned a promising acting career for a life as a cloistered nun, a decision that was tagged "sudden" by the media and predicted to be of short duration.

The question she directed to me that day came almost forty years after that decision and her entrance into Regina Laudis. Mother Dolores and I had known each other for forty-four years.

In 1957, just out of the army, I went to work for the photo agency Globe Photos in Hollywood. Globe's specialty was photojournalistic coverage of the film industry for domestic and international publications. In those days, Globe pictures were the mainstay of the movie fan magazines, now obsolete but in their heyday the most successful group of publications in the country. The editor of several of them, Bessie Little, assigned Globe Photos to shoot a layout on an ordinary girl caught up in the glamor of a night on the town in Hollywood. The girl was to be Bessie's niece Susie Grobstein. Globe was asked to supply a fresh Hollywood couple to host the evening and a young bachelor to accompany Susie as her date.

Jim Stevens, a publicist at Paramount Pictures and my contact at the studio, suggested, as the Hollywood couple, up-and-coming Earl Holliman and the new contract actress Dolores Hart, who had just completed a film with Elvis Presley. I was the only young bachelor at Globe.

The layout, which included dinner at Trader Vic's and Margaret Whiting's opening at the Moulin Rouge, was pleasant enough. Everyone had a good time, and Bessie Little picked up the tab. Earl and Dolores made an attractive couple, and Susie couldn't have been more starstruck. The young bachelor, for the first time in his life, was dazzled.

Not only was Dolores beautiful; she was bright and witty and very down-to-earth—a killer combination. Dolores didn't have starlet glitter. She had a glow and an openness that put me in mind of happy college days. She could talk about something besides herself, and I was impressed with the way she related to Susie that night—as if they were high school confidantes. A big plus was her wicked sense of humor with well-placed zingers that found in me an especially appreciative audience.

A short while after that introduction, a relationship developed between us, and there has been no time since that we haven't been in touch. She even invited me to participate in her Consecration in 1970.

But it wasn't until 1979 that our potential grew beyond what I had envisioned in 1958. A close friend was very ill and had returned home to Louisiana to die. That September I flew to Monroe to say goodbye, and while there I called Mother Dolores to say I was halfway across the country and would like to see her. She said I had better get myself to Regina Laudis the very next weekend because it was the last weekend before the Community's annual October retreat, when they did not have guests. I did just that.

Mother Dolores and I had a daylong reunion in one of the abbey's parlors. At the end of that day, somehow, with only a one-semester course in film editing at UCLA behind me—we're talking a gap of twenty-seven years—I agreed to edit a decade of 8 mm movie coverage of Regina Laudis into a film that would be the Community's contribution to the Vatican celebration of Saint Benedict's fifteen-hundredth anniversary. It would be the first of many ventures that would keep me close to Mother Dolores and Regina Laudis.

After the publication of Patricia Neal's book, whenever the subject of Mother Dolores' autobiography came up, I was afraid to commit, for fear I might not be as objective an editor as I would need to be. In truth, I was always secretly relieved when the subject was dropped, even though decades after her entrance into the cloister, press interest in Mother Dolores had not faded.

To this day, a month does not go by without some media request. Mother Dolores knows without a *TV Guide* when one of her films has aired on television because requests for visits to Regina Laudis increase overnight. She still receives what she jokingly refers to as "fan mail" from people around the world, admirers of long ago and young people who after seeing one of her movies for the first time investigate her on the Internet.

There have been invitations from movie producers to cooperate in a film of her life story, and in her forty-ninth year as a contemplative, she was named one of the ten most important Catholics by *Inside the Vatican*. In 2005 she was included in the exhibit *God's Women: Nuns in America* at the Pope John Paul II Cultural Center in Washington, DC. Just last year, she was recognized by the Breukelein Institute, which honors men and women whose lives "have illumined the human experience", and she was the subject of a documentary produced by Home Box Office that was nominated for an Oscar. This year, the Christophers presented her with their Life Achievement Award at their sixty-third annual ceremony.

With each request, each tribute, thoughts of a book would be revived. So it came as no surprise that, on that May afternoon, she was being forced to consider again that possibility. I just wished she hadn't asked it that way: "Do you think I have a *responsibility* to write my story?"

Of course she did. She is the only person who can tell what drew her to a life of monastic enclosure so strongly that she could sacrifice the realization of the dream she had since childhood and, more importantly, what has kept her steadfast and devoted for half a century. Additionally, her story can reach out to young people who find themselves living a contradiction between their inner truth and the values of the world around them.

"Yes", I answered.

"I won't do it without you", she said.

"Then," I said, with less trepidation than I would have expected, "you've got me."

"Be careful," she warned, her justifiably famous blue eyes sparkling as she nodded toward Mother Abbess, "I've got a good witness."

Work on the memoir began in the summer of 2002. We made the decision to compile her recollections in a Q&A format—I was the Q—recording the interviews and using as our research base the extraordinary archive she has maintained since she was very young. Early in her childhood, she heard a voice telling her to "keep everything; you will have need of it someday."

Her life from an early age to well into her monastic years is recorded in a host of spiral notebooks. She has kept every letter, and she was a prodigious correspondent; every note and sketch, and she was an inveterate doodler. Her mother had made a huge scrapbook about her career. There are leather-bound scripts full of notes in her tiny, scrunched up, analytically pregnant hand.

What she did not personally hoard came from family and friends. When her mother and grandmother died, all of her letters to them were returned to her. I found a box of her letters written to me the year she was on Broadway. A fan in Texas compiled twelve scrapbooks about her and generously sent them to her after she entered Regina Laudis. It took many, many months to sift through this treasure trove of memories.

You will hear two voices in the memoir—Mother Dolores' and mine. Occasionally interrupting the narrative are casual exchanges taken directly from the tapes of our interviews.

Half of this collaboration is not Catholic and, at the beginning, was lamentably lacking in many facets of Catholic religious life, notably in my misunderstanding of the term *call* as used in expressions such as "I had a call" or "I was called." I spoke to people in the Church and read what I could to enlighten me. But, frankly, it all sounded either highfalutin or fuzzy. I badgered Lady Abbess, the founder of Regina Laudis, to the point of exasperation—hers not mine. But after repeated queries, I hadn't found an answer that I could relate to personally. Again I approached the abbess, this time using Mother Dolores as my emissary.

Upon hearing that I had that same old question, Lady Abbess heaved a weary sigh and said, "Mother, you tell Dick that a call can't be explained any more than you can explain falling in love."

Richard DeNeut

The Road to Bethlehem

One

There is a tiny room in the basement of the abbey building at Regina Laudis, just down the hall from the laundry. It measures eight by ten feet but seems smaller because of all the things in it.

There are two tables that by themselves almost fill the space—one against a wall and the other, serving as a desk, in the center of the room. Half of the desk's surface is taken up by a huge cage, home to an African gray parrot named Tobiel (Toby for short) whose vocabulary consists of "Toby's sweet", "Go to church!" and "Mazel tov!" On the second table sits another, even larger cage, home to eight pairs of finches of various descriptions, next to a cage of normal dimensions accommodating a sick bird—a kind of finch infirmary.

There is a tiled sink from the time the room was used as an art studio and two chairs—both larger than necessary but all that was available when the room became an office. High up are cupboards—one of which contains leather-bound scripts of fifteen movie and TV productions and one Broadway play, and another crammed with videotapes and DVDs of films sent by the Academy of Motion Picture Arts and Sciences. File cabinets of various sizes and styles fill the remaining wall space, providing surfaces for a small refrigerator, a fax machine, three telephones, and a heater; a globe of the world as it was known in the sixteenth century; an anti-pirating DVD player (also a gift from the Academy); books, scrapbooks, journals and framed photographs; a twenty-eight-volume DVD collection of the Carol Burnett TV show, a gift from the star herself; Christmas ornaments that picture Bob Hope and play his "Silver Bells"; and several floppy, wide-brimmed garden hats.

Hanging on hooks attached to the door are heavy aprons, a raincoat, craftsmen tools, farm utensils, bits of electrical wiring and some hand-knit sweaters in pastel pink and baby blue.

This is Corpus Christi, Mother Dolores' office. It is where, as prioress, she communicates with the outside world, reads and evaluates requests from would-be visitors, arranges living accommodations for guests, oversees (she prefers to say "undersees") the dramatic productions of the abbey's Act Association and visits by professional artists who come to the abbey to give of their talents (the list is impressive), considers subjects for Education Deanery seminars, "undersees" the photo and video (now digital) recording of abbey life and, most importantly, gives her ear to any member of the Community who needs her. She is also available for anything the abbess asks of her.

—Might that include sweeping the floor?

She wouldn't ask that.

Too demeaning?

She wouldn't trust me with her broom.

Corpus Christi also served as my office for two or three months each year during the past ten years. In that time, for three hours each afternoon, it was the place where Mother Dolores and I worked together on this manuscript. Originally, out of respect for the cloister, we met in one of the abbey parlors, but taping her recollections separated by the grille, which was not recorder-friendly, became burdensome, so permission was given for us to work inside the enclosure—certainly a major exception to cloistered life and one that added a laptop and tape recorder to the room.

To describe the working area as cramped I need only say that when both of us were seated, it was impossible for either of us to move without the other having to move too.

Our chairs faced each other, which allowed me to study that face, framed by the wimple, as Mother Dolores spoke into the recorder. As a flattering device, nothing beats a wimple in focusing attention—and hiding wrinkles. Mother Dolores has very few of those, belying the fact that she is now in her seventies. Her face is still beautiful. Her blue eyes, large and expressive, settle into a thoughtful gaze as she delves into the past—now pensive as she conjures the odor of vanilla beans being ground into powder in her grandmother's home; now bright and mischievous as she recalls a tomboy acing out the neighborhood roughnecks by being the last kid to get out of the way of an approaching

4

train; now moist as she relives playing a clarinet solo on a late-night TV show for her grandfather as he lay dying; frequently troubled, hesitant at the prospect of speaking publicly about the mystery of enclosed religious life. They can flash, too, in an unexpected explosion of temper. The lady has a temper.

Now and then, my attention would be gently interrupted by the ever-so-slight movement of her feet. Her special shoes, sensible and protective, cannot conceal the motion of pain-plagued feet inside, moving constantly, trying without much success to find a comfortable resting place. It was something we never averred because this was our working time, our professional time.

— Where shall we start?

How about flashbacks in a movie? Tell me things I don't know.

Well, did you know I ran away from home once?

I ran away from home when I was four years old. I ran away in the middle of the night with my mother. We were leaving my grandparents' house on Hermitage Avenue in Chicago, where we had been living after Daddy left for Hollywood. He had gotten a contract with MGM studio, and Mommy and I were going to join him. We were running away because Granny and Grandpa were dead set against Daddy. They thought he was a good-for-nothing.

We sneaked out of the house very quietly, but as soon as we reached the street I suddenly remembered I had left my panda bear behind in Granny's bedroom. I started crying, so Mommy slipped back into the house and retrieved my beloved bear while Granny slept peacefully. I don't remember if Mommy handed the bear to me or me to the bear; I was only two inches taller than Panda. The two of us had to sit on Mommy's lap for most of the train trip because she could afford only one seat. But we didn't care. We were going to see Daddy. In Hollywood!

We rode for what seemed like years. It was the beginning of World War II, and I remember there were so many soldiers and sailors on the

5

train, all so much taller than Panda and I that it was like a forest of uniformed pant legs. I remember looking out the window and seeing the beautiful California desert for the first time and then, against the background of a bright sunset, tall slender trees with feathers blooming on top. They were palms, and I was to discover that California had thousands and thousands of them. Over the next several years this route would become a familiar journey, but the sudden magic of the palm trees against the Pacific curtain of the sky would never fail to take my breath away.

Four years earlier, in January of 1938, Dolores' future parents were just graduating from high school, where they had been sweethearts since the eighth grade. Edmund Burdell Lyhan Hicks, nicknamed Bert, was seventeen years old. Harriett Lee Pittman was sixteen. Both had eye-catching good looks and shared tattoos acquired in a moment of youthful recklessness, decades before tattoos on teenagers came into vogue. Harriett's tattoo, however, remained unfinished: while the tattoo artist was working on hers, Bert passed out and that ended the session.

Shared, too, were dreams of marriage and careers in the movies. The latter was put temporarily on hold when they had to marry earlier than planned. This circumstance caused Harriett's mother, Esther Bowen, and stepfather, Fred Kude, both of whom frowned on the relationship, a great deal of grief and spawned a serious but brief consideration of abortion. Harriett, in a characteristic show of defiance, totally rejected this advice. Esther and Fred reluctantly accepted "that wild good-for-nothing" as a son-in-law, even though there would never be any affection between them and him, and Esther paid for all the maternity expenses.

The newlyweds were forced to move in with the Kudes, but as soon as they could afford it, they set up housekeeping in a small apartment in Chicago, adjacent to well-traveled train tracks. Harriett found employment as a secretary, while Bert tried various endeavors, including truck driver, furniture mover and salesman for ladies' shoes. He did not, however, settle down to the responsibilities of marriage, and this, combined with his drinking, caused increasingly frequent arguments between the young couple. Instead of trying to work things out themselves, the two kids—which is what they were—took their gripes, *Rashomon*-style, to their respective families, who were not stingy with advice.

After particularly violent arguments when Bert, drunk, would strike her, Harriett would run back home to Esther and Fred. The next day, refusing their advice to leave him, she would go back to her husband. Despite the increasing abuse, sometimes provoking police intervention, Harriett remained in love with him.

The arrival of Dolores Marie Hicks at 10:30 A.M. on October 20, 1938, was cause for great celebration in both the Hicks and the Bowen clans. She was the first grandchild and served temporarily to patch the cracks in her parents' marriage. Bert adored his daughter. With huge blue eyes, she was a beautiful baby, beneficiary of the drop-dead-gorgeous genes that ran so generously through both sides of her family.

To my father I was "Punkin", but I was named after my great-aunt Frieda, who that same year became Sister Dolores Marie in the order of Saint Joseph of Carondelet in Saint Louis. Mommy brought me to her Investiture because my aunt was hopeful that I could be baptized in the Church at the same time. There was precedent. Daddy had been baptized Catholic. He was even an altar boy, though he had never practiced his religion enough even to be considered "fallen away". The baptism wasn't destined to happen, however, not then. The Church didn't allow it. So I wasn't baptized until ten years later.

Dolores was born into families that could easily be the hard-edged versions of the zany Sycamores in that year's Oscar-winning picture, *You Can't Take It with You*. Her paternal grandfather, John W. Lyhan, called Jack, came from a wealthy railroad clan. The family line dated back to nineteenth-century England and Sir Thomas Atkins, a member of Queen Victoria's palace guard. His service to the queen earned Tommy, as he was called, such royal affection that he was knighted. Additionally, Her Majesty presented him with the christening gown of baby Prince Alfred, which has been passed down through generations of Dolores' family. Legend has it that "Tommy", the universally used nickname for British soldiers, in wide currency from the 1880s through World War I, was in honor of Sir Thomas and immortalized by Rudyard Kipling in his 1892 *Barrack-Room Ballads*.

7

Added to the English mix were Dutch, French, Irish, Welsh, and Norwegian, as well as a touch of the exotic—a red-headed Jewess from Spain and an American Indian. In 1871 the Atkins side of the family settled in Chicago, where they saw their home burned to the ground in the great fire.

The entire Atkins-Hicks tribe was churchgoing with religious convictions as varied as their nationalities: Catholic, Jewish and Protestant, as well as Christian Science and Mormon. Dolores' great-grandparents, Reuben and Eliza Atkins, English converts to the Church of Jesus Christ of Latter-day Saints, moved from England to Salt Lake City to join Brigham Young, but when that leader espoused polygamy, Atkins refused to take another wife, earning the leader's wrath. The couple was ordered to leave Salt Lake City within twenty-four hours.

Jack Lyhan and Dolores' paternal grandmother met in college, where Jack was a blackface performer in minstrel shows, giving vent to an urge to perform that had been thwarted by his parents' insistence that he study to become a doctor. Mary Atkins, known as May, was the daughter of successful farmers. She had hoped to become an actress, traveling for a short time with a theatrical group performing at resorts in Indiana and Wisconsin. But, at the turn of the century, an actress was considered half a step above a trollop, so her family pushed her into a teaching career in speech and dramatic arts.

Jack, a Catholic, and May, a convert at marriage, produced three children: John, Bert and Betty. But Jack was not a model head of household. He was an abusive husband and father, whose main targets were his wife and second son, Bert, both of whom were subject to severe beatings. May, in turn, compensated for this abuse by overprotecting Bert, babying and spoiling him.

The cruelty and maltreatment over the next five years rose to such a level that finally even her priest advised May to divorce her husband. She took the priest's advice, repeatedly refusing Jack's pleas to reconcile, preferring to rear the children alone.

In 1929 May took a second husband, James Earl Hicks, whom she had met at a political convention. A tall man with Clark Gable good looks, Hicks didn't have Lyhan's formal education or moneyed background, but he promised to be a more affable family man.

8

May's second union added three girls, Gladys, Shirley and Virginia, to her first family of three, all of whom Hicks adopted. Hicks turned out to be only a sometimes jolly parent. Gladys and Shirley remembered that he could be "unbelievably mean". He too was rough on Bert, whose dependency upon his mother grew stronger. His siblings remember that Bert was always involved in some theatrical venture or another. He figured out early that all he needed to get by were his good looks and bad-boy charm, a tactic that separated him from his older brother, John, who was, even at an early age, ambitious and hardworking.

In the mid 1930s, after several successful years as a manufacturer of flavored butter spreads, Hicks lost his business. He was forced to move his family into a modest flat on the north side of Chicago. Money was scarce, though he managed to scrape together enough to have a nice Christmas in 1935. But on that Christmas Day, Hicks left the house on an errand and never came back, leaving May to raise all six children alone in the middle of the Great Depression.

> —*Of all my ancestral transgressors of laws or moral codes or commandments, the one I find difficult to forgive is Grandpa Hicks. He may have been suffering—he had just lost his business and couldn't provide for his family—and perhaps felt he couldn't live up to the tenets of his Christian Science beliefs. But he walked out on his family on Christmas, and, to my mind, that was not Christian. That was a sin.*

May Hicks could have taken her children and gone home to the family farm, but she was ferociously proud. She wouldn't ask anyone, including her parents, for anything. She resolved to leave teaching for better-paying employment, but she went from one low-paying job to another until she and her children found themselves and all their belongings on the sidewalk. Young Bert was especially upset, flying into a rage, breaking windows and creating havoc. It was the first time the family became aware of his violent side.

The Salvation Army came to their aid, moving the family temporarily into their Home for Women and Children and helping May land a job demonstrating Singer sewing machines at the Marshall Field's department store. May rose with regular promotions to the position of buyer in the furniture department. While she was working, her "first family" took on the responsibility of caring for her "second family" in their new home, a duplex on Chicago's west side. But she never forfeited her position as matriarch and maintained a strong influence on her children, investing them with a keen awareness of the hard realities of life. She saw to it that all of them attended church every Sunday, and she passed on her signature optimism. Even during the blackest days, her mantra was "Things are going to get better."

—I remember her as genteel and high class, in many ways the perfect foil for my other grandmother, who had more than a passing acquaintance with the mean streets of Chicago.

Esther Pittman Brown Kude née Bowen, though of a different class, was on a par in rank with May. She was also a beauty, but what made the two women close was that Esther was an equally proud and strong lady. Having been born poor, she learned early how not to get pushed around.

—She loved to tell the story of how she walked to school without shoes in 18-degree weather, not because she didn't have shoes—she had one pair—but just to show the kids how tough she was.

Esther was thrice wed, the first time at age sixteen to Lee Pittman, Harriett's father. Shortly after Harriett's birth, Pittman got a teenage girl pregnant. When Esther learned of this she did two things. She demanded he shave every hair off his body because "if he was going to behave like a baby, he was going to look like one."

—And he did as he was told.

Then Esther divorced him so that he could marry the pregnant girl, Helen, with whom he had a long, happy marriage and seven children. The resilient Esther remained friendly with her first husband, now a Catholic convert, and saw to it that Harriett did the same. Harriett and her father were close for his entire life, and she often brought Dolores with her when she visited his home in Williamsfield, Illinois.

When Harriett was nine, Esther married her second husband, Paul Brown, who was a preacher and a wife beater. One day Brown took off for California and never came back. Alone, with mounting bills, Esther got a job as a waitress at a local bar and grill called the Round Table, a job she would keep for the rest of her life.

After Esther's second divorce, Fred Kude, a projectionist at a local movie house, entered her life. This union would provide the stable core in Dolores' early years.

When Dolores was two years old, Bert and Harriett separated, the first of many partings in their turbulent union. Those two years had been frustrating ones for Bert, who drifted from one meaningless job to another, increasingly fearful that fame and fortune would elude him. He began to drink more and more heavily and was as abusive to his wife as his father had been to his mother. But, his brother remembered, "Bert had to get drunk to be as cruel as our father was sober." At one time or another, Dolores' paternal aunts all witnessed violent outbreaks, with Harriett running screaming from Bert's attacks, sometimes carrying tiny Dolores in her arms.

Harriett filed for divorce, charging cruelty. Before it was granted, however, the judge called the couple into his chambers and effected a reconciliation. He wrote up a Code of Conduct that both the eighteen-year-old wife and nineteen-year-old husband had to sign. Convinced that the paper was a good foundation for future stability, the judge dismissed the suit. The story made the Chicago newspapers, which printed the agreement. Under the terms of the Code of Conduct, (1) Bert had to attend church voluntarily for one year, (2) both had to agree not to run to their parents to settle future domestic problems but (3) allow Bert's lawyer to act as arbiter of any dispute.

The well-intentioned judge's code would not ultimately save the marriage, nor would it end Bert's violence toward Harriett. But the fresh start was benefited by Bert's getting a job as a commercial model, something for which he was suited. He posed as the attractive suitor admiring the soft hands of the beautiful girl in magazine ads for Jergens lotion. He filled the same role in ads for Lady Esther 4-Purpose Face Cream and Trushay hand lotion. He also began appearing in the popular, photo-illustrated romance novelettes, featured in women's magazines such as *McCall's* and *Good Housekeeping*. These photos dramatized scenes from the stories. They were not a particularly impressive showcase,

11

but Bert achieved minor star status, which fed his ego, and the jobs brought him into contact with a lot of pretty and available girls, which set him on the road to chronic infidelity. He basked in this attention and no longer minded having to take the occasional regular job when he wasn't working as a model.

While Bert was moonlighting as a soda jerk at the Aragon Ballroom, a job he took as a way of meeting influential people, he was discovered by the Chicago-based talent scout for Metro-Goldwyn-Mayer. Definitely the matinee-idol type at six foot two, Bert bore a striking resemblance to one of that studio's biggest stars, Robert Taylor, especially with the mustache he grew at the talent scout's request. Thirty-something Taylor was about to depart MGM for the army. Presumably as a twenty-one-year-old replacement for him, Bert was tested and signed by MGM to a stock player contract. In the days when studios had stables of actors under contract, it was a usual practice to keep their stars in line by having a similar—and often younger—type in the wings. James Craig was MGM's threat to Clark Gable. Warner Bros. had Dane Clark for defense against John Garfield. Sheree North, in her blonde-bombshell period, was signed by Twentieth Century-Fox when Marilyn Monroe was misbehaving. Rarely did any of the threats go beyond being just that.

Bert Hicks would not prove an exception. In his first year under contract, he did bit parts in four MGM movies before the studio dropped his option. Almost immediately he was signed by Twentieth Century-Fox, and he appeared in a walk-on with Betty Grable in *Sweet Rosie O'Grady* before World War II interrupted his career. He joined the Army Air Forces and took his training at Sheppard Field in Texas.

In 1943, Broadway's Moss Hart wrote and put into production the US Army Air Forces' *Winged Victory*, which followed a group of air cadets through their training to the nightly raids on Germany and Japan. A call went out to Air Forces servicemen who had been actors to fill the cast. When the show opened in November 1943, the cast featured 209 members of the armed forces, including future stars Karl Malden, Edmond O'Brien, Red Buttons, Don Taylor, Gary Merrill, Barry Nelson, Lee J. Cobb, Kevin McCarthy and Peter Lind Hayes. Two of those, Malden and Taylor, would work with Dolores a decade and a half later.

12

Private Bert Hicks had a small part in the play, and a close buddy, Alfred Arnold Cocozza, nicknamed Freddy, sang in the chorus. Malden and fellow cast member Phyllis Avery remembered Bert as being gregarious and fun but also an irresponsible actor. He would miss performances and, without his wife and child near, most of his free time was spent drinking and womanizing.

Winged Victory became the megahit of the 1943 Broadway season, winning critics and audiences alike. When the show closed in May 1944, Bert brought his buddy Freddy Cocozza home to Chicago to meet his sister Betty, whose photo had taken Freddy's fancy. He was a hefty man with a voice that had been compared to Enrico Caruso's and wasn't shy about showing off his talent.

> —*In fact, he used to sing so often—and so loud—that Granny once told him to shut up when he all but shattered her wine glasses. Aunt Betty, however, was more than impressed. Aunt Betty was in love.*

The entire cast of *Winged Victory* transferred to the screen when Bert's home studio, Twentieth Century-Fox, made the movie version in 1944. Bert's role barely survived in one scene. Directed by George Cukor, the movie is the typically patriotic, sentimental fare of the war years, but its cast includes five future Oscar winners: Malden, O'Brien, Buttons, Judy Holliday in her film debut and Cukor, who would also be one of Dolores' future directors.

Bert Hicks might have been starring in movies if the war hadn't interrupted his career at Fox. After the war, the return of Henry Fonda, Tyrone Power and Victor Mature shoved Bert back to stock-player status, acting in B movies and appearing opposite aspiring actresses in screen tests. But his name popped up with regularity in the columns, usually preceded with the words "heartthrob" or "sigh guy".

Harriett was always supportive of Bert, subordinating her own dreams of a career to his. After she and Dolores joined Bert in Los Angeles, she committed herself to making the marriage work, hoping that Bert would change. Bert's infidelity was, of course, beyond Dolores' comprehension. It wasn't until she was in her teen years that Harriett

13

confided to her that her father had been unfaithful during their entire married life.

I remember the fights, the yelling, but I don't think I really connected them with the bruises I would often see on my mother. I remember, too, long periods of silence and waiting for the next explosion. It always came. But as violent as he would get with my mother, my father never lifted a hand to me. He never struck me or even said a cross word to me. I was never afraid of him. I always knew that he loved me and had a sense of pride in me. But I don't remember Daddy being a constant presence in my life.

We did have happy times as a family, especially when things were going well for him at the studio. Most of those memories are centered on trips to the beach. Both my parents adored the ocean, Mommy especially because she loved looking tan. They would pack me and my new favorite toy, Bulgy, a huge pop-eyed red rubber whale who had replaced Panda in my affections, in the rumble seat of our secondhand car, and off we would go for a day at Santa Monica Beach. While Mommy and Daddy sunned and swam, I was kept literally under wraps because I would sunburn in five minutes.

Happy, though, wasn't the right word for our life. Frantic would be more like it. It seemed as if we were always running to get somewhere, as if we could keep ahead of threatening undercurrents.

Those undercurrents, Aunt Shirley remembered, reached a violent climax when her brother struck Harriett with such force that he broke her jaw. She was hospitalized and finally bowed to the fact that she was married to an unstable, sadistic man. She made the decision to separate for good, and fearful that Bert might come to the house when she wasn't there and take Dolores, Harriett sent her to Chicago to stay with Grandma and Grandpa Kude until the situation was finalized.

The only problem was I had to go alone. Granny would be at the Chicago station to meet me, but for the three-day journey I was on my own. Well, not really. Mommy made arrangements with one of the porters, a big black bear of a man, to take charge of me. You could do things like that then. She bought two seats so I could have room to sleep

14

and sewed a label on my coat with my particulars—identification, destination and into whose hands I was to be delivered. I didn't like having that sign on me, but I wasn't in the least frightened. It was another adventure. Even so, I was sad. I knew that Mommy and Daddy weren't going to live together anymore.

Dolores' visit to Chicago was cut short with the announcement that Harriett had once again reconciled with Bert and wanted her child back home, a request that Esther granted very reluctantly.

The reconciliation ended almost as soon as it began. There wasn't going to be another one. Harriett filed for divorce again. "This time it will stick", she vowed in a newspaper interview on the divorce, borrowing a phrase usually identified in Hollywood with reconciliation. With no meddling judge to intercede, this time the divorce was granted. It marked the end of the marriage, but it would not be the end of the relationship. Harriett may not have had success as a wife, but she could be a friend for life.

Harriett and Dolores moved to an apartment on Reeves Drive in Beverly Hills. The one bedroom and kitchenette was soon shared with Aunt Betty, who had relocated to the West Coast to follow her boyfriend, Freddy Cocozza, who was now pursuing a singing career.

Betty was my love when she lived with us. She had beautiful black eyes and shoulder-length hair that bounced when she walked. She was one of the best playmates I ever had. She tried to be stern, but whenever I didn't obey she would scoop me up and throw me, fully clothed, into the bathtub, turn the water on and shriek with laughter.

But somehow, no matter what Mommy and Aunt Betty did, I felt lost, uncertain. Divorce, remarriage and redivorce left me angry—not unwanted, but lonely. I remember Mommy bought a picture and hung it over my bed. It was a picture of a small boy carrying a large round globe. She told me it was Jesus and the globe he was carrying was the world. I thought to myself, "That's not the world; that kid just has a fancy basketball." Still, I would stare at the picture, maybe out of a real desire to believe, and little by little, I wasn't so alone. If that kid could carry such a burden, maybe I could too.

15

Bert would come back on numerous occasions—always uninvited and usually drunk—presumably to see Dolores. Harriett would complain that he came back just to quarrel with her. But she would always let him in. If he had been drinking, she would put Dolores in the bedroom and close the door.

When he would come back he was awful to Mommy. She never said anything bad about him to me, but I could see she was afraid of him.

Aunt Betty, who always sided with my mother whenever Daddy was around, said she thought I was a remarkably well-adjusted little girl in spite of the fact that my family life had not been a good environment. It was the first time I had heard that word, in-vire-ment. *I didn't know what it meant. Must be something awful, I thought.*

On our first Christmas Eve alone, Daddy came by dressed in a Santa suit and very drunk. Mommy wouldn't let him in, so he stood banging on the door, yelling and singing Christmas songs. He was making such a fool of himself in front of the neighbors that she was more embarrassed than frightened. She grabbed me, put me in the bedroom and opened the front door.

Fortunately Betty was there, for once inside Bert's holiday boisterousness turned menacing. Dolores could hear him bullying her mother while both women tried in vain to reason with him. She crept out of her hiding place and saw Bert holding a knife, threatening to use it on Harriett. Betty was trying to take the weapon away from him when the six-year-old child, crying, spoke to her father.

—I told him to give Aunt Betty the knife because what he was doing was not good.

Bert surrendered the knife. But the row continued. Clapping her hands over her ears to shut out the ugliness, Dolores hid in a closet and wrote a short letter to her grandmother: "Can I come to live with you? This is not a good *invirement* for a little girl to be in."

16

Two

It was a difficult thing for Harriett to do, but she sent Dolores' letter to her mother. Esther's response came back like a shot: "This is enough! You have to send her here."

Mommy and I were sitting on the steps at school, facing a big picture window, when she told me she was sending me to Chicago. Although I had wished for it, I was not happy to leave my home. As I sat there on the steps, I thought my heart would break, but ever so quietly I became aware of a lovely blue curtain that waved across the windows, and everything suddenly seemed peaceful. I asked Mommy what the curtain was for. She looked at the windows and said, "What curtain? There's no curtain." But I knew I had seen it.

—That image has stayed with me, and only as a contemplative did I come to associate the waving blue curtain with the protective image of the Madonna.

I was shipped off to Chicago, once again in the care of a porter my mother pressed into service. I wasn't bright-eyed with expectations. I didn't know that going back to live with Granny and Grandpa would turn out to be the start of a very happy time in my life.

Granny was especially good to me. She didn't spoil me—oh no, she was very strict—but she made me feel included. She taught me to wash and iron and clean house, to knit and crochet. She showed me how to brush and set my hair, and she helped me to learn to read by reading to me—every one of the Oz books. And she lectured me on the value of money and how to get the most for it.

An essential part of her costume was a garter into which she stuffed her tips. She made good tips because, as she frequently proclaimed, she was the best in the business and the only one at the Round Table who

17

could carry eight plates on her arms at once while, as an added treat, making her false teeth slide in and out.

—My favorite memory is of Granny on duty at the restaurant, standing on her head while she drank a martini. It was a performance she had perfected through many rehearsals.

If Granny was my best friend, Grandpa was my best buddy. Grandpa was German and, whenever he got mad, he would say the same thing: "Gott, ich bin ein dummer Esel. Schlag mich auf den Kopf und mach' mich wieder klug." He said it so often that I memorized it, but I didn't know what it meant, so I was afraid to say it. It was later translated for me, and I admit there have been many times over the years when I've said it myself: "God, I am a dumb ass. Hit me over the head and make me smart again."

Grandpa was also a heavy drinker when I came to live in Chicago. You would think I would have recognized the problem, but I didn't. I mistook his rosy cheeks as blushing. Later he joined Alcoholics Anonymous and successfully stayed off booze for twenty years.

Grandpa worked as a projectionist at the Drake movie house on Montrose Avenue and used to bring me with him to the projection booth on weekends. Whenever he would take a snooze, it was my job to wake him up in time to switch projectors. In between I would watch all the movies through the little projector window.

I was spellbound. I eventually got to know the stories so well that I could act them out myself, copying the expressions of the actresses. I began to work out the reasons for pausing or holding a certain look, which allowed for a feeling to be portrayed. I can't believe I was thinking about those things in the second grade.

My favorites were Myrna Loy, Gary Cooper and Loretta Young. I loved The Song of Bernadette. *I had never seen a human being as ethereal as Jennifer Jones. I loved* Miracle on 34th Street *and* The Bishop's Wife *and a year or so later,* The Snake Pit *and* Sunset Boulevard, *darker dramas I wasn't supposed to see. My very favorite movie, though, was* Blithe Spirit. *I loved the actress who played the ghost, and for years I thought she was Lucille Ball because of her bright red hair.*

—The single performance, however, that made me want to be an actress was Gene Tierney's in Laura.

Grandpa got me my first job—at age seven—washing tombstones at the cemetery behind our duplex. I got a nickel a marker, and when I earned two dollars I bought a Tinkertoy set. Grandpa was a mechanical mastermind and had a workshop in our basement. He motorized everything, including my Tinkertoys—together we built a working Ferris wheel. I would stand and watch him, and whenever he asked for a "gozinta" I would hop to it.

—Gozinta?

That's something that goes into *something else.*

Although Harriett thought that she was sending Dolores to Chicago on a temporary basis, when it came time to return her to Los Angeles, Esther balked. Harriett made a beeline for Chicago. Tug-of-war was declared.

I sensed very early that a battle was going on for me. Mommy and Granny were very much alike, each fiercely protective of her territory. The two of them could write the most affectionate letters to one another and exchange extravagant expressions of love on the phone yet, within minutes in each other's company, turn into snarling competitors. How often I heard "This is my daughter, not your daughter" or "She's more mine than yours." I instinctively knew I needed both of them and somehow managed to referee.

For five years, Dolores bounced between them like a tennis ball, except that the rackets were swung at one another. At first, she spent school terms in Los Angeles, vacations in Chicago. When she hit the third grade, the schedule reversed.

When Mother Dolores looked back on those years from the vantage point of a half century, she determined that she had had the best of both worlds. The Kude household provided her with family and stable roots. In Los Angeles, Harriett was a constantly available presence, as much a girlfriend as a mother—she was, after all, in her early twenties—and their time together produced a solid bond that stood strong against later assaults that would have permanently alienated most mothers and daughters.

Those years also provided Dolores with an opportunity to get to know her extended family, both sides offering dramatically rich characters. Her maternal great-grandmother, Louella May DeWitt Bowen, called Nellie, was another strong-willed beauty, five foot ten and as thin as the rails she would chop for firewood. She was of real pioneer stock, having come east from Kansas to Illinois in a covered wagon to marry Casper Bowen, a blind coffin maker and fiddle player who regained his sight in his fortieth year and found he had a wandering eye. Once, during World War II, a nephew went AWOL and fled to Colorado to hide out. Grandma Bowen, determined to help him but with no money to make the trip, accepted a friend's offer to take her the thousand miles—on his motorcycle. It's not difficult to see where daughter Esther got her pluck. Unfortunately, the parallel didn't stop there. During Grandma's absence, Grandpa Bowen dallied.

When I met them, they shared a three-room house—with warped linoleum-covered floors, a potbellied stove and an outhouse—across from the railroad station in Galesburg, some one hundred fifty miles from Chicago. There was one old, old rug on the floor that covered the area linoleum no longer did. The rooms didn't have doors, just curtains hanging on cut-off broom handles. The couple lived on Bowen's pension and the money Grandma earned by cleaning the local bank at night.

—Grandma Bowen was fierce of heart but a praying woman who could recite the chapters of the Bible from memory and could forgive a husband's unfaithfulness because she had married for life.

When she was in Chicago, Mommy would take me to see my Grandpa Pittman in Williamsfield. It was really the sticks, way out in the country, but I loved going there. Grandpa Pittman owned the only restaurant in town, and, boy, was he a handsome devil with his dark hair and mustache.

Fun times in Williamsfield were spent with Grandpa Pittman's new family (I called them cousins, but they were actually my aunts and uncles) mostly down at Murphy's Pond, which was just beyond the

Santa Fe railroad tracks. Bruce Pittman, the eldest, was several years older than I and a real cutup. One day he got me into the small shed next to the tracks for a little show and tell, but what I didn't know was that all the other kids were hiding to watch. They began hooting and hollering, and then they told my mother what had gone on. When we got back to Chicago, I was taken to the back bedroom. Mommy took off a belt and said, "Okay now, every time I hit the bed, you cry." While Granny eavesdropped outside, Mommy whacked and whacked the bed, and I screamed and screamed. I was getting some practical experience in acting.

—Are you still in contact with those cousins?

Yes. But no one ever mentions the incident. I'm the only one who remembers it.

And maybe not.

And maybe not.

My great-aunts and -uncle on my mother's side were nothing if not colorful. Aunt Ruth was an amateur tap dancer. On her eighty-fifth birthday, still going strong, she made a tape of her tapping, which she sent to me at the abbey. Aunt Ruby collected all kinds of guns and was expert with every one of them. Aunt Vivian was the only Bowen relative who was fond of Daddy and, to Granny's everlasting irritation, made her home available as a place he and I could spend time together when he was in Chicago. I adored Uncle Clyde. He had only two fingers on his left hand, the result of a childhood prank involving a firecracker. He always treated me as a little person, not a child, and he was so funny.

—When I became an actress he sent me a note: "I am your most loyal fan since you were a little girl. I have seen all your movies and the only thing I can't understand is where in the world you picked up a name like Natalie Wood."

During those years, Daddy came back into my life sporadically, sometimes in Los Angeles, sometimes in Chicago. He never brought me presents, not even for my birthday or at Christmas. Well, except once—an oversize, glossy publicity photograph of himself.

My father's halfsisters—Gladys, Shirley and Virginia—were teenagers when I met them. Unlike Granny's side of the family, which was church-living but not church-going, the Hicks girls went to church a lot. They took turns taking me to Sunday school—or schools, since each went to a different church. I think rather than confuse me, this gave me a sense that church was special.

Once a year, for two weeks, Sister Dolores Marie would come to Chicago. I looked forward to each magical visit. Sister smelled of lavender and dressed with starched linen around her face, which was like an aging peach, fuzzy and full of color. The linen was stiff as a board; you could bounce a coin on it.

Fred Kude, who never forgave his sister for "being taken in by the Church", had not spoken a civil word to her for years. It was Esther who paid for Sister Dolores Marie's annual trips out of her garter money so Fred could remain blissfully prejudiced.

She would read to me—stories of the Creation, of Adam and Eve, of the saints and, my favorites, the wonderful and gory tales about the Christian martyrs. One in particular fascinated me. Saint Tarcisius, known as the boy saint, was a twelve year-old-acolyte who lived during the Roman persecutions of the third century and met a grisly death rather than give up the Eucharist to an angry mob. I was fascinated by this story of youthful courage and devotion. So impressed was I that I told Sister I wished I could live my life all over again because I would be so much better.

—How old were you then?

Six.

Three

My most vivid early memory of my mother is the care she took in looking after every detail in her grooming. It made her special.

Something else that was special was the tattoo on her left thigh. It looked like an eye sitting on a triangle. I never ceased badgering her about what the tattoo meant, but she never told. Still I grew up knowing that most likely I had the only mother with a tattoo. She had a flair for glamor and created many faces for herself, each favoring the look of a current movie queen.

She would have a new boyfriend to go with each new look and always brought them home to meet me, introducing them as Uncle John or Uncle Joe or Uncle Whoever. I knew they weren't my real uncles, but I was too young to call them by their first names, and the situation was too informal for me to address them as "Mister". The one I liked best was Don Sebastian, a handsome Spaniard.

In Los Angeles I attended Beverly Vista Grammar School, which was ten blocks from our apartment, but Mom trusted me to take care of myself on the way to and from school. There was a boy, younger and smaller than I, who lived nearby. He was a nasty little fellow. One day he showed me a necklace he was wearing. It was moving. He had a necklace of live ladybugs around his neck! He had pierced each one, and the poor things were struggling to escape. I was horrified—and furious.

A few days later I lay in wait for this murderer at his house. I grabbed him and twisted his arms behind him and pushed him down into his basement. Now he would get a taste of his own medicine. I tied him tight to a pole with a clothesline and left him there, yelling his lungs out.

When I told my mother what I had done, she lectured me that I should have been more cautious. "Holy Toledo, sweetie, you should have considered that there could have been an accident while he was tied up, like the furnace exploding. No, you shouldn't have done what you did. You should have just beaten the crap out of him."

This is the child who once carried a ladybug ten miles on the streetcar to show her little friend Amy Godshaw and then brought it back to Beverly Hills so it wouldn't get lost.

Bert had remarried after the divorce but remained in nonviolent contact with Harriett, who was friendly toward Bert's new wife, offering sympathy and frequently first aid whenever Jan would appear with a black eye.

Bert lingered under contract with Twentieth Century-Fox for a couple more years without catching on. It was back to walk-ons for the rest of his film career with two exceptions. He played the heavy opposite Robert Montgomery in *Once More, My Darling*, and he had one scene, albeit silent, as Anne Baxter's cad of a lover in the episodic *O. Henry's Full House*. He did a little stage work at the Pasadena Playhouse and with the Los Angeles Civic Light Opera before calling it a day. Coincidentally, his old army buddy, Freddy Cocozza, was beginning what would be a spectacular movie career just as Bert's was fizzling out. Cocozza was now Bert's brother-in-law, having married Betty Hicks, and he had a new name. He was now Mario Lanza.

Dolores was spending most of each year in Chicago so the question of schooling was a chief consideration. The nearest public school was some distance from Hermitage Avenue, through busy streets and across streetcar tracks. Esther simply wouldn't allow Dolores to walk there. There was a Catholic school closer to home with a safer route. So, for practical rather than religious reasons, Dolores was enrolled in Saint Gregory's third-grade class.

I wasn't the only non-Catholic child in school, but there weren't many, and I sensed a difference, maybe that the kids who were Catholic

24

had a feeling of security that I lacked. I used to hang on every word they said when they talked to each other about their family life. It was different from mine. And I was shy and embarrassed that my clothes weren't as nice as the other kids'. Granny's philosophy was if you're dressed warmly enough, that's all that mattered.

The teachers were stricter than those in public school, expected more and, one way or another, got more. Sister Celine was my favorite. She took special care with me because I didn't have the advantage of a Catholic background and she didn't want me to fall behind the other students. She also considered me musical and thought I should play an instrument. I made up my mind on the harp, but Grandpa nixed it. He couldn't see me lugging the thing all over town, and he sure wasn't going to be my bearer. He made up his mind on the clarinet, so the clarinet it was.

Classes in religion were part of the curriculum at Saint Gregory's. Each child had a Baltimore Catechism, *a little blue book with questions such as "Who is God?", "How many Persons in God?" and answers such as "God made me to know Him, to love Him, to serve Him and to live with Him for all days and even unto eternity." It was something a child memorized—like the Pledge of Allegiance.*

Harder for me to accept was the edict that if you weren't Catholic you couldn't go to Heaven when you died. As taught in parochial schools then, you went to Hell and lived in eternal damnation.

> *—When I heard those words, that non-Catholics couldn't go to Heaven, I thought of Granny and Grandpa. It was a hard swallow.*

Students spent some time each day in the adjacent church, and I went along with them. I didn't understand the Mass but did pretty much what they all did, copying their postures. When they would stand, I would stand; when they kneeled, I kneeled. I found these prayerful movements and the ritual of the service very appealing. In fact, I was finding most everything about the Catholic Church engaging, and I started to go into the chapel when no one else was there.

As young as I was, I was taken by a special presence in the sanctuary, and I grew to understand that this presence came from the place

25

where the candle was lighted and was holy. It made me feel secure. Although that feeling certainly contributed to my entering the Church, it wasn't the main reason.

When I began school, all the children who received Communion at Mass in the morning, and most of them did, fasted from midnight until they broke the fast with Communion. Then they would all have hot chocolate and sweet rolls for breakfast right there at school. Non-Catholic kids were supposed to eat before Mass and weren't invited to breakfast. The sweet bread looked very good, so I asked one of the sisters if I could have bread with the other children. She thought I meant that I would like to receive the Eucharist and asked me if I wanted to become a Catholic. I said I would ask my grandmother.

Granny didn't care. She said whatever I wanted to do, I could do: "Just because we never found anything, that doesn't mean we should deny you the right to try." Mom gave me the same answer she always had as long as I could remember: "You should do what you know in your heart is right." When I learned that I would be allowed to convert, I got down on my knees and said aloud all the Catholic prayers I had memorized.

Dolores was entered in First Communion classes, a first step toward the conversion that began, not with a strong religious incentive, but two practical ones: don't cross dangerous streets and have breakfast with the children.

Sister Dolores Marie was ecstatic. Every day she would get me on my knees and teach me the Rosary, which we did in the back bedroom closet so Grandpa wouldn't hear.

At Mass I watched when the children received Communion. I began to put together the fact that the presence I experienced when I was alone in the church—the reassurance, the well-being—was somehow associated with the wafer the children ate. Soon I would be able to participate in a new way—not only going into the church but actually receiving the wafer kept in that box, the tabernacle. It was hard to explain as a child—there I was finding this wonderful thing, and there I was eating it.

26

—It's hard to explain as a grown-up too.

After school, some of the Saint Gregory kids would go swimming at the YMCA, and not wanting to be left out, Dolores went with them, never admitting that she didn't know how to swim. One day, she took a dare and jumped off the high board. She bumped into the side of the pool and was taken home, badly shaken and very groggy. When she didn't recover as quickly as Esther expected, a doctor was called. The doctor administered penicillin, unaware that Dolores was allergic to the new drug. That night she had a serious reaction and great difficulty moving. Esther was sure it was polio. In the 1940s there was a polio epidemic in America, and public swimming pools were high on the list of places to contract the disease.

I remember everybody being so sad. Granny slept on cushions on the floor next to my bed, and whenever she couldn't be there, her friend Lola Menary was. The atmosphere was decidedly gloomy, and I couldn't help but pick up on it. When a playmate slipped in and placed a lily on my chest, causing Granny to burst into tears, I believed I was going to die. I couldn't explain it, but I felt the presence of something that I accepted as the presence of authority—the presence of God. I spoke— not prayed, but spoke—to God: "If You want me to go to You, I'll go. I'm not afraid."

I had awakened to the possibility of that kind of direct communication during the times I had sat alone in the chapel at Saint Gregory's. But this was the first time I knew I could speak directly to God, that I had that privilege. Out of that moment I found the gift of faith. Out of that moment I became a Catholic.

That same day Dolores was given Benadryl to counteract the penicillin and decrease swelling. Within a short time she was fully recovered. She didn't realize until many years later, after her entrance into the monastery, that this unusual, casual, direct conversation with God had been her first interior response.

I was baptized at Saint Gregory's Church on October 4, 1948, a few days before my tenth birthday. When the priest sprinkled me with holy water, it was the greatest moment of joy in my ten years of life. I experienced a sensation of acceptance that any child, and especially a child in my circumstances, would find quite empowering. Even though my grandfather, grandmother and mother all had approved, I had crossed a boundary that was really of my own doing. I had found something that was now my own place, above and beyond all that had been cruel and dishonorable in my parents' home.

By the time I was ten years old, I had a very dramatic imagination. In becoming a Catholic, I thought of myself as part of a colorful new cast of characters in an exciting new story. I was a member of the Kingdom of God, the Kingdom of the Saints, the Kingdom of the Angels.

When I was first introduced to the sacrament of confession, I had difficulty grasping some of the things the sisters taught us. I knew stealing was wrong and sassing your mother, forgetting to feed a pet and being mean to somebody—that all made sense. But I did not understand why the sisters were always warning us to keep our bodies covered, as if there were something sinful about the body. Mom had always taught me that the body was natural, something to rejoice in.

I started to keep a list of usual sins, but when I looked at it, I found I hadn't done any of those things. So what to confess? I thought I could confess something I might easily do if I had the chance. If sins were expected, I would make up a few.

—I took it so seriously, so very seriously.

I was confirmed at Saint Gregory's on April 24, 1949. The bishop welcomed me to the altar and, after confirming me, slapped my face. The slap said: "You'll take a beating; be strong." My cheeks burned with bravery. Now I was a real soldier of Christ.

At confirmation you take the name of a saint who holds personal meaning for you. It signifies your devotion to that saint, who will help you in your mission in life. I took for my confirmation name Therese, after Saint Thérèse of Lisieux, who was just a little older than I when she entered the convent. She was described as a child who found Christ not through great healing miracles but through doing humble, simple things. She had such a sense of mission and purpose. The rigorous,

28

sticky French spirituality of her time made it difficult to be an individual, and I suppose her stamina was very appealing to me.

After my conversion, I had my first reflection about vocation: the act of being fully Catholic would be, of course, to become a nun. But I reasoned that that was what I should be thinking, so the reflection vanished as quickly as it had flared, not to materialize again until I was in college. Yet I still knew that I had something I had been missing. I had been deeply impressed by the sense of belonging that the other children derived from the practice of their religion; and as I participated with them, I began to feel that I too belonged there with them. My aunts had exposed me to other religions, but it was only as a Catholic that this sense of joyousness and purpose came over me.

> *—Some people are quick to say that any child who had no more stability than I would clutch at anything with a sound foundation. That never bothers me because they are only confirming that the Church has strength and solidity.*

Four

For the first time in her life Dolores had lived in one place long enough to have a sense of belonging. When Dolores was eleven, however, she returned to California to live with her mother, who was planning to remarry.

Harriett had been establishing a new life for herself, one that eventually would include Dolores, but since the divorce, she had enjoyed the single life that marrying at an early age had denied her. She played the field and had a number of suitors, but when she met Albert Gordon, a divorced man raising a nine-year-old son, she thought she had found the man who would give her a home and security.

Harriett met Al while she was working as a cashier at Gordon's, a restaurant in Beverly Hills. Al and his two brothers, Gene and Bernie, owned Gordon's, as well as liquor stores and a small deli.

I was unhappy about leaving Chicago, which I now thought of as home, but one thing cheered me: I would again be near Hollywood, where movies were made. I used to read the movie magazines all the time. I never let my family see me reading them, though. I was afraid they would think I was funny. The only Nancy Drew book I read was Nancy Drew in Hollywood, *and I read that under the covers.*

—If truth were known, my dream was to be a movie star. I used to say I wanted to be an actress, but that was just to hide the pretension of "star".

After the wedding, the two families moved into a bungalow on Hazeltine Avenue in Sherman Oaks. One of Al's liquor stores was on the corner. The cheery yellow house had a large backyard with fruit trees that supplied Harriett with an abundance of fruit for preserving.

Al Gordon was a good man—Jewish, but he did not practice his faith. At first glance, with his dark looks and large brown eyes, one might have taken him for a dandy. He was, however, all work. I liked my stepfather and wanted to call him something besides Al. "Daddy" would always mean my father, so Al became "Pop". Pop worked days at the liquor store and nights at the restaurant. Mom often joined him in the evenings to help out or just to have drinks with friends after closing.

Harriett soon made friends with the neighborhood coffee-klatch ladies, who had been accommodating enough to loan her a sewing machine. The kids in the area were mostly boys, but they immediately accepted Dolores. Some years later, in a magazine interview, Harriett remembered her daughter "played football with boys before she dated them. She was always taking bikes apart and putting them together again. She would get on the roof and fix the TV antennae. The boys thought of her not as a girl but as their equal, a comrade who could whistle through her teeth just like they did."

—Mom taught me how to whistle through my teeth—a loud, piercing, real-boy whistle that, later in life, I found effective for hailing cabs in New York City. I once whistled like that in the common room at the monastery, and food dropped from mouths.

Older sister and younger brother bonded easily. Dolores and Martin were close in age, so there was no awkward initiation period. She was also enough of a tomboy to make for comfortable coexistence and sufficiently pretty to make him feel proud. They shared a fondness for *Dragnet* and *I Love Lucy* on TV, which Dolores got Jewish Martin to join her in giving up for Lent. Together they built a small stage in the garage, where they presented puppet shows to family and neighborhood friends.

Pop took us on excursions to Rosarita Beach and Las Vegas. At holiday time, Mom would decorate the house like Macy's department store. She even accompanied me to Mass on occasion. I was starting to experience the things the children at Saint Gregory's spoke of when they talked about their families.

I had, at long last, a strong sense that Mom and I were going to be all right, that we were finally going to make it as a family. All the stressful years that had taken their toll on Mom were over, and she

31

seemed truly content for the first time in a long while. Our relationship, which had always been close when I was very young, got closer. I became her confidante, a younger sister.

Dolores saw little of her father during this period. Bert had married yet again but still had not settled down. His drinking and his wife abuse continued—a sympathetic Harriett often administering to his battered third wife, Deena—and he went from job to job in Los Angeles and Chicago. He tried selling used cars for a short time and then sold pots and pans door-to-door, pretending to be a religious man. That was a brief career, ended abruptly by the authorities. Forever chasing the butterfly of success, he even tried his hand at gold mining in Alaska, but the Hicks Gold Mining Company was another short-lived addition to his many failed schemes.

> *—We got one thing out of the mining company—a lot of free stationery. I'm still using it for note paper.*

When it came time to enroll in school, Dolores told her mother she didn't want to attend public school. Saint Francis de Sales was close to their Sherman Oaks home, but Dolores could not be enrolled because she was from a divorced home and had a Baptist mother and a Jewish stepfather.

This got Harriett's Irish up, and she confronted the priest at Saint Francis de Sales and read him the riot act. "I may be a Baptist," she said, "in fact, I may even be a heathen, and I am divorced and married to a Jew. But my kid is Catholic because she chose to be Catholic, and if you refuse her admittance because of me, you are defeating the message of your gospel. Jesus did not refuse the little children, and if you don't take her, between the Baptist and the Jew, this kid won't stand a chance. So you better find a way."

Dolores was entered into the sixth grade, impressed that her mother had gotten through to him with her impassioned speech. But Harriett later confided that, when Dolores was out of earshot, she fired a final salvo at the startled priest: "If you don't let her in, I'll be down here in the morning and personally throw a brickbat through every one of your god-damned stained-glass windows."

On my first day, I noticed a scroll on the wall of my classroom containing the words of Saint Francis de Sales: "The same everlasting Father who cares for you today will take care of you tomorrow and every day. Either he will shield you from suffering or he will give you unfailing strength to bear it." I felt that message was somehow meant for me.

Her favorite teacher was Mother Anthony. When, in 2004, I spoke to Mother Anthony, who had become Sister Dorothy Bartels after Vatican II, she sounded no more than thirty as she recalled Dolores in the seventh and eighth grades, some fifty-five years before. "I seem to remember Dolores always on a bicycle, wearing one of those beanies that were so popular with the kids, with the tiny propeller on top. A very good student, curious about everything—and not at all 'actressy'. I also remember that she used to doodle Shmoos—those shapeless cartoon figures in the *Li'l Abner* comic strip—on everything, including her homework and test papers."

Dolores became part of a small group of kids who earned the nickname "Can-do Gang", because of their fearlessness in tackling any challenge with humor and imagination. "Can-do" reflected the spirit of America at that time, having finally emerged from the Depression era. The Can-do kids became friends for life: Gail Lammersen, Arlene Howsley, Janne Shirley, Marilyn Finch, who also would become a nun, Judy Conway and Joseph Allegretti, the lone boy in the group, who had a reputation for helping people. A half century later, Joe remembered Dolores: "She was not only pretty but very quiet and serious and, yes, I thought, saintly."

At Saint Francis de Sales I came across a book on the French actress Eleanora Duse. I thought it was the most wonderful book I had ever read, and I locked some of her sage observations inside me. Her art depended on intense naturalness—"I did not use paint. I made myself up morally." That made sense to me. She recounted going to her mother's funeral and being aware of her feelings and reactions to use later when she was acting. At the time I was horrified at her heartlessness—but also fascinated. It did seem a means to pack away difficult moments into a memory bank that could be called up when needed later. I vowed to store up memories of all the things that affected me, so I could use them when I was playing a role. Eleanora also said something else that I wrote down in my diary: "When we grow old, there can only be one regret—not to have given enough of ourselves."

Way, way back in my mind, even that early, I was aware of the fact that my life was not for me, that it somehow was something outside of me. I remember walking up and down the ramp at the back of the Drake Theater and thinking that my life was meant for something else. I knew it was going to be ecstatic; I was sure of this because I had decided to be an actress. In my mind it was preordained.

Life was good for the next two years, living up to Dolores' early hopes. Then cracks in Harriett's marriage began to appear. Both Al and Harriett were social drinkers, but on occasion they would get what Dolores called "pie-eyed". Arguments increased until finally, in 1951, the couple separated, Al and Martin moving out of the Hazeltine house.

During the separation Harriett's drinking continued; her coffee-klatch sessions with the neighbor ladies were now afternoon happy hours, and her excursions to the beach were in the company of a beer-drinking buddy. Although Dolores knew the score, she euphemized Harriett's behavior to younger Martin, telling him, "Mom is sick."

The marital separation was short lived, and when Al and Martin moved back, Harriett went on the wagon. Dolores once again felt hopeful.

Hopeful, yes, but I wasn't stupid. I could see that our life wasn't going to be what it had been for that first little while. For one thing, Pop and his brothers opened two new restaurants, the Rainbow Inn in the Valley and the Beefeater Inn on restaurant row in West Hollywood. The Beefeater was Pop's very successful baby, and he couldn't be pried away from it night or day. Pop had expected Mom to give up drinking, but he continued to drink with his friends at the restaurant, coming home later and later. I resented his behavior because I felt he was giving her a reason to drink. Mom thrived on attention, and Pop just wasn't around to give that to her.

I got away to Chicago whenever I could. It was a godsend to be back with Granny and Grandpa. On one trip, I even got a job helping Granny out as busgirl at the Round Table. I think they created the job just to make Granny happy, but I got $2.50 a day.

Until she was fired. Customers would continually interfere with her work to tell her how much she looked like Grace Kelly. Finally, when she tried to avoid yet another Grace Kelly comparison, she backed right into a tray full of dishes. The management decided they couldn't afford her any longer.

Each time I returned to California, I would find the situation at home much the same. There was so much tension. So I went in for scholarship and all the school activity I could to keep occupied. I became active in dramatics and the band, and I began writing for the school paper. I also began a very happy relationship with my young Lanza cousins.

Mom had kept close contact with Betty and Mario while I was living in Chicago. Uncle Mario's movie career had skyrocketed, and he was becoming the most famous singer in the world. The Lanza family now included two daughters and two sons, whom I often babysat.

Colleen and Ellisa Lanza were not really babies at all but young girls with wonderful minds of their own. I don't remember Uncle Mario being present a lot, and the Aunt Betty I knew as a child seemed far away in the opulent Beverly Hills home. They were rarely there when I visited. The kids seemed almost orphaned, so I made sure they knew that I cared and that life was about something more than thirty-foot, Saks-decorated Christmas trees and wagons full of toys.

"We were pampered as children", Ellisa Lanza Bregman recalled. "Everything was done for us. My brothers couldn't even tie their own shoelaces. Our mother was a party girl and loved entertaining. Our parties were grand affairs with all the trimmings, and holidays were extravagantly mounted.

"But we wanted to be with Dolores on Sundays. She would pick us up for Mass and sometimes would even have breakfast with us after services or take us shopping. When she became an actress, I think we were more impressed with her career than our father's—because of

35

Elvis Presley. We would beg her to get his autograph for us and for our friends, and we loved to boast about our cousin knowing Elvis."

The bonding with Ellisa and Colleen was interrupted when Uncle Mario moved the family to Italy after his career in films began to wane. As his career declined, his drinking increased, and his excessive weight gains and losses did great harm to his health. So he quit Hollywood for Italy, where he enjoyed a resurgence in his singing career through concert performances. I was happy for Mario and Betty, but I missed the girls.

Two new pets helped to take my attention away from problems at home. One, a mouse I crowned Mouse Deputz, would actually pray with me. At least she seemed to. Whenever I said the Rosary, Deputz would lay her head down and looked as if she were praying too. The other was Doc Doc, a duck little more than the size of an egg, an Easter present from Mom. When fully grown he was a real pet, accustomed to wearing a red tie around his neck and waiting for me to come home from school. Doc Doc followed me when I went to the grocery store and waited patiently outside. But I could take him inside Pop's liquor store on the corner because they didn't mind.

Graduation from middle school to high school took Dolores from Saint Francis de Sales to Corvallis, an all-girl Catholic school in Studio City. The Saint Francis lads transferred to the all-boys high school, Notre Dame, but they were still present in the girls' lives.

I always trusted in God's power, so at Corvallis I did a lot of praying for Notre Dame to win football games. I may have said one or two prayers for help in religion and Latin too. I was getting good grades—As and Bs—in all my classes except religion and Latin.

—I did end up with an A in religion, but no amount of praying could help me with Latin.

Harriett became pregnant in 1954 and was optimistic that the baby would stabilize the marriage. But she suffered medical problems early in the pregnancy. She was in her third month when she was rushed to the hospital, in critical condition. Rather than take any risks, Al immediately decided to end the pregnancy.

Mom was bitter about not being consulted and carried her resentment toward Pop, that it was his decision and not hers, through her life. I didn't blame Pop, because he did what he thought best. He wasn't Catholic, so all that mattered to him was Mom's safety. Mom later admitted to me that this was when she knew their marriage was over.

Harriett's drinking accelerated after the loss of the baby, causing severe mood swings. She could be gay and friendly when Dolores or Martin brought chums to the house, preparing snacks for the visitors, yet within a split second, raging at them that she wasn't a hired hand to be taken advantage of. Dolores tried to explain to Martin, who was not aware of the abortion, that there was a cause for everything, even her drinking.

Dolores' first realization that her mother was a solitary drinker came as a result of caring for Doc Doc. The pet duck was housed in the orchard, and on a routine gathering of mulch for Doc Doc's nest, Dolores came upon a bottle of whiskey hidden under the straw and leaves.

I knew intuitively it was Mom's bottle. I had seen her drink with Pop at the Beefeater and sometimes come home tipsy, but the fact that the bottle was hidden scared me. I finally asked her about it, and she admitted to drinking but insisted that she wasn't drinking to excess and would stop. But every time she went out, I could always find a bottle somewhere. Angry and hurt, I would empty it down the drain. Mom invariably found out, which would result in a nasty confrontation. She said many times that she would stop drinking and over the years made repeated attempts to get help from Alcoholics Anonymous without success.

My elemental, deep-seated love for Mom was permanent—nothing would ever change that—but I became more independent, not only emotionally, but also financially. Mom inadvertently aided this goal. For my sixteenth birthday, she bought me a used '38 Chevy and taught me to drive. This new freedom allowed me to add tutoring to my résumé. I tutored a boy in the neighborhood and drove him on his early-morning paper route. I also got one part-time job in the bakery of

37

Ralph's Market for $1.75 an hour and another at a stable in Toluca Lake, grooming the horses and mucking out the stalls, for a dollar an hour plus free rides. Some evenings, on my own, I would drive up to Mulholland Drive, atop the mountain separating Los Angeles from the San Fernando Valley, and park just to watch the searchlights in Hollywood light up the sky for a movie premiere and pretend it was all for me.

At school, I volunteered for everything. I was on the student council and in the Catholic Scholarship Federation. I attended the Girls State conference in Sacramento, a program to introduce students to the workings of government. I was pitcher for the softball team—I couldn't hit or catch worth a damn—and, briefly, a cheerleader. Arlene Howsley and I volunteered at Saint Anne's Home for Unwed Mothers. We were Red Cross and Community Chest volunteers too. I found the time and money to enroll in a modeling course during summer vacation and, with three friends, formed a small pop band—piano, accordion, drums and clarinet. We wore outlandish old clothes and called ourselves the Ragamuffin Band.

I was a member of the Science Club, the Spanish Club, the San Fernando Valley Youth Band, the YMCA (yes, YMCA—this predated the establishment of the YWCA) and, still faithful to Al Capp, the Secret Society of Super Shmoo. I belonged to anything I could. The reason I was so engaged in all this extracurricular activity was, of course, to delay going home.

Her backbreaking schedule didn't stop Dolores from going to Mass almost every day, even if she had to get up at 6:00 A.M. to do it. In fact, when she did not make Mass, it was an occasion worth noting in her diary.

—The comfort I felt when I was alone with God seemed stronger in the church. I had come to rely on that direct communication with Him, which always reassured me that I would be able to deal with hard times.

Social life during high school was more problematic than anyone knew. I wanted to be accepted, but there was always the possibility that

38

someone would see Mom drunk. When girls would come over for slumber parties, Mom would curb the drinking, but as the evening went on, she would sneak enough drinks to be a little too giddy. My greatest fear was that I might be blackballed by my classmates. At the dances at school, I sat in the gym bleachers that were the farthest back. Then at least I could have an excuse if no one asked me to dance.

Attention wasn't as difficult to come by as she implies. There was a constant flow of boys at the Hazeltine door—Martin joked that it was more like a river. She didn't lack for dates to dances and parties and football games and—if it was up to her—movies. Decades later she could still remember names.

> *—Burt Glannon, Jim Adams and Donald Boyles were my movie dates. I would see a movie I particularly liked with each of them. I must have seen* Roman Holiday *and* The Rose Tattoo *ten times each. I was in a dance contest with Bob Saunders. We were second in waltz, third in rumba.*

Harriett always insisted that she trusted Dolores and her boyfriends. She gave them freedom. This modern approach, however, was undermined when, with a few drinks in her, Harriett would flirt with Dolores' dates.

This was so embarrassing for the boy and humiliating for me. She could also pick up the phone and very easily pretend to be me with one of my boyfriends, which she thought was funny.

Privately and soberly, Mom gave me one warning—"too easy, too late"—and that was sufficient. I wasn't in the market for a steady relationship anyway. It wasn't until Chris, a young telephone repairman, did some work at the house that I dated seriously. Two years older than I and a high school dropout, Chris had a way about him, a lively joie de vivre—and he was Catholic. I was infatuated. But when I showed up at a school dance with Chris as my escort, I got some flack from Mother Phillip, the principal at Corvallis, who thought Chris wasn't an appropriate companion, emphasizing that, as a dropout, he had no sound future. I've often wondered whether she sensed something about the direction my life was to take, if perhaps I had a religious vocation. She never mentioned that to me, but she minced no words

39

about the telephone repairman. She told me to get rid of him because my life was going somewhere beyond him.

Reluctantly, I did, which happily allowed me to meet one of the nicest boys I've ever known. On a trip home from Chicago, I sat next to Jack Lynch, a young sailor from Wisconsin en route to San Pedro Naval Base. For the few months that Jack was stationed in California, we dated and went to Mass together. I saw On the Waterfront *with him. I remember thinking my world had changed because of that film and Brando, Eva Marie Saint and Karl Malden, who showed us* truth. *Usually movies didn't speak to me that way. I was riveted and inspired by Eva Marie's performance. That was the kind of role I wanted to play someday.*

Jack was my date for the senior prom, which was a big deal. I mean, to show up at the prom with a sailor in dress uniform was a very big deal. That night Jack and I crowned the prom queen—which disappointed Grandpa. He wrote that I shouldn't have crowned the queen; I should have been the queen. The lovely part is that Jack Lynch became a wonderful friend to both Mom and me. Through the years we stayed in touch, until his death in 1998.

Father Charles White, a Paulist priest from a parish in Westwood, came to Corvallis to conduct a retreat, a series of seminars devoted to religious topics. He looked like a head-on collision between the youthful John Paul II and Bing Crosby. I admired him greatly; he was one of the most loving people I ever knew. He was an orphan, so the world became his family.

In her senior year at Corvallis, Dolores was elected president of the student body. She also began a relationship with Joan of Arc, first in a scene from George Bernard Shaw's *Saint Joan*, suggested to her by the new speech and drama teacher, Beverly Zanoline. Dolores had earlier won a speech contest and had gone on to represent Corvallis in a final competition at the Lions Club. There were so many contestants that evening that she was almost asleep when her turn came. Approaching the podium she suddenly realized she couldn't remember what she had prepared.

All I could do was stand there and say miserably, "I forgot my speech."
I ran from the stage and collapsed in tears in the backseat of our car. I
vowed to my mother that I would never set foot on a stage again.

"Cripes," she said, "it's no big deal. After twenty-five speeches,
everyone wanted to go home anyway. You're not a failure, kiddo; you're
a prize." Miss Zanoline apparently agreed with Mom because she
scheduled a scene from Saint Joan *for the class to present to the student*
body and cast me as the French Maid of Orléans. Everyone thought that
the kids would never sit still for the "King of Heaven" scene; but, with
reborn confidence, I insisted that they wouldn't dare not sit still. I was
the school president after all.

—It was a captive audience.

The fact that a nationwide search was going on for an unknown actress
to play the teenage Joan of Arc in the film version of *Saint Joan* may
have added to the attraction. This well-publicized search was second
only to the 1938 quest for an actress to play Scarlett O'Hara in *Gone
with the Wind*, with applications available in movie-house lobbies across
the country. The film was to be produced and directed by Otto Preminger, who in the recent past had been responsible for *Laura, Carmen
Jones* and *The Man with the Golden Arm*. He had lined up a strong cast
of internationally known actors including Richard Widmark, John Giel-
gud, Anton Walbrook and Richard Todd to support the unknown actress.
Dolores couldn't believe it when she received a letter inviting her to
read for *Saint Joan*. Her friends Gail Lammersen and Janne Shirley had
submitted in her name an application for an audition.

Mr. Preminger personally conducted the auditions at the Academy
Awards Theater in Hollywood. There were hundreds of girls lined up in
front of the theater. I waited five hours for my turn and overheard other
candidates saying the most frightening things about Mr. Preminger. I
was petrified when my name was finally called. His appearance was
intimidating; but he was astonishingly sweet to me during the interview,
and I started to feel at ease.

Just before the test began, Mr. Preminger asked me if I could cry
easily. I told him I thought I could. "Fine", he said and slapped my face

41

and called, "Action!" Stunned and humiliated, but with tears streaming, I did the "King of Heaven" scene. Mr. Preminger asked me back for a second reading. To put it mildly, I was reluctant. I was afraid he might hit me again. He didn't, but I was so nervous I read very badly, and that was the end of that. Jean Seberg, a young girl from Iowa, was the chosen one. From what I have been told, her life changed radically and so sadly. Over the years, I often prayed for Jean.

The "King of Heaven" scene was useful twice more: first, when the high school cast was invited to present it on the local Gene Norman television show, which put Dolores in a professional atmosphere for the first time in her life; and again when she presented it in a bid for a scholarship at her school of choice, Marymount College in Los Angeles.

Just before graduation, arguments between Mom and Pop accelerated to the point where divorce was talked about. I could hear them late at night calculating who would get the television set and whether the car was community property. She added and subtracted ironed shirts and hot meals, while he added and subtracted scotch and sodas. Their ears were closed to my pleas to try to work things out as they sat there and divided love. Pop wanted to sell the house—he always called it the "big house"—and promised to pay my Marymount tuition if we moved to an apartment. Mom vetoed that fast, and Pop walked out. Then he came back once again. That summer no people moved through the house on Hazeltine, just shadows.

I was peeved at Pop's constant reference to the "big house" as if it were costing a fortune and his using my tuition as a wedge. Although I thought of his financial support of me as my due, I wasn't about to ask for his help. I didn't ever want to beg for anything.

—There's a lot of Grandma Hicks in me.

Pop made good on his threat to withhold money. Still, I had to acknowledge that Pop had been very good to me; when all was said and done, I didn't dislike my stepfather, and my relationship with him continued to be affectionate.

42

Dolores and her mother scraped together $400 for the tuition and took it personally to Marymount. It was after hours, and they traipsed up and down hallways, peeking into rooms until they found a lone nun sitting at a typewriter. Dolores presented the money and was told she was $75 short. The nun, Mother Gregory, was not a clerk but the president of the school, and she assured Dolores and her mother that something could be worked out.

That was when *Saint Joan* came through for Dolores again. The scene won her a scholarship of $500, which ensured that she would be able to attend the college. Her freshman year at Marymount would begin in September 1956.

The scholarship would pay for the tuition, but I was still responsible for room and board. So I enrolled as a day student and planned to live at home the first semester.

On graduation day, I was valedictorian of the Corvallis class of 1956. I wasn't chosen because I had the highest scholastic average but because the nuns thought I could speak better. Everyone was impressed except Grandpa. He still preferred that I was prom queen.

During the summer between high school and college, I got a job at the Glen Aire Country Club in Sherman Oaks. They tried me out in several positions, but I ended up making hamburgers in the small pool café. It was a pretty boring job, so I daydreamed a lot about being an actress. The jukebox in the café continually played Bing Crosby and Grace Kelly singing "True Love" from High Society. *The kids at Corvallis had teased me about looking like Grace Kelly. But when Grace Kelly was my age, she was already modeling in New York and studying at the American Academy of Dramatic Arts. And there I was, making hamburgers.*

Five

Marymount College was founded in Los Angeles in 1933, separately from but parallel to Loyola, the Catholic men's university. These institutions would merge and become Loyola Marymount University in 1973, but in 1956 Marymount was still a small liberal arts college almost hidden behind eucalyptus trees in the hills above the UCLA campus.

The usual liberal arts curriculum was substantially supplemented by courses in religion, including apologetics.

— Apologetics?

> *Literally,* apologetics *means "defense of your faith". One way to think of it is how a person who has faith would try to explain to someone who does not believe why it is necessary to believe.*

There were also personal improvement classes such as charm and etiquette, with emphasis on how to comport oneself like a lady, how to carry on an intelligent conversation and how to set a table.

Most of the classes were taught by nuns, but there were "civilian" teachers too. The well-known modeling agent Caroline Leonetti taught charm and etiquette, and Roger Wagner, of the Roger Wagner Chorale, taught singing. Marymount also boasted a dramatic club. Virginia Barnelle was the head of the drama department.

Classmates Gail Lammersen and Maureen Bailey worked alongside Dolores and still remember her as "a vivacious comedienne who kept everyone in stitches with pantomimes made up in a flash—say, a bullfight, and she would play the bullfighter *and* the bull."

The school's living accommodation was Butler Hall, a dormitory with a nun in residence to "keep the girls safe", and only one public telephone, which imperiled their social life. Finances kept Dolores from moving into the dorm during her first semester, but later she became a Butler Hall resident.

44

In the mid-twentieth century, college girls were expected to be on campus at all times unless they had permission to leave. They signed out and signed back in. Weeknight curfews were early, but if grades were kept up, girls were allowed to stay out until ten o'clock. The deadline was extended two hours on weekends. Marymount didn't have uniforms, but its dress code was strict. Dolores and fellow class counselor Deanna Smith were monitors of the code, charged with reporting any classmates who were in violation.

—Neither of us ever snitched. In fact, one night we joined the rest of the Butler Hall residents in a protest over the dress code. We "decorated" the trees facing Sunset Boulevard with our garter belts and bras, which caused a traffic jam of hotrod drivers from both Loyola and UCLA.

I liked all my classmates, but especially Sheila Hart. When we met, Sheila was holding court in Butler Hall. I found her gay and witty, energizing, and I figured I would have to make a pretty big impression to get her attention. I followed an impulse and improvised one of my "scenes" on the spot. I pretended I had something important to say, opened my mouth wide, then clapped my hand over it, pantomiming with great distress that I had just swallowed a fly. I made my impression. Sheila made one too. She was the only girl who went for a glass of water.

Five decades later Sheila recalled that the chemistry between them was immediate: "There are some people who are a match from the first moment. Somehow you know you've just met someone you will cherish for the rest of your life." The girls shared like points of view. They also shared similar hurts—the divorce of parents as well as the devastating effect alcohol can have on a family. Both had gone through a polio scare. About the only difference between them was Dolores' lack of interest in fashion. "She just didn't care about clothes", Sheila laughed, "and relied on me whenever she needed to buy something."

Most importantly, we found in each other the same gentleness of budding womanhood and deep-rooted Catholic values, part of Sheila's

45

upbringing but a personal discovery for me. We could talk to each other on a level beyond usual freshman nonsense.

The two girls would walk up into the hills behind the school, trespassing on the nearby Bel-Air golf course. "It was on one of these walks", Sheila said, "that Dolores wondered out loud if possibly there was something more in store for her than just becoming a Catholic. Although she laughed it off—'No, thank you, I'm going to be an actress'—I was always aware that there was something about her, a longing. I used to think of it as her Hound of Heaven, and I was honored that she would share that with me. She hadn't ever talked about it with the nuns at school."

I did not understand or know how to describe what I was feeling because I was sure I would be a candidate for the loony bin. But I seemed to be searching for something. I felt I didn't fully have the understanding of the Church that I needed, so my pursuit would introduce me to a number of Catholic orders such as the Carmelites and the Franciscans. For a brief time I was a Dominican tertiary and took classes on the works of Saint Thomas Aquinas at a Dominican house of studies. To take on study of Aquinas was no small challenge.

—Throughout my life, I've had difficulty concentrating while reading. At school, I relied a great deal on synopses. I was able to pull out the pith.

Early in her freshman year, Dolores met Loyola philosophy major Don Barbeau, who was older than most of the students by some ten years. He had been a Trappist monk before he entered Loyola, and he drove a 1938 hearse instead of a regular car. He was also involved in Loyola's upcoming production of *Joan of Lorraine*, Maxwell Anderson's modern take on the story of Joan of Arc, and asked Dolores if she would be interested in reading for the lead.

Barbeau was genuinely convinced that Dolores had movie potential, and he promised to invite Hollywood producers to see the play. Dolores figured this was just a line, but the thought of doing that play did interest her because one of her favorite actresses, Ingrid Bergman, had played it in the original Broadway production, and, well, it *was* Joan of

Arc. The drama department's Virginia Barnelle, however, would be a formidable hurdle.

I knew Miss Barnelle would not permit a frosh to be cast over one of her senior girls. So I didn't ask permission but went to the audition in secret. I got the part. Miss Barnelle was not pleased.

Rehearsals, which occupied five nights a week, all but canceled Dolores' social life, but she didn't care. She admired the play and thought the part of Joan was perfect for her. The director was a priest from Hungary, Father Andrew Viragh, only recently liberated from behind the Iron Curtain. The cast included a young student, Bob Denver, in the role of the dauphin. Bob would make his mark in television a few years later as the star of *Gilligan's Island*.

Barbeau did not take lightly his promise to help Dolores land a movie career. He invested in a camera and took some head shots to include in the letters he wrote to studio executives, inviting each of them to a performance of *Joan of Lorraine* during its one-week run beginning December 11, 1956.

As astonishing as it sounds, there were some takers. Representatives from Warner Bros. and Twentieth Century-Fox responded to Don's invitation to see the play. I was asked to interview at both studios. The Fox possibility especially interested me because Daddy had been under contract there.

Neither studio followed through, but there was another name on Barbeau's list of invitees—Hal Wallis, one of the top producers in Hollywood. During his years at Warner Bros., Wallis had been involved in the production of over one hundred films, personally producing over half of them, including *Casablanca*. In the mid-forties he moved to Paramount, where he would rack up a total of sixty films, including *Come Back, Little Sheba*, *The Rose Tattoo* and the successful Martin and Lewis comedies.

Wallis was taken with the genuineness of Barbeau's letter and thought the girl in the photograph was fresh and pretty, so he asked the Paramount head of talent, William Meikeljohn, to check her out in the play. Meikeljohn's reaction was positive, so Paul Nathan, Wallis' associate producer, made a call to Dolores' home to invite her to come in for an interview. Since Dolores hadn't told her mother of Barbeau's plan, Harriett thought it was a gag and hung up on Paul. His secretary tracked Dolores down at Marymount. She was called from class to take a telephone call from "a Hollywood producer" and dutifully marched to the dean's office. She picked up the phone, and her life changed.

Nathan explained that she might be right for the new Elvis Presley movie that was about to go into production and asked her to come to the studio that very afternoon.

I nearly froze on the spot. I told him I would have to get my mother's permission. He said she had hung up on him. With heart pounding, I somehow managed to track down Don Barbeau, who excitedly agreed to drive me to the studio immediately.

As we approached the studio in Don's hearse, I recognized the Paramount gate as the same one through which Erich von Stroheim drove Gloria Swanson in that Isotta Fraschini in Sunset Boulevard. *Wow, some difference! I had on my usual school costume—navy skirt, white blouse, white bucks and, of course, my ponytail. Mr. Wallis and Mr. Nathan met us in a reception room.*

A few minutes later, she got her first look at the Wallis inner sanctum. Beautifully appointed, the huge room was full of trophies attesting to his lofty position in the film industry—twelve framed Oscar nominations for best picture plus the statue itself for producing *Casablanca*— and a number of original Remingtons and Russells reflecting his personal passion. He had a sense of humor too. At the threshold of his private john, there was a doormat with a caricature of Jerry Lewis.

Several executives joined us. Introductions were made, and we all sat down. The room fell into an immediate and prolonged silence. I could feel each man studying me. Mr. Nathan leaned over and whispered, "I didn't like your photo, but I like you." I began to blush.

The blush, which began at the roots of her hair, spread downward. Years later Nathan recalled, "Her ears looked like they were on fire. Everyone laughed, and the tension was broken. Her blushing had captivated us." The meeting ended with Wallis giving her a scene from his current production, *Hot Spell*, to study for an audition in a few days.

Don insisted that I needed to get an agent fast. He knew of one, Carlos Alvarado, who had a good reputation. Mom wasn't so sure that was the right move and asked friends—the Duncan Sisters—for advice. The Duncan Sisters, who were appearing at the country club Pop managed, had been headliners in vaudeville. They counseled against signing with Alvarado because they feared that, with a name like Dolores and an agent named Carlos, I would get offered only senorita parts. But both Don and I knew I wasn't in any position to be choosy, so we met with Mr. Alvarado, who agreed to represent me.

Mr. Alvarado got an acting coach and an actor to help me rehearse the scene. Just before Christmas, we presented it to Mr. Wallis in a Paramount rehearsal room called the "fish bowl" because of a large see-through mirror on one wall through which he could watch auditions without being seen. I got through the scene and waited for some comment. Nothing. Not even "Don't call us; we'll call you."

There was no call during the entire Christmas break. With midterms coming up, my attention went back to the books. On the first day back at school, as I was being raked over the coals for taking my shoes off in charm class, Mom arrived clutching a telegram from Paul Nathan. I was going to be given a screen test for the Elvis Presley movie.

A letter agreement for a test option was drawn up on January 8, 1957, giving Hal Wallis the right to screen-test Dolores Hicks and lock her into a six-month contract, should that option be exercised. The test was set for the following week. There was one major bugaboo in this too-good-to-be-true scenario. The test was scheduled the same day as the drama class finals. There was no way around Miss Barnelle this time.

I had to ask to reschedule my exam. "Forget it", Miss Barnelle warned. "If you miss the exam, you will not pass, and if you don't pass, you can forget the scholarship." I was a wreck and went to see Mother Jean Gailhac. "For Heaven's sake, go for it", she said. "This is what all the girls in the acting class would give their right arm for." Did I ever love Mother Jean Gailhac!

The test confirmed that Dolores was photogenic and projected an open, natural quality that Wallis liked. The option was exercised for a six-month period beginning on January 16, 1957—exactly one month from the date of the final performance of *Joan of Lorraine*.

It was all turning out exactly as Don had promised. When we finally came down from cloud nine, I tried to put my gratitude into words. Nothing I could say seemed big enough to let him know how much I owed him. Then I felt his arm, gentle and tentative, around my waist. I had been afraid that Don's interest was more than professional, but I couldn't respond. I simply didn't think of Don that way. But I couldn't hurt his feelings, so I merely moved from his embrace, and we looked away from each other in silence. A while later Don gave me a beautiful wooden crucifix that he had had for a long time, with the most thoughtful and expressive note promising he would always have my best interests at heart. Then he moved out of my life.

But I never forgot that Don's faith in me was greater than my own. I tried to repay him in the only way I could: I made sure that he was identified by name in all of the articles about the way I got into pictures. Even years later, when the story was repeated at the time I left Hollywood, Don Barbeau's gift to me was acknowledged.

I took the midterms and did well in every class—except one. Miss Barnelle, true to her word, failed me.

The Wallis contract was offered. Drawn up and signed before the six-month period was up, it was for seven years with a salary starting at $250 a week and going to $3,500. There would be an option pickup every six months, at which time Wallis could keep her or let her go. In addition, he could loan her out to any other studio or producer, paying her the weekly salary and pocketing the fee he charged for her services. Everyone celebrated, but no one more than Carlos Alvarado, who without having to pick up a telephone now represented a contract actress who would be paid forty out of fifty-two weeks a year.

I guess I was the only girl in America who wasn't insane over Elvis Presley. I had never been interested in rock and roll—it all sounded much the same to me. So when our director, Hal Kanter, introduced

50

Elvis to me, I wasn't meeting ELVIS!!!, but a very charming, soft-spoken and polite young fellow who was immediately on his feet. He took my hand and, in true southern-gentleman style, called me Miss Dolores. He called me that the whole time I knew him. He was the only one who did—except for Gary Cooper, but that was later. I thought Elvis was quite sweet, but truthfully, I was much more impressed meeting Wendell Corey and Lizabeth Scott. They were real movie stars.

Just before we started shooting, Mr. Wallis asked me to change my name. In his opinion, Hicks wouldn't look good on a marquee. For my first name, he favored Susan, the name of the girl I was to play in the movie.

That same day, Dolores went to Westwood's Village Delicatessen, nicknamed the VD by the students, with Sheila Hart and Maureen Bailey. Sheila had news. She had just become engaged to her Loyola boyfriend, Bob McGuire, and was deliriously happy. In the midst of the girls' hugging and shrieking, Sheila had a brainstorm. Since she was going to get a new name, she said Dolores could have her old one.

That's how I got the Hart. Mr. Wallis liked it and thought it went well with Susan, so I was introduced to the press as Susan Hart—"the girl other girls will hate"—because I was going to give Elvis Presley his first screen kiss. When Mom saw that in the newspaper, she exploded. She didn't object to the last name—after all, she had gotten rid of Hicks too. But she made such a fuss about my given name that Mr. Wallis backed down on Susan and I became Dolores Hart.

Dolores would legalize that name later, a move that pleased Grandpa Kude, who had always said that no Hicks would ever amount to anything. Her father, however, was displeased. Bert had not seen his daughter for almost a year and had become aware of her budding career through family members.

Production began on *The Lonesome Cowboy*, the title of the *Good Housekeeping* story it was based on. The film was renamed *Running Wild* during the shooting. It would subsequently be called *Stranger in Town* and then *Something for the Girls* before getting its final title from one of the songs in the film, *Loving You*. Dolores played Susan Jessup,

51

a young singer who falls in love with a truck driver (Presley) who becomes a rock-and-roll singer thanks to a bandleader (Wendell Corey) and a clever press agent (Lizabeth Scott).

From the very first day, I felt I was surrounded by a new family. Mr. Kanter couldn't have been kinder or more helpful. And he was funny to boot. Everyone was wonderful to me—makeup man Wally Westmore; our choreographer, Charlie O'Curran; and the lady who did my hair, Nellie Manley. Charles Lang, our director of photography, actually took the time to tell me that I was picking up movie technique in a snap. He wanted to know where I had studied. I told him nowhere. That night in a dream, Grandpa showed up and said, "Hey, kid, remember me? I showed you a thing or two." From then on, whenever I was asked about early training, I would give Grandpa his due.

Edith Head did the costumes for the film and took a shine to me. She nicknamed me Junior. She had six Oscars in her office then (she would win eight in all). Time had taken its toll on their glossy finishes as it probably did to most things in Hollywood. I picked one up. It was named Sabrina. *"God can be good", I thought, remembering nights I lay awake in the dormitory dreaming of holding my own Oscar.*

Edith once took me on a tour of the costume department, and as we passed the forms of the actresses she had dressed at Paramount, she had a running commentary. "Ingrid. Do you think that's her bust? I gave her that bust. Grace had a very flat fanny, but not when I got through. My motto, Junior: 'What God has forgotten, I fill with cotton.' "

Oddly enough, Edith never padded me. Not that I didn't need it. I think she just liked me as I was. She also approved of my homemade wardrobe: "You're so cute the way your mama put you together", she said with a smile. "We'll take advantage of that." She designed my movie wardrobe like the clothes Mom made for me.

Edith Head voiced the feelings of the rest of the studio personnel who came in contact with Dolores: "That girl had such a way with her that we were all pulling for her. We wanted her to be a success."

Two people at the studio were more than special. Edith's assistant, Pat Barto, who actually did a lot of the designing but got no credit, was someone I took as a role model. She had elegance and the charm of true womanhood, and I wanted to be like her. The other was the studio publicist, Jim Stevens, he of the dry wit and sly smile, who was largely responsible for my becoming known even before Loving You *was released. Jim remains a friend to this day.*

My first scene in front of a camera was my last scene in the film, the clinch with Elvis. The set was small but hardly intimate with the crew, of course, and all of Elvis' "boys"—four or five young guys; I think most of them were cousins—who followed him everywhere. Mr. Kanter stressed that we hold the kiss until he called, "Cut!" During the take, it seemed as if we held that kiss for ten minutes. Elvis himself finally broke away and called, "Cut!" He apologized but said he had to come up for air. Mr. Kanter said it was all right because the take was no good. It seems I began to blush, and my ears got bright red.

Another take, and the same thing happened. So production stopped while Wally Westmore fiddled with my makeup. Another take. More red ears. Mr. Westmore finally had to devise a completely new makeup that would mask my rosy countenance.

Elvis and I hit it off right away. He seemed to be in the same boat as I. He had just finished his first movie but was still way in the dark about filmmaking. He was a dream to work with. He had a marvelous sense of timing, which isn't so surprising, given that he was a musician. He took direction quickly, though it wasn't always from Mr. Kanter. "Colonel" Tom Parker, Elvis' manager, was on the set at all times, standing more often than not right behind Mr. Kanter. When the director called, "Cut", Elvis never failed to look first to the Colonel for approval.

On the set, Elvis always had his guitar within easy reach and would strum it and sing whenever the spirit moved him—which was often. You would never find him in his dressing room. He would walk around the set, almost childlike, talking to people and bumming dimes for the apple machine.

—Elvis Presley never carried loose change.

Almost as much as Elvis loved to sing, he loved to kid around—that's where his boys came in. Like all young kids, they were forever laughing at their own jokes. Theirs were always "in" jokes, and though I generally

53

didn't get them, they were never crude—as far as I knew. The boys themselves were very sweet to me and would shuffle their feet and look down at the ground—very "aw, shucks", "gosh golly"—whenever I was around. The one I knew best was Gene Smith, who kept in contact with me even after I entered Regina Laudis. His calls were just short hellos to tell me he and Elvis sent their love.

And, yes, Elvis did ask me out. We had been shooting for about a week when he thought it would be "nice for us to get to know each other". I did the unheard of: I turned him down. I didn't want to be thought of as an opportunist trading on his celebrity while we were working together.

> —There was a lot of Granny in me. I patted myself on the back
> for this estimable stand when I wrote her, "This Natalie wouldn't."
> I would have gone out with Elvis after the film was finished, but
> he obviously took no for an answer. He never asked me again.

Mom went with me to the studio frequently, but she was hardly a stage mother. She was just excited to be on a movie set. I think it gave her a feeling of fulfillment, that she was part of the entertainment world at last. Elvis liked Mom a lot. So did Wendell Corey. I had begun sharing tales of my family with Wendell, and he was genuinely fascinated. He really wanted to meet Granny and watch her drink a martini upside down. I didn't tell those stories to everyone. But I usually found at least one person on each picture I could share them with.

I wrote Granny a lot on the set, and my letters often concerned my finances. I was making $250 a week, less taxes and agent fees, more money than I had ever had in my life. I was determined to sock away in the bank at least fifty dollars every week and told Granny that even if this kick lasted only a year or so, I would probably have enough to return to school. I told her I was always on the lookout for other sources of income and once hinted that when Elvis got his hair cut on the set, I should sweep up the clippings and sell them to the girls at Marymount for a dime a piece. That was when Granny started slipping five or ten dollars into the envelope with her letters "to tide you over just in case". Bless her, she did that during my entire time in Hollywood in spite of my salary boosts.

My one and only extravagance was a new car. Through Paramount, I got a brand new Ford Skyliner convertible, light blue with those wonderful stripes. And I was able to buy Mom a sewing machine. I got Great-grandmother Bowen a rug to cover the holes in her linoleum and delivered it in person on a fast trip back to Illinois. I stayed the night, and the following morning I found her on the floor, stretched out on the carpet, and my heart stopped. Suddenly she sat up and smiled, "Honey, I'm fine. I jist wanted to sleep on this nice new rug b'fore everbuddy messes it all up."

When a movie finishes shooting and the director calls, "That's a wrap!", it's customary to celebrate with a wrap party. Hal Kanter hosted the celebration for the *Loving You* company on an empty soundstage, but when the guests arrived, they were greeted by a booth with a huge sign reading, "Thank You". In the booth was a beaming Colonel Parker, greeting everyone and handing out Presley albums. Kanter, still miffed after fifty years, recalled, "Everyone thought the Colonel was the host of the party. The next day I received a handmade card from Dolores thanking *me* for the evening. She was the only one who did."

For weeks after the production ended, I was in a blue funk. After months of being together like a very close-knit family, everyone was gone. It was more than disorienting. It was depressing.

Loving You was a hit, and Dolores reaped the benefits of giving Elvis his first screen kiss. Overnight Jim Stevens found he could pitch this newcomer to the fan magazine editors. She began a heavy schedule of publicity, interviews and photo layouts.

At first the interviews were about her take on Presley, with titles such as "What It Feels Like to be Kissed by Elvis". But her fresh personality and candor, especially about the pitfalls of teenage dating, connected with the editors, and soon the features bore titles such as "Flirting Can Be Fun—but Dangerous", "Going Steady—Shortcut to Heartbreak?" and "Be a Good Girl".

In interviews I frequently spoke about my conversion to Catholicism. I tried to convey my conviction that faith can be a great buttress to one's shortcomings and weaknesses, helping us to rise above them and giving

55

our lives true purpose. I didn't beat the drum. But it was part of my identity.

❦

Things at home were problematic at best. While Mom was sincere in her joy for my good fortune, she could, when she was drinking, be jealous and hostile. "You have everything—I have nothing; you are somebody—I am nobody" became Mom's mantra. She had a strong moral sense of her own value, but when she drank, self-pity blocked it out. She was alone much of the time. Pop left for the restaurant early every morning and stayed there late, way past closing, drinking with his cronies. I'm sure it was because he didn't want to face the situation at home, but the pity was that he wasn't there when Mom needed him. I thought he didn't love her enough to help her.

Usually I was able to call on my ability to detach myself from the unpleasantness, but with increasing frequency, I found myself confronting Mom and adding to the ugliness. I was jealous too—of the bottle. I would spit out hateful things and later feel awful about it. My faith in her basic goodness became my guiding principle; it kept me trying over and over. But each time I found in myself a growing resentment of my softening. When you allow those sentiments to creep in, when you soften, it makes you vulnerable all over again.

If it hadn't been for the good things happening to me then, I don't know what I might have done. I knew that this sudden fulfillment of a dream was a gift of grace that had to be carefully nurtured. It was given to me with a condition: that I not set up any false values or let the trappings of Hollywood delude me into forgetting the grace. It asked for all my attention.

Six

There's a saying around Hollywood soundstages that getting your first film is easy; getting the second one is hard.

During 1957 Paramount Pictures introduced several young actresses, only to drop each after one film. Norma Moore was Anthony Perkins' leading lady in *Fear Strikes Out*; Elaine Aiken played opposite Perkins in *The Lonely Man*; Mary Webster was the ingenue in Jerry Lewis' *The Delicate Delinquent*. And that was it for each of them. Dolores had the advantage of being under contract not to Paramount but to Hal Wallis, whose associate producer was the savvy Paul Nathan.

Paul liked me from the first moment and was always honest with me. He carefully monitored the rushes of Loving You *and decided I should spend some time in the studio gym and pay attention to a diet. I was five foot six and weighed 126 pounds. Since the camera adds about ten pounds, Paul thought I should get my weight down to 117. So I began living on lettuce and cottage cheese. Paul also got me into cheek exercises so I wouldn't look like a chipmunk in close-ups.*

More important, Paul watched out for her career. There was a role in the new Jerry Lewis movie Wallis was producing that she could do. And she would have too and then possibly have bitten the dust if not for Paul.

There was another film on the Wallis slate, one that was shaping up to be his most important for the year. *A Woman Obsessed* was to be Anna Magnani's follow-up to her Oscar-winning American debut in *The Rose Tattoo*. The cast included Anthony Quinn and Anthony Franciosa. The director was George Cukor. The film had prestige written all over it. The story concerned an Italian immigrant (Magnani) who, in old-country tradition, comes to America to marry her late sister's husband, a rancher. A romantic triangle ensues, involving the Magnani character, the widower (Quinn) and a young ranch hand (Franciosa) betrothed to

57

the rancher's daughter. The role of Angie, the nineteen-year-old daughter, had not been cast. Cukor agreed to Paul's request to let Dolores test for the part.

Dolores' test impressed Cukor and Wallis enough to cast her as Angie. That bit of casting, coming so early in her career, stamped the young actress as a contender, someone due a respect that wasn't going to be given to the latest Elvis Presley or Jerry Lewis girl. The chances of her fading from view, like the contract actresses before her, got smaller.

My character figured in only a few scenes, but I was in major company now and aware of my inexperience as an actress. Loving You *had been a game. This film made me realize how much more I would have to learn if I was to be any good. I vowed to study, but the film was about to start shooting. I had been given a great gift in being able to work with these extraordinary people, so I spent every moment I could watching the rehearsals and filming. On days I wasn't scheduled to work, I would show up anyway just to absorb as much as I could. This began my dependence on people who were more experienced and willing to share their knowledge with me. No one was more generous in this regard than Anthony Quinn.*

The first day of filming was devoted to my short scene with the two Tonys. Then my character was shipped off to school so the grown-ups could thrash around in love and lust. I would have no scenes alone with Tony Franciosa, which was just as well, since every time I was in his company my ears turned red.

I was to have only one scene with Anna Magnani, but she had not been on the set yet. I looked forward to working with this actress who had captivated me in The Rose Tattoo, *and I felt I was prepared. I had spent days working with Pamela Danova, the dialogue coach, who carefully translated the lines into Italian so I would recognize the words if Anna spoke them in Italian, which I was told she sometimes did.*

The day we were to do our scene was the day I met Anna Magnani. I remember thinking this was going to be the most important day of my life.

The lady was having one of her so-called disturbances when Mr. Cukor introduced us. With her mane of dark hair and those deep-set eyes, shaded by sunglasses, she appeared larger than I had anticipated.

Before I had a chance to kneel at her feet, she glared at me and shook her head, "No, no, no." The corners of her mouth drooped while she looked me up and down over the dark glasses. She stared at my eyes and threw up her hands. "No!"

She already hated me, I was sure. Mr. Cukor artfully pulled her away and spoke very quietly—so quietly that I had trouble eavesdropping. But Magnani did not speak quietly. Her English was not good, so she yelled in Italian, with Pamela translating as fast as she could. I could catch only bits and pieces of the tirade—words such as inexperienced *and* amateur. *I was devastated. Mr. Cukor was equally firm but without the hand waving: "Her inexperience can work for the scene."*

"She's not Italian", Anna shouted, and then I heard Mr. Cukor say, "But she is *Italian. She could do the entire scene in Italian!"*

"Oh, dear God," I thought, "what is he saying?"

"The eyes, they're blue!" she barked.

But Mr. Cukor insisted, "I believe in her, and I want her in the picture, and those adorable blue eyes are all over northern Italy, Anna."

Suddenly, with a thunderous laugh, she turned to me, grabbed my shoulders in what I prayed was an affectionate gesture and said, "Hokay! We try one day, today, hokay?" Then she was gone. Apparently Anna Magnani would do anything for George Cukor, even work with me.

Mr. Cukor quickly took me aside and said, "The scene is scheduled for two o'clock. You have the morning to work with Pamela to learn the lines in Italian just in case. And I think it would be a good idea if hairdressing darkened your hair even more. So get going. And don't you think it's time you called me George?"

While my hair was being redone, Pamela flew into action, script in hand. "Papa non piace parlare Italiano", she would say, and I would repeat it. Every line of the scene was translated into Italian, and I would repeat and repeat until I was dizzy with the words.

The scene takes place outside the ranch house under a tree, where Anna flees after being humiliated by Tony Quinn's character. Angie runs after her in sympathy, and the two women bond. At two o'clock we began to rehearse. We rehearsed the scene over and over, and each time

59

Anna would do it differently. I was at a complete loss. When Mr. Cukor called for a take, I was trembling, afraid that I would lose my lines. In the first take I did lose them. Anna looked at me but not in anger. She penetrated me with those eyes, and I listened, really listened, to her silence. Suddenly, I could feel tears welling up. "What am I crying for?" I thought. I remembered my first line but said it in tears. George yelled, "Cut!"

"Oh, God help me", I muttered. "I've ruined it already."

But George whispered, "Darling, do it that way—but we can't hear you."

Anna took my hand and whispered, "All you have to do is respond from the heart."

Again, we started from the top of the scene, but this time Anna began speaking in broken English, going in and out of Italian, and the scene began to take on a life of its own, different from rehearsals. I found myself listening carefully and responding on a gut level, the lines coming easily. Anna and I were both weeping now. She was allowing me to reach a genuine catharsis with her. That was her gift as an actress. I will never forget her for that.

We worked until eight o'clock that night. When the scene was over and the takes marked for printing, Anna said nothing to me. She simply got up and went to her dressing room.

As I walked to my dressing room, I was close to tears. There was a small note pinned to the door. Its message had been hastily scrawled: "I just saw you shoot the scene. I was tremendously proud of you. Now I not only love you as a person but love you as a talented young actress. You've made your 'papa' proud." It was signed "Tony". I hadn't even known Anthony Quinn was there watching. His words coming at that moment meant more than I could ever tell him.

The next day I bumped into George and Anna on the lot as they emerged from a screening room where they had been watching rushes, the assembled prints of the previous day's shooting, including my scene with Anna. In 1957 it didn't occur to me to watch rushes. As George and Anna approached, I looked around for an escape, but there was none. Anna stopped in front of me. "Here it comes", I thought. She looked me right in the eye and then, laughing, took hold of both my ears and shook me as

60

hard as she could. Then they continued on. George, looking back for a moment, gave me a wink and the okay sign. Dear George. I hardly ever mention his name without prefacing it with "dear". He was one of the kindest men I ever worked with, and I simply forgot he was the big man. He was just somebody who liked me very much. Later, when he wrote to me at the monastery, he would sign his letters "Old Uncle George".

By the time the company moved to Carson City for the exterior scenes, I had begun feeling a real part of this family of actors. Anna and the Tonys became comrades, and I was their mascot. Even Anna couldn't have been warmer to me. On location, invitations for dinner came from all sides, which helped in my constant concern about finances, given that per diem then was six dollars. Being the only young girl in the company meant nobody would let me pick up the check.

Away from the studio, Anthony Quinn was more attentive, his interest hinting at something other than paternal. Frequently he would ask her to dinner alone. But although he enjoyed flirting with her, he couldn't shrug off his role as protector, so he kept hands off. Dolores enjoyed his company, especially hearing about his occasional forays into the theater, which started her thinking that she should investigate working on the stage.

One night, after dinner in nearby Reno, Tony showed me the town— that meant the casinos. I watched while he gambled, and every time he was ahead he would slip a silver dollar into my hand to play the one-armed bandits. I hit a jackpot, and the machine began spitting silver dollars all over the floor.

I called to Tony to come and see my good fortune, but before he could join me a man came up and asked how old I was. I very proudly announced I was eighteen just as Tony reached my side. He grabbed me by the arm and rushed me out, leaving my winnings on the floor. "But," I protested, "my money!" "Never mind", Tony said. "Good God, Dolores, you have to be twenty-one to gamble. We'll get arrested."

Sometimes Tony and I would drive to Lake Tahoe and just sit by the lake watching the sunset. Mostly we talked about acting. Acting was a religion to Anthony Quinn. He felt passionately about it and spoke often of wanting to establish a class for actors who needed an outlet when

61

they weren't working. He believed that talent must never be allowed to become stagnant and the only way to keep it alive is to act.

It was on one of these evenings that Tony confided that he once had the desire to become a priest. He told me he actually had begun to study for the priesthood, but the call to acting had been stronger. "Occasionally," he said, "I'm sorry I didn't continue, but judging by what my life has been and has become, the Church might say it is better off for my decision." He said he hadn't thought about that for a long time but somehow felt I would understand.

On our last evening, we were aware of a huge rock in the water that, as the sun set, began to hide the colors reflected on the lake's surface. I asked him if there was anything in the world he would like at that moment. "I would like to move that rock," he answered, "so we could have the reflection a little bit longer." Lovely thought. Lovely man. We remained friends for the rest of his life.

What was it about Dolores Hart that persuaded adults, many years her senior, to confide in her? Anthony Quinn was but one of several. Paul Nathan also communicated with her at a deep level. Paul had been in analysis for a number of years, a fact not generally shared with his professional colleagues, but he was quite candid about his problems when he and Dolores talked.

> *—Paul was blessed with an enhanced wittiness that enabled him to reveal some mighty heavy pain and still get a laugh. Perhaps Mom was wise when she demanded I not be renamed, that* Dolores *was essential. You see, Dolorosa, the Mother of Sorrows, bears witness to man's redemption. A Dolores has to be a listener.*

After the film wrapped, Dolores was free to join Paramount's talent program, run by Charlotte Clary. Mrs. Clary maintained a family atmosphere in the talent school, which became for Dolores an enclosure within the enclosure of the studio itself. Classes were held in voice, dance movement and acting. Her classmates were Earl Holliman, George

Chakiris, Ursula Andress and three young actors who would become lifelong friends: James Douglas, Valerie Allen and Jan Shepard.

The first project for Clary and her young players was Arthur Laurents' *A Clearing in the Woods*, which was to be presented once only on a Paramount soundstage for all of the studio's producers, directors and casting personnel. When the play was performed, however, only Paramount's talent scout Milt Lewis was in the audience.

Dark, good-looking James Douglas had the leading male role in the play. At the time, James was separated from his wife, Dawn, and turned to Dolores—not for romance but for comradeship. Theirs was a friendship that would become even closer when James and Dawn reconciled and would fully blossom when the couple moved to Connecticut after Dolores entered Regina Laudis.

Dolores, Jan and Valerie were inseparable on and off the lot. Contract player Valerie was a former Las Vegas dancer who had every one of her options picked up for four years straight, though she made only one film for the studio. Valerie was very pretty window dressing, the one who cut the ribbons at openings and posed with visiting dignitaries. She could be relied on to add glamor and sex appeal to any studio function.

Although Jan Shepard appeared to be Dolores' contemporary, she was a little older and already married, to actor Ray Boyle. In an odd coincidence, Ray had been a buddy of Dolores' father when both were recently discharged servicemen hanging out at the Actors' Lab and Schwab's drugstore on the Sunset Strip with other aspiring actors. Jan was a devout Catholic and shared Dolores' appreciation for church buildings. Jan recounted, "Many times we would be driving around LA and spot a Catholic church we had never seen and, on the spur of the moment, stop for a quick look-see."

She also remembered waking early one morning to find Dolores sleeping in her car in the Boyles' driveway. She had been there all night, having escaped from a drunken row with Harriett.

It was the same old "Big movie star, you have everything—I have nothing, not even a marriage." I shouted back, "Why should anyone want to stay married to you if you're just a drunk?" I grabbed a framed picture of myself, one that Mom treasured, and threw it to the floor, smashing it. Then I stormed out of the house. I drove around aimlessly for a while and finally found myself at the Boyles' and parked outside.

"It scared me to death", Jan said. "I brought her into the house and made her promise she would never do that again." Jan and Ray turned their den into a guest room that Dolores often used as an escape from Harriett's chain rattling.

Like *Loving You*, *A Woman Obsessed* was renamed just before its release because of the title song. As *Wild Is the Wind* the film got a major premiere in Los Angeles, which was everything Dolores had dreamed of on Mulholland Drive.

My whole family was there—my mother and stepfather and Granny and Grandpa, who was puffed out to here with pride because this was better than being prom queen. Mom had made a beautiful dress for me, and I remember thinking when I looked at myself in the mirror, "The Father has put me in the limelight as the lady I dreamed of becoming. God has been good in letting me have these things for now." And then I wondered why "for now". I was being given the life I always wanted, wasn't I?

By the end of 1957, Dolores had two movies in release: *Loving You*, which introduced her to Presley's massive teenage audience, and *Wild Is the Wind*, which would be an Academy Award contender with nominations for Magnani and Quinn as well as Dimitri Tiomkin and Ned Washington for their song.

Dolores had struck a note with reviewers, getting positive notices for both minor roles, and when lists of the most promising new female personalities of the year began appearing, her name was there alongside Joanne Woodward, Sophia Loren and Lee Remick.

When the annual *Photoplay* magazine awards were handed out to the most promising newcomers of 1957, Dolores was in the company of Woodward, Franciosa, Pat Boone and Tony Randall. Hollywood columnists Hedda Hopper and Louella Parsons each published end-of-the-year lists of future stars. Both included Dolores. She was one of the 1957 Deb Stars, debuting movie actresses for whom stardom was predicted by the Motion Picture Hairstylists and Makeup Artists. Essentially a publicity event, the Deb Star Ball always got a great deal of domestic and foreign press coverage.

Dolores Hart was just about the most envied teenager in Hollywood, and she had been a professional actress for less than one year.

It looked as if Hal Wallis just might have gotten himself a star.

Seven

Dolores was again cast opposite Elvis Presley in the musical drama *King Creole*, loosely based on Harold Robbins' *A Stone for Danny Fisher*. The property had been announced numerous times for production with various young actors slated for the lead role, James Dean and Tony Curtis among them.

Before filming started, I caught up a little on Elvis. I listened to his recordings and went to my first and only Presley concert. The next day I was surprised and not a little outraged when I read a review that called him "vulgar". I found nothing vulgar in his performance. I thought that his rather innocent sexual energy moved to the soul of the new youth culture and that he gave that culture a voice.

Her casting interested several of the bigger agencies in Hollywood, all of which came calling. The advice from Wallis, Nathan and others at the studio was unanimous: she should change agents. The most recommended name among them was Phil Gersh at Famous Artists. Dolores liked Gersh and agreed that a stronger agency could certainly do more for her. Alvarado immediately sued Gersh for stealing his client and damaging his reputation. Ultimately an arrangement was worked out, though Alvarado privately felt Dolores was an ingrate. At this point, she was hardly a moneymaker for any agency, but everyone at Famous Artists, especially Harry Bernsen, was convinced she was going to make it big. Bernsen began canvassing the town for TV roles for their new client before *King Creole* started shooting.

I trusted Harry's counsel because he was obviously more interested in building my career than he was in the money. I mean, there was no money. He wanted to put me into big pictures eventually but felt exposure on television could only help make me better known.

66

Remembering what Tony Quinn told me about the theater, I asked Harry
if he could also check out summer-stock possibilities for me.

Dolores' first TV job was on the popular anthology series *Alfred Hitchcock Presents*. In the mystery "Silent Witness", she played a babysitter who was murdered in the first act. Her costar was Don Taylor, who fifteen years earlier had worked with her father in *Winged Victory*. "Silent Witness" was followed by "Man on a Rack" with Tony Curtis and Everett Sloane on the *Schlitz Playhouse of Stars*.

Dolores would ultimately appear in only two other filmed television shows—in 1959 on *The Dupont Show with June Allyson* and in 1963 on a segment of *The Virginian*. She also made three appearances on *The Christophers*, the long-running Sunday morning program of interviews and readings featuring Catholic stars such as Rosalind Russell, Ann Blyth and Pat O'Brien.

With the release of Loving You, *I started to receive fan letters, ten or fifteen a week, most of them requesting autographed photos. I took them home and answered them myself in longhand. I ordered and paid for personal copies of publicity photos shot by Paramount's portrait photographer, Bud Fraker, and purchased the needed envelopes and postage.*

But Dolores soon found that she couldn't keep up with the demand for photos and enlisted her stepbrother Martin to autograph them, paying him a nickel for each one he signed. He had to sign a hundred to make five bucks, but he did it. Years later he saw a "genuine autographed photo of Dolores Hart" offered for sale on the Internet and recognized the signature as one he had forged. Harriett got into the act too. She set up a makeshift office in the family garage and formed The Dolores Hart Fan Club with herself, under a pseudonym, as president.

Dolores kept some pieces of fan mail, which turned up in shoe boxes when I was researching her archive at the abbey. One I particularly liked was short and sweet: "You are my favorite movie star and Jane Russell is my second favorite."

—Well, we were the same type.

As the fan mail increased, Dolores became concerned about the dollars-and-cents aspect. One day on the lot, she confided this to another Hal Wallis contractee, Shirley MacLaine, who told Dolores that the studio was happy to pay for fan mail expenses, including photos, envelopes and postage.

I had no sense at all about perks in the movie business. Because of Granny's influence, I never lost sight of what something cost; even if the studio was footing the bill, I was careful not to take advantage. I preferred not to be thought of as an irritating property who made expensive demands.

Whenever the studio would send me to, say, New York for publicity, however, I would ask to be routed through Chicago. It didn't cost the studio anything extra, and I could visit Granny without having to pay for my ticket. Not wanting to be thought of as uncooperative, I never turned down a request from the publicity department, though I was fast finding that those assignments had nothing to do with making movies. I shot a layout with Valerie Allen in Sun Valley to promote the popular winter resort as a year-round vacation spot and got an education in being a starlet. When you're a Hollywood starlet, you're expected to do cheesecake—slang for bathing-suit art in those days. The difference between Val's figure and mine hadn't escaped me, so each time the photographer would ask for more cleavage, I would cheerfully pass him on to her. I knew I looked better in jeans and boots than I did in a bikini.

She was also growing weary of another aspect of starletdom. She didn't much like going to parties as window dressing. She could understand cutting ribbons at an opening. She had something to do, a function. But she thought mingling at parties was like being a geisha.

It was about this time that Dolores and I met. I was just out of the army, having done to the day my two years of drafted service following graduation from UCLA, and I was working for Globe Photos, which led to our meeting at the Susie Grobstein night-on-the-town photo layout.

A week after our meeting, I was still thinking about Dolores and dropped her a note. She replied in kind. A flurry of short notes were exchanged that led to our first date, after which I received a handmade card "from D to D", which is what we began calling each other. It featured a big-headed figure with a silly grin saying: "I'm so happy." On the inside, it read: "And it's all your fault."

Soon we were going out a lot, mostly spending time alone or with my close friends, all of whom took to her. I knew very few of her friends. I was uncomfortably certain that I had to be making half of what she was earning, so our dinner dates were at Villa Frascati, on the Sunset Strip, because I had a press card that gave me a discount there, a perk of my profession. And I was able to take her to press screenings of upcoming films and to play openings, also perks. Her knowledge of theater was woefully lacking, and I found her taste in movies suspect. I made a list of essential films that we began tracking down—not a simple task in the days before DVDs. Her favorite actors then were Kim Novak and Rock Hudson. I made sure she was aware of Kim Stanley and Jason Robards too. And I was happy to set her right about the red-headed actress in *Blithe Spirit*—Kay Hammond, not Lucille Ball.

We enrolled in extension classes at UCLA, our favorite being a course in film criticism taught by the dean of West Coast critics, Edwin Schallert of the *Los Angeles Times*. We both still adhere to Schallert's rule that the word *unique* does not take a modifier.

During the next several months, Jim Stevens and I set up photo layout after photo layout with Dolores. For "date" layouts, a staple of the movie magazines, we paired her with every young actor in town: Tab Hunter, Tony Perkins, John Saxon, Patrick Wayne, Ty Hungerford (who became Ty Hardin), Earl Holliman. Usually it was the only time she would ever see the actor. Holliman was an exception. He became a close friend.

Thanks also to Jim Stevens, I began accepting "handouts"—studio production stills—of Dolores to beef up Globe's features on her. The publicity departments at all the studios then handed out photos to agencies in hopes that they would be published. Globe Photos had not accepted these before, preferring (somewhat snobbily) to represent only exclusive material produced in-house. But I now had a personal interest in helping Dolores' career along.

Unless the studio deemed it essential for her to be on the arm of a young actor, I would escort Dolores to occasional Hollywood functions. At those events, she usually kept her hand snugly in mine, not only as a romantic gesture but so she could squeeze my hand whenever someone she recognized, but whose name she couldn't remember, approached. Dolores rarely wore her glasses when she went out, and her desperate squeeze signaled she needed identification before her glazed expression gave her away. I was more than repaid for this service; Dolores gave a great neck massage.

I took her to meet my family in Eagle Rock, a suburb of Los Angeles, and Dolores and my mother connected straightaway. Mom took me aside after dinner and confided, very seriously, that she had "just met an angel". An angel, I might add, who helped with the dishes that evening and, a week later without my knowing, drove back to Eagle Rock and spent the day helping my mother scrape wallpaper off the dining room walls.

I ate Thanksgiving dinner that year with Dolores' family. The meal was wonderful—Harriett was a great cook—and the house looked festive. But there was something unpleasantly familiar about the gathering. I realized that, as the dinner progressed, the atmosphere grew more and more tense. Based on my experiences with my father, I recognized it as the tension that all families of a drinker share at holiday time. Harriett had been nipping in the kitchen, and watching Dolores watch Harriett was depressing.

>*—Mom would spend days meticulously decorating the house, and I loved her for that effort, but I got so angry that the preparations were ultimately such a fraud. She usually got so drunk she didn't enjoy the celebrations. Neither did anyone else.*

So D and D were "going together", but few people in the Industry were aware of it. About the only studio folk we saw were Jim Stevens and his wife, Delores with an *e*. Once in a while, there would be a mention of us as a couple in a gossip column, but that was offset by the many published date layouts with young actors (most of which I was setting up). As our relationship grew closer, the subject of religion came up with increasing regularity. As a non-Catholic I was not the most promising suitor she could have chosen. Dolores and I would discuss religion in general, Catholicism in particular. Actually, "spar" might be a better word because we would keep it light. Never did we argue about it. As long as we kept company, that subject was earmarked "to be continued".

Our romance was marked by a series of those delightful cards she drew. Ever since she was a tot, she doodled little cartoon figures and fashioned them into personal cards for friends and family. She sent one to Paul Nathan that crossed the desk of a coworker, Don Bradford, who had once worked for a card company and thought her sketches were terrific. One day he asked if she had ever thought about turning her doodles into commercial greeting cards.

> *—He said that I should think of doing something as a sideline because actors are always without jobs and need some way of getting an extra dollar. Of course, the minute he said that, he had my undivided attention.*

For a combined investment of $250, Don and Dolores went into the greeting-card business. Hal Wallis smiled his consent and suggested that she use her own name in the trademark in order to cash in on her movie publicity. The line was christened Sweetharts. Decision making was left up to Don. Dolores' contribution, apart from the sketches and greetings, was to appear at gift shows to promote the line. They didn't make Hallmark nervous, but Sweetharts was doing well until Don's untimely death in 1960.

King Creole began shooting exactly one year after *Loving You* and found Dolores in a part that was an extension of her first two roles, though Nellie had a pinch more dimension. Nellie, unlike Susie and Angie, was desperate to change her life. Nellie was also faced with a decision that neither of the other two ingenues had to make: Should she do it with Presley's character or not?

Filling out the cast were Carolyn Jones, Walter Matthau, Dean Jagger and her friend from the studio talent department, Jan Shepard. Jan credits Dolores for her being cast as Presley's sister. "She went right to

Hal Wallis and said she had a girlfriend who would be perfect for the role, which got me a test."

The veteran director Michael Curtiz was signed to direct. Dolores hadn't heard of Curtiz, although he had directed over a hundred American movies, including the classic *Casablanca*. For his part, Curtiz was not happy with the cast Wallis had handed him. He didn't want Dolores in the film, or Jan, or, for that matter, Presley, whom he thought too inexperienced for such a dramatic role. It was the second time that Dolores faced being fired before she even started.

There was no question that Presley would remain in the film, but Curtiz took his case about the actresses to Wallis himself. Wallis stood by the girls and told the director that they would stay, but if Curtiz wished, he could leave. In the end, they all stayed and worked well together. The only disappointment for the two actresses was that some of their dramatic moments were cut in order to expand musical numbers.

The girls also didn't care for Curtiz' manner, finding him a vulgar man and a bully on the set. Although the Hungarian-born Curtiz had been in America for forty years, he hadn't lost a week of his native accent. At best, he was difficult to understand; at worst, he needed subtitles.

Mr. Wallis flew the entire cast and crew—except Elvis, who didn't like to fly—to the New Orleans location on a chartered flight. When we arrived at the New Orleans airport, we got our first look at what was going to envelop us for the next several weeks. Kids. Hundreds and hundreds of screaming kids.

New Orleans remained a madhouse for the entire shooting schedule. On the very first day, Elvis was mobbed when he tried to enter the hotel. The police had a bridge built connecting the roof of the hotel to the roof of an adjacent building, so he could enter and leave without being engulfed by a sea of pubescent humanity.

Elvis was much more serious this time around. He was getting quite knowledgeable about the movie business, much more than I was. He knew Mr. Wallis made important pictures, and he wanted to be associated with quality. He desperately hoped that King Creole *would be the*

72

beginning of a new direction for his movie career. He loved James Dean and wanted to have a career just like his, but he was afraid the Colonel would lock him into run-of-the-mill schlock, which is what ultimately happened.

One morning, while we were waiting to be called to the set—we had to wait in one of the rooms in the hotel because the fans made it impossible for Elvis to wait on location—Elvis suddenly took the Gideon Bible out of a drawer and opened it at random, letting a finger fall onto a verse. He read it and turned to me and said, "Now, Miss Dolores, what do you think of that?" We talked about the verse and what it meant to us personally. He did this several times more, opening the Bible and casually selecting a passage. I was impressed to find that Elvis was no stranger to the Bible. He quoted from it quite often. Of course, he came from a deeply religious background; he was raised attending camp meetings and revivals.

In the evenings after production wrapped, Elvis and I would share a limo back to the hotel. There were always hordes of shrieking teenage girls reaching out to touch him. He reacted politely, but of course he couldn't stop or we would be stranded for hours. Once, however, he did stop for a moment and spoke to a girl who had just called out, "You're the king!"

"Don't call me the king", he said to her softly but firmly. "There is only one king, the Lord Jesus Christ." I thought that was lovely and wanted to say something to him, but I was too shy.

Another evening, just as the limo pulled away from the crowd, a girl thrust her arm into the backseat, hoping to touch him. Her sleeve caught on the door handle, and she was pulled along with the car. Elvis shouted for the driver to stop. The car came to a halt before she suffered any injury, but Elvis got out anyway and made sure she was all right before we went on.

—Thirty-five years later, I received a letter from that girl, then a woman with a family of her own in Canada, reminding me of that "horrendous but wonderful" moment. I am always touched when I remember that experience because many random hands must have reached out to him, yet he was so sensitive to one in trouble.

73

Although her visits were less frequent than they were during Loving You, *Mom did come to the studio to watch filming now and then. Sometimes she would be included in a cast shindig, something that made me nervous, for fear that she might misbehave. But Mom watched the drinking whenever she was part of a studio celebration. It was at home that the drinking was a problem. At home the chain rattling continued.*

As soon as King Creole *wrapped, Mr. Wallis wanted to team me with Elvis a third time. I wasn't keen on making a career out of being "the girl" in Elvis Presley movies, and besides, I got a look at the script. It wasn't just "the girl"; it was the same girl. So I went to Mr. Wallis and asked him not to make me do that film. Surprisingly, he didn't.*

The last time I saw Elvis was at the birthday party I gave for Jan Shepard at the Hazeltine house. I invited Elvis and warned him that he had to be on time because it was a surprise party. He said he would try, though I didn't think he would come. But on the night of the party he was there, on time, laden with gifts and, of course, his guitar. For most of the evening, we had a private Presley concert. I dragged out the clarinet, and we played duets of "Danny Boy" and Grandpa's favorite tune, "Whispering". Elvis went into the army when Creole *wrapped.*

The Paramount Talent Department folded in the spring. Never as strong a department as those of other studios that had rosters of young television actors to bolster the classes, it was deemed too expensive for Paramount to continue to subsidize. Charlotte Clary recommended that Dolores join a private class taught by a respected actor, Jeff Corey. A few years earlier, Corey had been called before the House Un-American Activities Committee to answer charges of Communist sympathies and name others in the Industry who attended Communist meetings. Not only did Corey not name names; he criticized previous witnesses who had and promptly got blacklisted in Hollywood. He began teaching acting in the garage of his home for the affordable fee of $25 a month. Dolores was thrilled to be accepted into the class, which included her pal Valerie Allen plus Jack Nicholson, James Coburn, Sally Kellerman and John Gabriel, who coincidentally had been a classmate of mine at UCLA.

Harry Bernsen was hustling as if he had only one client. He had Dolores testing all over town. Anthony Quinn, who was making his directorial debut, tested her for the remake of Rafael Sabatini's *The Buccaneer*. Inger Stevens got the part. Dolores tested for the role of Gary Cooper's daughter in *Ten North Frederick* at Fox. Diane Varsi was under contract to that studio and was cast. Dolores was amazed when she was asked to test for the young Jewish woman in William Wyler's *Ben Hur*. Wyler himself spoke to her following the test, judging that she came across as the least Semitic human being he had ever seen.

—Heck, I could have told him that!

Things had moved so fast for me career-wise. I knew I had to learn faster. I reasoned that I didn't have the luxury of time, but I did have easy access to some of the world's best actors. Even if I didn't know what I was searching for, something was bound to rub off on me.

What Dolores failed to realize was that, as relatively inexperienced as she might have been, she had something that was connecting with audiences and with filmmakers. Paul Nathan recognized it: "Sincerity. Honesty. That's what brought her so far so fast."

At this time, Anthony Quinn fulfilled his dream of offering a class for working actors who wanted to stretch and hone their craft. Dolores joined the acting class alongside Carolyn Jones and Dennis Hopper every Wednesday night in makeshift quarters above a bedding manufacturing company.

I had begun to think that my career was destined to be briefer than I had imagined. I didn't like the testing process—not so much the actual test or even the "thanks but no thanks"; I hated the waiting for an answer. My cup looked decidedly half-empty, not half-full, when Harry arranged for me to audition for two rather important projects.

Writer-producer Dore Schary, who had run two major studios, RKO and MGM, was now heading his own producing unit. The first production under his banner was to be the film version—albeit none too faithful—of Nathanael West's best-selling novel *Miss Lonelyhearts*. Harry felt Dolores could do the role of the girl in love with the protagonist, a reporter relegated to writing the lonely hearts column for a metropolitan newspaper, and knew she could benefit from being in a cast that included Montgomery Clift, Robert Ryan, Myrna Loy and Maureen Stapleton. He pitched Dolores to Schary, and an interview was set up for the following week.

Simultaneously, Harry had learned that Roger Stevens of the Playwrights' Company and actor-director Cyril Ritchard were in Los Angeles auditioning actresses for a new Broadway play, *The Pleasure of His Company*. Ritchard had already conducted six auditions for the role in New York and had scheduled two for Los Angeles. Ultimately five hundred hopefuls would be seen and considered. Harry got Dolores an audition for *Pleasure* on the same day as the one for *Lonelyhearts*.

The first interview was with Mr. Schary. I dressed for the part of the conservative daughter of a middle-class family and brought a suitcase with a change for the play's more sophisticated girl, who was very upper-class San Francisco, just in case there was no time to go home. And there wasn't. I made the transformation in the women's restroom at a gas station.

The audition for The Pleasure of His Company *was held at the Huntington Hartford Theater in Hollywood. It was my first time backstage in a real theater. I seemed to sail through the reading, and Mr. Ritchard, who was the director and the star of the play, asked me to stay and read again. I waited with another young actress also trying out, Sandy Dennis. Two hours later I read once more. By then I had had time to get nervous. That reading was a resounding flop.*

Ritchard would tell her later that if she had read so badly the first time she would never have gotten the part. But get it she did. In fact, she got both parts. At least three people were elated by the news: Dolores, Harry Bernsen and Hal Wallis, who had nothing for her, film-wise, and could demand substantially more by loaning her out than he was paying her. There was no profit in negotiating her Broadway salary. The Playwrights' Company would pay her minimum, period. Wallis let her keep the Broadway money herself. But, of course, he took her off salary for the duration of the play.

This exciting good fortune was all but wiped out by accelerated confrontations with Harriett. Their intensity grew until, finally fed up,

Dolores decided she had to move out of the house. She packed two suitcases and made two calls, one to Paul Nathan, who arranged for her to live temporarily in her dressing room at the studio, and the other to me, asking me to pick her up right away.

She remained in residence at the studio for several weeks and loved the arrangement. I saw her almost every evening, after my work and her daily search for new quarters. At night we had the dark and virtually deserted Paramount studio as our personal playground. We would walk hand in hand on the back-lot city-street set, and once, on a lark, we recreated a scene from *Sunset Boulevard*, the one in which William Holden and Nancy Olson strolled that same set—the "I will now kiss that nose of yours"/"If you please" scene.

There was no time for Dolores to find a suitable apartment, since *Lonelyhearts* was scheduled to start immediately. She settled on a one-room studio with a Murphy bed in a nondescript building on tree-lined Flores Avenue in West Hollywood. The location was quiet and convenient to the studio and within walking distance of my apartment, but there was nothing attractive about her new home. We nicknamed it the Black Hole of Calcutta.

I didn't stay angry at Mom for long. I never did. Rarely did a fight go more than a day or two without a reconciliation, usually sparked by a note or a cartoon sketch one of us would send the other. Soon I was driving over the hill to Sherman Oaks for visits in a friendlier atmosphere. But I wouldn't move in again, and I didn't take back anything I had said to her.

From the first day, Lonelyhearts *was an unusual experience for me. It was the first time that the entire script was read by the cast before any work started, and then we rehearsed for two full weeks before anyone stepped in front of the camera. What a glorious opportunity to become really familiar with the character I was playing. I was used to rehearsing a scene once before it was shot. The picture could be half-over before I realized what I could have done, and it was already in the can.*

77

More rehearsals made it easier to become more friendly with my cowork-
ers too—a big help in the love scenes.

The director, Vincent J. Donehue, came to Hollywood from Broadway, where he had directed *Sunrise at Campobello*, produced by Dore
Schary. Dolores thought he was a nice man, but he was not as helpful
to her as Cukor and Kanter had been, probably because he was enthralled
with Clift.

The young Montgomery Clift had also come from Broadway in the
late 1940s, making a tremendous impact in his first two films. Clift was
very good-looking, a fact especially obvious when he and Elizabeth
Taylor shared close-ups in *A Place in the Sun*. Tragically, just three
years before Dolores met him at the first reading of *Lonelyhearts*, Clift
had suffered major injuries in an automobile accident. Plastic surgery
had repaired his face but couldn't restore it.

Montgomery Clift was a man I admired, loved and disliked with equal
intensity. I sensed he found little repose in living, and acting seemed a
self-torture that obsessed him. But I knew there was much I could learn
from this haunted young actor.

I was aware of the talk that his eccentricity had taken on a veneer of
bitterness. I found him very intense and somehow disconnected. Fre-
quently, we lunched together in his dressing room—he would always
have raw hamburger and a little booze, which gave him a peculiar
odor—and he would sit and rock. Without talking. And I would be
absolutely positive that he wasn't listening either. Just rocking. But then
he would say something that was perfectly appropriate to the moment,
proving I was wrong—he had been listening.

Other times he would ramble on nonstop, almost as if he were talking
to a doctor, or perhaps even his mother. I suspected that Monty related
to most of the women in his life in a filial way. He never talked about
acting, though. He was aware that I was going to Broadway, but as
much as I wanted him to, not once did he offer advice.

He could become morose: he was terribly conscious of the difference
in his looks since the accident and spoke to me of his fear that he no
longer had a future in films. He could cry at the mere mention of a
heartbreaking experience, yet he could be callous and hard. It was as if

he could touch a flower with the gentleness of a mother's caress and then trample that same flower in an embarrassed retreat from the garden.

I listened because my faith told me it was right to do so. I deeply responded to his internal pain, and more than once thoughts of Saint Thérèse flashed through my mind. I was giving a great performance in the dressing room, and it was never going to be seen on the screen.

Dolores and I would spend evenings in the Black Hole going over lines. Her first scene with Clift was scheduled early in production, and forewarned by rehearsals in which he never set what he intended to do, she knew she had to be well prepared. Those evenings were wonderful dates. I read Clift's part, and she was spontaneous and quite inventive with hers, enjoying the process immensely. Eager to see her shoot the scene, I visited the set.

After a brief blocking rehearsal, Donehue called for a take. Dolores' Justy was bright, strong and very real. Clift, however, didn't know his lines. On the second and third takes, Dolores repeated her performance with equal intensity. Clift still didn't know his lines. By take ten, I realized that as Clift became more confident in his performance, Dolores was losing the freshness in hers. If Donehue was aware of this, he chose to ignore it. His focus was on Clift.

Finally—painfully for me—Donehue marked take twenty-seven for printing. After twenty-six tries, Clift finally gave an interesting performance. But by this time Dolores was drained. She had nothing left to give. I wasn't prepared for such selfishness and was so convinced that it would continue that I didn't visit the set again.

On the screen, Clift's performance is intriguingly quirky, though not near his best. Dolores manages to project an appealing character, but not as multidimensional as she had been in our nightly rehearsals. Claudia Belmont, in *Films in Review*, was one of several critics who disagreed with my assessment.

"There is one example of good casting in *Lonelyhearts*", Ms. Belmont wrote. "Dolores Hart in the part of Justy Sargent, the girl Adam wants to marry. The well-proportioned features of Miss Hart's face combine into what used to be called 'an open countenance,' in which we think we see not only implacable honesty but also animal strength. It is an appealing and magnetic combination. If Miss Hart ... holds out for the right roles, she can have a long and profitable career depicting the normal, feminine and loving woman every man desires."

Dolores would be better served by her other costars. Myrna Loy had enjoyed a long career in films. Originally employed as an exotic beauty in silent pictures, she reinvented herself as a sophisticate in the thirties and again in the forties as the perfect wife in movies such as *The Best Years of Our Lives*, the film that had made her one of Dolores' favorite actresses. The fifties found her moving into character roles.

Myrna was the lady. She was the epitome of graciousness and charm. We had our tests for makeup together, and she looked almost like she did years earlier, only I thought that age had given her an air of calmness, which is flattering to anyone. She took me under her wing and tried to broaden my intellectual horizons. She loved getting me into a discussion of current events. She was quite political and very aware. For several years she was film advisor to UNESCO, the first actor to be associated with that organization.

I genuinely shocked Myrna when I let it slip that I didn't go to rushes. She couldn't believe it. She said that all actors should view rushes. "You always must watch yourself—even if it's only to make sure your stocking seams are straight!" I made a point to go to rushes after that.

Robert Ryan, whose movie career spanned three decades and more than seventy films, was one of the screen's most dependable stars. He was frequently labeled "an actor's actor", a term that reflected his versatility as well as the high regard in which he was held by his peers.

Bob Ryan was the friendliest. He was so kind to this newcomer, even giving me tips whenever he could without stepping on Mr. Donehue's toes. I thought he had much the same calmness that Myrna had and, unlike Monty, was a very contented man.

As it turned out, Bob gave me what would be the best advice I ever got. When I told him I was going to be in a play in New York, he said that if I ever needed vocal coaching I should contact Alfred Dixon. "He's the best", Bob stressed. "Remember the name."

The coworker Dolores bonded with most strongly was, surprisingly, Maureen Stapleton, cast as the frustrated housewife who seduces the lonely hearts columnist. Stapleton was a smoker, a drinker, a belcher, and she boasted a vocabulary that turned the air around her blue. On the surface, little about her should have appealed to Dolores, and little about Dolores should have appealed to her. But they became fast friends for the duration of the filming. They had no scenes together, but Dolores came to the set to watch Stapleton whenever she was working. They would spend time in one or the other's dressing room, both of them savoring this odd-couple camaraderie, and at the end of the shooting day, Dolores would drive the license-less New York actress home. Maureen Stapleton was the one with whom Dolores shared her Granny Kude stories.

Years later, Karl Malden told me that their bonding was inevitable. "Maureen and Dolores were mothers in capital letters. They both radiated trust—you could tell them anything. And they had taste in the people they chose to befriend."

—I treasured Maureen's company, and on my last day of filming, thoughts of her friendship intensified the letdown I always had when relationships ended.

Does that still make you sad—when people who have been important in your life don't relate anymore?

I think that's the centerfold of my vocation. Early on I grasped the pain of that aspect of making films. Bonds would form. The film would end, and then suddenly that relationship I trusted would be gone. It was, to me, shattering. I felt there had to be some centering in my life in which there was continuity.

With barely a week before I had to leave for New York and rehearsals for the play, those hectic last days were mercifully interrupted by a tiny vacation that was both exhilarating and calming. I was a bridesmaid at Sheila Hart's wedding at the beautiful old Mount Carmel Church in

81

Santa Barbara, and Dick and I decided to make a weekend of it. We drove up on Friday so we could attend the rehearsal and dinner planned for the wedding party that evening.

The wedding took place on Saturday morning, and the happy occasion became even more so for me by introductions to the officiating priest, Father Michael Doody, a Jesuit, and Father Armando Salazar, with whom Sheila had worked at the Catholic Welfare Bureau in Los Angeles. Both good men would remain forever firmly ensconced in my life and in my heart.

Dick and I spent the remaining time sightseeing in Santa Barbara, starting with Sunday Mass at the mission and walking hand in hand through its famous rose garden, which was in bloom. The whole weekend seemed filled with love. I knew I would never have told Dick I loved him in a moment of flightiness. It had to come from deep inside, and I thought I had no reservations.

Yet, looking back, a distant cloud hovered, and it confused me. It made me question if I was really able to commit to a relationship and made me wonder what would happen if I were asked to commit myself to something else.

Eight

Less than a week after Dolores completed her work in *Lonelyhearts*, she was en route to New York on a late-night flight. That journey would change her life in ways she could never have imagined.

One of the four stewardesses was Winnie Allen, who had been alerted about the VIPs on board. She saw the names Patti Page, which registered, and Dolores Hart, which did not. After dinner service, Dolores asked for an Alka-Seltzer. Winnie supplied the tablet, which could remedy any number of airborne discomforts from heartburn to anxiety, and later checked if her passenger was feeling better. Since Dolores was neither sleeping nor showing any signs of illness, Winnie asked if she felt like talking. The answer was affirmative, so for several hours, while the other passengers slept, the two young women bonded.

Winnie learned that Dolores was headed to Broadway for her first professional stage appearance and that the Alka-Seltzer had calmed a nervous stomach. Dolores found that Winnie came by her concern for others naturally, being the daughter of a missionary. By the time the plane landed at New York's LaGuardia Airport, the two new best friends had agreed not only to share a taxi into Manhattan, but to share digs as soon as they could find them. Winnie accepted Dolores' invitation to stay overnight at her hotel, the venerable Algonquin on West Forty-Fourth Street, famed as the site of the Round Table luncheons of literary wits Robert Benchley, Dorothy Parker, Marc Connelly and Oscar Levant.

It was late morning when they checked in, and both girls were bleary-eyed when they finally got to the room and were met by an oversize bouquet of flowers bearing an invitation from Cyril Ritchard asking Dolores to join him for supper that evening. The girls turned the single room into a double by pulling the mattress off the bed. One slept on the box spring on the frame, and the other on the mattress on the floor.

When Dolores returned from Ritchard's that night, she wrote me:

New York! I love it! Cyril—I am to call him Cyril—had me over to his Park Avenue suite (ahem!) for "a simple bit of goodies" before we start rehearsals tomorrow morning. I just love him. The cab driver took me through Central Park on the way home, and I pinched myself in case I was dreaming but it is all true. Oh, PS, Cyril is Catholic.

—How did you know that? Did you ask him?

Catholics always know other Catholics.

The next morning, at precisely 10:00 A.M., I walked onto the stage of the Longacre Theatre on West Forty-Eighth and was introduced to the cast of The Pleasure of His Company.

Cyril made the introductions as I ran down the collective résumés in my mind. Cornelia Otis Skinner: famous for her performances in Major Barbara *and* Lady Windermere's Fan, *acclaimed for one-woman shows she had also written; stately carriage; gracious. Walter Abel—my step-father in the play—had a forty-year career in theater and movies. I remembered Charlie Ruggles from movies I watched in Grandpa's pro-jection room. He twinkled in movies. Still did, I noticed. Cute Jerry Fujikawa was in the original* The Teahouse of the August Moon. *What with Cyril's twenty-year career, which included* Visit to a Small Planet *and Captain Hook in* Peter Pan *on Broadway, I was meeting over a century of theatrical stardom. Talk about intimidation.*

The other newcomer in the cast was George Peppard, who would be my fiancé in the play. I didn't know a thing about him, but he was one good-looking guy—single, too, but it turned out we had no social life outside the theater. I always felt as if he was looking down his nose at me.

The only familiar face that morning belonged to our costume designer who was also making her Broadway debut: Edith Head, who greeted me in front of the whole company with "Hi there, Junior!", which gave me a stamp of approval.

The Pleasure of His Company may have been the last of an honored Broadway genre, the sophisticated comedy of manners that had nothing more serious on its mind than a good time. The drawing-room comedy presented simple human truths with wit and charm and was usually environmentally restricted to the upper class. *Pleasure* was written by Samuel Taylor—who had established his flair for the form with *Sabrina Fair*—and the coauthor was the show's leading lady, Cornelia Otis Skinner. Ritchard, too, did double-duty as the director and star, playing Pogo Poole, an irresistible rogue of a playboy who descends on the San Francisco home of his ex-wife and their about-to-be-wed daughter he has not seen for many years. The plot concerns the giddy rapport of the reunited father and daughter, which threatens to break up her engagement, as well as his brief attempt to rekindle a spark in her mother.

Producing the play were the Playwrights' Company and Fredrick Brisson. Prior to *Pleasure*, Brisson, the husband of actress Rosalind Russell, had produced only musicals. Two of them—*The Pajama Game* and *Damn Yankees!*—had been anointed with Tony Awards as the best musicals of the two preceding seasons. The Playwrights' Company boasted a formidable list of founding members. Individually, Robert E. Sherwood, Elmer Rice, Sidney Howard, S. N. Behrman and Maxwell Anderson had written the most honored and respected American plays of the first half of the twentieth century. They founded the Playwrights' Company in 1938, producing their own works and those of other major playwrights. In the seasons since, they had been responsible for more Tony- and Pulitzer-winning plays than any other producing organization.

—Also, Maxwell Anderson had written Joan of Lorraine.

The company rehearsed on the Longacre stage they would occupy when the show opened. Within a few minutes of the first day, Ritchard called out to Dolores, "We can't hear you, dear child." She would hear that same remark, said with growing concern, throughout the day.

I seemed incapable of projecting my voice past the first few rows. At the end of rehearsal, Cyril came down to the stage and, in front of the entire company, announced that I would have to improve overnight or he would send me back to Paramount "jangling rosary beads". I was devastated. The other actors politely smiled it off, but I was humiliated. I remembered Anna Magnani's judgment: amateur.

Suddenly I heard the echo of Robert Ryan's voice. "If you ever need a vocal coach, call Alfred Dixon. Remember the name." I contacted Mr.

Dixon immediately, and he agreed to see me that same evening. He was a very pleasant man who tried to put me at ease by telling me even Katharine Hepburn had needed help.

He looked over the script and asked what I was being paid. When I told him my rehearsal salary was $75 a week, he was stunned. He couldn't believe that I had contracted for so many sides for so little money. Highway robbery, he called it. I confessed I had no money at the moment but promised he would be paid when I began receiving a performance salary, which he also found shockingly meager. He told me not to worry, promising that he could raise my projection level overnight.

We worked for four hours on proper breathing exercises and making very loud mooing sounds. When I got back to the Algonquin, I continued the exercises in earnest. Within fifteen minutes, there was a gentleman from the front desk at the door, asking if there was anything wrong. Neighboring guests had complained of distressed sounds coming from my room. I assured him all was well. But I spent the rest of the night in the shower, water on full blast, mooing into a pillow until I was exhausted.

Unbelievable as it seems, there was a small improvement in my projection the following day. Cyril didn't mention the rosary beads once, and Robert Ryan became my patron saint. Cyril was so relieved, he promised that the company would pay for additional coaching. Mr. Dixon admitted he could teach me all I needed to know in three lessons, but to protest their "slave wages" he charged the Playwrights' Company for ten weeks of tutoring.

—To this day, whenever I have to speak at a special occasion, I do Mr. Dixon's exercises. The only difference is that here at the abbey we have a dairy, so there's never a complaint.

We rehearsed six days a week, from ten in the morning until six in the evening. Our elegant genius worked us like a madman, but I adored him. After rehearsals, I would meet with Mr. Dixon. On some days I didn't seem able to get anything right, which made me wonder out loud why they picked me in the first place. On those days, Cornelia and Walter would be especially sweet, and my pet, dear Charlie, would shuffle over and, with a wink and an "Oh, phooey", tell me not to let

86

my disappointment get me down. All through the production, Charlie was my living report card. When I was good, I got a kiss.

Cyril was a hands-on director. He would virtually act out my part, with the precise line readings he wanted as well as every pause and reaction. One might expect an actress to be annoyed at being given every inflection and gesture to copy, but I was grateful.

Privately, Ritchard remarked that Dolores had something he couldn't teach her: "She had this quality of light. She shone from inside."

To create a real girl to inhabit, I began a diary as Jessica and filled a sizable volume. I got up enough courage to show the entries to Cyril, and he said he liked them! I think he liked more the fact that I bothered than what I wrote, but it looked as if he would put up with me after all.

By the tenth day, it seemed as if I were spending all my time either rehearsing or sleeping. I couldn't remember ever working as relentlessly in my life. I was always fearful that my lack of stage experience would be broadcast to the entire company if I slowed down even for a moment. I was really giving two performances, one as Jessica and one as Dolores Hart, actress.

Jessica crept into Dolores' almost nightly letters to me, too.

The play has become so much a part of my life. I don't think I've set foot outside the role since we started. It's like I'm in a coma called Jessica Poole. Today was the first day I became myself again. All of a sudden I was terribly lonely, and that's when I called you. It is pretty bad when you are lonely in your own company and can only remedy the situation by becoming someone else for a while. But maybe that's why I like this business so much. Jessica can do all the things that I find so terribly difficult to do. Maybe I will learn something from her. She is so completely enraptured with everything in life. There is not a tiny thing that she lets go by unappreciated. She can live and laugh and love a great deal. Sometimes I wonder what I would do if I find this isn't the business for me, or if I find that I am not any good. That I couldn't stand. I think I would quit on the spot. I hate halfway houses. Oh, phooey, as Charlie would say, it's getting on to the wee hours, and I am just writing down a lot of aimless thoughts. I am afraid my mood is quite similar to a few I had when I was with you on Flores Avenue—couldn't make much sense then either.

The "sense" Dolores yearned for concerned our personal relationship. Although what we felt for one another had not been diminished by our separation, it was coming in for more critical evaluation, and small craft warnings were posted.

Shortly after arriving in New York, Dolores had searched for a church near the hotel where she could attend daily Mass. Saint Patrick's, on Fifth Avenue, sufficed for a while until she found Saint Malachy's Church on West Forty-Ninth Street. It was known as the Actors' Chapel because it had a late-night Mass actors could attend after their final curtain. Announcements of auditions could be found near the entrance alongside the religious tracts and envelopes for donations.

Because the Algonquin was within walking distance of the theater, Dolores continued to live there through the rehearsal period and the opening of the play. She had the hotel's cheapest rate, $10.50 a night, which was still above what she could afford on her rehearsal salary, so she cut corners wherever she could to keep from dipping too often into her Hollywood reserve.

   —The hotel laundry charges were way too rich for me, so I smuggled mine out in paper bags and took it to the Chinese laundry down the street.

I knew no one in Manhattan except Winnie and the actors in the play, who invited me out infrequently. Once in a while, I would have to attend some professional function, and on those occasions dear Ray Powers, my agent with Famous Artists in New York, would be my escort. But most nights, when everyone went home after rehearsal, I went back to the Algonquin and ate dinner alone in my room.

New Haven was the first stop for the company's out-of-town tryouts, and their first dress rehearsal at the Schubert Theater was also their first time in front of an audience. There were only four hundred invited guests, but that was enough to render Dolores a mass of nerves. That day she wrote me two letters, before and after the performance.

[before] All day I've been waiting for the curtain to go up tonight. I feel like ... every bone in my body, every corpuscle, every part of me has been put into a vat and bleached. And the sense of terror. Wanting to run so fast and so far. I think that I would if it wasn't for the absolute duty to what I promised and the sense that this was a moment I have waited for since I can remember. Just before curtain, I went up to Cornelia backstage and told her how nervous I was and asked if there was a way to calm stage fright. She didn't answer, just kind of stared at me. Then, suddenly, she snapped to and apologized, "I'm so sorry, dear, I didn't hear a word you were saying. I'm too nervous."

[after] When I made my first entrance I found the sight of those people in the dark absolutely breathtaking. Throughout the whole performance it was amazing to realize that you don't lose yourself completely in the part because you are constantly aware of the audience too. It was an education to know those lovely moments when you have those people in the palm of your hand as well as the panic whenever you've let them slip away.... It was great to discover I could be funny. I have this witty line about my fiancé who raises prize bulls—"He sends his semen all over the world." I got a big laugh.

Opening night in New Haven was spectacular in more ways than one. During a scene between Dolores and Cornelia Otis Skinner, an overloaded electrical switchboard blew out with a heavy report and a brilliant flash. The stage went black. In the audience there was not a sound, and no one moved. Elliot Norton, in the *Boston Herald-American*, reported it was because the two actresses went on with the scene, "missing not one syllable, much less a line."

— Not entirely true. When the lights went out, I immediately froze. And then I felt Cornelia's hand on mine. She whispered, "Stay right where you are", and began improvising lines about the San Francisco power failure and the beauty of mother and daughter sharing moments in the dark. She knew the characters inside and out, so she wasn't in any danger of running out of ideas. The one thing she didn't do was pose a question, out of fear that this novice might attempt an answer. When the lights were restored, she just picked up the scene as if nothing had happened.

Out-of-town tryouts give companies the advantage of audience reaction and insight from local critics. It is the period when last-minute—and often major—changes in the production are made and, as a result, the most exhausting time the players face. During the New Haven and Boston tryouts, *The Pleasure of His Company* went from a three-act to a two-act play. This necessitated long daily rehearsals to take out and put in dialogue Samuel Taylor had written late the night before. The changes would be performed before the audience that night. Then more discussions occurred after the show, and additional changes were made.

Her nightly letters continued:

> George and I would hear Cyril, Cornelia and Walter speak about their "crust" and the fear of losing it. We had no idea what they meant. Cyril later explained that they were on guard to falling prey to becoming too involved on an emotional level. If that happened, he said, "the soufflé wouldn't rise, and if the crust crumbles, there will be no edge to the performance." That sophisticated "crust" apparently is what makes the show funny. George and I aren't as worried as they. Maybe we aren't old enough to have a crust.
>
> Last night, when the play still had three acts, Cyril and I had just started a scene in the second act when I realized that he was doing a scene from Act III. Or at least I thought he was. He was so confident that I assumed I must be mistaken and continued along. When we were backstage he realized what had happened and oh, the relief I felt. He was human after all. I asked him what we would do in Act III and he said, "The Act II scene—they won't notice." And they didn't.
>
> Oh, remember the "semen" laugh? I thought it was my delivery that was responsible for it. Wrong. It's Cyril's reaction.

I planned to go to New York for the opening, and as the date grew near we were on the phone nightly making plans. Luckily, the three-hour time difference worked in my favor. She was the night owl. I was the one who retired early. She told me that she was getting last-featured billing in the ads and on the placards. I was not happy. I don't think it's too much to expect that billing be appropriate. Dolores' role was a major one and warranted commensurate billing. But the decision had been made, and she felt it was too late to ask for a change. I begged her to ask that her name be the last in the lineup—"*and* Dolores Hart"—as even big stars were getting in movie ads—"*and* James Mason as Rupert of Hentzau". I stressed that she also ask for a box around her name and larger type than Peppard's and Fujikawa's.

I had been to New York City only twice before, but I knew a handful of places that I wanted to share with Dolores: Charles à la Pomme Soufflée, courtesy of Carol Burnett, where the pommes exploded in your mouth in tiny puffs; Frankie and Johnnie's, where you entered through the kitchen; a tiny club called The Baq Room, thanks to Tony Perkins and Gwen Davis, to hear the wonderful Janice Mars.

The place Dolores was eager to show me was the Cloisters, a museum devoted to the art and architecture of medieval Europe. Overlooking the Hudson River, the building incorporates portions of monastic chapels dating from the twelfth century. There are thousands of pieces of art, but the most famous are the seven Unicorn Tapestries.

I had been drawn to the unicorn since Sister Dolores Marie told me the legend of a princess who brings a unicorn into her garden. She leaves it alone, and hunters kill it; but she plants a tree where the unicorn dies, and the animal comes back to life. Then the princess binds the unicorn to the tree with a golden chain.

The Unicorn Tapestries depict scenes from the hunt for this elusive, magical being, its death and its resurrection. I responded instinctively to the purity of the unicorn's image and wanted to share the experience with Dick.

The seventh tapestry, The Unicorn in Captivity, *is the most famous. In this tapestry the unicorn is miraculously alive again, and I had been told that the risen unicorn is symbolic of the risen Christ. Dick didn't buy that because the animal, though resurrected, is chained. I tried to reason that the unicorn, like Jesus Christ, is forever tied to life everlasting, but Dick insisted upon being literal.*

Mostly we walked around the city, which Dolores preferred to taking taxis because it was good exercise and so my ego wouldn't be subjected to her superior cab-catching skills. My polite, rather timid raised arm was no match for that piercing whistle of hers.

At the theater I got my first glimpse of the placards in the lobby, with major stars Ritchard, Skinner and Ruggles above the title; below it, the top-billed costar, Abel; and featured players Peppard and Fujikawa followed by—in letters no larger and unboxed—"and Dolores Hart". It looked ridiculous considering that on the corner of Forty-Eighth and Broadway, half a block away from the Longacre Theatre, a giant bill-board trumpeted four stars in huge print above the title of *Lonelyhearts*. Dolores Hart was one of them.

—And you were surprised that I was unhappy.

But, Dick, I got the "and".

The Pleasure of His Company opened at the Longacre Theatre on October 22, 1958, just two days after Dolores' twentieth birthday. It rained on opening night, but inside the Longacre it could not have been sunnier.

It was buoyant—like moving through space—crowned by the trium-phant moment when we knew we had won our audience. Whatever the critics might say, there was no doubt when the curtain came down that The Pleasure of His Company *was an audience-pleaser.*

It is traditional for Broadway companies to party on opening night to give them something to do while waiting for the newspaper reviews, which in those days always appeared in the next morning's early editions. The opening night party was held at Cornelia Otis Skinner's townhouse. I got my first taste of the tension that lies beneath conviviality as the cast dined and drank and laughed while keeping an eye on the front door. When it finally burst open, someone was waving a copy of the *New York Times* with not only the first review of the night but also the most important one, that of Brooks Atkinson, the dean of theater critics.

As the youngest member of the cast, Dolores was called to read the *Times* review. She took off her shoes, and I helped her onto a chair in the middle of the now silent room. She read the notice, which was an unqual-ified rave for everyone involved. With each superlative mention—"Mr. Ritchard is in great form", "Miss Skinner gives her best performance",

"Charlie Ruggles is wonderfully droll"—the room exploded. Perhaps the biggest ovation came when she read, "Dolores Hart, a fresh young actress with a magnetic personality, is excellent as the mercurial Jessica."

As I helped her off her perch, my slightly dazed girl leaned over and whispered in my ear, "Who is Brooks Atkinson?"

For her Broadway debut, Dolores could not have wished for a warmer welcome. Douglas Watt, in the *New York Daily News*, anointed Dolores "a superior ingenue in all respects". John McClain, in the *New York Journal-American*, called her "a most entrancing lady". Walter Winchell, in the *New York Mirror*, said she was "one of the most believable actresses" he had "ever seen". The *New York World-Telegram*'s Frank Aston simply called her "a sugar plum".

The *Herald-American*'s Elliott Norton again tipped his hat: "Dolores Hart has had a good deal of success in pictures. That is no guarantee that she can act on the stage for the theater demands a different kind of performance. But she is just as much at home and as convincing in her way as is Charlie Ruggles, the comic veteran."

Each notice was met with her surprised smile, but there was a question in her eyes. She finally asked what I thought. I was able to tell her, in all honesty, that her Jessica Poole was everything she was meant to be: lovely, bright and altogether enchanting. In truth, she was even better than I expected she would be. When I left New York a few days later, I knew that night had been one of the happiest of my life. Fifty-five years have passed, and it still is.

Harriett was also at the opening and the party and was one happy— and well-behaved—mother, nursing a single glass of wine the entire night. She came to New York bearing a birthday gift—a pure white, pedigreed toy French poodle, which Dolores immediately christened Pogo, after Cyril Ritchard's character in the play.

I had never seen such a belligerent, determined animal in all my life. In spite of his size, barely six inches long, he would challenge every dog in Central Park. Each order I gave became a fight. I was sure that making him mind would be a full-time job.

But Pogo surprised me: he would soon be my obedient companion and a welcome guest at the Algonquin. He accompanied me wherever I went, even to the theater, where he stayed absolutely quiet in the dressing room while the show was on. Pogo was my unseen date at Manhattan restaurants and galleries and other no-pets-allowed venues. I had a large pocket sewed inside a coat into which Pogo easily fit. Pocket time meant sleep time.

Dolores got another surprise a few nights after the opening. Her father sent a note that he was in the audience and wanted to come backstage. It had been almost two years since she had laid eyes on him. The two went to supper after the show, a father and daughter reunion, which was coincidentally the theme of the play. But Dolores noted with some irony that Bert was no Pogo Poole. He now seemed quite seedy, and a blowhard. He told her he had come back to collaborate on her career. He wanted to be her manager.

I thought the Lord must have a black sense of humor. It made me sad, but no way did I want him in my professional life. I just reminded him that the people responsible for my career had contracts that I couldn't break and gave him an out.

At the end of the evening, Bert found he couldn't pay the check and asked if she would, insisting he would pay her back.

Apartment hunting became a number-one priority for Dolores and Winnie. By virtue of her freer schedule, Winnie took responsibility for finding a flat. They settled on a place on West Forty-Fifth Street, a large apartment whose two rooms were separated by glass french doors, giving the appearance of being one huge room—with a bathroom, of course, but no kitchen or closet and not a stick of furniture. The rent was $150 a month, which they split. At that time Winnie was making more money as a stewardess than Dolores was as a Broadway actress. Upkeep was not fifty-fifty. Dolores didn't like cooking or cleaning; Winnie did. So the actress chipped in a little more for food and such, and the stewardess took on the household chores.

The immediate problem of a kitchen was solved by laying a wooden board on top of the bathtub for an electric hot plate, toaster, and coffee maker. When we wanted to bathe, we had to remove the so-called kitchen to fill the tub. Instead of a closet, we had nails in the wall. For the longest time we slept on mattresses on the floor.

We felt like a couple of college girls in our first apartment, and together we set out to clean and redecorate. I suspected that the previous tenants were color blind—the rooms were painted pink and black. Beneath the paint we discovered a rather nice marble fireplace, so we both got down to scraping the pink away.

Furniture was added gradually. They did some bargain hunting at the Third Street Auction House. Cooking utensils and tables came from Cornelia Otis Skinner and Charlie Ruggles. Hal Wallis' New York–based partner, Joseph Hazen, supplied lamps, and an older gentleman named Irving Sachs gave them chairs.

Winnie had met Irving Sachs, who was a regular passenger on a shuttle flight from Roanoke to New York City. Mr. Sachs was somewhere in his seventies and brought a bag of berries to eat on the plane. Winnie insisted upon washing the berries, and when she brought them back in a bowl on a tray with a white linen cloth, Mr. Sachs was impressed. He was the owner of a big clothing store in Roanoke and traveled to New York on buying trips. By the time the plane had landed, Mr. Sachs and Winnie were friends. That friendship soon included me.

In a Gregory La Cava movie, Mr. Sachs would be a sugar daddy. In reality, he was a surrogate grandfather who was so enchanted with the girls and with what they were doing with their lives that he made them beneficiaries of many kindnesses, not the least of which was a trip to New York's garment district to pick out some stylish additions to their wardrobes "on the house". Irving Sachs remained a treasured friend to Dolores for the rest of his life. When she became a nun, he transferred his generosity to the Regina Laudis Community, and upon his death his sister continued his visits and his gifts.

Dolores soon found herself in a comfortable routine. She would arise late and go to Mass, then spend afternoons reading or writing letters or scraping paint. She still did publicity layouts for the fan magazines with young actors who were making movies in New York, such as Tab Hunter and Tommy Sands, and when *Newsweek* proclaimed her "Broadway's newest star", doors opened to the national magazines. She got her first cover—with Pogo—on *Parade*, followed by another on the *New York Mirror*. She appeared with Cyril and Cornelia on the covers of *Gotham Life Guide*, *Host* and *Where*. *Look* did a photo essay on her life with Pogo. Famed fashion photographer Francesco Scavullo shot a feature for *Cosmopolitan* of Dolores pub crawling in high-toned Manhattan, dressed to the teeth in Scaasi—after which she returned the fancy wardrobe and went back to her Forty-Fifth Street hovel.

She still walked to and even from the theater, which could be done without fear in the 1950s. On matinee days, she would be at the theater from noon until well after eleven at night. Still keyed up from the performance, she usually had a snack of matzoh, cream cheese and ginger ale, then wrote letters or did laundry until she was tired enough to sleep—usually around 3:00 A.M.

She was always the first of the cast to arrive at the Longacre, usually more than two hours before curtain, to give her time to do her makeup and hair and an hour to relax.

—Did you ever use the time to meditate or pray?

I was not inclined to pray in that circumstance. I wanted to clear my mind to prepare for the evening's performance, and prayer does just the opposite. It engages the mind.

On January 3, 1959, *The Pleasure of His Company* was declared a bona fide hit. On that day, the producers repaid the entire investment of $80,000, only eleven weeks after opening night, at a top ticket price then of $6.90.

Down the street, *Lonelyhearts* had opened to disappointing reviews—it was called grim, gloomy, bitter. Dolores received fewer valentines than she got for the play. *Variety* said she "glows with a spirited sensitivity", but most reviewers just acknowledged her presence in the cast. I had inconsiderately sent my less-than-enthusiastic assessment plus reviews from the Hollywood trade papers and got this reply:

> I received the trade reviews you sent. Sort of gave me a bit to think about in the *Reporter*. I haven't had a blow in a review yet, and the first time is kind of stunning. However, after the newness wore off I had to laugh at myself for acting like such a typical actress type. The only salvation in this business is to learn early not to take yourself too seriously.

Every now and then, I would see Father Michael Doody, the priest who had officiated at Sheila's wedding, because he was now living in Boston. Father Mike, as I called him, was the quintessence of Irish, right out of a John Ford movie. I thought of him as a continuity of my grandfather. He thought of himself as my guardian Jesuit.

Mom and Pop, making yet another attempt at reconciliation, took a second honeymoon at the Kentucky Derby and stopped off in New York. Of course, they saw Pleasure *and that served to sharpen a self-analysis of my performance. The excitement I felt when I was onstage had not flagged, but I became aware that the cause of my nightly nerves had changed. It was still generated by fear, but now I was going onstage afraid that I wouldn't be as good as I was at the beginning or even as I might have been the previous night.*

I strongly and repeatedly suggested that Dolores investigate acting teachers in the city that boasted the best. High on my list was Uta Hagen, who was a major acting force on Broadway. In the late 1940s she and her husband, Herbert Berghof, had founded the well-respected HB Studio, and by 1958 few teachers equaled Hagen's impact on the quality of acting in America.

Initially, Dolores resisted the suggestion. She felt classes were for actresses who wanted to do what she was already doing. I prevailed—nagged—pointing out that Jason Robards, Geraldine Page and Hal Holbrook still studied with Hagen. I think I was more delighted than she was when the Actors Studio coincidentally invited her to observe some classes taught by Sandy Meisner and Bobby Lewis. Those few classes whetted her appetite. She contacted Uta Hagen, who told her she would have to audition for the class. Now determined to be accepted, Dolores spent the next several days working up a scene from Sherwood Anderson's *Winesburg, Ohio* and was accepted. For the remainder of her time in New York, she met with the actress-teacher once a week.

Uta's classes were a highlight of those days in New York. I was sharpening my craft, inspired by her on-the-money critiques, though I admit the best feeling of all came from hearing her say, "No criticism."

Her challenge to me was to preserve a kind of innocence in my work. In a long run, you can become too comfortable, but there needs to be an edge so that the audience can feel that what's happening in front of them is happening for the first time. Uta Hagen instilled in me a new and nearly unshakable respect for myself as an actress.

Yet I remained restless. The weekends presented a special problem. With Sundays and Mondays off, everyone else in the cast left town after the Saturday night performance, not to return until Tuesday. Everyone except me had someplace to go to unwind.

I mentioned to Winnie that I would like to find a nice, quiet retreat of sorts, a resort perhaps. Her friend Faith Abbott knew of a monastery of cloistered nuns in rural Connecticut, about two hours from Manhattan. It was an ideal setting, Faith said, for a devout Catholic woman to relax and meditate, and she would be happy to introduce me. I told her that I had had my fill of nuns and declined. But the idea of that kind of retreat kept creeping back into my thoughts.

With the play such a major hit, leaving no question that Dolores would fulfill her year's commitment, she and Winnie moved uptown to a new apartment on the east side.

It was a real New York apartment with a real kitchen, dining room, bedrooms, everything—and it was furnished too. The rent was $500 a month, now affordable because I was earning a performance salary of $425 a week, and expenses and responsibilities were split as before. I rationalized the extravagance to Granny by enumerating the advantages

over our former home: a safer address with a doorman and an elevator
man, both of whom you had to pass before you got to the seventh floor.
Granny would not have been pleased to know that, although East
Sixty-Eighth Street was some twenty blocks from the Longacre, I still
walked to and from work. But I now had a place to host cast members,
and a frequent guest was the pert Sandy Smith, my understudy.

Sandy once told me she had taken the job as an understudy *and had*
no ambition to play the part. She would regularly call to make sure I
was showing up and would panic if I arrived at the theater a few
minutes late. No Eve Harrington, she. When the East Coast winter
introduced me to sinus problems that would plague me for years, Sandy
would check on me several times a day. But the only performance I
missed my entire year was the night Sandy was asked to go on so the
producers could see her play the role in front of an audience.

When the Tony nominations were announced for the 1958–1959
season, *The Pleasure of His Company* racked up four. Cyril Ritchard
was nominated for Best Director and Best Actor, and Charlie Ruggles
made the Best Featured Actor list. But the nomination that most thrilled
the cast was Dolores' as Best Featured Actress.

I flew back to be with her at the awards. She was exquisite that night,
in fur and jewelry freebies offered by designers to nominees on the
chance that someone would mention their names to the press. That was
a cottage industry in 1959. Today it is a major business.

Not one to be impressed by celebrity, Dolores knew, nevertheless,
that she was going to be in the company of some of the history-makers
in her profession. The Broadway experience had increased her respect
for stage actors, and she loved being a part of their tribe—whether she
recognized them or not.

After dinner—and before the awards were announced—Dolores was
in the ladies' room with another nominee in her category, Julie Newmar.
Julie found she had no money to tip the attendant, so she borrowed fifty
cents from Dolores.

Dolores and I sat at *The Pleasure of His Company* table, which at the
end of the evening was graced with a Tony. Charlie Ruggles was named
the Best Featured Actor that season, the most popular award of the

99

night. Dolores was not named Best Featured Actress. That honor went to Julie Newmar.

—And she still owes me the four bits.

With Dolores' evenings committed to performing, I took in some of the other plays that were on that season. She was in very good company. The 1958–1959 season included *The Visit, A Raisin in the Sun, Look Back in Anger, The Most Happy Fella, Sweet Bird of Youth* and *Look Homeward, Angel.* I was also able to catch a dress rehearsal of a new musical opening off-Broadway, *Once Upon a Mattress,* which began the enduring career of my UCLA pal Carol Burnett. Dolores couldn't accompany me to the rehearsal, but I was finally able to introduce my two favorite ladies.

I was amazed at how closely their lives paralleled. As youngsters in Los Angeles, both Carol and Dolores had hidden away to avoid the violence of alcoholic parents. Both were reared mainly by grandmothers who were real characters. (I've always thought, given the chance, Granny Kude would have taught Nanny White to drink a martini standing on her head.). Carol and Dolores also share a wicked sense of humor, a down-to-earth sense of responsibility and the passion necessary to bring each to her ultimate dream.

D and D were able to go to the theater together only once, to the Actors Fund benefit performance of *Redhead* with Gwen Verdon. On a Sunday, we "attended" the Academy Awards together. Richard Altman, my friend from UCLA days, now living in New York and teaching at the American Academy of Dramatic Arts, threw an Oscar party at his Greenwich Village pad. Several other transplanted Uclans were there, including Merv Kaufman and Larry Swindell, who was then the reviewer for the Westchester County Newspaper Group (and, fortunately, had called Dolores "enchanting" in his notice). Altman always maintained that he threw the party just to be able to say that Kaufman and Hart attended.

William Perlberg and George Seaton came backstage late in the run of *Pleasure.* The Perlberg-Seaton Company, which was headquartered at Paramount, had just bought the movie rights to the play, and that night they promised Dolores that she would repeat her role in the film.

I literally floated above the ground for the next several weeks. Then one night Debbie Reynolds appeared backstage with the news that she had just been cast in the movie—in my part. I was totally devastated. I barely managed smiles and congratulations. It was the only time I've ever experienced the urge to kill. All the original actors would be replaced save one. Twinkly Charlie Ruggles repeated his role in the movie. I could never bring myself to see it.

George Peppard was the first cast member to leave the show, and I tried to get my friend James Douglas the part. James was a perfect fit for it and flew to New York to audition. I read with him. But Jim didn't get the part. I had to call him to break the news, and it was the hardest thing I had ever done.

Richard Altman contacted Dolores about the possibility of one of his students auditioning for the role, and they met Dolores for coffee after a performance. Thinking he looked wonderful for the part, she arranged an audition for him. But Robert Redford didn't get it either.

In June, wedding bells were going to ring for Winnie, setting off an alarm in Dolores. She had met the groom-to-be and thought she recognized her father in him and cautioned Winnie, who would not be dissuaded. Winnie's family was against the marriage but waited until just four days before the wedding to withdraw their support, taking back her grandmother's wedding dress she was counting on wearing.

"I'll never forget," Winnie said, "Dolores took me by the hand to Lord and Taylor, where we saw an ideal gown on a mannequin. It fit me perfectly. Dolores bought it on the spot as a wedding present. She was supposed be my bridesmaid, but the wedding was scheduled in upstate New York on a matinee day, which made it impossible. Still, she drove up early that morning just to see me in my wedding dress. She had to turn around and drive back to Manhattan immediately."

As the end of her contract grew near and the play was showing no signs of fading, the producers asked Dolores to extend until the end of the run and then go on the road with it. Since Hal Wallis had nothing in the offing for her at the studio, she strongly considered extending, especially since her New York agent, Ray Powers, had arranged for her to test for the TV presentation of Edith Wharton's novel *Ethan Frome*, which would be done in New York. I was excited at the prospect because the book was a favorite of mine and I thought she would make a fine Mattie Silver.

—I didn't get the role—Julie Harris did.

Back in Hollywood, however, Harry Bernsen had lined up a test with director Henry Koster for the lead role in *The Story of Ruth*—a biblical drama—and both he and Hal Wallis felt Dolores should return sooner rather than later.

I had to agree that I would be better off in Hollywood, even if I wasn't working, because at least I would be available. And I had come to the realization that, as much as I loved the Broadway experience, I did miss making movies.

I was told that one of the rewards of a long run on the stage is that it gives you the opportunity of tiring of everything and everybody gradually, and you don't feel the letdown when it's over. Don't believe it. I think it's the biggest scourge of show business. I felt completely empty, and nothing filled the space for a long while after.

Her last engagement before departing New York was to join other young players named by *Theatre World* as the most outstanding of the season for a group photograph. *Theatre World* has been, since 1944, the official chronicle of each Broadway and Off-Broadway season and acknowledges its best debut performances. Among the other actors photographed that day were William Shatner, Ina Balin, Larry Hagman and Rip Torn.

So, with 364 performances in *The Pleasure of His Company* behind her, a Tony nomination and a *Theatre World* award, "Broadway's newest star" headed back to Hollywood, with a very tiny, very quiet, very secret Pogo in her pocket.

Nine

The year in New York was one of the great learning experiences of my professional life. I had worked with a gifted company of actors and had studied with a master. I was coming back to Hollywood with confidence in my craft.

I was also coming home with a heart filled with unanswered questions. I prayed that if the answers remained beyond my comprehension at that moment, God would give me the grace to live with the questions.

The questions concerned that monastery in Connecticut that Faith Abbott had recommended. While Dolores was still in New York, the idea of visiting the monastery surfaced in her thoughts from time to time. What could it hurt to find out more about the place, she would wonder, but then she would turn her attention to something else.

Until the chilly autumn day she stood on a crowded corner in midtown Manhattan and stared as the traffic light turned green, then red, then green again and she couldn't move a muscle. A policeman approached her and asked if anything was wrong. She said she was only daydreaming, but when she got back to the apartment she told Winnie that it was time she did something about Faith's suggestion.

When Faith first mentioned Regina Laudis, I thought it would be "blue" Catholic—you can't get any more Catholic than that. Faith had been drawn to its traditional ways—Latin prayers and full-length habits. Still, it seemed to have potential as a getaway to massage the kinks out with meditation and prayer, and the fact that the order was contemplative happily meant that the nuns would not be constantly available.

Dolores wrote to Regina Laudis for permission to visit overnight. The guest secretary, Mother Columba, thought the letter sounded very nice and shared it with the guest mistress, Mother Placid, who had grown up in New York City and was not unfamiliar with show-business folk.

103

Both women were convinced that actors and artists felt comfortable at Regina Laudis. Mother Placid had recently spent time with a visiting group of aspiring actresses who all lived at the Rehearsal Club in Manhattan. "The play *Stage Door* was about that place", she was quick to tell me, sharing a bit of insider information. "Performers are always fun, if a little affected, and that group was particularly 'actressy'—you see, they had all seen Ingrid Bergman play a nun. Frankly, I expected the same from this Dolores Hart. But I agreed that the letter was thoughtful and sincere." An invitation to visit was extended.

Very early on my next day off—Monday, November 12, 1958—Pogo and I boarded a bus at New York's Port Authority. I knew I was not supposed to bring pets into the guesthouse, much less on the bus, but Winnie was on call with the airline and I couldn't leave him alone. He rode in my pocket. Two hours later we were deposited at the Regina Laudis "outpost", Phillips Diner, in the small town—a village really—of Woodbury, Connecticut. At that time, Phillips resembled what it was, a real 1940s Pullman car. It has changed over the years but is still there. Out front was a phone booth. I had no small coins, so I splurged and dropped my sole quarter into the slot to call the only taxi listing in Woodbury.

I shared with the driver, Herbie Robertson, the directions I had been given: "You'll drive through Woodbury and up Flanders Road toward Bethlehem, to the monastery. If you get to Bethlehem, you've gone too far."

The drive up Flanders Road was short but, to my artist's eye, full of God's beauty. Although mid-November was late for the Technicolor extravaganza of a New England autumn, more than enough color remained in those woods, sparsely dotted with neat Connecticut houses, to inspire a greeting card or a calendar.

As we turned onto the rugged grounds of the monastery, a small red-and-white farmhouse with a stone chimney came into view. Beyond and above the little house was a large, imposing building that looked like a factory, which, I was to learn, it had been. This was the monastery. Herbie deposited me at the entrance with cheerful assurance that I would enjoy my visit. I followed the handwritten instruction tacked to the door and knocked, then entered.

104

I stood in a small entry. There was another door inside, the top half of which was a grille. The room certainly evoked a sense of the past.

A nun appeared behind the grilled door. "Benedicamus Domino" ("Let us bless the Lord"), she said in an imposing, accented voice. I would later learn this was the portress, Mother Mary Aline, but at this moment there was no conversation. I was simply informed that Mother Placid would meet me in a parlor and was directed outside to an attached building just beyond a small chapel. Again, following printed instructions, I knocked and entered a tiny, dimly lit room of the same dark wood, divided by a grille of wooden lath, with straight chairs on either side. Not the parlor I was expecting. In a cloister, the word parlor, *from the French* parler, *which means "to talk", refers not only to the special room I was in but to a conversation with a nun. I sat and waited. Before long, a small—almost tiny—nun bounced into the parlor on the other side of the grille. She had a soft, round face with a very open smile under bright, twinkling eyes.*

"When I entered the parlor," Mother Placid remembered, "I saw this lovely young woman with no trace of artifice about her. 'You must be Miss Hart', I said, with a hint of relief. During the next hour we talked about theater and films and found we shared an interest in art. She was very down to earth, direct. There was no mention of vocation. She was interested only in a place to come and get the cobwebs out. But I remember I had a feeling that she would return."

Mother Placid thought her religious name was wonderful because, as she put it, "Guests expect a tall, willowy lady, and they get this pygmy who seems to have a screw loose somewhere." I didn't tell her that, with my sense of irony, I had expected a nun with the name Placid to come equipped with a ruler to whack my knuckles.

She was from Brooklyn, last name Dempsey, an art major on scholarship at Marymount College, particularly drawn to medieval art. She also had been a regular at Broadway matinees and had worked on sets for the Blackfriars Guild. For a monastic nun she was very current on what was happening in American theater, even able to tell me what was coming to Broadway, because actresses would write to have prayers said for auditions. I guess you could say she had one foot in the Middle Ages and the other in Greenwich Village.

105

Dolores met one other nun that first visit: the guest secretary, Mother Columba, whose family name, coincidentally, was Hart. Mother Columba came from an intellectual Yankee family of no small accomplishment. A graduate of Smith College with a master's degree from Radcliffe in a day when such a thing was rare for a woman, she had been a teacher in the English department at Smith. She spoke French fluently and had a passing knowledge of theater. In fact, she had known the famous stage actress Maude Adams. Mother Columba had produced some major scholarly contributions to monastic studies—especially in regard to the monastic women mystics of the twelfth century. She had translated and published the works of Saint Hildegard, which have, to this day, continued to earn royalties. Like Dolores, Mother Columba was a convert to Catholicism.

Mother Columba had a tiny voice, wore thick glasses and was almost completely hunched over from, I would learn, endless hours at her desk. She was a scholar. She had a romantic imagination and a drive to which I immediately responded. I found her a very dignified lady.

I don't remember having any problem with conversing through the grille, and in those days the grille separating the enclosed nuns from the guests had a double row of lath. You could not put your hand through it, and you could not pass a nun a piece of paper without crumpling it. But the grille didn't obliterate the feeling of intimacy for me.

The chapel at Regina Laudis was quite different from Catholic churches I had seen in LA, Chicago and New York that were similar in their adornment. This one was small, almost cozy, its stained-wood walls lending a decidedly country feel. It smelled like roasting pine nuts and was sprinkled with golden light shining through yellow stained glass, which dotted the two or three small windows in no particular design. Entering the chapel was like walking into a warm piece of toast.

I wasn't wearing my glasses, so the entire room appeared to be lit by teeny sparkling lights, which were, in fact, candles burning in cut-glass vases. The altar was a simple wooden table with a runner of crisp white linen. At the back of the chapel, behind a large wooden grille, curtained off from view, was the choir area where the nuns prayed. The chapel had a cleanness about it, a simple waiting room where I felt the Lord was waiting.

Women guests were housed in a nearby white farmhouse named Saint Gregory's. It was comfortable and spotless. Vegetarian meals, simple and filling, were taken in the guest refectory. Although I was a steak eater by preference, I was always on a diet, so the fare was pretty well down my alley.

Regina Laudis was the only Benedictine monastery for contemplative nuns in the country (there was one other in North America, in Canada), and the Community followed the Primitive Observance—Saint Benedict's fifth-century Rule. It was an ancient pattern of ora et labora, *"prayer and work".*

Prayer consisted of singing the Divine Office according to the monastic breviary seven times a day and once at night beginning with Matins, at 2:00 A.M., and continuing through Lauds, Prime, Terce, Sext, None and Vespers to Compline at 7:40 P.M. Interspersed were periods of Lectio Divina—holy reading—and private prayer.

Manual work included all the tasks necessary in a large monastic household: the charge of the sacristy, library and storerooms; cooking and baking; cleaning, laundering and sewing. During the summer there is outdoor work in the orchards and gardens and indoor work of preserving. A large place was given to arts and crafts such as painting, bookbinding, vestment making, ceramics and printing.

Intellectual labor consisted of study of Holy Scripture and the Church, the Rule of Saint Benedict *and the history of monastic life as well as of Regina Laudis itself*

The history of the founding of Regina Laudis is thought to be the basis for the Clare Boothe Luce magazine story that became the successful 1949 film Come to the Stable. *I remembered having enjoyed that movie as a child, but it bears no relationship to the actual events. Loretta Young and Celeste Holm play nuns, and it is set in Connecticut. The similarity ends there. The two screen nuns are not quietly devoted to a life of contemplation, prayer and work. These ladies toot around Bethlehem in a jeep, seeking support to establish a children's hospital, and they get their building from a New York gangster.*

The roots of Regina Laudis are found in the seventh-century Abbey of Notre Dame de Jouarre in France. In 1936, a young American woman, Vera Duss, had just received her medical degree from the Sorbonne and was beginning a career in medicine when she stunned her family by entering religious life at the Abbey of Jouarre. By an unprecedented decision by the abbess, Miss Vera, even though only a postulant, became the abbey's doctor.

During World War II, Jouarre was seized by the German Army, and the abbey was occupied by Nazi officers. After the United States entered the war, the now-consecrated Mother Benedict Duss was forced into hiding. Because she was an American, her mere presence in the abbey was a constant danger, and more than once she was kept from falling into the hands of the Gestapo by the quick thinking of her loyal friend, Mother Mary Aline Trilles de Warren, who had wanted to be an actress before entering monastic life.

On August 27, 1944, the Abbey of Jouarre was liberated by the Allied Forces under the command of General George S. Patton. As Mother Benedict watched the convoy of American soldiers moving through the village, she vowed to make a commensurate response to their victory over oppression. She was determined to find a way to bring contemplative Benedictine life to the land of the liberators, her native country.

That vision was never out of her thoughts or her prayers through the long, slow and difficult period that followed. She finally received support from two important men—Angelo Giuseppe Roncalli, the papal nuncio to Paris who would later become Pope John XXIII, and Cardinal Giovanni Montini, the future Pope Paul VI.

Fortified with their blessings and practical advice, Mother Benedict and Mother Mary Aline sailed to New York, arriving with exactly twenty dollars between them plus the names of two Americans, Frances Delahanty and well-known artist Lauren Ford, who became their benefactresses, not only taking the nuns into their farmhouse near the town of Bethlehem but also bringing their mission to the attention of Robert Leather, an industrialist living in the area.

Leather was a devout Congregationalist who owned a large piece of land there. He wanted his land to be held intact in perpetuity, and he gave it to the nuns, knowing that they would care for it as a sacred place. This wooded hill became the center of the eventual 450 acres of land, both cultivated and wild, that the Abbey of Regina Laudis comprises today.

There was a large barn on the land that Leather had converted into a brass polish factory but which now stood unoccupied. The factory was eventually remodeled and became the monastery building. Before long, the Community grew to eight with the arrival of six nuns from Jouarre. A small farmhouse on the land was converted by the nuns into their first chapel as well as their living quarters. This little red-and-white house, my introduction to Regina Laudis, later became the guesthouse for male visitors.

—That story would make a better movie than Come to the Stable.

The Benedictines are named after their founder, Saint Benedict, who was born in the Umbrian town of Nursia in the year 480. Benedict came from the aristocracy and was a student of law in Rome, but, abandoning family wealth and career, he set his mind on serving God, joining a community of similar seekers in a village at the foot of Mount Affile, where a miracle occurred. This miracle concerned an earthenware colander his nurse had placed on a table. It was knocked over and broken, which left the nurse distraught. Seeking to comfort the distraught nurse, Benedict picked up the pieces and began to pray. When he rose from his prayers, he saw that the colander was once again whole.

The occurrence caused Benedict to become so renowned that he left the village. He made his way to Subiaco, where he lived as a hermit in a cave for three years, choosing a life of hardship. It was this coming together of holiness and hard work that was to become his great legacy.

Benedict founded a monastery at Monte Cassino, where he wrote his Rule. The Rule stressed living in community, and over centuries like-minded groups who lived by it became known as the Order of Saint Benedict.

I did not have an educated opinion about the Benedictines or what set them apart from the other orders with which I had come in contact. During my first visit, I didn't really discuss Benedictine life with either Mother Placid or Mother Columba, so when they mentioned the Rule of Saint Benedict *I was curious about it. As neither sister offered me a copy, I bought one in the monastery art shop, where it was hidden behind jars of honey and bags of tea and skeins of wool—all prepared by the nuns.*

— Obviously, no one was trying to "sell" me.

I read through the Rule while I was visiting. It grabbed me with the first words of its prologue: "Listen, O my son, to the precepts of thy master, and incline the ear of thy heart." I found it a simple commentary that spoke to me about the dignity of being human. We are meant to serve God with the gifts He has given us. Sin is not so much doing something wrong; sin is not being true to who we are. That someone would have that light in the fifth century was a discovery for me.

My grasp of Benedictine life would develop more fully after I entered the monastery, but somehow even then I found it very right for me. I felt a tremendous rapport with the Rule's basic premises–simplicity, discernment and praise of God. When I left that weekend, I thought that, however Regina Laudis interpreted the Rule of Saint Benedict, *I could accept it personally.*

Upon reflection back in Manhattan, my hoped-for mission had been fulfilled at Regina Laudis. I had found it restful; I had recharged my batteries and now was eager to get on stage again. Latent thoughts about a vocation had not been stirred up.

I was again taking bows with the cast every night, holding hands as applause rolled over us—what was it Anne Baxter said in All About Eve?*—"like waves of love". I loved the theater, and I loved the movies, and I wanted more than anything else to grow in my career. Why would I look anywhere else?*

Memories of the monastery, however, remained in my thoughts. Regina Laudis was the perfect place to go to integrate the weariness of a long run and the anxiety over what awaited me back in Hollywood. But I had to admit that there was something more.

I didn't know then that I could have walked into any other Catholic convent or monastery anywhere in the world and walked away, keeping the life I had intact.

For the remainder of the play's run, I made repeated visits to Regina Laudis. I attended Mass and Vespers and occasionally some of the other Offices, though never the 2:00 A.M. Matins. I took walks—either alone or with another woman guest—exploring the land. I helped to clean Saint Gregory's. I meditated. I had parlors with Mothers Placid and Columba but no other members of the Community. Visitors then were not passed on to other nuns with shared interests.

On each visit, Mother Placid greeted me with the same question: "Why have you come?" I always wanted to answer that I needed a first-rate catechism course. In her own splendid and lofty way—camouflaged a bit by the twinkle in her eyes—she smiled and said, "You return to give of yourself. When a person gives of himself, he gives what he is, his essence, just as God continually reveals to us His essence, which is love."

That's how it had felt to me ever since I sat all by myself in the church at Saint Gregory's School. I knew then I was not alone, that God's presence was close to me. That feeling had grown stronger over the years. I had come to rely on it. I had come to want God even closer.

During my third visit, I met the founder of Regina Laudis, Reverend Mother Benedict Duss. She was a handsome woman and had the most incredible skin, soft and smooth, unlined. She seemed ageless. Her gray-green eyes were cool in the sense of remote—sometimes distant, sometimes thoroughly amused. She was radiantly joyful and spoke so positively about life. My first impression was that she was a very happy person. But as I left the parlor my estimation of her was harsher. How could she possibly believe that life is that beautiful? How could she be so naïve? She was a woman with professional experience, a doctor. A person that old and with her background should have some cynicism. Doesn't she know how painful the world can be? Either she was enlightened or she was a boob.

I felt like walking and headed in the direction of lush green woods, which I happily discovered opened onto a golden field. I was locked in my thoughts and hadn't seen the young nun coming toward me until she suddenly appeared at my side.

It was Mother David Serna, who is now the abbess of Regina Laudis. "I was walking on the road next to Saint Pius Field," she recalled,

111

"when I saw this young woman, probably, I thought, a visitor at the monastery who had wandered off the beaten path. Not all the grounds surrounding the monastery buildings are open to visitors. There are areas that are within the enclosure and should not be trespassed upon. They are marked with signs, which she had obviously ignored. I simply said to her, 'I don't think you want to be here.' She retreated immediately. But later that day, Reverend Mother Benedict said to me, 'I've just met your blond counterpart.' I had no idea what she meant."

Throughout 1959, I had several parlors with Reverend Mother Benedict, who, I quickly learned, was anything but a poor, naïve woman. On the contrary, this woman was well educated and cultured. She had learned the works of Bach and Ravel when most kids were learning to play with blocks. Her mother took her at age nine to the Louvre to appreciate the French Impressionists. American thought, as far as Reverend Mother was concerned, was overly linear and childish.

Both introspective and pragmatic, Reverend Mother shared stories of her early life as a medical student in Paris and then as a Benedictine nun and doctor at the Abbey of Jouarre. She and Mother Mary Aline were true heroines during the German occupation of the abbey, and I listened with fascination as she told of chilling exploits in dodging the Nazis. Once, late at night, on a street with no place to hide from view, she and Mother Mary Aline had to cling like shadows to a wall to conceal their white wimples from Gestapo soldiers driving by on patrol.

It was from one of her hiding places, the abbey bell tower, that she heard sounds of an advancing army and looked over the casement to see which troops were approaching. At first, she couldn't identify the convoy, and then, there it was, on the back of a military truck: an American flag.

At that precise moment she vowed to establish a Benedictine monastery in America. She chose the name Regina Laudis, *which means "Queen of Praise", even before coming to this country because, she told me, "Mary is the exemplar of praise for the Lord; she did nothing else but live to meet God's terms."*

Life at Regina Laudis was extremely difficult in those early years. Many nights their supper consisted only of soup made from nettles that

112

grew profusely on the property. The nuns planted vegetable gardens and orchards, raised a flock of sheep, and pursued various crafts—carpentry, spinning and weaving, even blacksmithing—out of necessity. Monastic life may be the summit of holiness, but the realities of such an existence make considerable demands.

I wondered how she had managed to keep from feeling defeated, and Reverend Mother told me, "I had no special method to do it, except to do it. The secret to keeping this place going was to do the next thing that had to be done—without wasting time worrying. Founding a monastery is a continuous process of sawing to build and, at the same time, trying to dispose of the sawdust. If you do something concrete, that opens the possibilities. You don't know what God is doing on the other side, but He's doing something. You have to keep a sense of obligation on the one hand, and trust on the other. I lean on one of Saint John of the Cross' basic principles. He said that in a situation where there is no love, you put in love and love will be there."

Each parlor with Reverend Mother made me recognize that there is another kind of confession other than sacramental confession. One can be open to confession to people of wisdom and understanding, which allows one to share the concerns of one's heart.

Reverend Mother had a depth of understanding that astounded me. Without reciting "absolutes", she could put the tension I was feeling into perspective for me. She had an incredible capacity for womanly assimilation, which made it easier for me to share my struggles to maintain a relationship with the Church and the Industry—with a capital I, which is what insiders called Hollywood. I hadn't truly been able to integrate my professional life with what I was feeling about the Church. I had so many questions—though not theological ones. Mine were more like "What do you do when in confession a priest tells you your profession is an occasion of sin?" The bourgeois mentality in the institutional Church—that rigid, Jansenist thinking—was confusing to me.

I remember she smiled—even chuckled a bit—at that priest's ominous caveat. She was completely down to earth in her replies—and very modern. She could be worldly in the most sophisticated, delightful way, but she could cut to the bone too. Above all, she communicated the

113

sense that she lived in the presence of God and that was the central fact of her existence.

At first, my visits ended with a sense of tremendous satisfaction, the kind I used to have as a kid after a good report card or, later, when I knew I had done a good job in front of the camera or before an audience. It was the feeling that something good had happened and now I was free to look beyond to another cycle. That was comforting, but very much at a naïve level of intensity.

Over the next months, during the bus trips back to New York, my thoughts were more about what this Regina Laudis experience might mean in terms of seriously clarifying what it was that my life was about. Would I reenter my professional life with new values? Was the experience giving me a sense of further direction?

Or just more questions?

One thing I knew: what I was finding at Regina Laudis was the peace that had first attracted me to the Catholic Church, and when I went away I carried it with me.

When my contract with Pleasure *was up, I knew I had to visit Regina Laudis before I returned home. With no performances to rush me back to New York, I took a full week there. It was odd—at the end of each day, right at 7:30, my thoughts ran back to the "half hour" call when I would be dressing and finishing my makeup. Instead I was in the tiny chapel listening to the nuns sing Compline, which had become the Office I liked the most. It is the only Office that doesn't change; it is the same throughout the year. It is sung in the dark with eyes closed. I felt as if I were being rocked back and forth in a sea of feminine rhythms.*

What, I asked Reverend Mother Benedict, is the meaning of the Benedictine expression contemptus mundi? *"This does not mean contempt for the world," she assured me, "but detachment from the world. We think of fruit as food but, to the tree, the pulp of an apple or pear is a cushion of protection around the seed's life forming within. That is why a monastery is enclosed, to protect and nourish the life of the spirit*

114

that is forming inside you and to help it to grow, in its own terms, to its fullest expression."

I came to appreciate that in Reverend Mother—this woman who had spent nearly twenty-five years in monastic enclosure—I was in touch with a spiritual master.

It was during our last parlor that I suddenly blurted out, "I worry that I might have a call. I know I've been looking for something deeper. I wonder, Am I material to enter the monastery? Could this be where I belong?"

"No, Dolores," she replied, "go back to Hollywood, return to your career. And from time to time, come back and visit."

Reverend Mother passed a card through the grille. I glanced at it as I left the parlor, but her handwriting was difficult to read—she was, after all, a doctor—so I put it away in my jacket pocket to examine more carefully at a later time.

At the end of my visit, Mother Placid gave me a gift—a card she had drawn in her strong, unique style. It said that a cross is planted in the soul. It takes root and grows.

On the plane home I felt exhausted. The end of this visit found me spiritually and physically dried out, and I didn't know why. Looking back, I think it was just the Lord turning me inside out to shake off all the old clinging vines before He planted His bumper crop.

Ten

When she left Hollywood a year earlier, Dolores had just gotten her first star billing. Now she was returning home from a year's run in a major Broadway hit, with a Tony nomination to boot.

She had a right to expect that producers would be knocking down her door with offers. But there was nothing waiting for her, not even with her boss, Hal Wallis. Her agent, Phil Gersh, told me that Hollywood producers fall all over themselves to grab a spanking-new Broadway actor for a movie debut—think Brando, Clift or Streisand—but the same moguls couldn't care less about a movie actor returning home after an appearance on the New York stage.

Gersh recalled, "Lee J. Cobb, who was firmly established in movies, left Hollywood for Broadway, where he created the role of Willy Loman in the great American play *Death of a Salesman*. When Lee came back to Hollywood a year later, one producer greeted him with, 'Good to see ya, Lee! Wha'd'ya been up to?'"

The shoulder Dolores cried on was Paul Nathan's. He was genuinely upset that Perlberg and Seaton had passed her over for the movie version of *Pleasure*. But he said not to worry. They would find something.

> —*I made a suggestion:* The Debbie Reynolds Story—*and I would play Elizabeth Taylor.*

Wallis, in fact, was considering loaning her out to Hammer Productions, the English company pumping out low-budget horror movies that were very successful at the box office. The film was *Never Take Candy from a Stranger*, starring the fine Shakespearean actor Felix Aylmer, who was obviously slumming.

The test for *The Story of Ruth*, deemed a success by producer Sam Engel, who was less interested in Semitic authenticity than William Wyler had been, immediately cancelled her horror-flick career. It looked as if the part of Ruth was hers, but the next thing she knew, another actress, Elana Eden, was given the role.

> —*You know, shortly after my entrance into Regina Laudis, annual donations to the monastery were received from Sam Engel. As there was never a note with the checks, no one associated the contributions with me. I learned of his gifts only upon his death in 1984.*

I met with King Vidor for the role of a young Jewish girl in Solomon and Sheba, *to be filmed entirely in Europe. Just the possibility of seeing Paris sent me to a bookstore, where I got one of those little French-made-simple books and pored over it for days. Much of the emphasis was on pronunciation, and coincidentally I was asked to read for a part that called for a French accent at the La Jolla Playhouse, the Southern California summer-stock company formed by Gregory Peck, Dorothy McGuire and Mel Ferrer. I had visions of spending four weeks in lovely La Jolla and twelve more in Europe. I didn't get either part.*

When she was asked to test for yet another Jewish character, the daughter in the screen adaptation of the play *A Majority of One*—her Broadway neighbor the previous year—she joked to friends that maybe she should convert. She was passed over for Madlyn Rhue. She was then up for the role of the nice girl opposite Paul Newman in *From the Terrace* but lost out to Ina Balin, who would become a close friend after Dolores entered Regina Laudis.

> —*I often felt that there were not a whole lot of happy stories that came out of Hollywood. Careers fade and people are discarded and some end up tragically. Ina was one of the good people of the world. She did fine work in films yet found her true calling outside of Hollywood. During the Vietnam War, she became involved with an orphanage in Saigon that she helped evacuate before the city fell to the Communists in 1975. She saved 217 children, three of whom she adopted.*

Dolores was then announced for a movie about the Mafia, *Brotherhood of Evil*, to star Louis Jourdan and James Mason, which was already of

117

concern to both the Legion of Decency and the world of crime. Some cast members, Dolores included, received anonymous letters—and not from the Catholic Church—"suggesting" that they not participate. For whatever reason, that script never made it to the screen.

There was a role in an upcoming Wallis production that I coveted: the seductive young girl in Tennessee Williams' Summer and Smoke. *Mr. Wallis thought I was too young for the role—which I took to mean not sexy enough—but agreed to let me do a test for the director, Peter Glenville. Paul warned me that I probably wouldn't get it, but I wanted to prove I could do something for Mr. Wallis besides Presley girls. Mr. Wallis liked the test. But Mr. Glenville thought I was too old—which I took to mean not sexy enough. Pamela Tiffin was very good in the part.*

Although I made light of being "at liberty", I was pretty depressed. I had gotten used to being on the fast track in Hollywood without much effort. I had come back full of expectation, and the disappointment was enormous. Was I going to be just a flash in the pan?

Our first date following Dolores' return from New York was at the funeral of her uncle Mario Lanza, who had succumbed to a heart attack at age thirty-eight in Italy but whose body had been transported back to this country for multiple services, ending in Los Angeles at the Church of the Blessed Sacrament some two weeks after his death. We had to file by the open casket, which bothered Dolores a great deal. As for me, I was completely oblivious to what a "funeral date" portended.

The open casket held a bloated, gray semblance of my uncle. Did fame make it necessary to show him in such a state? My adored, now distraught, Aunt Betty, who had fallen for the phony glamor of Hollywood, would join him in death barely five months later.

My father was an usher at the funeral, and I was aghast to see him take Mom to a front pew, where he seated her next to his second wife, who was seated next to his third. Throughout the Mass I prayed to keep my temper, but I was shaking with anger when I confronted my father. "You bastard!" I said. "How could you embarrass Mom that way?" He was unfazed and merely whispered in my ear, "Don't be angry with me. You have to understand. Your mom was the only one. She was the virgin." That he could understand the value of virginity surprised and actually touched me. For all his offenses, he did understand that, and before God that was going to be to his advantage.

When I got back home that night, Mom had already had a few scotches. She had been behaving since my return, but why should I have expected that to last? I knew I couldn't stay at the house permanently. I had gotten too used to living on my own.

I helped Dolores move into a new apartment below the Sunset Strip, modest but nicer than the Black Hole and within walking distance of Saint Victor's Church. As she was loath to buy new furniture because of low funds, we turned to garage sales to find cheap "antiques" such as an oak dining table that we cut down and refinished as a coffee table. She did purchase a nice print of Andrew Wyeth's *Christina's World*, which was hung in the bedroom. It had special meaning for her.

— *To me,* Christina's World *had always represented my geneal-ogy. I saw all the Bowen women in her. The girl in the painting is reflective, contemplative, and I used to wonder if she was mov-ing* toward *something or* away from *something?*

Dick and I had become very close in a short time. A strong motivation for my going to New York to do the play was to make him proud of me. His praise for my performance meant more to me than anyone else's, and by pleasing him I pleased myself.

To love is the most wonderful thing in the world. But the gift of love has to be like a fountain that flows between two people, and I believed with all my heart that the water that flows must have an eternal source or it will dry up.

I trusted Dick completely and found it easy to confide in him on professional matters and personal problems, including the reality that his not being Catholic would jeopardize a permanent relationship. But I didn't speak to him of my thoughts of vocation or my visits to Regina Laudis. I was afraid to. I felt there was no way he could understand.

119

I had tried to reach Dolores in New York by phone one Sunday and the following Monday, too. When I finally reached her, she told me she had been out of town—she said "upstate".

Over the next several months, there were times, always at the end of a weekend, when she was unreachable. I was under the impression she was regularly spending time with Cornelia Otis Skinner at her upstate New York home, and Dolores never corrected me. In fact, when I was in New York for the Tony Awards, I personally thanked Cornelia for taking care of my girl, which was met with a blank stare. "She is such a dear," Cornelia said with a smile, "poor Catholic thing." I thought it was a funny line and left it at that.

I had been advised against our liaison often by priests in the confessional, but Dick felt strongly that two adults could adjust if they worked at it. I didn't doubt his sincerity, but I knew he would have to discover for himself what demands would be asked of him. I had written to him from New York suggesting he speak to the pastor at Saint Victor's Church. And then I had a Mass said for us—a prayer that our Lord might deign to help out a couple of wandering waifs who are stranded all alone and three thousand miles apart to boot.

I did meet with the priest. I was not as serious as the situation merited and didn't earn any points when I admitted that I was unable to buy in wholeheartedly but would "join up" if necessary. The good padre recommended I not fake it and ended the meeting then and there. Then, as usual, I put off thinking about it.

I remember that Dolores and I once discussed children. She had concerns about children growing up in a divided family and getting different signals from each parent. I asked her, since she had been allowed to decide for herself about religion, why she wouldn't give her children the same opportunity. She answered in a flash: "Because I found the true way, and I am able to show them the truth so they won't have to struggle to find it."

I recalled wonderful mommies and daddies that I used to watch as they came to church with kids my age. Those kids didn't have to wonder why they had to get up and go to church when one parent didn't. That

120

unity is what I missed then, and it was what I was missing now. The only thing I was ever able to believe and trust in completely was my faith. It was sad that Dick and I saw eye to eye on everything except the one thing that meant most to me in life. For me that was an insurmountable problem.

One thing I was sure of: I could never marry outside my religion. It would be like sand and ball bearings. If we did go forward, I would only box him into a corner by inflicting my answers on him, and I knew it would never be fair to him. The only answer I could come up with was to move out of the relationship.

My option was dropped. We separated as loving friends, but I was convinced that it was not the end of the line for us. I felt confident that, in time, we would be together again.

As it turned out, I saw Dolores only twice in the next three years. The first time was when she visited me at UCLA Medical Center, where I resided for three months following a 1961 New Year's Eve accident. She and Jan Shepard, Valerie Allen and artist-actor Bill Stephens brought me a huge poster Bill had painted duplicating the ad for the film *Ben-Hur*. My poster read, in huge stone letters, "BEN-HURT".

The second time was in the fall of 1962, when she invited me to lunch at Villa Frascati—"our place", she said. My euphoria at the prospect of seeing her again didn't last long. She only wanted to tell me she was going to be married before it broke in the newspapers.

I did continue to set up photo layouts, though, and kept up with her career. It looked pretty shaky for a while. There were frequent mentions in the trades of possible roles, but nothing materialized. Finally I saw her name in the cast of a movie called *The Plunderers*.

The Plunderers, for which Wallis had loaned her out to minor league Allied Artists, was a low-budget western that fell in a gray area between the top and bottom half of a double bill. It featured Jeff Chandler and John Saxon, one of Dolores' fan-magazine "dates". Also in the cast was Marsha Hunt, a bright lady with an infectious sense of humor who immediately became Dolores' buddy and the beneficiary of the Granny stories.

Marsha recalled, "I was so taken with Dolores that I could think of no better gift to give my husband, Robert Presnell, than an introduction.

121

For a while we were the Three Musketeers." This friendship is the only reason *The Plunderers* remains a memorable experience for Dolores. Coincidentally, Marsha Hunt had been the star of *A Letter for Evie*, which featured an early Bert Hicks appearance. Bert, as a matter of fact, visited the *Plunderers* set, the only time he ever watched his daughter work in a film.

All through the filming of The Plunderers, *I knew there was a lack of the nervous energy that usually kept me edgy, but I chalked my listlessness up to the difference between a movie set and the stage. I thought that was what was bothering me.*

I had been in constant touch with Mother Placid, and she suggested I visit another Benedictine abbey, Saint Andrew's, in nearby Valyermo. I thought it made sense, but I didn't go to Saint Andrew's with the conscious objective of testing Benedictine life against, say, Franciscan or Dominican. There was no doubt that, since my visits to Regina Laudis, I thought of myself as Benedictine. But that weekend at Saint Andrew's made one thing crystal clear: other places did not have the meaning for me that Regina Laudis did.

On the set of The Plunderers *I experienced the first in what would become a frequent where-am-I-going-what-am-I-doing sense of desperation. I was in my trailer dressing room combing my hair, and as I stared at my image in the mirror, I distinctly heard these words in my head: "You know this is not what you want."*

"What is this?" I said to myself and then actually spoke back to my reflection: "I want to do this for the rest of my life." I got up and moved away from the mirror, thinking I had gone cuckoo, and simply dismissed it.

But that "voice" would be heard again and again over the next two years, never in the same way but bearing the same message.

Eleven

As soon as The Plunderers *wrapped, I crawled back into the uncomfortable certainty that I would never work again. I needed activity to take my mind off the pain.*

Thankfully, Jim Stevens had some publicity assignments for me at the studio. I also signed up to participate in charity events.

One was a benefit for parochial schools in Palmdale, California. I was partnered in a soft-shoe dance with a young actress I had met at a Cardinal McIntyre Communion Breakfast in Hollywood. Gigi Perreau had been a child actress in the movies since her debut, at eighteen months, in the 1943 film Madame Curie. *Our performance that day served to make us friends for life.*

At another charity function, Dolores was seated at a table of young women whose conversation was about as stimulating as the Waldorf salads they were eating. Across the table, though, was a beautiful girl Dolores didn't recognize, but from her manner and her quick wit she was obviously someone worth knowing. For the entire meal Dolores found herself wanting to converse with Maria Cooper, who was an art student at the Chouinard Institute in downtown Los Angeles and the daughter of Gary Cooper. As Maria felt the same way about Dolores, they set a luncheon date for the following week.

Lunch day arrived, and I stopped by the Chouinard campus to pick up Maria. I found her waist high in a trash can, collecting paper. "You know, these students are terrible", Maria called out to me. "They put two lines on a piece of paper and throw it away. Do you know how much paper costs?"

—A person after my own heart.

Maria was only a year older than I, but when I was in her presence I felt protected in a gentle and loving way. She knew her way around our

123

town and was careful that I was taken care of, although I'm sure she
never saw herself in the role of protector.

Sometimes the girls would just walk a couple of blocks from Chouinard to nearby MacArthur Park, in recent years an area to be avoided
because of gang activity but in 1960 a quiet, picturesque forty acres of
green slopes, a small lake and loads of pigeons.

"We brought sketchbooks, pencils and brown-bag lunches", Maria
recalled. "We would eat and sketch the pigeons in the park. She drew
better pigeons than I did—ones with more character. And we would talk
of life and meanings, turning our eyes and souls to the Mystery. There
was such an ease of language between us. Were there other friends with
whom I could discuss—or even bring up—the Mystery? No.

"There's a passage in *The History of Impressionism* by the art historian John Rewald that perfectly describes our friendship: 'The two
friends saw each other almost daily and communicated as much in the
silence of their sensitivities as in the exchange of meditations or in the
fraternity of enjoyment shared.' That was us."

We talked a lot about books that dealt with the big questions of life,
books by Pierre Teilhard de Chardin that had meant a lot to us indi-
vidually and which we now read over together, underlining meaningful
passages. I introduced Maria to The Thirteenth Apostle, *by Eugene*
Vale, because the story is about a painter, and she pointed me toward
Evelyn Underhill's Mysticism. *We both admired Francis Thompson's*
"The Hound of Heaven" and anything by Thomas Merton.

> *—Merton's* No Man Is an Island *had been tightly woven into*
> *my life. When I was younger I found him very appealing. But he*
> *found his way to God in isolation, and although I still appre-*
> *ciated his writing, ever since I visited Regina Laudis I realized*
> *that his search for God did not coincide with the way I needed*
> *to find Him.*

Maria and I usually attended Mass together, alternating between my
West Hollywood parish, Saint Victor's, where I now taught catechism
class to youngsters, and her Church of the Good Shepherd in Beverly

124

Hills. I was seeing so much of Maria that Mom finally asked who my new friend was. I said her name was Maria Cooper and left it at that.

As Maria's mother was curious too, it wasn't long before Maria invited me to tea at her home. I sensed that her mother wanted to check me out to see if I was the right kind of person for her daughter to spend time with. When I told Mom where I was going she couldn't believe it. "You mean that girl you see is the daughter of Gary Cooper!?"

When I arrived at the Cooper home, there was a gardener working outside. I asked him if this was the home of Maria Cooper. "Yup", he answered. I was looking into the face of Gary Cooper! I barely managed to introduce myself as Maria's friend. He grinned and pointed the way to the front door.

Maria showed me around the house, which was all warm wood and lots of glass, with Matisses and Gauguins and van Goghs on the walls and sofas splashed with colorful needlepoint pillows she and her mother had made themselves. We sat in the living room waiting for Maria's mom and, as usual, I slipped off my shoes. When Mrs. Cooper entered, the first thing she said to me was, "Shoes are worn in this house."

— "Uh-oh," I thought, "this isn't Galesburg."

Maria's mother was beautiful. She had been an actress when she met Maria's father and gave up her career for marriage. She was charming, knowledgeable on many subjects—and mean as hell. That afternoon, she found a lot to criticize, including the way I dressed. "If you want to be an actress, you've got to learn how to dress. Obviously nobody taught you." I was a little annoyed because Edith Head thought I looked nice. But I took it.

—She wasn't nicknamed Rocky for nothing.

Over the next weeks, however, Mrs. Cooper thawed. I think the thing that broke the ice was that I could be submissive to her, and that made her comfortable. She enjoyed taking me on.

Gary Cooper cottoned to me immediately. He was the second person to call me "Miss Dolores", a name I had liked when Elvis used it. Now I loved it. I am proud to say that Gary and I enjoyed a

125

very special relationship. He even asked me to be his godmother at his baptism when he converted to Catholicism in early 1961. He treated me like a daughter but also as a contemporary in the business. Always interested in my career, he would, as long as I knew him, greet me with the actor's standard salutation: "Working?"

❦

Playhouse 90 was the most ambitious and arguably the most prestigious show of television's Golden Age. Ninety minutes of theater broadcast live every Thursday night, the program spawned emerging writers and directors such as Rod Serling, Abby Mann, Reginald Rose, Arthur Penn and Sidney Lumet. During its four-season reign, *Playhouse 90* produced 133 programs—all but four of which were originals, *Judgment at Nuremburg*, *The Miracle Worker*, *Requiem for a Heavyweight* and *Days of Wine and Roses* among them.

John Gay's World War I love story *To the Sound of Trumpets* was part of *Playhouse 90*'s last-ditch effort to remain the stronghold of live original drama. The program held a hard core of loyal viewers, but when ratings were falling in its fourth season, producer Herbert Brodkin scheduled eight high-budgeted plays to lure its audience back. Sadly, the fourth season was its last.

Playhouse 90 also presented the cream of the acting crop from both coasts. Since the actors had to be trusted to perform live, almost all had stage experience. After her disappointing reentrance into Hollywood, Dolores' fortune picked up when she was cast in a lead role in *To the Sound of Trumpets*. Brodkin and the director, Buzz Kulik, cast Dolores in spite of opposition from both the CBS brass and the sponsor's advertising agency, both concerned over lack of name value. She joined a distinguished company that included Dame Judith Anderson, Boris Karloff, Dan O'Herlihy and Stephen Boyd.

Stephen Boyd played a disillusioned British Army officer, wounded on a French battlefield, who plans to desert his unit. In a military hospital near Paris, he meets a young American volunteer nurse, Dolores' character, who has been wrongly accused of administering unauthorized

126

drugs to a patient. The two desert together and, through the ordeal of their flight, fall in love.

As challenging as it was, I was emboldened by the thought of performing live. It brought back the excitement of theater. The daunting fact was that I would be seen by more people in one night than had seen me on Broadway in a whole year.

I was both thrilled and intimidated to work with Judith Anderson, who played the head nurse. Our scene together was her only appearance in the play and, as written, was my scene. I had all the fireworks. We rehearsed several times, and she played the scene exactly the same way in each rehearsal—menacingly soft-spoken, petting a cat she held in her arms. During the live performance, however, just as she was exiting, she took hold of the cat's paw and pretended to scratch my arm, then sweetly scolded the animal, "Bad pussy. Bad pussy", and walked off with the cat and the scene.

Later, I approached the venerable actress to tell her what an honor it was to work with her and casually mentioned the surprise business with the cat. "My dear," Dame Judith purred, "I had only one scene. I had to do something."

Stephen Boyd was extremely attractive and very professional. We shared most of the scenes in the play, and he was such a generous actor. He was also a bit of a cutup. As we approached performance day, I confessed my habitual stage fright to him. Just before air time, a telegram was delivered to me. It was from Stephen. "Relax dear. Twenty million Chinese don't give a damn."

On February 9, 1960, *To the Sound of Trumpets* was aired live from CBS Television City to the East Coast at 6:00 P.M. Pacific Time. The show ended at 7:30 P.M., which gave the actors the opportunity to see the performance when it was aired on the West Coast at nine o'clock. Actors had to scramble to get out of costume and makeup and rush to a TV monitor somewhere. Maria Cooper, Gigi Perreau and her husband, Frank Gallo, actor David Hedison and young actress Judy Lewis, the daughter of Loretta Young, threw together a TV viewing party, giving Dolores this advantage over stage actors, who never get to see their own work.

127

If her Elvis Presley connection would be the one most recalled by the press at the time of her entrance into Regina Laudis, her next picture would be the movie most mentioned. *Where the Boys Are* was a modestly budgeted comedy-drama about the annual Easter pilgrimage of college students to Florida beaches. Coming as it did at the end of cinema censorship by the Hays Office, it was one of the first teen films to explore premarital sex. Its producer was the veteran Joe Pasternak, who had his own unit at MGM, producing among others the films of the studio's top star of the fifties, Dolores' uncle Mario Lanza.

Directing would be Henry Levin, a serviceable craftsman who specialized in frothy sex comedies and enjoyed an enviable reputation of bringing films in on budget. As Levin was handled by the Gersh Agency, Harry Bernsen got an early look at the script and felt the pivotal role would be perfect for Dolores. Levin agreed and suggested her to Pasternak, who coincidentally had just met Dolores at a party and was struck by her charm. Up to that point, Pasternak had had his eye on Jane Fonda for the role.

Hal Wallis was only too happy to loan her out, and Paul Nathan thought exposure in a glossy MGM film aimed at the massive youth audience could only enhance her status, especially since she would have top billing. Harry Bernsen was sure this was the break he had been working for since her return from Broadway.

Her coworkers were Paula Prentiss, Yvette Mimieux, Connie Francis, Jim Hutton, George Hamilton and Frank Gorshin. It was Henry Levin's style to run a happy set. He felt strongly that if the actors liked each other, it would come across on the screen. This worked especially well for the girls, whose on-screen chemistry was complimented by several reviewers.

Paula Prentiss has bright memories of those days. "Shortly after the start of the movie, which was my first one, I came down with one lulu of a cold. Dolores would drop by my apartment bringing chicken soup and sympathy. She was so open and loving. As I was fresh out of school and not acquainted with Hollywood, her caring gesture was as surprising as it was welcome.

128

"I had been raised a Catholic but had been away from Catholicism for a while. I felt deep down that if God really wanted me back, He would send a sign. I've always thought that Dolores was that sign. I knew I should cling to such a person." Though Paula didn't return to Catholicism then—she married Richard Benjamin, a Jew, and raised two children in the Jewish faith—she is once again Catholic and visits her former costar at Regina Laudis.

In an interview with *Night Moves* on the occasion of the film's thirtieth anniversary, Mother Dolores made the statement that she has always thought *Where the Boys Are* was a "message film".

From the first reading of the script, I felt it took a strong moral tone, which was passed on to its youthful audience in a comedic way. Teenage girls, especially, could find something to think about as they struggled with personal-relationship puzzles, and most of the "message" lines were spoken by my character, Merritt Andrews, a liberal-thinking but strongly moral student.

Where the Boys Are *was a very good experience for all of us at a time in our country's life when we trusted our innocence and believed in the meaning of lasting friendships. That is the one lingering memory I have of that film—that we all did become friends.*

One man may have hoped for more. Some cast members were sure Henry Levin entertained romantic notions about Dolores. She remains mum on this subject.

—All I know is I got a lot of close-ups.

In the final days of production, I experienced a second "haunting". Sister Dolores Marie visited during filming. She was on the set for the hospital scene with Yvette. It had gone well, but I hadn't felt any satisfaction. I seemed to be separated from what was happening on the soundstage and had to struggle to relate to what was going on around me. Suddenly I had this overwhelming feeling not to fight it, to let the drifting apart happen. Inside me, I heard the words, barely whispered, "Don't fight it. Don't fight it."

I felt I had to share these odd happenings with someone who might possibly understand. I told Sister Dolores Marie about the "voice in the mirror" and what had just happened and confided that I feared I might have a vocation to religious life. Sister looked into my eyes and warned, "You better think that over, Dolores. Give it a long, long thought."

The *Film Bulletin* trade review judgment that MGM's comedy was "sure-fire box-office magic" was prophetic. *Where the Boys Are* was a bona fide "sleeper"—the once-in-a-while movie that opens unheralded and ends up a commercial hit. It was MGM's highest grossing picture of 1961.

Paula Prentiss got the lion's share of good notices, but Dolores' reviews fully justified her top billing, with *Box Office Digest* proclaiming, "Dolores Hart proves she is stellar movie material." Mainstream critics were generous in their estimation that she was "refreshing", "charming" and had a "bright future". Columnist Sidney Skolsky labeled her "the Junior Miss Princess Grace". The film went on to receive a Golden Laurel Award from the Producers Guild of America as one of the year's top comedies. *Where the Boys Are* is now considered one of the classic teen flicks.

Dolores' fan base had been building consistently since *Loving You*. Two studios, Paramount and now MGM, were forwarding bags of fan letters to the Hazeltine address. Going nuts trying to keep up with photo requests, Harriett was relieved when a woman by the name of Gladys Hart asked to create a national fan club. The official Dolores Hart Fan Club was formed, with Gladys as its committed president. Gladys became a friend whose relationship with Dolores continued after she entered the monastery.

Dolores' social life was again in an accelerated mode. There were the usual potential suitors in the Industry and a couple outside the business, Adlai Stevenson Jr., the son of the two-time presidential candidate, and the young Aga Khan, son of Aly Khan, who, a decade earlier, had turned movie queen Rita Hayworth into a real-life princess. Then, one night Dolores went on a blind date.

Don Robinson was supposed to meet Dolores on two separate occasions before their actual meeting. He was a high school friend of Sheila Hart's husband, Bob McGuire, and had been invited to their wedding in Santa Barbara but had been unable to attend. Another friend promised an introduction during the Broadway run of *The Pleasure of His Company*, but Dolores had left the cast before Don made the trip to New York. He also might have met her through Maria Cooper or Judy Lewis, both close friends of his, but neither had mentioned her name.

The introduction was finally arranged as a blind date by mutual friends Jody McCrea and Jennifer Lea. It was to be a double date with Jody and Jennifer, but at the last minute they had to cancel. Rather than miss another chance to meet her, Don kept the date with Dolores.

"When I picked her up at her West Hollywood apartment, Dolores wasn't quite ready", remembered Don. "There were clothes hanging on strings stretched across the living room. The place looked more like the home of a costume assistant than a movie star." Don took her to dinner at a little French restaurant on the Sunset Strip. It was an evening when everything clicked.

Don put me in mind of John F. Kennedy. Not so much in looks as bearing. Like JFK, he was tall and lanky and had that same attractive brotherly quality that made girls like him. He also had a glint in his eyes.

Don Robinson was a deeply religious Catholic who went to Mass almost every day. He was born in Los Angeles to strict Catholic parents who had married young and were still married to each other when death parted them. The family business, Robinson and Sons, was in moving and trucking. The foundation of the Robinson family was as solid as Dolores' was shaky. As for the glint in his eyes, Don proposed to her on that first date—even before the salad had been served.

—When he said, "You know, I'm going to marry you", I was bowled over.

I laughed, but just to keep the door open, I suggested he ask me again at a later time.

131

We began dating, and I found that Don was basically one of the happiest persons I knew and, without a doubt, one of the finest. He was a fabulous catch. I can say that today because it is only in the light of consecrated life that one can see the grace of any man clearly.

Don had been educated by the Jesuits at Loyola Prep and Loyola University. He graduated in 1955 and had already served two years as a second lieutenant in the Air Force when he met Dolores. "I had more than a passing acquaintance with show business," Don said, "having dated several actresses, including Margaret O'Brien and Anna Maria Alberghetti, and working at the William Morris Agency for a short period—long enough to realize that the agency business was not for me. I had a deep-seated love for architecture and design, but when I quit William Morris I joined my father in the family business, giving vent to my dream by decorating my parents' new home which appeared on the cover of one of the top shelter magazines of the day. That opened up another career as a designer and decorator."

Don was a member of a social club that I found snobby—I think he did too—and the Bel-Air Bay Club, where everyone played tennis except me. I sat, as I did as a child, covered up with a towel. Our favorite times were just dinner together and a movie. And I was truly grateful that I had someone dear to me sitting beside me at Mass every Sunday. Sundays were reserved for dinners at the Robinson family home.

—I attended my second Oscar ceremony with Don. I joked that I didn't want to go unless I could come home with an Oscar. And I did. I swiped the gold centerpiece from our table and put it under my coat. On the way out, I noticed Mrs. Charlton Heston had a centerpiece Oscar under her coat too. But hers matched the one her husband carried, unhidden, as the year's best actor.

Coincidentally, Harry Bernsen got his first look at my apartment. It put him in a state of shock. He insisted that I move into more suitable quarters immediately, something that said "rising young movie star". Don knew of a beautifully designed Georgian building in Westwood with a vacancy. He helped decorate the space in Grecian mode—shades of white and my favorite color, lavender.

132

At this time, Mom and Pop were finally divorcing. The "big house" was sold, and Mom moved into an apartment in Beverly Hills, but Mom and Pop continued to see each other—for Mom it was another case of "can't live with him or without him". Since the divorce had left her financially shaky, she went back to work, at first as a manicurist and then as an assistant to a tailor. Most importantly, she didn't feel sorry for herself and was staying off the booze.

The year 1960, which had gotten off to a shaky start personally and professionally, now offered optimistic change. Dolores had a new friend, a new beau and a new home. The *Playhouse 90* was a critical success, and *Where the Boys Are* was a commercial hit. Dolores was invited to become a member of the Academy of Motion Picture Arts and Sciences. Harry Bernsen was braced for an onslaught of offers for his client, who seemed poised to become the cinematic successor to the actress she had been likened to since high school. Things were decidedly looking up.

—So, of course, there was an actors' strike.

Twelve

Dolores took advantage of the strike to study, this time with Actors Studio mentor Sandy Meisner, who was conducting classes at the Twentieth Century-Fox acting school. Her fellow students were Don Murray, Hope Lange, Joanne Woodward, Richard Beymer and Diane Varsi.

While she was studying at Fox, the studio head, Lew Schreiber, contacted Phil Gersh to say he had seen Dolores in *The Pleasure of His Company* and was interested in signing her to a two-picture contract for $100,000. At the same time MGM, reacting to studio buzz about her performance in *Where the Boys Are*, began negotiating with Harry Bernsen for four pictures at a total of $250,000. The sums would be paid to Wallis, of course, who was paying Dolores $1,250 a week at that time. He could hardly afford to put her into one of his own pictures when he was making that kind of a profit loaning her out.

The proffered contract at Twentieth Century-Fox included the role of Saint Clare in its upcoming religious drama, *Francis of Assisi*, based on the book *The Joyful Beggar* by Louis de Wohl. Not only was it planned as one of the major films for the year—by the studio that had produced *The Robe* a decade earlier—but the entire production would be shot in Italy, with exteriors in the actual locales of Assisi and Perugia and interiors at Cinecittà Studio in Rome.

The fact that one of Dolores' favorite films, *The Song of Bernadette*, had also been made by Fox figured into the mix, as did the circumstance that she would be working at both studios where her father had once been under contract. The strongest attraction, however, was the European location. She had never been out of the country and had long dreamed of seeing London, Paris and Rome. To say she was jubilant would not be overstating it.

I revered Saint Clare as a holy woman and respected the order she founded, the Poor Clares, but I didn't have a personal devotion to her

134

as a saint because my particular orientation was Benedictine. The Benedictines, I was pleased to learn, came to Clare's personal aid during her flight from her family, which opposed her desire to become a nun.

The first thing I did was read The Joyful Beggar. *Then I enrolled in a Berlitz course in Italian. Next, I went to see Father Salazar, a priest I met at Sheila's wedding, who had become a close friend. Father Sal had a parish in downtown Los Angeles, near Olvera Street, and had begun coming with me to see Mom. He was young and hip and didn't scare her off with church posturing. She liked and trusted him. Lately, she had been bouncing back and forth between good days and bad. I would feel I could trust her one week and the next be afraid to go even a short distance out of town. It was an immense relief when Father Sal assured me that he wouldn't forget her while I was away in Europe.*

Then, as quickly as it was on, the film was off. The studio pitched instead a bit of fluff called *A Summer World*, pairing Dolores with another young singer whose popularity had catapulted him into movies, Fabian. She was so disappointed that she rejected it, one of the rare times she did not cooperate with the management. To ease her frustration, she decided she needed to go somewhere. If not Italy, why not New York?

I had no sooner checked into the hotel than Harry called with the news that the Fox negotiations were on again. Before I could sigh with relief, however, everything was off again, apparently for good. It might have seemed funny, but when I was out the second time, I got mad. To heck with it, I decided, I would go to Europe anyway because it had always been my dream. With Paul Nathan's help, I made all the necessary arrangements in a matter of hours and, with stuffed suitcase in hand, had a bon voyage dinner with Winnie in her Manhattan apartment.

Winnie and her husband had barely poured the second martini when we discovered I was overweight. Well, not me, not on two martinis. The bathroom scales showed thirty-seven excess pounds in my suitcase and given that it would cost me eighty-seven cents a pound, we decided to remove thirty two dollars and nineteen cents' worth. Out came the travel iron, a book on Umbrian civilization and my riding boots. Smaller items, such as the travel clock, umbrella and a one-pound guide to Europe were stuffed into the clothing I would wear or carry on the plane.

Seven hours later I landed in France full of misplaced confidence that the gift of tongues had been miraculously bestowed upon me, until I was speeding toward Paris in a car arranged by Paul and didn't understand one word the driver said in his flowing travelogue. I couldn't get enough, however, of the beautiful way he said "Mademoiselle" before every exclamation. Soon I was checking in at the Palais d'Orsay, which I am embarrassed to admit I pronounced "Palace de Horsey". The spacious lobby reminded me of hotels Ginger Rogers stayed at in her movies. I had $800 in traveler's checks, one suitcase and shoes that hurt my feet. But I was in Paris!

It was hard to believe that, from my window, I could look out over the Seine and see the Eiffel Tower in the distance. Too excited to sleep, I got out the guide, which proclaimed Paris the city to walk in, and bravely ventured out to find a church, keeping for reference the Tower within navigating view.

I must have walked for a couple of hours when I began to feel hungry. I stopped at a small bistro. The menu, of course, was in French, and I got out my French for Tourists. *When the meal arrived, it was a bowl of dreadful-looking tiny fish in what could pass for motor oil. The full reality of my linguistic ignorance had sunk in. I paid the bill, fled the café and bought an apple from a street vendor. I just held out my hand full of francs, hoping he would take the proper amount. But he took the handful and was so effusive in his appreciation that I figured I must have just subsidized the education of one of his children. What was I doing in Paris? Alone! I had really gotten myself into a mess. I went back to the hotel and had a good cry.*

The telephone interrupted my tears. The caller was Earl Holliman, who was on a vacation in Paris and had learned from Paul Nathan that I was en route. He put himself at my disposal for my entire stay. That dried up the tears very quickly.

Earl was at the hotel in twenty minutes. He brought along a friend, Bob Oliveira, a musician and conductor who lived in Paris. I could not have had more attentive—or attractive—escorts. Knowing the city inside and out, Bob led us to Saint-Germain-des-Prés and a little sidewalk café for omelettes and martinis rouges and a fascinating parade of straggly haired French girls and gaunt, bearded young artists.

Overnight, I went from being Cinderella with only an apple for supper to the belle of the ball. With Earl and Bob, I got to experience not only the magnificent Louvre, Montmartre and the great flying buttresses of Notre Dame, but also special little places Bob knew. His favorite, L'Abbaye, was a tiny basement club on Rue Jacob where the audience showed its appreciation for the folk singers not by clapping, but by snapping fingers—in consideration for the upstairs neighbors. We stayed out until dawn and ended up at Les Halles, the early-morning flower market. Now I was really in Paris.

Oliveira suggested what would be the highlight of Dolores' French adventure. As a conductor, he admired Gregorian chant, and he thought she should hear the chant sung at the Abbey of Solesmes, several hours outside of Paris. The three of them piled into Oliveira's car and headed there, stopping in Chartres to see the legendary stained-glass windows of its medieval cathedral.

I'll never forget my first sight of the famous mismatched spires of the Chartres Cathedral, which seemed to appear suddenly on the horizon. It was like seeing Oz.

As we approached Chartres, a storm was threatening. It got so dark that by the time we drove into the city, it was like night. Then began the rain. We were allowed into the cathedral but warned that it was a waste of our time, for without sunlight we would not get the full impact of the windows. We went in anyway, and as we entered, a flash of lightning lit up the entire church. The magnificent windows looked as though they had been ignited.

The moon was high when we reached Solesmes, the abbey outlined against the now clear sky. We stood on a riverbank transfixed by the abbey's wavy reflection in the moonlit water as its bells tolled a welcome. The next morning we went to ten o'clock Mass at the abbey. For the first time since I was at Regina Laudis, I heard Gregorian chant— but now sung by monks. With the sound of their voices I thought my heart would swirl up into the arches of the ancient Gothic church.

137

I could not have asked for more: first, the sight of the Chartres spires all but puncturing the floor of Heaven, then those massive glass windows illuminated by God's light and now the simple beauty of His music.

But more was coming. There must have been an angel on my shoulder. A message from Maria Cooper was waiting for me when I returned to Paris. Maria and her parents were in the city, and I joined them for dinner that very evening.

That night I became the Rocky Cooper project. Rocky is impossible to condense into a Reader's Digest *character. She's the flavor of a delicious soup as well as the sting on the tip of the tongue when the soup's too hot. She had long been displeased with my wardrobe. At dinner she asked how much money I had with me. About eight hundred dollars, I told her. "Good," she said, "we'll spend it."*

Rocky was an astute shopper with incredible taste in clothes—I was her paper doll, and she didn't give a damn about my budget. She selected; I handed over the francs—at Givenchy, the House of Dior, Balmain, Lanvin. The eight hundred was gone in a day, but at the end of our spree I had the smartest wardrobe any young woman could wish for.

The on-again, off-again Fox contract and *Francis of Assisi* was on again. Bernsen wired that the part of Clare was definitely hers. Plato Skouras, the producer of *Francis*, sent a wire welcoming her to the company and instructing her to stay put because arrangements were being made for her hair to be done by the famous Alexandre de Paris. Her light-brown tresses were to be dyed to match Saint Clare's blond hair, locks of which still existed in Assisi.

Since she still had four days before she had to report for costume and makeup tests at Cinecittà, she was invited to spend them with the Coopers in London, where Gary would be filming what would be his last movie, *The Naked Edge*. The Coopers were living at the Savoy and booked Dolores there.

Everything in London looked like a CinemaScope movie shown on a regular screen. The people were long and thin, with long, thin umbrellas and shoes and mustaches. Even their words were long and thin. My a's were already broadening by the time I checked into the Savoy and "awsked" if there were any messages.

All the clichés fell beautifully into place. Maria and I went to the Tower of London and London Bridge, saw the changing of the guard at Buckingham Palace, visited the London Zoo, and browsed art galleries and antique shops. Maria found a little church all but hidden on a small side street where I joined the Coopers for a lovely Mass. On the spur of the moment, Maria and I decided to have a picnic in spite of the threatening clouds amassing above. We bought chestnuts, tarts, cookies, ice cream and, as a concession to our waistlines, a grapefruit, and headed for Hyde Park. Raindrops began just as we were spreading our blanket. A short while later, the same blanket and goodies were spread on the floor of my hotel room and the English picnic commenced. There were so many golden moments like this with the Coopers that complemented the dream of mine that was coming wondrously true.

Between costume fittings and makeup tests in Rome, I went sightseeing, once again in the company of Earl Holliman, whose extended holiday had taken him to Italy. But all the monuments and statues and fountains we saw paled before the highlight of my time in Rome—the day I spent at the Vatican.

I received an unexpected invitation to tour the Vatican from Monsignor William A. Carew, of the Vatican Secretariat of State. I was overjoyed and assumed that the invitation was extended at the request of a VIP at the studio. Imagine my surprise when Monsignor Carew told me that my friend Father Salazar was behind it and that the tour would also include an audience with Pope John XXIII.

On the day of the audience, I met Monsignor Carew, who not only was as courteous a gentleman as I had ever met, but was as handsome as George Peppard, with wavy blond hair and a broad smile that showcased his glistening teeth. If he had been an actor, he could have gotten any part he wanted. During the tour, I asked Monsignor Carew what it took to be a successful Vatican delegate. He winked and said,

"The Holy Spirit". *Then he reached in his pocket, pulled out a small comb and added, "And this, of course."*

Monsignor Carew escorted Dolores and Earl into the Hall of Benediction, where a number of people were already assembled. Pope John XXIII was the pontiff who had announced from the pulpit that everyone—not only Catholics—has a way to Heaven if the condition for Christ is in his heart. Thus, he was the man who had relieved Dolores of a troubling concern ever since her conversion.

The pope was carried into the room on his portable throne, and just as he passed us, his slipper fell to the floor. His Holiness rocked with laughter, and Monsignor Carew seized that moment to introduce me as the Hollywood actress who would be filming a movie on the life of Saint Francis. "Ah," Pope John smiled, taking my hand, "Chiara."

I thought he had misunderstood. "Oh no, Your Holiness, my name is Dolores Hart."

"No, no," he repeated, "you are Chiara."

"Dolores, Your Holiness."

"Chiara."

Years later I recalled that, up to that moment, I had not the slightest awareness of any religious significance that my involvement in the film might have for me personally. I thought of my participation on a professional level only. Might there have been another level of meaning? It was a piercing thought.

—You don't usually get your vocation from the Holy Father.

Thirteen

Production on *Francis of Assisi* began on October 26, 1960, one week after Dolores' twenty-second birthday. The cast included Bradford Dillman as Francis, Stuart Whitman, Pedro Armendáriz, Finlay Currie and Cecil Kellaway. The director was Michael Curtiz, who three years earlier had tried to get Dolores fired from the cast of *King Creole*. This time he was enthusiastic about her casting.

But Dolores, mindful of how crude Curtiz could be, wondered about *his* suitability for this particular film. Brad Dillman voiced a stronger opinion. "He was a calamitous choice. Foul-mouthed and vulgar and here he was, directing the life of a saint."

Almost immediately upon their introduction, Brad learned to rely on Dolores, because of her past association with the director, for translations of Michael Curtizisms. On a shared ride to Assisi, Curtiz looked out the car window and said, to no one in particular, what sounded like "The ships are crazy." Dolores saw Brad's face go blank. She pointed out the window and whispered, "The *sheep* are *grazing*."

I settled in on the top floor of the Subiaco Hotel, overlooking the most beautiful city I would ever see. Only 115 miles from Rome, Assisi was another world. Except for traffic lights and telephone poles, which were camouflaged for the filming, little had changed in the town's narrow, winding streets since the thirteenth century. I can't remember ever having been so moved by the realization of the existence of God on earth. It was no wonder Francis and Clare were saints. They lived in paradise.

Not a hundred feet from the hotel stood the Church of Saint Francis. I heard the bells ringing in the tower in a voice grown rusty over eight centuries. I closed my eyes, and suddenly the words of Saint Paul were with me: "Eye hath not seen, ear hath not heard, nor has it entered into the mind of man the things that are waiting for them that love him." It made so much sense there.

The weather was another thing. During the entire month they shot in Assisi, cold, drizzling rain greeted the actors every morning. But when they reached the location for that day's filming, Dolores and Brad remember vividly, it was always bathed in sunlight. "It was sort of supernatural", said Brad. "Maybe not a miracle, but Dolores would tell me God was certainly watching over the production."

The third star of the film, Stuart Whitman, was very sweet and attentive from the first day—so attentive that I began to steel myself for a pass. But Stuart wasn't a pouncer. He was the perfect gentleman. As a matter of fact, in my entire time in Hollywood, I had to fight off advances only once. I think it was simply that the men were afraid to risk being rejected, and their assumption was that they would be. Their egos guarded against the embarrassment of being turned down, and as a result, they treated me like a lady.

Besides my friendship with Brad, another lasting relationship came out of Francis of Assisi—*with Geraldine Bogdanovich Brent, the only other American woman on location. Gerry had a small role as a nun but did not have sights on an acting career. Gerry was the Tuna Queen; her family owned StarKist. In fact, she created the character Charlie the Tuna for the ads and became known as "Charlie's mother". After I entered Regina Laudis, Gerry became a patron of the monastery, subsidizing many practical needs of the Community.*

Great pains were taken to ensure the film would be historically and geographically accurate. With the cooperation of the Franciscan fathers, the company was allowed to film in Assisi's ancient churches and shrines. The Palm Sunday prayer of Saint Francis was recreated in the Church of San Pietro, which necessitated clearing the building of pews because thirteenth-century worshippers knelt on the floor. Even a number of the Franciscan monks appeared before the camera.

To make sure the film was ecclesiastically correct, the company had an adviser assigned by the Vatican, Father Vincenzo Labella.

When I first read the script, I thought the screenwriters had added a romantic tone to the personal relationship between Francis and Clare to titillate the audience, but after studying The Joyful Beggar *I found that*

142

the love between them was, in fact, addressed in the book. Nevertheless, our Vatican adviser kept close watch lest delicate lines be crossed.

Father Labella specifically instructed Brad and me to watch our language when we were filming in the town and never to smoke when we were in costume. I didn't smoke anyway, but Brad did and was very steadfast in maintaining the proper image. I got a kick out of watching him sneak behind buildings to smoke like a guilty teenager. The reason for Father Labella's request was obvious. The deeply religious towns-people were proud of their heritage and were very respectful toward Brad and me. We could not risk offending them. The children, not as sophisticated as their elders, behaved in an almost worshipful manner, certain that the saints had come to life. When they asked for auto-graphs, they wouldn't be satisfied until we also signed "Saint Francis" and "Saint Clare". It was very humbling.

One morning a group of children, each with an animal in tow, arrived on the set. The young spokesman for the group asked Brad to bless his pet. Brad turned to Father Labella and said, "I can't do that."

"Oh yes, you can", the priest assured him. Filming that day was delayed for over an hour while Saint Brad of Assisi blessed all those dogs and cats, pigs and goats, donkeys and cows, even chickens.

Whenever I wasn't scheduled to work, I would walk alone through the town. It took no time at all to tour Assisi; what took time was appre-ciating what I saw and stamping it in my memory. Very special was Santa Chiara, the Gothic church that contains the tomb of Saint Clare. Her 708-year-old body was laid out in a glass coffin. It was a wonder to see, uncorrupted and amazingly beautiful.

One evening about dusk, I was roaming the crooked streets and happened to pass a church that looked closed. As a tiny gate was open, I decided to investigate. Inside the darkened church, I followed a faint stream of light and found myself in a frescoed archway lit by a single 60-watt bulb. Just as I turned to leave, a sound swelled into the room; it was so overpowering that I almost jumped out of my skin. The sound came from an organ in a dark corner where a lone padre was playing with the aid of a tiny flashlight. I stood transfixed. It was quite exciting there in the dim glow of the church, hearing his music and feeling the vibrations throbbing in the floorboards. I could feel a part of it myself,

143

maybe because I was an actress. Somehow an actress absorbs a moment like that. I watched and listened for a long while and then left silently. I never made my presence known to the priest.

Little by little these private experiences were beginning to have a disturbing effect on her enthusiasm for the film she was making and even on the life she was living. There were no voices, no reflections in a mirror, but a growing awareness that the comforting sanctuary of her work was eroding.

We would shoot inside a church where Clare and Francis actually stood and watch its sanctity stripped away as it was "cleansed" for the movie. The dignity of the frescoed walls was compromised by being made too perfect. It seemed to me that the old Gothic arches winced at the repeated hosannas echoing from the portable record player.

A prop man lighted dummy wax candles on the altar, and the shadows they threw were too even. I knelt in front of a real altar now made phony. I knelt alone, but there were a hundred people watching. I pretended to believe what I do believe so thoroughly. I caught a reflection of a caricature in a mirror and thought, "I'm the caricature, a dressed-up form of this lady who existed outside the whim of a director."

I wanted to cry out, "Here is a soul. They're not easy to find, and I have this wonderful one for a while. Please don't trample it with reloading and retakes because there's a hair in the aperture."

Years later, I would often be asked if one particular scene in Francis of Assisi *had any influence on my decision to enter religious life, if somehow it had been a mystical moment. The scene in question is when Clare has her hair cut off during her Investiture. The queries usually came from people not connected with show business. Professionals recognize that, although I wore my own waist-long hair throughout the film, it was plastered down and a wig placed over it for this scene. It was the wig that was cut. I can't deny that a moment like this is poignant for the actress recreating it, but the only mystical impact the scene had was the realization that an actress, like a religious, is a servant.*

After production wound up at Cinecittà, Christmas 1960 was spent in Rome. Christmas Eve approached under the tide of a violent rainstorm.

144

Boredom and frustration set in among the cast and crew. I was pained because the work on Francis of Assisi *was ending. Our makeup man, Hal Lierley, sadly confided that it would be an especially hard Christmas because most of the company was planning to go out carousing.*

Almost simultaneously, we decided that this Christmas could not end up a dead end for our friends, that we had to do something to keep the company together. We pooled our week's salary, jumped into a cab to Piazza Navona and bought gifts and Christmas decorations by the box load. Back at the hotel, the Spirit seemed to take over, and soon everyone was decorating the tree and wrapping presents. My Assisi *family celebrated the birth of Christ together, and on Christmas morning everyone felt clean. It was, for me, one of the most piercing experiences of community I had ever known.*

I seemed to be forever searching for a way in which committed relationships could come to a holding pattern together—a continuity. I believe that search was the drive that brought me to Benedictine life.

Fourteen

Twentieth Century-Fox gave *Francis* a major send-off with both a world premiere in the saint's namesake city, San Francisco, and simultaneous premiere showings in twelve international cities—from Dublin to Bombay, Manila to Johannesburg, Boston to Sydney. The mayors of each proclaimed the day of the opening Saint Francis Day.

Dolores attended the premiere in Los Angeles, a benefit for the Sisters Servants of Mary Guild, where she was grateful for compliments from the evening's hostesses, now her good friends, Irene Dunne and Loretta Young.

The critical reception for *Francis* was fair, the best being the *Motion Picture Herald*'s assessment as a "first rate example of the art of motion picture making." *Newsweek* complimented the film's "pervading beauty". The *New York Times* singled out the cinematography's "reverence, spirituality and adherence to fact as authentic as the Giotto frescoes and Umbrian landscapes the film so vividly captures" but also found the film "as static as ancient tapestries". Personal notices for the players were respectable, with Brad Dillman coming off particularly well.

For the second movie under her two-picture contract with Twentieth Century-Fox, the studio offered Dolores the part of Rosemary in the film adaptation of F. Scott Fitzgerald's *Tender Is the Night*. Thinking she wasn't right for the part, she asked Harry to pass on it.

I was shocked when I got a phone call from the studio's president, Spyros Skouras, who bawled me out for turning it down. He told me it was their most important picture of the year, and the part of Rosemary would make me a star.

As a mea culpa, I agreed to go on a personal appearance tour for Francis. *The gesture was not magnanimous; I was eager to visit the monastery again. I arrived in time for a parlor with Mother Placid, and*

then, before Vespers, I was able to do something I had become accus-
tomed to and looked forward to—take a walk in the quiet hills around
the monastery. I think I began to love the land of Regina Laudis long
before I met its nuns.

There were a number of other guests at Saint Gregory's, including
Helen Boothroyd, who had served as an army nurse in World War II. In
fact, she was among the Americans who stormed the Normandy Beach
on D-Day. When she met Dolores, she was a nurse at Boston Hospital.
"I was mulling around the monastery because God was calling me
there", she said. "I was aware that Dolores was an actress and found her
very sophisticated. I was also impressed with her humanness and her
considerate way of integrating with all of us in Saint Gregory's."

Dolores' follow-up to *Francis of Assisi* was *Sail a Crooked Ship*, a
contemporary farce by Columbia Pictures. It was not a big film and
hardly in the same league as *Tender Is the Night*, but it fit in with a
series of minor comedies currently in vogue that were low budget and
earned a nice profit.

Crooked Ship was based on the novel by Nathaniel Benchley, son of
Algonquin Round Table's Robert Benchley and father of Peter Benchley, the future author of *Jaws*. The cast included Ernie Kovacs, Carolyn
Jones, Frankie Avalon, Robert Wagner and Frank Gorshin. Jean Seberg
had been originally penciled in for Dolores' role; thus, their professional
paths that had begun with *Saint Joan* were still crossing.

When I reported for work at Columbia, there was a lot of discussion
about my hair and makeup to make me more glamorous. I overheard
suggestions to pluck my eyebrows and bleach my hair. I also heard
myself referred to as "the Wallis girl", something I thought identified
me as his girlfriend but soon learned meant "hands off; leave her
alone, or you'll have Hal Wallis to answer to". My "look" remained
natural.

Pat Barto, my role model from Paramount, designed my wardrobe,
this time getting full credit. She also picked out a silver mink coat for

me to wear. The price tag read $6,500. I remember seeing my reflection during costume and makeup tests and thinking, "Wow, this is a different person!" I looked like a glamor girl even if I didn't feel like one. I was hardly a sex goddess.

> *—I once went to a costume party as Brigitte Bardot, and nobody guessed who I was. Just as well. Any actress who has so much attention focused on her has to get away from herself to survive. Otherwise she just joins the worshippers.*

I thought the script read like a screwball comedy of the thirties, but the movie deteriorated into slapstick. Even so, making it was a lark. It marked a happy reunion with my King Creole *costar Carolyn Jones, thus strengthening a happy relationship on screen as well as off. This time I got the better billing, but Carolyn again had the better role.*

My favorite was that consummate clown Ernie Kovacs. He kept everything moving at breakneck pace, always taking an improvisational detour from the script that kept the rest of us on our toes—when we weren't cracking up. He was probably the most inventive actor I've ever worked with, an absolute joy. Sadly, Sail a Crooked Ship *would be his last film. A month after it was released, Ernie was killed in an automobile accident.*

About halfway through the shoot, Pat Barto began hinting that now was the time I should finally ask for a perk—specifically the silver mink. Other actresses asked for and got their movie wardrobes, she noted—why shouldn't I? I was too embarrassed, but she wouldn't let up on it. She nagged and nagged until I finally screwed up enough courage to "suggest" to Mr. Wallis that I wouldn't turn down the coat should he feel I had earned a bonus. He didn't reply, but asked me to lunch at the studio the next day.

That morning the coat was delivered to the apartment, and I was wearing it when I arrived at the commissary to find Mr. Wallis at the head of a long table of company men I didn't know, and no other women. My boss introduced me as his new star and then suggestively added, "She's the first one who got the mink and didn't." The guys howled. I thought I would die. Mr. W. looked pleased as punch. He got his laugh from the men and the mortified blush from me.

148

—But it cost him sixty-five hundred bucks to do it.

At the 1961 Oscar ceremonies, James Stewart all but broke down accepting an honorary award for Gary Cooper. Stewart's emotional words to his old friend alerted the Industry that the ailing Cooper was near death.

The last time I saw Gary was in his Brentwood home, where I had once mistaken him for a gardener. He was a man who just fit in with nature, yet was so comfortable around people. To me, Gary Cooper was comfort. He always treated me with respect, kindness and affection. It was devastating to say goodbye to him. As I approached his bed in the dimly lit bedroom, he reached out and took my hand. "Hello, Miss Dolores," he said with a smile, "working?"

Gary Cooper was laid to rest on May 16, 1961. At his funeral, I held a religious relic in my hand. A relic is a sacred piece of matter from the body of a saint—it can be a bit of bone or hair or something that was close to that person's body in life. The Church considers relics very precious because through them we can come into contact with the holiness of the person. The relic I held tightly was Gary's relic of Saint Thérèse. Rocky had given it to me at the time of his death. It means a great deal to me still.

Maria Cooper recalled, "My father had felt very paternalistic toward Dolores. He knew how close we were, and he felt kind of like she was a younger daughter, maybe much younger than her calendar years because she had not had the family environment that would have given her a kind of sophistication about the 'ways of the world' that her beauty and talent were leading her into. Although he recognized that she had the 'street smarts' her difficult life had provided, he still felt protective of her in terms of the 'business'; he knew she didn't have the training to move easily in the circles he foresaw as her road to being a really big star."

Near the end of production of *Sail a Crooked Ship*, Dolores got a call from Harry Bernsen telling her that producer Mark Robson and director Philip Dunne wanted to meet with her to discuss their upcoming film *The Inspector*. She had been aware through the trade papers that the film was in preproduction because Natalie Wood was scheduled for it. Wood had abruptly pulled out of the project, and Robson and Dunne were interested in Dolores for a lead role.

The problem was that the film was scheduled to begin almost immediately, and I was shooting Crooked Ship. *It didn't seem possible that I could ready myself for another movie so quickly. But when I read the script, I knew I should do it, that it was decidedly a major jump toward the more demanding roles I coveted. I did note with some trepidation that the heroine was Jewish and feared that, once I tested, out I would go.*

But the meeting was not an audition. I wasn't asked to test or even to read for the part. Mr. Dunne and Mr. Robson had already decided they wanted me for the role of the Jewish refugee, Lisa Held. The meeting was to see how soon I could get ready for the European start of production, scheduled in three weeks. Amazingly, Sail a Crooked Ship *was to wrap in exactly three weeks.*

Mr. Dunne and Mr. Robson asked if I would object to having my hair practically shaved off for a flashback sequence in a concentration camp. Apparently they thought I would be horrified. If they had only known how glad I would be to have it off. On this film, I wouldn't have to check it constantly.

—Besides, I was finally going to play a Jewish girl.

I finished my last scene for Sail a Crooked Ship *on Friday evening. The next morning I was on a plane for London and shaking with more fear than I had had since the night I left for Broadway.*

Fifteen

Based on the novel by Jan de Hartog, *The Inspector* was a straight-line suspense drama of a Dutch secret policeman who rescues a World War II concentration camp survivor from the clutches of a white slaver and smuggles her into Palestine. The production was scheduled to shoot in the Netherlands, London, Wales, Tangiers and along the Mediterranean. Interiors would be shot at Elstree Studio near London.

In her previous films, Dolores radiated health. As Lisa, she would be required to appear ill and worn. Getting the externals of the character is easy enough for a good craftsman. But healthy radiance can be masked only so far with makeup, and Dolores was concerned about projecting Lisa's interior pain.

A producer friend, Bobby Cohn, suggested she meet a woman he had recently met at a party. He had noticed tattooed numbers on her arm, and she told him she had been in Auschwitz. Since her arrival from Hungary, Suzanne Zada had been working as an assistant to a beautician and knew little about Hollywood. She had no idea who Dolores Hart was but agreed to a meeting as a favor to Bobby.

Suzanne remembered, "The meeting was set up at the Beefeater Inn, and as I was escorted to a red-leather booth Dolores rose and said, 'I think you should slap my face.' I stood stunned as she explained, 'I don't know why we thought we could ask you to relive your suffering just so we can make a movie. I apologize.'

"I was totally overwhelmed by the fact that she should be that sensitive, but when she said that, I suddenly knew that I wanted to share with her because I knew my help would allow this sensitive woman to get it right. If one person in the audience could appreciate the real degradation, if just one person realized the most tremendous cruelty is depriving a person of his humanity, I would be happy."

Suzanne's eyes still carried that wound. "Why me?" she had asked repeatedly. "Why didn't God choose another?" That question was what had made her suffering so hard to bear. "It wasn't the daily beatings that hurt" she said. "It was the hurt inside, the knowledge that I had no reason to be proud, that I wanted to be loved but who could possibly love me? I learned constantly to avoid being noticed because if you're noticed, you could be gassed. I trusted no one."

At that moment, the film became a personal crusade. I wanted to be able to show Suzanne I really did understand how deeply she was hurt. If she understood, it would make the work more than worthwhile. Alone, I spent hours staring at myself in a mirror, trying to remove all life from my eyes, leaving them hollow and dead. Suzanne's words "I trusted no one" never left my consciousness.

En route to our Dutch location, I caught sight of something I had seen only on cans of kitchen cleanser—a windmill. "Oh," I cried aloud, "there's one!" Others appeared on the horizon. "There's one and there's one!" My traveling companions began to laugh, amused at my naïve enthusiasm. "My child, you are now in the land of windmills", they assured me. "You'll soon see so many of them, you'll hardly notice them at all."

My good fortune to work with respected actors continued with this film. Stephen Boyd was the inspector, and the other players read like a Who's Who of the acting profession: Leo McKern, Marius Goring, Donald Pleasence, Hugh Griffith, Robert Stephens and Harry Andrews.

I remember long rehearsals before each scene. Philip Dunne was not stingy with rehearsal time, and Mark Robson's background as a director made him a generous producer. Their frequent and considerate notes to me were gifts of encouragement that I will never forget.

Most of the location filming took place on Dutch canals or at sea, on barges and boats and a diesel trawler that the company named Madre Dolorosa as a compliment to Dolores. Although she and Stephen were constantly queasy, they were denied the solace of seasickness pills because Dunne felt they made his actors drowsy and interfered with their performances.

It was a good thing that Dunne had a contented company. It would bode well for the production when they moved to Swansea in Wales, the exhaustingly uncooperative location that doubled for Palestine. That single location resulted in the film's going over schedule.

The weather proved so unpredictable that it forced Dunne to "double take" scenes to keep outdoor filming going whatever the conditions. He shot alternate takes of every scene both dry and wet so that sequences could be matched up in the editing room.

I didn't like Swansea. I thought of it as the sinkhole of Great Britain. For fifteen days we sat in pup tents and trawlers, fighting seasickness, rain, wind and sun. I was feeling the effects of going from one film to another without a break, and at the end of each day I didn't know if I was seasick, sunstroked or hung over.

Anything that could jinx our company did. One night, a storm grew to such massive proportions that our camera longboat washed away, the Traveler *got stuck in a sand dune and our transformers conked out. When the sun at last peeped through, a huge swarm of bees took over the beach. Mr. Dunne was forced to reshoot the entire day's work.*

Crowds of people from Swansea lined the hills above the location, watching the filming, all of them within critical camera range. It was annoying—and expensive—when we lost shots because a boy scout troop waved or light flashes from binocular lenses were caught by the camera.

— You know, forty years later, I received a touching letter from a Welshman named Alun Rees, who was a child of seven on that hill above our location. He wanted me to know how special that day still was to him. You're welcome, Alun.

On top of all this, a letter from Granny confirmed that Mom had gone off the wagon again. I exploded. I wrote her that I couldn't care less what was going to happen to her. God knows we all want love and attention and someone to care, but my mother—and my father, too, for that matter—seemed to go through life thinking they were the only two people on earth with those needs and the rest of us were created to serve them. So I was in a blue funk when we came to the climactic scene in which I'm shot and Stephen carries me onto an army tank. The crew promised to put real bullets in the gun to put me out of my misery.

I was relieved when the company moved to London for the remainder of production. I took a comfortable flat in Eaton Square, a far cry from the tent on the Swansea beach.

There was a sequence in Waterloo Station that had to be shot on a Sunday night because the facility could not be closed down during the day. It took most of the night, and at the end of the shoot, I was so tired I didn't bother to take off my costume or remove my makeup before I was driven to Eaton Square. After the driver dropped me off at the flat, I realized I had left my purse in the dressing room. I had no money and, more important at the moment, no key to the building.

While I was standing forlornly on the street, a London bobby drove by and asked what I was doing in that neighborhood. Mind you, in my costume—a tattered wool skirt, crumpled blouse, stained trench coat—I looked like one of the hundred neediest cases. I told him I lived in the building and didn't have my key. He asked for identification, which of course I didn't have; he told me to be on my way or he would have to take me to the station. I walked away slowly until I saw him leave, then I turned back. I was desperate to check the back door in case it was unlocked, but as soon as I reached the rear of the building the bobby was beside me, and I was taken to the local police station. I protested to anyone within earshot that I was an actress making a movie in London and they could check all this by calling Elstree Studio.

Someone noticed the "tattooed" numbers on my arm and was momentarily sympathetic. I asked for a washcloth. As I removed Lisa's identification numbers, someone at Elstree finally picked up the phone, and this jailbird was released.

—The next day, the studio publicist put out a story that screen actress Dolores Hart had been arrested by London police who mistook her for a streetwalker. It was picked up by newspapers all over the world.

154

During production, the film had its title changed from *The Inspector* to *Lisa* to focus on the character of the refugee for the European audience that would have a deeper acquaintance with the war-scarred and the displaced.

Lisa marked a reunion with Stephen Boyd, with whom Dolores had enjoyed a rapport during the *Playhouse 90* production two years earlier. The lengthier production schedule of a movie provided time for the two to nurture a personal relationship denied them by the fast pace of television.

A romance between Dolores and Stephen began in the press, with gossip items suggesting that the two must surely be having a love affair. Photo layouts, following the fan-magazine formula, gave credence to the gossip. But indeed, something real was developing. Dolores' relationship with Stephen Boyd would be her only professional relationship that would also become a romantic one.

Stephen was an amazingly gentle man for his brawn and size. He wasn't tall but had substantial bulk—which I was gratefully aware of when he had to carry me. Most of my scenes were with Stephen, and we were frequently together for publicity interviews and photo layouts. But we also seemed to seek out each other's company in private time. When I was working, I usually didn't date, but on Lisa, *I saw Stephen for supper almost every night.*

At first, Stephen found it difficult to open up, but gradually he became willing to speak about his private life. When I was agonizing over Mom's fall off the wagon, he told me I shouldn't waste my time shaking my fist at her. He admitted that he also had a problem with alcohol and bluntly said that I couldn't help my mother, that only she could help herself. He had stopped drinking only when he *wanted to.*

I found him deeply spiritual. We had many discussions about religion, mostly in a general way, but occasionally we spoke of Catholicism. Stephen was adamant that although he was genuinely interested in the broad spectrum of religion, he was not attracted to any specific church. He would come to change that stand.

Our dinners grew to two and a half hours of soul-searching and reaching out, which Stephen acknowledged as a gift of understanding.

155

Most men are dominant and directive. They're threatened by a woman's inner sense of authority. Stephen could expose his vulnerability. He let me show my authority. It didn't make him feel less masculine. I was grateful for his trust and began to feel that our relationship had a potential future.

By the time we got to London, I knew that my feelings for Stephen had gone as far as they could go on a friendship level. I felt I had an obligation to indicate I was ready to move to a more personal one. Up to this point, there hadn't even been a kiss. Not that I had never kissed Stephen, but it had never been that *kind of a kiss.*

One evening, returning from one of our walks in Saint James' Park, we stopped at the front door as we had on so many evenings, and I suddenly said, "Stephen, would you like to come in?" He looked at me and said, "Yes." He leaned forward to kiss me, but the kiss was placed on my forehead. "Yes," he repeated, "but you're marked. Don't you know that?"

I was confused. I felt hurt. Had I exposed my vulnerability, my trust, only to be rejected? I wondered what he had meant by saying I was "marked", but I didn't ask for an explanation then. I never did. Our dinners and talks continued, but we never mentioned that evening. When the film was over, our lives moved apart. But I heard his voice— "You're marked"—often.

I was surprised when Don Robinson called and told me he was coming to London and wanted to see me. I wanted to see him too. It did seem a good time because I was scheduled for several days off after we filmed the pivotal sequence where Lisa is forced to relive the medical experiments performed upon her, and I was sure Don would be a welcome break. I couldn't be sure, however, whether my eagerness to see him again wasn't merely a rebound response to Stephen.

The scene was highly emotional, and the fact that Mr. Dunne wanted to film it in a single close-up scared me. It was further intimidating that Arthur Ibettson, our cinematographer, planned to use a special camera lens, one usually used for film inserts—extreme close-ups, such as a

156

shot of a person's hand writing a letter—which would mean the camera was going to be only twenty-one inches from my face.

We got through the first take, and Mr. Dunne wanted to print it, but due to an apparent technical problem, Arthur wanted another take for insurance. I felt I had used up all my voice in the first take, but I did it again. This time everything went well, thank God, because by then I had lost my voice completely. I was certainly ready for that four-day break.

It had been several months since Don and I had seen each other. It was a lovely reunion. We took several day trips outside of London—I did the driving because I was now used to driving on the wrong side of the road—saw plays in the West End and dined at wonderful restaurants. More importantly, Don's presence served to remind me of all that we had in common. I liked being with him.

"We had only one disagreement", Don recalled. "I was appropriately angry at poor service we had received in a restaurant and purposely did not leave a tip. When we left the restaurant, Dolores excused herself and went back inside, obviously to leave one."

—I did not apologize. I did it for Granny.

In the days following his return home, I thought a lot about Don. I even fantasized our running off and getting married as in a romantic comedy. Why did those thoughts come only in an imaginary way? Why couldn't I really think of myself as a part of them except in a reflective sense?

During the entire production, Dolores bombarded Harriett with tough-love letters that resulted in Harriett's renewed effort to stay sober. Dolores was encouraged enough to invite her to the last week of shooting in London and then on a vacation to Paris, Madrid and Rome before returning home.

I picked up Mom at Heathrow Airport, and I was so nervous I could hardly drive. I was always holding on to the hope that she would straighten out, and I was always disappointed. But Mom was in great shape, trim and buoyant and full of "piss and vinegar", as she used to say. In the time it took to drive from the airport to the flat, we were giggling like girls again.

The next morning, just minutes before we left the flat, I got a call from a man who said he was Frank Sinatra. Sure, sure, I thought, and I'm Princess Margaret. He said he wanted to take me to dinner to discuss a part in a movie he was going to make. I told whoever it was that I was in a rush and to send the script and hung up.

The vacation was a great success. Mom loved London, Madrid, Rome and especially Paris—she fit the Paris scene like a cup on a saucer.

Harriett was blissfully peaceful because she was the center of attention. She was the star, not just a nobody basking in reflected glory. Making sure Harriett got that notice was Dolores' gift to her mother.

When we finally arrived back home, I was able to tell Granny that during the entire trip I was proud to introduce Mom as my mother.

Waiting for me at my apartment was a large envelope that had been forwarded from London. Inside was the script of The Manchurian Candidate. *It had been Frank Sinatra on the phone! I called Harry at once, but it was too late. Leslie Parrish had been cast. Mr. Sinatra never called again.*

Lisa wasn't a hit in United States, in spite of the lurid ads that Fox hoped would entice audiences—"They experimented on me, sold me like human cargo" and "Why am I terrified every time a man touches me?"—blurbs that *New York Times* critic Bosley Crowther charged gave the wrong impression of the film he found "an uncommonly colorful and tense adventure".

However, *Lisa* did well in Europe, where its thesis was still being lived on a daily basis. It was nominated for a Golden Globe by the Hollywood Foreign Press Association as one of the best films of 1962. Dolores received strong notices, her best to date, although the only review she still remembers called her "too apple-pie American".

For Dolores, more important than the judgment of the critics was Suzanne Zada's assessment. Dolores invited her to the first screening of the film and afterward, in the studio parking lot, she found Suzanne weeping. "It was there," Suzanne told her, "the hopeless, lost feeling I had, there for people to see. I thought that God was trying to make up for what He did to me." The friendship between these two women has lasted to this day.

Lisa had an impact on Dolores. Never before had she felt such compassion for a character; nor had she ever gotten so emotional about a role that tears became a standard part of each day's work.

It wasn't the acting of the role that affected me so deeply. It was the humanity of it, the undeniable sense of life I found in the character. I felt more motivated to visit Regina Laudis after Lisa *was over. Luckily, Columbia wanted me to make a personal appearance tour on behalf of* Sail a Crooked Ship, *which meant I could steal a few days at the monastery.*

It was when Dolores was on that publicity tour that her best buddy died. Grandpa Kude suffered a heart attack and was in grave condition in a Chicago hospital, with Esther, Harriett and Sister Dolores Marie at his bedside. Aware that he was dying, Fred asked his sister to summon a priest, who came and administered last rites and Holy Communion.

I was appearing on a TV talk show but remained in contact with the family through the evening. I had asked them to make sure the TV in his room was tuned in to the show because I was going to do something just for him. I had arranged with a band member to borrow his clarinet, and when I stepped into the spotlight, I said, "This one's for you, Grandpa", and played "Whispering".

Moments before, however, Grandpa had slipped into unconsciousness, and Granny was afraid that my gesture would go unrecognized. But, miraculously, he revived while I was still playing. He didn't see the performance, but Sister Dolores Marie was sure he had heard it. With her crucifix in his hands, an unmistakable look of tranquillity on his face, she told me, he had made his peace with God.

159

Grandpa always said Sister Dolores Marie would probably pray him into Heaven. I think she did. As a boy he regularly went to early Mass before he began his paper route, but somewhere down the line he lost his faith, and Sister spent years praying that he would return to it. She told me she was gratified that he experienced a conversion at the end. Her words "at the end" troubled me for a long time. Was it "the end"?

I arrived at the monastery with my mind cluttered with garbage that can filter out the silent beauty of the place. I had left five hundred bucks in traveler's checks at the hotel and couldn't get out from under the ridiculous bother of that. At the monastery, one's selfishness is so apparent. Vanity becomes a piece of fat that can't be digested. Even if it is spat out, the disgusting evidence is too ugly to face. There it made me feel unreal—phony.

"By this time," said Mother Placid, "it was no secret that our regular guest was a famous actress, but to my knowledge no one in the Community had ever seen her on the screen. I would never have asked to see one of her movies, but Mother Maria Joseph, who was in charge of our monastic art shop, was less inhibited. Once, when Dolores was in the shop, Mother Maria Joseph said she was sure the Community would appreciate seeing one of her films."

I was surprised but, frankly, pleased by her request, and I asked Fox if a screening of Lisa *might be arranged. I thought it would be the most appropriate of the movies I had made, and it was the one of which I was most proud.*

As before, I met with the nuns in parlor through the grille. Mother Columba had become solicitous of my privacy and assumed a protective attitude. She was very dear, so concerned about keeping my visits a secret that, when we would meet in Saint Placid, one of the three parlors, she would always remove her cloak and hang it over the window that looked out onto the road to keep prying eyes from peering in. It was the era of La Dolce Vita *and the rise of the paparazzi, but I couldn't fathom how she knew about such things.*

—I think she just enjoyed the dramatics of it.

I stayed mostly to myself. I walked in the woods and sat in sunny green fields watching lazy clouds overhead and wondering whether I would be able to come to grips with my life. Hours passed in a strange calm—one that preceded a terrible storm? I sat in the sun like a lizard waiting, waiting. I began a diary:

> *Lately, in much company, I can hardly wait for solitude. Yet in my own company, the time does not pass quickly enough. Is it loneliness I want to leave or learn to embrace? Comradeship that I am looking for or fleeing from? I wonder, what would it be like to be free to exist solely to find God? But, would I know what to do even then? ... I want so desperately to run away from this place—but to where? Back to the wasting of moment to moment, awaiting the temporal alleviation of boredom by trivial excitement? No, I must stay here and wait for another signpost. Listen, you fool. But to what am I listening?*

I pondered the strange new awakening in my heart that cried for explanation. I had been so relieved that I hadn't had one of those "visitations" during Lisa. *Yet I couldn't get Stephen's words out of my mind: "You're marked." He had spoken softly but with such sureness.*

When I returned to Los Angeles, I began to realize that the élan I once carried back from Regina Laudis was no longer transportable. The all-embracing experience of peace that I had been able to leave with, I was unable to take with me now. The absence of these consolations was so intense, I ached. All that I could hope for was a little grace.

161

Sixteen

Catholics of the Motion Picture, Radio and Television Industry handed out annual awards—gold medals of Saint Genesius, the patron saint of actors—to show appreciation to outstanding members. The occasion for the award-giving was James Francis Cardinal McIntyre's annual Hollywood Communion Breakfast, which featured a parade of Catholic movie stars whom we in the press referred to as the "Catholic Mafia".

The breakfasts began in 1951 and migrated from a small affair at the Jesuits' Church of the Blessed Sacrament to the Beverly Hilton Hotel. At her first breakfast in 1958, Dolores was introduced to a Mrs. Tom Lewis and told her how much she looked like Loretta Young. Mrs. Tom Lewis *was* Loretta Young.

At the eleventh gathering in 1962, Dolores received a medal and was one of two speakers; the other was Clare Boothe Luce, the writer not only of *Come to the Stable* but also of the hit Broadway play *The Women*.

Dolores' message was to urge the Industry to maintain a high standard of morality while fulfilling its role in the worldwide communications sphere, but she veered from her text and reminded the starry audience of a more personal responsibility:

> Our problems, worries, frustrations are nothing but pride. Every one of us has too much pride to put our trust in God. No matter who we are, no matter how big a star, we must trust humbly in Him and by doing so, we will reach that ultimate reality which is in Him.

The stars in the audience—Jane Wyman, Pat O'Brien, Jimmy Durante, Rosalind Russell, Ricardo Montalban and Ramon Novarro, as well as two close friends now, Loretta Young and Irene Dunne—rose to pay tribute to the young actress.

❦

Although I would look forward to the times when Don and I would be together, I was always on guard. Was I avoiding the prospect of marrying Don or the prospect of marriage itself? Looking back, my deeply unsettled feelings about a vocation wouldn't allow me to make any commitment unless I was backed into a corner, which certainly wasn't the most encouraging proposition for Don, or the most flattering. His patience was wearing thin, and he deserved to have some indication that my feelings would be resolved one way or another.

I did have a practical reason for pushing back the thought of marriage. I had a real conscience problem about being a good wife and mother and at the same time having the kind of career I knew I wanted. This was something I would have to work on during our upcoming separation. I was set to do another film for MGM that would take me to Europe in the spring, and Don had issued an ultimatum. He felt it would be wise for us not to have any communication with each other while I was in Europe.

In Europe I plunged feverishly into work. Still, Don lingered in my thoughts. Several times I would start to write him and then remember I wasn't supposed to. I wished for the phone to ring and to hear his voice at the other end. But Don stuck to his self-imposed quarantine.

Come Fly with Me is a pleasant, if routine, addition to the enduring Hollywood formula of three pretty girls in search of love and security. Lightweight but attractively cast, with travelogue-like locations in London, Paris and Vienna, it marked the second time Henry Levin directed Dolores, who was again top billed, not a small consideration in the Industry, in which billing is currency.

Dolores, Pamela Tiffin and Mariette Hartley were cast as three airline stewardesses on a New York-to-Europe run who are looking for Mr. Right, played by Karl Boehm, Hugh O'Brian and, surprisingly, Karl Malden, whose presence made the movie look more substantial than it was.

With their shared theater backgrounds, Dolores, Mariette and Malden rehearsed unofficially for a few weeks prior to production, frequently at Malden's Brentwood home. Years later Mariette recalled, with lingering disappointment, that she was replaced just before shooting began. "The

163

physical required by studios for insurance purposes showed I had hepatitis. A subsequent examination proved I had been misdiagnosed, but by then it was too late." A talented New York actress, Lois Nettleton, had stepped into the role. Mariette lost the part, but her budding friendship with Dolores was only put on hold.

The company was probably the happiest I had ever worked with. Pamela and I bonded quickly at Grace Down's Airline School in New York, where we took classes to prepare for our roles as flight attendants.

Pamela Tiffin recalled, "It was only my fourth film, and Dolores was so experienced. I looked up to her. She was decent and sensible—and a bit of a smart aleck, which I liked. She was fresh bread."

Pamela was surprised to learn that Dolores had tested for her role in *Summer and Smoke.* "She never mentioned it. And she was so helpful to me, not the least bit competitive or jealous. Well, that was Dolores. I used to think, if we had to send a perfect example of American womanhood to Europe, it would be Dolores."

During the early days of production, Twentieth Century-Fox came through on my request to screen Lisa *at the monastery. I must say, the studio was very generous. They sent not only a 35 mm print, but a screen, a projector and a projectionist as well.*

"It was quite unusual", Mother Placid remembered. "Movie showings were extremely rare, and we had never had a professional projectionist. The two movies we had seen were on a tiny black-and-white television set. We were in the midst of building a new wing in the monastery, and we were practically outdoors. We had to wait until it was dark to begin. We sat on boards placed across the holes in the floor. Most of the Community was present and found the film very moving, but there were some women who preferred not to attend."

Although Mother David, the nun who had months before directed Dolores out of the enclosure, shared her sisters' opinion that movies had no place in contemplative life, she did attend, but she sat with her back to the screen.

Mother David recalled, "I had left the world and had come to this Community, which was very eremitical in its orientation, with this desire for a purity of life, so, yes, I was making a protest. I sat in a window frame and looked out. Of course, I heard the whole thing and was intrigued."

Three lifelong friendships were born during the making of *Come Fly with Me*. One was with Lois Nettleton, who made her movie debut in that film. "I was intimidated at first", Lois recalled. "I was so new to films and Dolores was a star. I was cast late and rushed to the Paris location where filming had already begun. I didn't even have time to pack properly and had only one nice dress with me. Dolores was an absolute darling. For the first week or so, she loaned me her clothes like we were old roommates."

Dolores didn't speak of her visits to Regina Laudis to many people. Lois was one with whom she did share her feelings about the monastery. "I was a lapsed Catholic when I met Dolores. She told me that whenever things got a little rough, when she needed some comfort, she went to Regina Laudis. 'Don't forget this,' she said, 'if ever life gets too much for you, they'll look after you. They'll put you up and you can refresh yourself.' I've followed that advice many times.

"In Vienna we were all invited to a prince's birthday party at a castle. I remember we met Peter Sellers that night, and he monopolized Dolores. He had seen an early screening of *Lisa* and told her he wanted to find something they could do together."

When the company moved to London, Dolores received a script from Sellers and, a few days later, a call—presumably to see if she had read it, but actually to ask her on a date.

I accepted his invitation to go to the Ascot races, and it was a fun afternoon that stretched out to include dinner at a very "in" place. Afterward, we went to his Dorchester hotel suite, where there was a

165

party going on. It was London in the Swinging Sixties, and I felt out of place, but it wasn't until a young waiter leaned over and whispered to me, "Miss Hart, I don't think you should be here", that I realized what kind of a party it was and slipped out.

Sellers called her later to apologize and asked her out again. They had dinner in a small, quiet restaurant this time, much more to her liking, and at the end of this pleasant evening, he saw her to her flat. At her door, Sellers asked to come in, but she begged off, saying she had an early call.

Sellers then asked for a glass of water. Dolores went to the kitchen, and when she returned with the water he was gone. Bewildered, she locked the door, kicked off her shoes and went into the bedroom. There, waiting in her bed—starkers—was Sellers.

It was a scene in a farce, and I couldn't help laughing. Peter said it would be a lovely way to end the evening and insisted—somewhat immodestly, I thought—that it would be the experience of a lifetime for me. I asked him to leave. Peter politely conceded and—now suddenly modest—asked if I would turn my back while he got dressed.

When he came into the living room he shook my hand very formally and said good night. Billy Wilder couldn't have written it better. Actually, we did have dinner several more times, but we never repeated that scene. We maintained a friendly—and decent—relationship.

The second person with the film in whom Dolores confided was pert and pretty Valerie Imbleau. Val was a purser for Pan American World Airlines on a flight from Istanbul to London when Henry Levin was a passenger. Levin took a shine to her and asked if she would like to be technical consultant on *Come Fly with Me*. Val saw no way the airline would grant her a leave of absence; consequently, Henry got MGM to contact Pan Am. The next thing Val knew, she was on the company's Vienna location.

Val was immediately embraced by the entire cast, but a firm bond was formed with Dolores, whom Val thought of as "the great listener, the great empathizer". Dolores called Val her "little sister". They shared

166

a deep spirituality, and when Dolores spoke of Regina Laudis to Val, she planted a seed that would have an unexpected yield.

Karl Malden was the third lasting friend Dolores made during the filming of that movie. Dolores had admired Malden's work; the mere fact that he was in the cast, she felt, continued her good luck of working with the best.

More than forty years after they worked together, Malden reminisced, "She was more than a friend. She was family. During filming in Paris, I had my wife, Mona, and daughters, Mila and Carla, with me; and whenever Mona and I wanted to go out, Dolores babysat the girls."

—It was like being with girlfriends. If we stayed in, I would tell them ghost stories, and when we went out, it was usually to shop. There's no better place to shop than Paris.

"Dolores", Malden told me, "had a lot of talent, but she had something extra. I'm referring to the fifty percent needed for the audience to like you. She had that. She could have been as big as Elizabeth Taylor. But ultimately, she didn't belong in that environment, not with the kind of heart she has. I love her for her decision. I always felt she wanted to be taken care of. She now takes care of others. And I'm sure she's good at that because she understands the need."

With continued press interest in Dolores, and since she was constantly on loan-out from Wallis, it was decided that she should get a personal press agent rather than rely on the studio. Her present salary of $3,000 a week permitted the extra expense, and Harry felt it was necessary not only to keep her in the public eye, but to ensure that her name was kept in front of producers, too. Veteran publicist Frank Liberman was hired, though at first he didn't want the job. "I once handled Shelley Winters and didn't much like representing actresses", he said. "When it comes to paying me or buying a new dress, the new dress always wins out."

Meeting reporters was always a bit of a fencing match, but I learned to enjoy sparring over provocative questions rather than becoming

167

argumentative. I could always count on reporters to ask old-hat questions such as, "What kind of books do you read?" Since I was into the works of Teilhard de Chardin and Saint Thomas Aquinas, the discussion would usually open up the area of personal belief. I became very conscious that I could utilize interviews to promote Catholic action.

I really thought that might be my place in God's scheme—to throw light on the Church. I hadn't experienced one of those "hauntings" during the production of Come Fly with Me. *Unless you count the day I picked up a Paris newspaper whose headline read, "Marilyn Monroe Morte". That news affected me more profoundly than I would have expected, and for the rest of the filming those old questions, the ones whose answers had been withheld—or avoided—troubled me: What am I doing? Where am I going?*

Come Fly with Me hit the top-ten moneymakers the week of its opening in seventh place, just below *To Kill a Mockingbird* and above *The Longest Day*. Reviews were mixed. Bosley Crowther in the *New York Times* called it "bright, colorful and fun". The *Daily News* added "appetizing". The *Hollywood Citizen News* called it "the kind of film Ernst Lubitsch used to do". *Time*, on the other hand, warned that it boasted dialogue "right out of a high school play". But the cast came off well with Dolores rating high compliments, from "a delectable sugar-coated pastry" to "one of our more exciting young actresses". The only out-and-out knock she got was for the awkward way she smoked a cigarette in the movie. Ironically, that role got Dolores—a confirmed nonsmoker—listed on the website *starswhosmoke.com*.

Seventeen

"When I marry, it will be for all time."

That was what I told Louella Parsons, arguably the queen of the gossip columnists in those days, during an interview just after I returned from Europe. I didn't have a dewy-eyed concept of marriage that young girls usually have. I balked at the notion that a woman is incomplete without the love and companionship of a man. Don thought I was afraid of marriage because of my father's behavior. I thought he could be right. Deep hurts don't heal easily.

Don remembered that, at their first meeting, Dolores spoke of her visits to Regina Laudis during her year on Broadway. "I knew when I started to date her that she had had feelings about a vocation. She told me about her visits to the monastery, but I didn't give them a second thought."

It was what she didn't say that was important. She did not tell Don about her subsequent visits after she had moved back to Los Angeles.

When Come Fly with Me finished, Granny joined me on a motor trip to Rome with Henry and Ethel Levin. We had a brief stopover in Monte Carlo, where I won at roulette and thought of how happy Tony Quinn would be now that I was legal. In Rome I rendezvoused with Harry Bernsen, a very happy agent indeed, who had a small fistful of film possibilities. So, in the summer of 1962, I wasn't concentrating on my love life. I was riding high on my career.

How could she not feel confident? Wherever she turned she heard herself referred to as "the new Grace Kelly". Even in Monte Carlo, people stopped in their tracks and stared when she entered the casino. Dolores was dressed to the teeth—in the mink, of course, and very blond—but she had never incited that kind of reaction before. The gambling tourists had mistaken her for Kelly, and the shocked reaction was because the princess never set foot inside the casino.

MGM was eager to rush her into another Henry Levin project, *Honeymoon Hotel*, as her third film on the four-picture deal. It was a vapid comedy that featured Robert Goulet in his movie debut and Robert Morse, riding the crest of his breakout Broadway appearance in *How to Succeed in Business without Really Trying*. Additionally, Dolores' boss, Hal Wallis, finally had something for her to do. After threatening to regress her career by teaming her again with Elvis Presley in *Girls, Girls, Girls*, Wallis instead penciled her in for the second lead in *A Girl Named Tamiko* for director John Sturges.

Earlier in her career, any movie had seemed okay to her. Now she was beginning to set her sights on better films. Wallis had also just purchased film rights to the Neil Simon play *Barefoot in the Park*, a hit on Broadway with Elizabeth Ashley and the young actor who had been passed over to replace George Peppard in *Pleasure*, Robert Redford. It wouldn't go into production for many months, but Dolores already coveted the Ashley role in spite of Paul Nathan's cautioning her not to hold out hope because Wallis wanted Jane Fonda.

I returned to LA just before my twenty-fourth birthday. It had been weeks since I had seen Don, and I was looking forward to our reunion. We connected again, and I was reminded that he was one of the most contented people I knew. He possessed a simple and uncomplicated faith that I mistrusted at first. I used to wait for the crack in the veneer, as I believed everyone is fighting something that threatens to scratch up the pretty surface.

Marriage quickly became a topic of concern once again. For the first time, I admitted to myself that thoughts of a religious vocation were keeping me from committing to this relationship. I vowed to face that once and for all so that I could come to a decision—before it drove me crazy! I sat down and wrote a letter to Reverend Mother Benedict asking—officially—if I could come back and talk to her about a vocation.

I had asked once before, back in 1959, if she thought I might have a religious call, and she had responded that she thought I should return to Hollywood and do my best there. But that October morning I felt I had to face the dilemma again.

I was about to drop the letter into the mailbox near my home when Don drove by and stopped. I was so happy to see him. We talked for a while, and he asked me to dinner. I suddenly had this strong feeling that my earlier determination must have been wrong. No, I thought to myself, I'm not supposed to go in that direction. I put the letter back in my pocket and said yes to dinner.

Don had the engagement ring with him when he and Dolores dined that night. At the end of the meal, he offered her the ring and asked her again to marry him. They both were disturbed when she couldn't give him an immediate and unqualified yes. Don remembered, "I asked if she had that other situation—the thoughts of vocation—behind her, and she told me yes, it was behind her." Dolores then offered a compromise. They could be engaged secretly for six months, and at the end of that period they would decide whether they were doing the right thing. Don subordinated his masculine ego and agreed.

—It was like a six-month option. I accepted the ring that night.

Within days, however, Hollywood columnist Harrison Carroll announced the engagement in the *Los Angeles Herald-Express*. Dolores has no idea how Carroll had learned of it, but once the news was out, all hell broke loose. Paramount's publicity department worked overtime to report every detail of the couple's plans. The wedding date was set for the following February 23 at the Church of the Good Shepherd in Beverly Hills. Hal Wallis would put a yacht at their disposal for the honeymoon. The official engagement portrait was shot by Bud Fraker. Bridesmaids and groomsmen were chosen. Friends gave parties. People had opinions.

Mom wasn't keen on my marrying Don, but her attitude had less to do with Don than with her hope that I could somehow avoid her errors in the marital ring by waiting a few more years. Mr. Wallis thought I should marry Don, though he added, in typical Hollywood style, "If it doesn't work out, you just get divorced." Paul Nathan thought Don wasn't right for me. He was sure it was a bad choice. The news that I was venturing into the state of marital bliss while continuing in the

171

glamorous world of the movies prompted Father Sal to warn me that I "should remember the dictates of the Baltimore Catechism, take up knitting and be resigned to growing fat at home." My professional friends didn't know Don well; they thought he cut a good-looking figure and seemed solid. Most of my close friends were all for the marriage, though years later some would confess that they didn't really think it would happen.

Count me in the group that thought it wouldn't happen. Dolores invited me for lunch at Villa Frascati. She wanted to tell me herself about the engagement. The lunch was pleasant, and she was a knockout in very smart couture. We talked about her work, and her perceptive analysis of *Lisa* in particular left no doubt that she now knew a great deal more about her craft. Her report of the big event, on the other hand, was like a press release about the perfect wedding—all peripheral, no center. As I drove back to my office, I remember consoling myself that she was not going to marry Don Robinson.

Granny was downright sceptical—and prophetic. "Don't marry a man because you want to live with him", she warned. "Marry him because you can't live without him." I would come to realize that, though I loved Don, the only thing I could not live without was my religion.

Everything began moving at an overwhelming pace. In mid-November Don bought a house for us on Benedict Canyon and moved in. Wait a minute, I thought, we were going to be engaged for six months and then decide if we were committed to each other. But maybe, I hoped, this is good, this is the way it should be; go with it. I would go over to the house and try to relax. I would wash my hair and let it dry in the sun while Don cooked dinner. Don could cook; I could make cold bean salad. But at the house I was forced to face decisions about furnishings and decorating. I began to feel like Alice falling down the rabbit hole.

Edith Head invited me to lunch in the commissary to tell me that, as her gift, she was designing the wedding dress, which she was going to make from a bolt of antique Spanish lace she had been hoarding for years. She showed it to me, and it was exquisite. "I'll tell you something, Junior," she said, peering through her outsize horn-rims, "if you have any thoughts of changing your mind, you better do it before I make the first cut."

172

Four generations of Bowen women. I'm in my grandmother Esther Kude's lap, with great-grandmother Nellie Bowen next to us. My mother, Harriett Pittman Hicks, at the top.

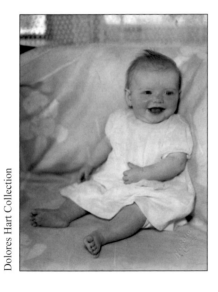

Dolores Marie Hicks ("Punkin" to Daddy) at seven months

I wasn't unhappy about the toothless look. I thought it made me look like Granny.

*Mommy and Daddy loved the sun whether at the beach or in the backyard.
They loved being tan. I was always fully clothed because I sunburned easily.*

Mommy and her shadow

A portrait of Daddy and Mommy and me at the time we all thought Daddy was going to be a movie star. He sure looked like one. And Mommy did too.

At St. Gregory School in Chicago, Sister Celine suggested I learn to play a musical instrument. I wanted to play the harp. Grandpa favored the clarinet because it was easier to carry.

At the age of nine, with Grandpa, in my First Communion dress. We're in the cemetery where Grandpa got me my first job— washing tombstones!

At St. Francis de Sales School, I was the pitcher (far right) on the girls' softball team. But I couldn't catch to save my soul.

With Chicago pets, parakeets Timmy and Tico, at Granny and Grandpa's house

My second family with Mom: "Pop" Al Gordon and my step-brother, Martin, at our home in Sherman Oaks

The poster for Loyola University's production of Joan of Lorraine

The photograph taken by Don Barbeau that led to my interview with Hal Wallis at Paramount Pictures

This photograph was passed out to the press when I was introduced to them as Susan Hart—"the girl other girls will hate" (because I was going to kiss Elvis Presley in Loving You*).*

*Our wonderful director, kind, helpful
and funny Hal Kanter, shows Elvis how.*

*At the end of the day,
Elvis escorts a lady
in true Southern-
gentleman style.*

My true mentor at Paramount, Mr. Wallis' associate producer, Paul Nathan, was responsible for getting me cast in Wild Is the Wind, *an important career-building film, for my second movie.*

Paramount costume designer Edith Head nicknamed me Junior and loved the clothes Mom made for me so much that she designed my wardrobe for Loving You *in similar fashion.*

I did a lot of magazine assignments, some pretty silly, for the Paramount publicity department. This is one I wouldn't want to repeat even for ready money: I had to wait in movie house lobbies all over town and when Loving You *was over climb the staircases and sign autographs for audience members. Then I would move on to the next movie house and do the same. (Oh, my aching feet.)*

*I liked the fashion layouts and even
drew huge sketches for one of them
as a backdrop.*

*I also enjoyed "home sittings",
especially when I could get some
of my buddies involved, such as
Valerie Allen, Jan Shepard and
Ray Boyle.*

*Another "home sitting"
photo (I did a lot of those):
My beautiful Duke made
his professional debut in a
bathtub.*

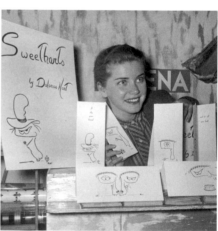

*Some promotion for my moonlighting
career: hawking Sweetharts greeting
cards at a gift show.*

With my boss Hal Wallis on the set of Wild Is the Wind. *I drew this caricature of him—and he didn't fire me.*

*With Dick DeNeut at
the beginning of our
relationship. We had
just started dating.
Our bond has lasted
over fifty years.*

A dramatic moment from Wild Is the Wind *with Anthony Quinn,
a consummate actor, an inspired teacher and a loving friend*

On the Carson City, Nevada, location for Wild Is the Wind *with Anna Magnani, an actress I was in awe of, and the two Tonys (Quinn and Franciosa)*

Granny and Grandpa came out from Chicago for the premiere of Wild Is the Wind. *Granny took it in stride, but I had never seen Grandpa so proud.*

A publicity photo for King Creole, *my second movie with Elvis. True, it was a much darker film than* Loving You, *but this situation is not in it. It was strictly for promotion.*

Elvis was a surprise guest at the birthday party I threw for my friend Jan Shepard at the Hazeltine house. Yes, he brought his guitar, but that's actor Ty Hardin playing it.

Valerie Allen and I wish Elvis good luck at the studio farewell party before he left for military service. While he was gone, I hosted some screenings of our movies for his fans.

*I was thrilled to work with "the lady", Myrna Loy, one of my all-time
favorite actresses. She let me draw a caricature of her. We were with our
producer, Dore Schary, on the set of* Lonelyhearts.

Listening (as usual) to Monty Clift between scenes. I waited and waited for him to share tales of his experiences on Broadway, but he never did.

At Myrna Loy's suggestion, I started going to rushes with the cast, which included a Broadway actress I came to like very much, Maureen Stapleton. Maureen made her movie debut in Lonelyhearts *and got an Oscar nomination.*

The Pleasure of His Company *cast on Broadway's Longacre stage*

With my stage mother, Cornelia Otis Skinner, a grand, majestic lady with a sense of humor who did, in fact, remind me a little of my own mother

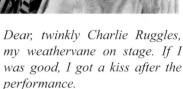

Dear, twinkly Charlie Ruggles, my weathervane on stage. If I was good, I got a kiss after the performance.

George Peppard and I made our Broadway debuts in Pleasure. *He was a fine actor but an incorrigible prankster. I had to take him to task a couple of times.*

Pogo was my constant companion in New York. I took him everywhere, including to the theater, where he watched me put on my makeup in the dressing room.

With my New York roommate and dear friend, Winnie Allen, on her wedding day. I couldn't be her maid of honor because of a performance, but I managed to drive upstate in the morning so that I could see her in her wedding dress.

Globe Photos

My first movie when I returned to Hollywood after a year on Broadway was The Plunderers, *a Western. I had to shoot John Saxon—in the back!*

Dolores Hart Collection

Daddy made his first-ever visit to watch me work during the production of The Plunderers.

Playhouse 90 *rescued me from the doldrums and got my movie career going again. "To the Sound of Trumpets" was aired live (and teamed me with Stephen Boyd for the first time).*

Where the Boys Are *was a stroke of luck career-wise. It was MGM's highest grossing movie for 1960, and, as I wrote Granny, it never hurts to have your name connected with money. Equally surprising was the bond that resulted with my costars Connie Francis, Yvette Mimieux and Paula Prentiss— a little unusual among actresses in Hollywood. (After all these years I'm still in touch with Connie and Paula.)*

I had a new beau in the new decade. Don Robinson and I met on a blind date arranged by friends. A year later we were engaged.

Having never been outside the United States, I wanted very much to do Francis of Assisi *because of its Italian location. I played Saint Clare to Brad Dillman's Saint Francis, and we became lifelong friends.*

The Investiture scene in Francis *later raised a lot of queries about how it might have influenced my decision to become a religious. It didn't.*

Before Francis *started, I had a holiday in London with the Cooper family—Gary, Rocky and Maria. Here we are at the Earl of Dudley's estate.*

My next movie was a change of pace—the wacky Sail a Crooked Ship *with Carolyn Jones, Robert Wagner, Frank Gorshin and, my favorite, the irrepressible and irresistible Ernie Kovacs (here in a personal photo that I treasure).*

Lisa, *a suspense drama about a Dutch secret police officer and the Jewish concentration camp survivor he smuggles into Palestine, reunited me with Stephen Boyd—and put me in the company of a virtual Who's Who of the finest European actors.*

Mom visited the location for the concentration camp sequence in Lisa. *She said I looked like the way she felt on her "mornings after".*

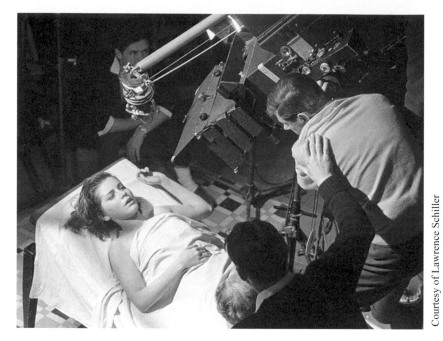

The scene of Lisa's re-creation of the experiments performed on her in the concentration camp was harrowing to do and was shot in one take. Our cinematographer, Arthur Ibbetson, equipped his camera with a special close-up lens, which meant the camera was placed only twenty-one inches from my face. Lisa *is my personal favorite of the films I made.*

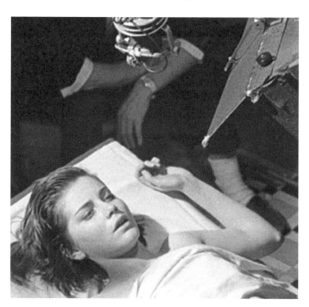

The official engagement photo of Don Robinson and me was shot by Paramount's top portrait photographer Bud Fraker.

Come Fly with Me *was the latest addition to a familiar Hollyood staple, the story of three girls in search of love and security, but it was a well-produced and gorgeously filmed travelogue of our European locations. It had one of my favorite casts including Lois Nettleton, Pamela Tiffin and my beloved Karl Malden. It was my last film.*

A second portrait of the Bowen girls—Granny Kude, great-grandmother Nellie Bowen and Mom—the three women who made me what I am. This was taken several months before my entrance into Regina Laudis. I was holding a secret.

Portraits capturing my evolution from teenager to twenty-four-year-old glamor girl

L'Osservatore Romano Photo Service

Earl Holliman and I were the guests of Monsignor William A. Carew (to my right) at the audience with Pope John XXIII in the Hall of Benediction. This was the moment when, just as the pope passed by us, his slipper fell to the floor and Monsignor Carew took advantage of the interruption while the slipper was retrieved to introduce me as the American film actress portraying Saint Clare in the film on the life of Saint Francis. His Holiness smiled and took my hand and called me "Chiara". I've been asked if his calling me "Chiara" might have influenced my decision to enter religious life. Who can tell?

Daddy invited us to an engagement dinner at the San Fernando Valley home he shared with his fourth wife, Liliana, the Italian woman who had been nanny for the Lanza children. I remembered meeting her at Uncle Mario's funeral and thought she was very sweet. Liliana was now expecting my half-brother.

The evening was a disaster. I had expected an intimate family dinner, but the house was filled with people I didn't know. I soon realized that I had been invited, not as a daughter, but as a movie star on display. Daddy was three sheets to the wind when we arrived and got drunker as the evening progressed, playing "lord of the manor" with phony bravado, even shoving a cigar in Don's face. Don rolled with the punches, but Liliana, who had prepared a lovely dinner, was embarrassed. I was offended. Don and I left as soon as we could. It was the last time I would see my father.

I moved through the days like an actor who forgot to study his lines and finds himself on stage in a spotlight. There were times when I didn't talk to anybody. Whenever I could, I would escape. I sometimes got into my car, as I had when I was a teenager, and just drove somewhere, anywhere I could to remove myself physically from the turmoil I perceived as my life. One day I decided to drive to Santa Barbara.

I needed so much to be alone that even a gloomy sky couldn't deter me from the trip. I sat on the beach for most of the day, oblivious to the storm clouds that were gathering, when suddenly there was a hand on my shoulder. I turned to see an older man smiling down at me. He and his wife had noticed me on the beach and became concerned. There was quite a rainstorm coming, he said, and they wondered if I had any shelter. If not, he said, I should wait it out at their house. The invitation was punctuated by the first drops of rain, and I took refuge in the home of Mr. and Mrs. Monte Healy just as the downpour arrived. It worsened into the night, which I spent, warm and protected, in the bedroom of the Healys' daughter, who was away at school. The next morning, refreshed by their kindness, I drove back to LA.

Within a week I was back in Santa Barbara, this time with Don, for Sheila and Bob McGuire's anniversary party at her father's home. After a gorgeous California afternoon with a barbecue on the patio, the evening sun going down over the Pacific created a perfect setting for young people, very romantic. Yet, I was ill at ease; I felt I was suffo-cating. I remember feigning a headache and retiring to a bedroom to rest. In the room, I caught my reflection in a mirror and remembered the incident in the dressing room. "This is not what you want to do." I thought I had made up my mind! At that moment, I put my life in God's hands and waited for lightning to strike.

Don had a clear memory of the night his parents hosted an engage-ment party in their home: "Dolores was distant from the minute I picked her up, and during the entire party I never felt she was truly with me. On the drive back to her apartment, I suddenly stopped in the middle of the street and asked her if she loved me."

I said, "Of course I do." He repeated the question, and again I answered, "Of course I do", but clearly it wasn't enough. "Then what is wrong?" he demanded. Obviously the effort to hide my feelings of discontent and desperation wasn't accomplishing anything except drain-ing me and hurting Don. He said he felt as if he were sitting on a fence, and he just couldn't sit there any longer. He thought we should make an announcement of a postponement right away. I agreed, though I knew I could not stand up under any media scrutiny that that kind of item would provoke.

"You're still thinking about the monastery, aren't you?" he asked, and without waiting for an answer he added, "Dolores, I think you have to go back there and get everything straightened out in your mind."

I could not get to sleep that night. It was one o'clock in the morning when I made reservations on the day's first flight to the East Coast. En route to the monastery, I was held by a kind of madness that I could not express. I say "madness" because there was no way I could intellectu-ally explain the hound that yapped at my heels. There was no earthly reason why I was shunning the life I wanted most—only that Regina Laudis had gradually seeped through my body like some mysterious liquor and I was at peace only on its taste.

Arriving back at the monastery was one of the strangest experiences. At first, I felt completely foreign. Los Angeles in January is warm and sunny. Everything here was cold and white. As the day drew itself

174

together, things settled down into a familiar framework, and finally a tiny sense of comfort began to fill the picture.

My visit coincided with Reverend Mother Benedict's twenty-fifth Jubilee—the twenty-fifth anniversary of her First Vows. There was an atmosphere of activity that surrounded me, as if the impact of her years with God had swelled up into a crescendo and its sound burst out from every heart, including mine. But the days changed. One day would pass smoothly, unstained by tears. The next would plunge me into despair.

During the entire visit, not once did I feel pressured by Reverend Mother to make up my mind. To the contrary, I was constantly being told, "Do what you want to do." It was maddening that I was the one left with the decision. I would have felt happy if someone would have taken that task away from me.

On my last morning, at Mass, I was handed a folded note from Mother Placid: "You can ask for me anytime if you want. However, I will expect you to spend the day quietly with Christ and our Lady in prayer, and in relaxed recollection, trying to present yourself and the problem to them alone."

It was cold that day. There had been a snowstorm during the night, creating a world of white, blessed with a glorious stillness. I bundled myself up against the light snow that was falling and left Saint Gregory's. I just began walking—to no place in particular. And, for no particular reason, I took my camera. I walked in the snow through the fields and up through the pine forest, to the top of the hill overlooking the monastery. I sensed I was in a sacred place, in union with a higher call, expectant that I would hear the voice of God direct me. I stayed there all afternoon and wept my heart out over the jumble that filled my head.

I was on the threshold of a career I had dreamed about. I couldn't imagine what it would do to everybody if I said, "Yes, I have a religious vocation." I had just signed a new contract with Mr. Wallis, and he would certainly be furious with me. Wedding invitations were printed. We had the house, and I had written Granny and Grandma Bowen, inviting them to come and stay there while Don and I were on our honeymoon. Edith was poised to make that first cut.

175

Oh, this could not be real! I just could not believe that God could possibly be asking me to give up all that was waiting for me in California. All He would have to do is tell me. But there was only silence.

As I started back down the hill, I felt suddenly and strangely relieved. I paused a moment, took out my camera, turned and shot a picture of the snow-covered hill and continued down to Saint Gregory's. Back in my room, I wrote a letter.

My Dearest One,

This morning I walked through the fields in the snow and the cold and called Your name. You refused to show even a part of Yourself or allow me to hear Your voice. I could hear only the echo of snowflakes touching the branches of the trees. I could not see You or hear Your voice, and my heart ached from the need. You want me for Yourself—this I know without any doubt, but how—how—in what way can I—the person You, my Dear One, have created—give You my heart and soul? I can't understand Your ways, if this is love! I stood in the clearing and silently shouted—and played the best scene I've ever played. I played to You and to the trees and the birds and the sky, the snow and the earth—to everything that is. I'll never forget that moment as long as I live. No actor ever shared such a moment with his audience.

Later Dolores met with Reverend Mother Benedict. She spoke of her walk and finding herself at the crest of the hill and standing still, not knowing why she was there. The founder of the monastery told her that years before, in 1947, when she and Mother Mary Aline came to Bethlehem with the mission to found a Benedictine order, they stood at that same place, holding medals they had carried from France. They buried those medals beneath the ground Dolores had stood upon and photographed.

"What is it that you want?" Reverend Mother asked me.

I told her that was what I was trying to find out. I said, "I want my career. I want to get married. I want to have a home. I want most of all to do the will of God." I think I hoped that she would not accept me but just say again that I should go back to Hollywood.

176

"I can't tell you what the will of God is", she said. "You must decide what you want to do, and in your deepest desire you will find the will of God. What is it that you want?"

Again I said, "I want my career. I want to marry. I want to please God and to serve Him with all my heart."

"You will find the will of God when you find what it is in your own heart that you know you must do", she repeated. "Don't look for God in some abstraction. The answer comes from within yourself, Dolores. What is it that you want?"

In his Rule, Saint Benedict cautions against granting newcomers to monastic life an easy entry. A pilgrim must knock on the door three times to be recognized.

When I got back to my room I began packing. I felt the decision had been made for me. God had not spoken. Reverend Mother had not invited me in. I was going home to pick up my life, and I was very relieved to have the whole thing off my back.

That evening I went to supper in the refectory. Mother Placid was serving. She smiled and said, "Well, Dolores, you won't be able to chew gum when you come in." I hadn't realized I was chewing gum. We both laughed.

"But I'm not entering", I told her.

"Oh," she said surprised, "Reverend Mother said you were. She said it was clear that you had a monastic calling because you were fighting so hard. I'll let her know she was mistaken."

She turned to leave, and I suddenly stopped her, "No, don't."

That was it. My answer didn't come in a lightning bolt. I simply knew at that moment what Reverend Mother was trying to tell me when she insisted that I say what I wanted to do. If I was honest about my answer, I would give God a point of departure He could work with. This is the exact opposite of the way many people think the spiritual life proceeds.

Back in Los Angeles, when her photos were developed, the one she had taken after wrestling with her decision, the one of the hill and its snow-laden trees that she turned around to shoot as she was leaving, was nowhere to be found. Instead, there was a photo of only her own footprints in the snow.

Eighteen

When Don met Dolores at LAX, he was in good spirits. Nothing in Dolores' letters from the monastery indicated he would not have a fiancée when she returned.

When he saw her, however, his mood changed. "She looked like a refugee, pale and drawn, no makeup, and her hair wasn't even fixed. We stopped at a steak house near the airport. It was packed, and we were seated smack in the middle of the room."

Dolores hadn't planned on telling Don her decision that evening, and she tried to keep up a conversation that, before long, gave way to silence. Don remembered, "I began thinking, 'Where are we heading?' I finally asked point-blank if she was entering the monastery."

Don's perception was so strong that I knew I couldn't put it off. I told him I was.

"I just fell apart," Don said, "right in the middle of the packed room."

We resolved that we had to see Monsignor Devlin right away. Monsignor was the pastor of our parish who was to officiate at the wedding. He couldn't understand why, after four months of our engagement, I would suddenly change my mind. He almost hit the floor when I told him that I planned to enter monastic life. He obviously didn't believe me.

"There is an aura of flightiness about Hollywood", he warned and, citing the movie actress June Haver, moved in for the kill. "Catholic actresses are prone to do things like this for publicity."

I didn't know June Haver then but was aware that, in 1952, she had walked out on her movie contract and entered a convent, only to leave a few months later. I held my tongue and merely assured him I wasn't looking for publicity, but he went on.

178

"So you think you want to be a contemplative. You know what contemplative life is all about?"

"I think so", I answered. "I've been there a number of times."

"You know they work with their hands? They garden. Do you garden?"

"No."

"They cook. Do you cook? They sew. Do you sew?"

"No."

"They have a life that is quiet, austere. They live in silence. They don't talk on the phone. They don't travel. They do without modern conveniences." He gave an exasperated sigh and turned to Don. "Not only do I not recommend this girl to the contemplative life; I don't know why you want to marry her."

"Dolores," he said sternly, "you must think this over for a long, long time. It's too big a step right now. I think you should see the archbishop as soon as possible. It's more than I can handle."

When we left Monsignor Devlin, I told Don I was not going to see the archbishop. I couldn't go through that again.

"It tore me apart at the time," Don said, "but, even then, deep down, I could see the other side. Having the background of religious vocations in my life, with friends who had entered the Jesuit Order, who had struggled with their vocations, I think I could understand. I felt that if I loved Dolores, I had to show her my support, whatever she was going to do."

I think that if Don had not been so blessed—I really mean that because he was given a great grace to stand behind me—my decision would have been even more devastating.

"The next weeks were a difficult time for both of us", Don remembered. "We went through the motions. We talked on the phone but did not see each other much. She got on with her life. I got on with mine."

Mom was disappointed when I told her the engagement was off, though underneath I think she was relieved. I decided not to tell her about my decision to enter religious life at that time. I wasn't sure what she might do, and I just couldn't face whatever that might be. I was also afraid that she would call Granny. No way did I want to fight both of

179

them. Mom might start drinking and getting ugly about it, but Granny would fling her body between me and the monastery gate. I knew I would have to face that situation eventually, but as the days passed I kept putting it off.

Don told his mother the whole story, and she was very shaken. She had known when we had the appointment with Monsignor Devlin that something was wrong, but the reality shocked her. I think it affected her more than anybody. She scalded me with her anger.

The only friends Dolores told immediately about ending the engagement were the ones involved in the wedding: her bridesmaids Sheila Hart McGuire, Jan Shepard and the Malden girls, Mila and Carla—and she wasn't completely honest with them. She couldn't risk even a hint about Regina Laudis because Reverend Mother Benedict had made secrecy a condition of her acceptance.

Frank Liberman set up only one interview—with Louella Parsons—to get the word out about the end of the engagement. The official story was that Dolores believed marriage should be a total commitment, and when she realized that she wasn't ready to make that complete a commitment, she felt the only fair thing to both Don and herself was to call off the engagement.

The first order of business was filling out the Regina Laudis application form—yes, an application form very much like the ones I filled out for employment when I was a teenager.

> *—Except Ralph's Market hadn't asked me for my baptism and confirmation certificates.*

All the things that might be problematic in beginning monastic life were actually covered in the application, but they didn't appear as dire warnings. It didn't say: Are you aware that you will have to work under absolute supervision without questioning or that you will not be able to speak to your coworkers? Rather, it quietly asked if you had been able to do certain things.

180

The five-page form included inquiries into her family background, health history, education and past employment, with emphasis on her work ethic:

Do you find it easy, moderately easy, hard, moderately hard to take orders, suggestions, contradictions, criticism and complaints from coworkers?

Moderately easy and moderately hard, depending upon circumstances.

Do you find it easy, moderately easy, hard, moderately hard to take orders, suggestions, contradictions, corrections, criticism and complaints from your employer?

Moderately easy and moderately hard. In my work my employer's suggestions and criticisms were often contrary to my temperament, and occasionally my convictions had to stand the test of a clash. I therefore had to become overly independent in my thinking.

How do you find taking orders, suggestions, contradictions, corrections, criticism and complaints from your subordinates?

Easy to take suggestions. Hard to take orders. I find it extremely difficult to take any complaint or criticism from someone whom I have tried to please, and I find my pride stands in my way when I know I am right.

—You can't say they weren't forewarned.

I just wanted to present as honest a picture as I could. I felt deeply that they had every right to know the truth before accepting someone into their house. I insisted that they be aware that I had adapted myself from childhood in the art of disguising true feelings as a protective barrier and feared that this instinct probably couldn't be erased spontaneously. So, I suppose it was a warning. But it was also a plea: Don't wait until I'm inside with no defenses and then decide you don't want what you're getting.

Dolores' answers also revealed that she was nearsighted, had no notable debts and could provide the dowry required then by Canon Law as well as her trousseau. Dowries are no longer required at Regina Laudis, but at the time Dolores entered the usual amount was roughly $2,000, which was calculated as the legitimate need for any one person. Dolores would turn over $20,000 as her dowry.

181

One question sought to determine if she wished to enter as a choir sister aspirant or an oblate sister aspirant. The distinction was an ancient one and firmly based in the European class system. The choir sister came with a background of wealth, and her sizable dowry supported the monastery and added to her family's prestige. She was also usually educated and could therefore read the books necessary to sing the Offices. Historically, the oblate sister was usually an older woman from a poor or peasant background that automatically excluded her from certain activities. The oblates were not obliged to sing or even to attend every Office and performed mostly manual labor. They were the only ones allowed to go in and out of the enclosure, to do errands and to serve guests.

> —*This system continued for a long time until it reached the point of perversion. Choir nuns could sit around all day having tea and doing petit point while the others did all the hard work.*

Regina Laudis never observed the distinction between choir and oblate sisters in its full demeaning implication. Still, since the oblate sister did not participate in chapter meetings, at which important decisions regarding the life of the Community were made, the feeling of "second class" remained. Thus, from the late 1960s, there has been but one class of nun with two "accents" of call. These accents are known as "enclosed" and "*missae*", which comes from the Latin word meaning "sent". Within the present understanding, the missae are women who have a gift for being the Community's interface with the world and thus are "missioned".

At the time Dolores entered, the age of the applicant determined her position. Being under the age of thirty meant she would be a choir nun.

In addition to my age, another reason Reverend Mother Benedict decided that I would be a choir nun was because, as such, I could not even casually come in contact with the media. I responded to the questionnaire that I had a strong, but not loud, singing voice—second soprano—and that my background in Latin was limited to one high school course. But I promised that I would apply myself to the study of Latin during my novitiate.

❧

182

On the surface, her life in Hollywood appeared to be status quo, close to what it might have been if she didn't have that decision hanging over her. She continued to fulfill every commitment she had made with the studios and, at the same time, immersed herself in the exhausting details of closing her life in California. Her lawyer, Sidney Williams, who was to have walked her down the aisle at her wedding, organized legal matters, including her dowry to Regina Laudis and a trust for Harriett. He also orchestrated the termination of her lease, while Dolores disposed of the apartment's contents.

She took a few days in January for the first of two pre-entrance retreats at the monastery, with Mothers Columba and Placid and now Mother Anselm, the mistress of novices, who would be her formation mother during her postulancy. Mother Anselm was one of the group of nuns from the Abbey of Jouarre.

I met a young woman, Catherine Nugent, a guest in Saint Gregory's. Catherine was a researcher at the Center for Naval Analyses in Washington, DC. She also was considering the possibility of a religious vocation at Regina Laudis, and when I learned she not only was fluent in Latin but had even taught it, I said a few prayers for her to reach an affirmative decision.

> *—In 1965, she did enter the monastery and is now Mother Maria Nugent, our dean of liturgy. And she has been, on occasion, my Latin tutor.*

Back in Los Angeles, it was a hectic time—yet delicate. I felt constantly out of breath from all the juggling. I didn't see much of Don. I wasn't avoiding him; I just had much to do. I had little time to see friends, and when I did see them, I had to be mindful of how little I could share with them. I was so absorbed in preparing for the monastery that my heart was hardly able to contain anything else. It was the only thing I thought of, and it was the one thing I couldn't speak about.

Besides her lawyer, only four friends were privy to Dolores' decision: Maria, Winnie, Suzanne Zada and Valerie Imbleau, the young woman who had been the technical consultant on *Come Fly with Me*. Valerie had earlier relocated to New York, begun a new career as a photographer and revived her friendship with Dolores. She had even accompanied Dolores on a visit to Regina Laudis.

Maria remembered, "I felt her call deeply. We had spoken of it metaphorically as hanging on to a branch of a tree, letting go one finger at a time. As long as she had one finger on the branch, she hadn't let go completely. I knew at some moment a decision had to be made to keep holding or finally to let go." Winnie was not surprised either; she had been aware of Dolores' visits to the monastery. "I felt her decision was thoughtfully made over a period of time," Winnie said, "and I was proud of her daring to run toward a genuine calling."

Valerie felt Dolores' call on a profoundly personal level. Val was seriously considering entering religious life herself.

Suzanne Zada, however, was aghast. "It was horrible that she was giving up a life that had so much promise. She was in full blossom, and to dig a hole and go into a monastery where she could be seen only through a grille—to me that was horrible. I looked upon the nuns at Regina Laudis as the enemy."

> —*Monastic life is a difficult and mysterious concept for many people and conjures up frightening images of austerity and isolation. I would come to hear over and over the concern that I had not chosen a more active life in the Church—teaching, nursing, social service. But I had thought of these only fitfully. There were areas of the active life that I found distracting and personally insufficient for my aims. I was choosing a contemplative life because of a desire to seek God in a pure and direct way and because of an instinct that I could neither define nor explain, except to say that it was the Spirit of God pressing me to find Him—and Regina Laudis was the way.*

It was decided that "D-day"—the date for my entrance—would be June 13, 1963. That would give me less than six months to close down one life and prepare for another.

—Your cloak-and-dagger period.

Don't laugh. I probably would have made a good CIA agent.

184

"Scripts and offers were being received with a regularity that should have put Dolores on cloud nine," recalled Harry Bernsen, "but she kept putting everything off. I couldn't understand why she was behaving that way. Just a few months earlier she had been ecstatic about the way the career was going." Harry had four scripts from MGM alone. Joe Pasternak sent two scripts for comedies boasting major directors: *A Ticklish Affair* directed by George Sidney and *The Courtship of Eddie's Father* directed by Vincente Minnelli (Shirley Jones got both roles). Boris Sagal was interested in her for *Twilight of Honor* (Yvette Mimieux was cast). And Henry Levin was still waiting for her to sign on for *Honeymoon Hotel*. Although Harry had no scripts on his desk from Twentieth Century-Fox at that moment, Dolores still owed that studio a third movie on her three-picture deal.

Robert Rossen asked her to test for the title character opposite Warren Beatty in *Lilith*. He thought Dolores' natural girl-next-door quality would make for an intriguing contrast with the character of a young schizophrenic in a New England sanatorium. Harry urged her to do the test for Rossen, but she asked him to beg off for her (Rossen's other choice for the role, Jean Seberg, was cast).

Hal Wallis changed his mind again. Instead of casting her in *A Girl Named Tamiko*, he decided to loan her to Universal Pictures for the romantic comedy *King of the Mountain* opposite Marlon Brando and David Niven. Its release title was *Bedtime Story*, but it didn't ring any bells until it was remade in 1988 as *Dirty Rotten Scoundrels* and later musicalized for Broadway. That offer carried a deal for two additional films that would have given Dolores multiple-picture commitments with three major studios plus Hal Wallis, who had drawn up a new contract giving him a picture a year for four years and put Dolores in line for a pay raise to $7,000 a week.

I knew I was creating chaos, but I didn't know what to do. I didn't know what to tell Harry, or anyone in the business for that matter— certainly not the truth. Harry was under pressure and in a constant state of frustration. I knew the agency was going to be furious and not only over lost commissions. I could make them look foolish by letting them negotiate commitments that I wasn't going to fulfill.

185

But how could I sign those contracts? I couldn't tell the truth because I hadn't yet been officially accepted into the monastery; I would have been burning bridges behind and in front of me. Professionally, I was walking a very precarious tightrope. How I wished I had the security of knowing the thing was going to happen. No one was telling me, go ahead; this is right! Or no, it's not to be; hold on to your day job.

The only one I could unburden my heart to was, of course, Maria. I must have written her every other day. I told her I had to know that if everything fell through, and I was in the poorhouse instead of the monastery, she would bring me an ice cream cake—with a file in it. I was also speaking pretty regularly with her father during my prayers, asking him to advise me or, if he already had influence upstairs, to put Someone Else on my case.

Even though she had no intention of doing the Brando film, in order to quell any suspicions at the agency she did keep an appointment with Larry Germain, the hairstylist at Universal, for preliminary wig fittings. Jan Shepard went to the studio with her, and afterward the girls stopped at nearby Du-par's restaurant. There, over hot-fudge sundaes, Dolores confided that she wasn't going to do the film.

"I couldn't believe it when she said she was turning down a costarring role with Marlon Brando", Jan related. "I thought she had gone off the deep end. I asked her why, and she answered, 'Because I'm getting married.'

"Well, knowing the engagement with Don was off, I asked Dolores whom she was marrying. She said, 'Christ.' It was then she told me about her visits to the monastery and that she had found there what she had long been searching for. She also swore me to secrecy. I didn't even tell my husband."

Without giving any explanation, Dolores asked Harry to put everyone off as long as he could—which he reluctantly did. The agents were having a tough time buying her vague references to "personal reasons", but the head honcho, Phil Gersh, was sympathetic. In his best fatherly manner, he told her that the agency would give her a hiatus from professional involvements and slow down on drumming up activity in the business—stop the pressure but remain behind her with no questions asked. Gersh told me many years later that he thought that Dolores was going through a severe depression over the breakup but that he and Harry were confident that she was on the threshold of becoming a major star.

There was one offer Harry had that I could do. It was a segment on the filmed TV series The Virginian, *which would take only a week. It was the least I could do for all of Harry's efforts on my behalf, and the timing couldn't have been better. The show was the perfect answer to the disorder in my life, and the role so undemanding that I could have phoned it in.*

Shooting began the week of February 23, 1963. February 23 had been the date for the wedding. I wrote to Mother Columba,

> *Wow, I really don't know how the people on the series maintain their sanity. We don't finish shooting until 7:30 or 8 at night, and by the time I get home and study the dialogue for the next day, it is past 11, and up again at 5:30. The routine at Regina Laudis will seem easy in comparison— well, I can dream, can't I? By the way, James Drury, our leading man, got an attack of the flu yesterday right after our love scene. Couldn't help but think it was the Regina Laudis bug and he didn't even know it.*

It was necessary for me to get the approval of my parish priest to be eligible for acceptance into the monastery. Monsignor Devlin had left no doubt that he would reject that request. When I advised Reverend Mother that I was empty-handed as far as approval was concerned, she felt my best course of action would be to get permission from the Archdiocese of Hartford on my next trip east, using the monastery address as my residence. Mother Columba wrote to the archbishop of Hartford and received an appointment for me to meet him at the end of the month.

—It was the right time. I had just found a gray hair, which I took as a sure sign of a vocation to monastic life.

I had agreed to go out on the road for a twelve-city personal appearance tour for Come Fly with Me, *and I hoped staying out of Hollywood for a few weeks would contribute to my disappearing act. I arranged to have some time off during the trip in order to spend the few days on retreat and sneak up to Hartford. In anticipation, I packed an extra*

suitcase with country clothes I would need in Connecticut and sent it
ahead to the monastery to keep Sonia Wolfson, the publicity woman on
the tour, from wondering about my two wardrobes. I felt guilty about
hiding something from Sonia, who had become a good friend and, as a
press agent, always seemed to go that extra mile for me.

We hit three cities a day, doing radio and TV spots, newspaper
interviews and autograph sessions before climbing back into a plane for
the next stop. I was relieved to have gotten through each day without
any serious gaffes. Whenever someone backed me into a corner about
my plans, I would mention that I would like to take some time off in the
south of France. This was usually interpreted as my wanting to get "a
breath of fresh air" after the broken engagement. I did nothing to
correct the misconception and even began to have a little fun with the
Q&A. If a reporter asked if I was seeing anyone new, I would admit that
there was someone in my life. It was then assumed I was getting
married, and I couldn't honestly deny it. Once, I was asked if my
intended was wealthy. Oh, yes, I said, very rich.

MGM gave Dolores time off when she finished the Chicago leg of the
tour. As always when she was in Chicago, she used her hotel room for
interviews but stayed with her grandmother. All through the visit, Dolores
was gleeful about the roaring success of the *Come Fly with Me* preview.
The studio, she told Granny, felt it was going to be very successful
commercially—good news, she confided, for it never hurt to have her
name associated with money, and she hadn't had a hit since *Where the
Boys Are*. She coolly chattered on about having to be careful to choose the
right projects and not just take whatever was offered—with full knowledge that *Come Fly with Me* was going to be her last film.

Her New York agent unintentionally abetted her ruse when he tracked
her down in Chicago to tell her he had two possibilities for a return to
Broadway. One was a comedy entitled *Cloris*, and the other was a
revival of *John Brown's Body*, Stephen Vincent Benét's narrative poem
of the Civil War that had been a success on Broadway ten years earlier
with Tyrone Power, Judith Anderson and Raymond Massey. The director, Lloyd Richards, wanted to meet Dolores about appearing in his
restaging of the piece.

It was the perfect excuse! I would go to Connecticut via New York City. I told the agent that I didn't think I would be available for a play, though I did confess that I was planning on a little getaway for a day or two and needed an alibi. Bless him, he thought I was having a clandestine affair and said not to worry, he would take care of it. MGM gave me the use of a car and driver to take me to see "friends in Connecticut".

First stop was the monastery, where I finally got Reverend Mother Benedict's official invitation to enter—on the condition of Archbishop Henry O'Brien's approval. The friendly but clueless MGM driver was happy to take me to Hartford and didn't bother to check with the studio first. During the trip, I had but one thought in my head: if I've come this far, turned down so much, gotten rid of everything and spun my life upside down, and I walk into his office and he says no—oh, my God—I will be so relieved.

I waited over two hours to find I didn't have an appointment with Archbishop O'Brien, but with Monsignor Joseph Lacy, the vicar for religious. The archbishop didn't waste his time on candidates; the monsignor evaluated whether someone had a vocation.

Monsignor Lacy was somewhere in his fifties, and I thought he resembled actor Paul Douglas. From the first moment, when he asked, "Who are you again?", we hit it off beautifully. He listened sympathetically as I spoke of my family situations in Los Angeles and Chicago, my introduction to the Catholic Church through a grade school I attended primarily for convenience, my conversion at age eleven. I rattled off anything I hoped would support my quest and assured him that Mom's drinking, which I had lived with for a long time, had nothing to do with my decision about religious life.

When he was satisfied that my call was real, Monsignor Lacy said that full approval was indicated. He also cautioned me to keep my name out of the newspapers and stressed that it was an important condition. I left with high expectations, but also a hollow feeling in the pit of my stomach. I still did not have the official letter of approval.

—What do you think the specific concern of the Church was regarding all the secrecy?

189

I think it's mainly the attention, the light that is shone on a monastery when a person in the public eye enters. If that person leaves an order, there's the laughableness, which reflects upon their capacity to advise someone coming in. It indicates poor judgment. Jokes are made.

❦

Over the weeks Dolores had been absent, Harriett had slipped back into hard-drinking mode. Several times, when she was smashed, she had made calls to Regina Laudis in attempts to play private eye. Mother Placid and Mother Columba had been alarmed and thought Dolores should try to get Harriett to visit the monastery.

I thought she had chalked all my absences up to publicity commitments and didn't connect them to trips to Regina Laudis. I would occasionally call and mention that, since I was "in the neighborhood" I had gone with Valerie to the monastery for Mass, but I continued to delay confiding in Mom. As long as she was in the dark, I thought I could avoid that confrontation.

Harriett, in fact, was too close to her daughter not to have had an awareness of what was going on in Dolores' mind. She was holding on to the hope, however, that something in Dolores' career—a part that was too good to miss out on—would interfere and push any thoughts of becoming a nun into the background. She didn't know the decision had already been made.

When I returned to LA, with so much to do and so little time to do it, I found Mom in a pitiful state. In the past, I had been successful in getting her to the hospital when she needed help, but this time she wouldn't listen to my entreaties. I remember thinking that, save a miracle, she was approaching the end of the trail. I told her that Mother Columba had invited her to the monastery and that it would make me very happy to be there with her. I said it could put some of the shattered pieces of her life together.
"Yes," she said, "I want that."

190

"But for crying out loud, kiddo," I warned, "you can't come to the monastery like this."

What may have made the difference to Mom was Mother Columba's invitation, but that miracle happened because she dried herself out all alone and enthusiastically began making plans for us to take the trip together.

Approval from the Archdiocese of Hartford came, leaving only two more hurdles. A complete physical examination was necessary, and Dolores would have to make the required final retreat. She went to a new doctor for the exam, again agonizing over a possible diagnosis that would keep her from entering, yet joking to Maria that she was "considering making excessive and repeated trips to Blum's ice cream parlor to court the gout". The final retreat, set for the first two weeks in May, would leave her only a few days to close up the apartment and dispose of all her personal property.

—How did you manage to keep so focused?

I was afraid someone would stop me.

I didn't want to have to defend my decision. But, in fact, I did leave myself open for some voice of authority to tell me not to do it. I respected authority and had accepted decisions made by others. As an actress, I did movies I was assigned without question because I was under contract and did publicity I wasn't crazy about because it was part of my job. Once the decision was made for me, I made the best of it.

With each step that brought me closer to the monastery gate, I wondered if it might be the obstacle I couldn't overcome. When Monsignor Devlin said no, it won't do, part of me was relieved. During the physical examination, I wondered if the doctor would tell me I wouldn't have the strength to endure monastic life. Might Monsignor Lacy be the one to end my quest? Could Maria have told me I was making the wrong decision?

I lived those days in a dichotomy of purpose: I am afraid someone will stop me—someone please stop me.

Nineteen

God, the founder of my successes and joys, of my gaiety and love,
forsake me not in this quest that is wrought of my need for You ...
and allow me the satisfaction of only one thing—the complete and
unshakeable belief that is so necessary for all that is to follow.

—Journal entry, June 7, 1963

The slow fade-out of Dolores Hart was hardly noticed at all. Everyone
in the Industry seemed to have gotten used to not seeing me around, and
no one was asking any questions.

In May I excused myself one last time for "a breath of fresh air"—
and headed to Connecticut to make my final retreat. It was an abso-
lutely joyful two weeks because I had little fear that the hounds would
be on my trail. My previous anxieties were like so much confetti, just
blown away on the breath of a breeze. I looked upon that time, which
could have been tense and nerve-racking, as a great blessing.

The final retreat is the one during which the candidate meets the
Community council, and the council votes on whether she should be
accepted. In Dolores' time, if Reverend Mother Benedict said yes,
acceptance was a sure thing, and she had already said yes.

The candidate also meets with the zelatrix, the nun who will help her
with personal needs through the days of postulancy, and the mistress of
novices, who has canonical responsibility for religious development and
growth. The mistress of novices was Mother Anselm Beaumont, one of
the original French nuns who came from the Abbey of Jouarre.

It is also usual for the candidate to meet other novices in residence.
In Dolores' case, however, this did not happen. Mother Columba, ever
vigilant, didn't want to risk one of them mentioning to a guest in parlor
that a movie star was entering Regina Laudis. Keeping her entrance
hush-hush was also the reason Dolores did not have the required second
physical examination.

192

Lastly, during the final retreat all preparations for entrance are made.

Had I expected to be clued in about monastic life, I would have had to think again. During the retreat, I was told almost nothing about what to expect once I was inside the enclosure.

The Rule of Saint Benedict *presents a map for the journey through monastic life, but it leaves to the individual to travel at his own pace, according to his own nature. As an actress who had been constantly required to adjust to different temperaments and egos during the crisis-fraught production of a movie, I was looking for a guide to help me find my way to that vital destination, the union of the soul with God. At what would be my last meeting with Reverend Mother before entrance, I asked if she would explain monastic life to me. "No", she said with a smile. "It is so simple, Dolores, but you have to live it to understand it."*

Mother Miriam Benedict, the zelatrix, did give me a list of items that would make up my trousseau and granted me permission to send any of those items in advance. They would be put in my cell. But I did not see what would be my cell. In fact, I still had no idea of what the inside of the cloister looked like.

Included in my trousseau were two blankets—dark gray—twelve sheets and pillowcases and six towels, also gray. Clothing included sandals, heavy wool socks, undergarments, which were made of seersucker then—now they are made of more comfortable material—a dark-gray winter jacket, two black sweaters, black work shoes, blue denim material for a work habit, and a pocket watch, a gift from Jan and Ray. Wristwatches were a no-no. Luckily, Mother Miriam, who was only a few years older than I, was very aware of the concerns of young women. She gave me permission to bring my electric razor, which was not on the list of approved personal items, so that I could shave my legs.

Dolores also needed to supply black material for her postulant tunic, one of two she would have, the other being a hand-me-down from within the Community. Usually the candidate had the dress made outside Regina Laudis, but again to preserve secrecy, her tunic would be made inside the monastery. Maria offered to buy the material as a gift.

Maria, in fact, bought several yards of very fine black wool gabardine at Bloomingdale's. It was quite expensive. When the salesgirl asked what it was for, Maria told her it was to be a costume for a play. "As she wrapped the cloth," Maria recalled, "she said she hoped it would be a long run, and I said, 'So do I.' A few days later, I was surprised to see an item in a gossip column that said Gary Cooper's daughter was planning to enter a convent."

At the insistence of Mother Columba, Dolores spent many hours during the retreat writing letters to family members, friends and professional colleagues explaining her decision to enter religious life. The letters, sealed and stamped then, would be posted only after she was behind the walls.

When I returned from the final retreat, I had less than a month to tend to all the remaining details of my disappearing act. The final few days were a jumble of shopping, travel arrangements and last-minute goodbyes. The goodbyes were hard and had to be kept in my heart because nobody could know. The letters I had written in Saint Gregory's were difficult goodbyes too, but not as hard as the ones face-to-face.

I said a silent goodbye to one I considered my spiritual father. On June 3, Pope John XXIII, "the good pope", died. I had a special love for Pope John because he had given me a real push to enter religious life when he called me Chiara. I had planned to write him after I entered and tell him that his prediction had come true. Now I would not have that opportunity.

Thank God Mom was behaving herself. She had calmed down and put her suspicions to rest, although she accused me of being withdrawn and referred to me as "Garbo". I don't know what I would have done had her energies not been directed toward her first visit to Regina Laudis. While she was planning her wardrobe, I was frantically putting together my itinerary, which was extremely tight as this diary entry shows:

Martin graduates June 7. New York June 8.
Mom to come on 10th.
To RL June 11 if all goes as I hope God wills.
Ask Maria if she'll come.

Knowing that Maria could be a great help to Mom, I asked her to be there when I entered. I also asked her to save a couple of afternoons for us before Mom arrived. I thought we both needed and deserved some fun out of all of this.

I packed everything I would need in two suitcases and then, in the happiest part of my evaporation, proceeded to give away everything else I owned. That was fun—picking out what should go to whom—this piece of jewelry to this friend, a sweater or dress to another. The mink, of course, was for Mom, along with my beloved Pogo. Fortunately, because she had cared for him whenever I was away on location, he was as comfortable with her as he was with me.

I later regretted giving away two items. One was my desk lamp, which was much better than the one I found in my cell. The other was my typewriter; it would be years before I would have another.

One of the two last engagements I had was a very happy luncheon with my Malden family. The second was the baptism of Gigi and Frank Gallo's firstborn, Gina. It was a bittersweet occasion for me. When Gigi had asked me to be Gina's godmother, I accepted even though I knew I wouldn't be able to fulfill my obligations as a godparent. What could I do for the child when I'm in a monastery?

Two weeks before her entrance, Dolores surprised her publicist, Frank Liberman, with her decision to leave Hollywood. It would be Frank's task to make the official announcement to the press—but only after she was inside the enclosure.

Frank's plan was to plant the story of her entering religious life with Associated Press rather than give one journalist an exclusive. But Hedda Hopper almost sabotaged his plans. Hopper called him a few days before Dolores was scheduled to leave to check on a whispered rumor that she was planning to give up her career for the Church. Press agents who lied to Hedda Hopper courted disaster, but Frank denied the story.

On her last day in Los Angeles, Don came to her apartment to say goodbye. "During the weeks following the end of the engagement, I had to be alone", he related. "I felt it was important for both of us in order to begin to reconstruct our lives." The farewell was not easy. "In the future there would be a lot to say, but not at that moment. We embraced. It was quick. It was difficult."

❦

In New York, Dolores was able to unwind in the Park Avenue apartment Maria shared with her mother. "I already felt a terrible sense of loss", Maria said. "Dolores had been the instigator in my life, the avenue to activity, the one to say let's do something—let's go to the park, read this book. And she wasn't going to be around anymore."

The parting from Maria clarified for me that I was going to miss her as much as I was going to miss Don, but strange as this may sound, this realization did not make me sad. When we were alone, Maria and I commemorated the winding down of the conspiracy with a celebration on the terrace. Giddy as teenagers, we devoured chunks of ice cream cake as we laughed away the nervous tension of the past weeks. We even began throwing gobs of ice cream at one another and then down onto Park Avenue, twenty-one floors below.

Refreshed by our childish outburst, we faced the real world again and took a cab to JFK to meet Mom's plane. That evening the three of us dined together as we had many times in the past, Mom referring to us as "my two daughters". It was such a pleasant evening that I was almost able to ignore completely that I was keeping a secret. The next morning, Mom and I took the bus to Connecticut.

The road to Bethlehem was a familiar one by now, but this was the last trip I would be making on the bus. Mom seemed content and quickly settled down to enjoy the New England countryside whizzing past us. She didn't know she would be returning alone.

—How about you? As D-day grew closer, were you at all fearful? Did you experience any angst?

I did not fear the completely different life I was heading into, nor did I feel a sense of loss for the life I was leaving. I simply didn't have the feeling of pain that might surround the kind of step I was taking. I felt quite excited, in fact, not

196

unlike what I felt on opening night of the play. It was a time full of love. So no, Dick, there was no angst. I was surprisingly lighthearted. As I understand it now, where there is a true sign of the Spirit, there is peace and joy. There may have been an underlying sense of anxiety about entering into a new cycle. I didn't know exactly what the feeling was, but it wasn't bad or ugly—it didn't have those qualities about it. There was a fundamental happiness.

One of the nuns met us at the new bus depot—in Southbury. It wasn't actually a depot—we were deposited in a vacant lot near a gas station. The short drive took us up Flanders Road toward Bethlehem. I couldn't help but remember—"If you get to Bethlehem, you've gone too far."

Mother Mary Aline directed us to Saint Gregory's, where Mom and I would spend the night. I was grateful there were other guests. I hoped they might serve to inhibit an outburst from Mom.

There was a box waiting in our room. It held my postulant's tunic. Made of the most expensive-looking material I had ever seen, it had a sheen that almost sparkled. I could have worn it to any Hollywood party. The problem was that I had to wear it as a lowly postulant in a cloister. I had been so careful about the movie-star bit, and now I was going to look as if I were flaunting it. I was embarrassed to wear it.

Mom looked at the garment and said, in a very matter-of-fact tone, "When are you going in?"

"Tomorrow," I answered, "before Vespers."

She took my hands in hers and said, "That doesn't give us much time."

This was the moment I had been dreading. "Mom, you mustn't refuse me the freedom of pursuing life on my own terms. We're all searching in this life to fill the void in us. That void is the absence of love, and I've found it in God."

"It's my fault, isn't it?" she asked.

"There's no fault in this. I am not running away from anything. I am running toward something—with all my heart. I'm counting on you to understand. I have given myself up to all kinds of pursuits, and they have led to only a glimpse of the happiness I now feel. I can find no

197

substitute for the love that has brought me to this place. So please don't be sad. Be glad that I have found my true home."

I don't know what I expected—an argument, tears, hysterics? But she simply said, "Dolores, I can't take back what I've always told you. You have to do what you know in your heart is right and true."

As I unpacked I discovered an opened envelope in the pocket of a jacket I hadn't worn for a long time. I recognized Reverend Mother's unmistakable script and realized it was the note I had stuffed into my pocket back in December of 1959—and had neglected to read.

Reverend Mother had written: "Dear Dolores: I know you are knocking, but you have a lot to do before you'll be ready. You'll have to wait."

The entrance ceremony took place at three o'clock in front of the Great Gate—the lower entrance to the monastery. Harriett, sad but composed—after all, nuns do sometimes leave orders—stood beside Dolores, as did Maria.

I wore the shiny, showy new tunic, and I felt as if there were a spotlight on me. I was close to tears. Mother Anselm, recognizing my discomfort, told me not to worry, that the tunic would not be noticed or commented upon.

Father Paul Callens, then the monastery chaplain, escorted Dolores to the gate and gave her his blessing. Dolores knocked at the gate. Reverend Mother Benedict opened the small grille and asked, "What do you seek?" Dolores spoke from her heart.

"I seek the face of God through the Lord Jesus Christ in your Community, Reverend Mother."

Reverend Mother opened the gate. I knelt on the ground before her and received her prayer and blessing. Then she invited me inside, and I walked into the enclosure alone. The Great Gate closed behind me.

Inside, the members of the council were lined up on either side of the road to the monastery building. I walked with the nuns in procession to

198

the chapel, where the entire Community was waiting. I was shown my place in the choir and knelt again while the Community sang Psalm 47: "Receive me, O Lord, in the midst of Your temple according to Your name." Then I was escorted from the choir to Reverend Mother's office, where I was officially greeted by the members of the council. I signed a formal paper requesting acceptance as a postulant, which was then affirmed by each member as she introduced herself. I was sure I would never remember all the names.

"We live by the Rule of Saint Benedict", Reverend Mother said to me. "Do you respond to the Rule?"

"Oh yes," I replied, "I greatly respond to the Rule. Saint Benedict thinks like I do."

The silence in the room was deafening, broken only when one of the nuns berated me: "Saint Benedict, young lady, does not think the way you do. Don't you think you should have said you think like Saint Benedict?"

Reverend Mother Benedict stepped up. "Wait a minute", she said. "This is a new era, and we should listen to what the new generation is saying. I think Dolores said it right. Saint Benedict thinks like she does."

In the *Rule of Saint Benedict*, the abbot hears the counsel and opinions of all of the brothers and then follows what he judges to be the wisest course. The reason he calls on all, from the oldest to the youngest, according to the Rule, is that "the Lord often reveals what is better to the younger."

Mother Miriam then took me to the refectory where I was assigned my stool, at the rear. Nuns move up nearer the prioress with seniority. Mother Miriam showed me how I was to sit on the stool, how to place my napkin, where to wash my dishes and silverware and where they were kept.

The napkin placement was unusual. One corner of the napkin is pinned to your tunic collar, and the opposite corner is placed on the table. Your plate then sits on the napkin, which conveniently catches the crumbs. How functional, I thought. After the meal, the napkin is unpinned and folded—first in thirds and then in half—and then the plate is removed.

199

Finally I got my first look at my new home. Saint Anthony's, which was formerly a barn, housed the three parlors in which the nuns met with guests, including myself when I had been a visitor. Above the parlors, on the second floor, were the cells for the novitiate.

My cell was tiny—about eight-by-five feet—and wasn't painted. It contained a cot-size wooden bed—no bedsprings, just a three-inch mattress on a wood platform—with drawers beneath for blankets and personal items. There was one table with a small lamp and one chair, a shelf with a wash bowl and towel rack, no closet but three hooks on the door to hang clothing. The cell had a window, very small, from which I could see the top of a tree. I would soon discover, to my dismay, that the tree was home to a noisy frog.

The door to my cell had a number—47—coincidentally the same number as the psalm sung at my greeting. I would be expected to embroider that number on all my clothing and mark or scratch it on everything else, such as buckets and garden tools and the like.

—I can't tell you how happy I was when felt-tip pens were invented.

June in Connecticut was already hot and humid, and there was no air conditioning—there still isn't—but there was a fan in the corridor. The cells had no running water. I had to fetch water from the sink in the bathroom to fill my washbowl. The first time I walked into the bathroom, I almost cried at the barrenness of it.

Vespers was the first Office I attended as a postulant. After Vespers, there is a half hour put aside for personal pursuits—meditation or perhaps a walk. Mother Miriam shepherded me back to the novitiate quarters, where I was finally able to meet the five women I would be living with—Mary Misrahi, whom I had met during an early visit and who was now Sister Rachel; the novices Sister Mary Peter, Sister Patricia and Sister Gratia; and Julia, the other postulant. Of the six women in the novitiate, I would be the only one to remain.

We went back to the common room, where I was once more assigned a place that would be mine. This was the time that the Community heard the news of the day, mostly about monastery events. Some world news was included, courtesy of Mother Ida Hurkins, a tiny Dutch woman in

200

*her seventies, who was the Community's bell ringer and the only nun
with access to the single monastery radio. The news was the news that
Mother Ida judged was news.*

> —*I remember that evening we were saddened to learn that
> human rights activist Medgar Evers had been murdered in
> Mississippi.*

*Supper was my first meal with the Community. We eat our food in
silence, although we are usually read to at mealtime from books selected
by Mother Benedict. The day I entered was the feast of Corpus Christi,
when recorded music takes the place of the reading. On feast days, a
small amount of wine is served. It might as well have been Old Taylor
on my nervous, empty and sleep-deprived stomach. At the end of the
meal, I rose too quickly, forgetting I was still pinned to my napkin. The
plate flipped onto the table. In a frantic attempt to keep it from falling
to the floor, I kicked over my stool. The quiet of the refectory was
shattered. I stood there, mortified, waiting for a harsh reaction to my
clumsiness. But all I heard were a few barely audible giggles from those
who, I guessed, had been there and done that.*

> —*Postulants still fall prey to the treachery of the pinned nap-
> kin, and we all can't help but wait for that moment to happen.*

*Somewhere along the line, I received the books I would study, four in
all:* Antiphonal, Psalter, Gradual *and* Breviary. *These would guide my
way through the chants of the Divine Office.*

*Because I was not expected to attend Matins at 1:50 A.M., the last
Office of the day for me was Compline at 7:40 P.M. Compline is sung in
the chapel in the dark. It is the only Office that can be sung with eyes
closed because it is the same every day, and you don't have to refer to
your book.*

*Mother Miriam escorted me to my cell and said good night. I was
finally alone. For the first time since I walked through the Great Gate,
I thought about Mom and the deep pain she must be feeling, and I
couldn't pick up a phone and comfort her.*

*I undressed and got into bed. Suddenly I was consumed with over-
whelming loneliness.*

201

All through the hectic months of preparation, I was being held to my decision by a life source far beyond my own self. My experience of God ever since my conversion to the Church had always been intensely personal. From the moment I accepted, as a child on my "death bed", that I had God's favor to speak directly to Him, I came to depend on His abiding presence.

That presence disappeared when I walked through the gate.

I knew absolutely that everything that had ever happened to me had not been the result of luck or coincidence or my own doing. Everything had resulted from the presence of God in my life. When I told the sister at school that I wanted to have bread with the other children, and she mistook my request for a desire to receive the Eucharist, that was God's will. When I stood, unmoving, on that Manhattan corner and felt compelled to go to Regina Laudis, that was His will. And when I stopped Mother Placid in the refectory that evening, that too was His will.

But God, who had nurtured me all along the way to this very moment, was no longer there. I could not feel *His presence. Had I been childish in my awareness of God's omnipotence and fatherly protection?*

I lay awake on the cot for a long time. I reached out my arm in the darkness. I could touch the opposite wall with my hand. I lay there, terrified by the enormity of the step I had taken. I began praying as hard as I could that, in spite of the isolation engulfing me, the love in my heart was God Himself trying to strike, if not lightning, at least a match.

I cried myself to sleep that night. I would cry myself to sleep every night for the next three years.

In the Open

Twenty

It was hard to believe that I was going to be in one place for the rest of my life. I would come to know that being in the monastery is never being in the same place—not ever in the same place in the same way.

When you live in the center, you find that everything around you changes with amazing reliability. If there is one thing you can be sure of, it is change. That is the lesson of real stability.

Stability, however, was not a condition that related to me that first morning. My night's rest had hardly been uninterrupted. The cells, I discovered, have such thin walls between them that you can hear a zipper being zipped; it's impossible to ignore your neighbor getting up at 1:30 for Matins. That kind of intimacy can make for stressful moments. But even if I had slept in the Plaza's most luxurious accommodations, that night's slumber would have been fitful and troubled.

I thought I was experiencing that same queasy feeling—those butterflies in my stomach—that I always had before a performance, intensified because I had had no rehearsal for what lay ahead that day. But those weren't butterflies. I was in a real panic. All the fears of the previous day were still with me, but the feeling of God's presence was not with me. I felt abandoned and utterly alone.

In this state I stumbled through the first day, as if I were in the middle of a jigsaw puzzle with no idea how the pieces could possibly fit together.

At the beginning, I didn't fully comprehend what it would be like to have the Divine Office as part and parcel of my life in the monastery. When I walked in, I was walking to God—to find communion with Him. I had no inkling what the matter and substance of that experience would be—what it takes to become a cloistered nun. I hadn't asked commonplace questions about the day-to-day routine because my drive—to find that spiritual union with God—was, I thought, of a higher order.

205

The Divine Office is the name of the hours of communal prayer observed by monastic communities, which are rooted in the Jewish tradition of prayer at regular times of the day. The prime mission for contemplative Benedictines is to pray the Divine Office, keeping the words of the psalms resonating through the day and night, every day of the year.

Because I didn't have to get up in the middle of the night for Matins—postulants are eased into Matins over a period of time—I was awakened at 5:45 A.M. by a bell I would learn to call the Rising Bell. I had little time to bathe and dress because the next bell, announcing Lauds, would ring at 6:10. There was only one shower stall in the bathroom, but I noticed no one stood in line at the door. Some of the women showered in the evening before bedtime. Eventually I learned to keep one eye out for the moment the bathroom was unoccupied and then make a dash for it.

My cell contained no mirror. The only available mirror was on the medicine cabinet in the bathroom. I used to be so annoyed at having constantly to check my appearance in a mirror, but doing without one was a difficult adjustment. In all my years at Regina Laudis, I have never seen myself full length in a mirror. Fortunately, a mirror wasn't crucial. Although my hair was long, it could be pulled back and held by a rubber band for easy maintenance, and the postulant headdress covered it like a kerchief. And there was, of course, no need to apply makeup.

When I walked into the choir for Lauds and took my place, I realized I did not know the first thing about the Office. I did not participate in the Latin chant, but I listened to and tried to follow in my breviary what the nuns were singing. I was appalled by the discovery that I was now required to sing prayers eight times every day. It was a blow, one I didn't get used to for a long time. Or rather, one that I didn't submit to for a long time.

Lauds is followed by Prime. As with Lauds, I understood not one word. After Prime most of the Community takes breakfast at 6:45. At 7:25, the bell rings for Terce. There is no need for a bell to announce Mass because it immediately follows Terce. Mass was familiar territory for me—and the readings and the homily were in English.

After Mass, the Community begins its first work period at nine o'clock. Benedictine work is twofold—Lectio Divina, which means "sacred reading" or study, and manual labor.

At first, with the other novices and postulants, I met with Mother Anselm for a variety of reading and study programs in a small novitiate common room adjacent to our cells. Afterward, we younger members reported for our manual work assignment—known as an obedience. Mine was in the vegetable garden or the orchard or, from time to time, the flower garden. The nun in charge was Mother Stephen Prokes, who was responsible for the maintenance of all the monastery land. Mother Stephen was tall and fit—and very much in charge.

Fruits and vegetables are raised for the Community's needs. The flower garden was Reverend Mother's domain; she would arrange flowers daily in the chapel. When I was assigned garden duty, I had a variety of tasks. One day I would harvest string beans, the next pick apples or cherries, the next shovel manure—and weed, weed, weed.

—Was the work assigned in a communal or democratic way?

It was "Do as Mother Stephen says." And she was unchallenged.

Was any particular area of gardening your favorite?

No, I hated it all. I have always hated getting dirt under my fingernails. I was such a ninny that I believed the sisters when they said that each bean had to be planted with a specific side up or it would not grow out of the soil, but down to China. It took me ages to plant the damn things.

The bell for Sext rings at 11:50. I was getting a little tired of the bells. As with the other Offices, I listened to the nuns sing the prayers while I stared at, but didn't connect with, the Latin in the book. Sext is followed by the midday meal. This time there was a reading. The Community had just begun Gone with the Wind.

After the meal, there is an hour set aside for Sabbath at one o'clock. This is personal time and, for a postulant, time for more study. The texts—always something that will aid monastic growth—are chosen by

207

the mistress of novices and, for me, included the psalms, the Rule, and The Life and Miracles of Saint Benedict.

The sixth Office, None—it rhymes with bone—*begins at two o'clock. More chant. More Latin. At 2:15, there is another half hour for personal development and study before the afternoon obedience begins. My assignment was in the laundry. I gathered the clean laundry and sorted stockings and underwear according to the numbers sewn on them. This was long before an individual's clothing was kept together in bags for laundering. The clean items were placed in numbered cubbyholes on the wall—I still have the same cubby I was given my first day. Some garments, such as the linen caps and wimples and bandeaux, had to be ironed. Thanks to Granny I was a pretty fair ironer.*

At the conclusion of our work period, it was traditional to sing the Salve Regina, a well-loved Catholic hymn. Sister Fides, who was in charge of the laundry, knew exactly how long the Salve took to sing, and she would count the seconds before beginning the hymn so that she could let us go at precisely 4:45.

—*Really, it was 5-4-3-2-1-Blast off! Salve Regina! And out!*

At 4:45 we take tea, also in silence, but there is no time for talk anyway because Vespers begins at 5:00 on the nose. After Vespers, there is a period for meditation from 5:30 to 6:00 and then supper. Again, there is no conversation but another reading. Everyone always does her own dishes. But there is a "dish list" posted every week with the names of three persons who are "invited" to serve on KP. From 6:30 to 7:15, there is scheduled recreation—either indoor or outdoor.

—I'm getting visions of nuns dribbling basketballs. What was outdoor recreation?

It was dismal.

Indoor recreation was generally left up to each of us—personal reading, letter writing or listening to the news of the day. Conversation in the novitiate was limited to the period of recreation. We could never, for example, go into another's cell to visit. When conversation did take

208

place, it was about the work we were engaged in. It was never personal and never gossip.

In those days, postulants and novices did not mix with the professed nuns. We had to stay in our own area. In fact, a postulant was not permitted to speak to the mothers ever—unless she received a note indicating that one of the mothers wished to speak to her. In monastic custom, postulants were addressed as "Miss". So, for the third time in my life, I was called Miss Dolores.

Compline follows recreation at 7:30 and is the last of the seven Divine Offices. As with all the other Offices, I was completely adrift. But I did remember it as the Office I had liked when I was a visitor. From the end of Compline to Lauds the following morning, the Great Silence is observed. No one is supposed to speak after Compline.

About thirty minutes after Compline ends, another bell rings to announce early bedtime—ridiculously early for me. It isn't lights out—I could read or write letters—but it wasn't long before I wanted to get to sleep as soon as possible because the bell for Matins would sound in just a few hours.

When I crawled into bed after my first full day inside the monastery, I was amazed that every waking moment had been rigidly accounted for. The monastic timetable put a movie production schedule to shame. Its steady and deliberate pace had, overnight, replaced the swift whirling pattern of motion that had filled my days for eight months—ever since the October morning when Don drove up and I put that letter back into my pocket.

Again, in the dark of my cell, that gnawing sense of abandonment returned. Confusion, complete bewilderment gripped me. I did not understand what I was feeling. This was supposed to be the place where I was going to have my meeting with God. Something was going to happen—an immediate change, a promise fulfilled—the quest that had been torturing me all these months would stop, and I would find some peace.

I had been certain that once I entered the gates of Regina Laudis, God would be waiting for me—to reveal Himself completely. But I never imagined how, and now I felt as if I were in a movie playing a patient with bandages on her eyes, desperate to have them removed so that she

209

can see again. As an actress I would have a place to go with that, but I wasn't playing a part in the monastery.

"What have I done? I have to leave." That thought dogged me to tears every night. It would disturb my peace of mind and heart for a long time.

Twenty-One

"Star Driven into Nunnery by Her Love for Elvis" was the headline on the *National Enquirer* story. Most of the media played it in more realistic terms, using as a centerpiece Dolores' own statement in the press release: "I am not leaving anyone or anything behind me. I am taking with me a full and grateful heart."

Frank Liberman's phone rang off the hook with calls from every reporter in town but one: Hedda Hopper. Frank told me Hedda had sent him a note instead. It was simple and to the point, with only two words. I didn't need to ask him what they were.

The impact of the story was one of shock. Many of Dolores' friends and colleagues would soon receive the letters written during her final retreat but they, too, felt the initial jolt. Telephone calls streamed into the monastery. Phone calls to a postulant, especially in the first days after entrance, were extremely rare but, given the surprise nature of her entrance and the media attention it received, it was clear that there were some people on the outside Dolores should speak to personally; she could return those calls that she felt required an immediate response. It was not permitted for a nun to take one step outside the enclosure, but Dolores was allowed to make these calls at Saint Gregory's guesthouse because there was only one telephone inside the monastery and she simply couldn't tie up that line.

Paul Nathan was one of the first people to whom she spoke. Paul hadn't been surprised at all. Years later, he told me he had seen it coming. "Deep down," he said, "I felt that her heart had never really been in Hollywood. I'm not a religious person, so I was envious of her. I think that most people, if they're honest, envied her ability to do what she knew was right."

In London overseeing his production of *Becket*, Hal Wallis learned of her decision from a news announcement on the BBC and called Paul immediately. He was apoplectic, Paul told Dolores, vowing that, if she ever changed her mind, she would not work again in the Industry. Over time Wallis mellowed, and he let her know on many occasions that he would welcome her back at any time with open arms.

I was allowed to take two calls that just happened to come in during a period of free time. Neither was monitored. One was from Elvis. "I don't want to bother you", he said. "I just want you to know I'm very happy about what you are doing and to tell you I'm praying for you." After that I would hear from him only occasionally, usually in post-scripts on letters from his cousin Gene Smith, who remained a faithful friend and correspondent over the years.

The other call was from Stephen Boyd, who tried to sound supportive but, I could tell, was not thrilled with my move. Still, he promised to visit as soon as it was permitted.

By the third day, mail to Dolores began trickling into the monastery. As was the custom, all her mail was read first by Mother Anselm, not to censor her letters but to be aware of their content so that she could discuss with Dolores its significance to her interior life.

— Still, my immediate reaction was that she was going to get quite an education.

After the tremors subsided, reactions took over. They varied from happiness to cautious support to rage. Bert Hicks was furious, less perhaps over his daughter's decision than that Dolores hadn't told him herself that she was entering religious life. His wife Liliana remembered, "His mother called to tell him. He immediately began drinking and tried to reach Dolores at the monastery, but he wasn't allowed to speak to her. Fuming, he then tried to call the pope in Rome, and he complained to anyone who would listen to him that his daughter shouldn't be there. Bert never got over this. He drank even more heavily following Dolores' entrance."

After he had calmed down, Bert did send Dolores a telegram containing a brief message—a quote he dimly recalled from his Catholic boyhood: "Remember, honey, in the words of John of the Cross, 'In the evenings you will be judged on love.' "

212

—Daddy got it wrong. Saint John of the Cross wrote, "In the evening of life you will be judged on love."

Phil Gersh was stunned. "I couldn't imagine she would want to give up the most promising career of all of the young actresses then. I thought she was doing that to avoid getting married." Harry Bernsen sent her a gold-plated razor blade with a note: "You've just committed suicide." Letters of encouragement were received from coworkers Lois Nettleton, Paula Prentiss, Brad Dillman, Hugh O'Brian and Myrna Loy. Industry friends—Joan Crawford, Irene Dunne and Loretta Young—sent affectionate notes of support.

Dillman remembered being happy for Dolores. "It was wonderful casting. I was always aware that she was deeply religious, but she never forced her beliefs on anyone." Dillman's "wonderful casting" observation was echoed by others who had worked with her, among them Connie Francis, Anthony Franciosa, Stuart Whitman and Frank Gorshin.

Paula Prentiss recalled, "It felt right. It's not easy for any soul to find God. And Dolores had a full life in Hollywood, a skyrocketing career, a future. But she heard another call." Lois Nettleton learned of Dolores' entrance when she was on a personal appearance tour for *Come Fly with Me*. "Our publicity man just casually said to me, 'Did you hear about Dolores? She became a nun.' Well, I was totally shocked at first, but very soon everything slipped into place. I always thought of her as being close to God."

Her movie papa, Anthony Quinn, wrote that she had his "hopes, prayers and love.... May I write again? I need your help so often. I'm about to start [the movie] *Barabbas*, and I am finding a lot of myself in him. Like Barabbas, I am in constant turmoil and long to meet Peter and find rest."

Sister Dolores Marie was not surprised by the news; neither was she overjoyed. I don't think she objected to my decision—she did, in fact, support it over the years—but down deep she loved being the aunt of a movie actress. She had shared stories of my career with her community and became, I suspect, somewhat celebrated vicariously.

Father White was surprised, "happily so", he wrote. "I knew you had a fine sense of values, but I did not realize it would reach as high as the religious life." Father Mike Doody did not believe my decision was the right one. He thought my position in Hollywood enabled me to do much for the Church. "There are so many nuns already", he said. "You don't need to be a nun."

Her Marymount school chum Gail Lammersen kept the letter Dolores sent to her, which said, "With all my heart I believe it is my real vocation. All else has been a rehearsal for the big number. But rehearsals are always shown up for what they are—a pretend game that never quite generates the spark of opening night." Sheila Hart McGuire remembered, "I wasn't prepared to hear that she had chosen a cloistered order. A life devoted to prayer was baffling to me. Eventually I came to understand and support her choice."

Don Robinson had gone through a rough patch. There were times when Don was deeply angry. Much of his anger was directed at Mother Benedict and Mother Placid for what he perceived as their meddling. "I felt Dolores and I had a holy commitment to God in one another that should be honored by the monastery, not one they wanted her to break. I was angry with God, too. I remember going to the altar rail one morning at Mass. I knelt to receive Communion, and I couldn't receive it because I thought that is what took her away. I got up and walked out of the church. I had to work things out within myself. I couldn't work it out with a friend and certainly not with a priest. It had to be me and God."

At Dolores' instruction, Frank Liberman had called me with the news several days before her entrance, explaining that she didn't want me to learn of her move in the papers. I kept my mouth shut. If the news did not extinguish the feelings I continued to hold since our breakup, it did put an end to the expectation that eventually we would be together again. Somehow I had no doubt that this was for keeps.

It fell to the portress, Mother Mary Aline, to fend off the media. Requests for interviews were made mostly by telephone, but some reporters—and fans too—actually came to the monastery door and asked to see Dolores. Mother Mary Aline was nothing if not formidable; her "Miss Hart is not available" left no doubt that there was nothing further to say.

214

Letters from family and friends were given to Dolores. But there were also many letters from people all over the world whom Dolores did not know. At first members of the Community attempted to answer them with a form letter: "Dolores Hart is not able to take mail at this time, but she appreciates your interest and wishes you to know that you are in her prayers." But there was soon such an avalanche of letters that the nuns couldn't handle it all. Dolores received permission to contact Gladys Hart, the woman who had organized her fan club. Gladys agreed to help, and the letters addressed to Dolores Hart at the monastery or at the studios were forwarded to her.

—Gladys replied to every letter and faithfully continued to respond throughout the next two years. When all the letters were eventually passed on to me, I was moved to find that many were from young people expressing their renewed faith.

Harriett remained at the monastery for fourteen days, and guest mistress Mother Placid was in charge of her. "We didn't want her to be alone unless she wished to—you don't just leave Mom hung up on a tree limb. When someone has entered, I often talk with a mom or dad and try to air out all the scary things so that they can begin to recognize something they can trust. We worked through her feelings together, and she made a good show of understanding them."

Since I had known Harriett pretty well, I wondered aloud if she had presented a sympathetic face while inside she was churning—in short, a performance. Mother Placid replied, "She made a great effort to be supportive of Dolores' decision, but I didn't think it was something she felt she ought to say. Harriett was still able to see Dolores, of course—we're pretty civilized around here. We don't just say, "You've lost your daughter—bonk!" But now, of course, she had to see Dolores behind the grille."

That separation made Mom very uncomfortable. She said it was going to be hard to relate to me if she had to do it through bars and said she could not find a reason why anyone would keep a mother from her child. I let her go on as long as she needed and then tried to explain as best I could that this was not something Regina Laudis had thought up but was an age-old custom. The grille was not meant to cut us apart. Quite the contrary, the grille is a sign of life.

With tears streaming, she said, "Well then, kiddo, I guess I will have to start thinking of it as a kind of trellis holding up my roses."

—Interesting that she used the analogy of a trellis. The grille could be understood as a sort of trellis supporting the life growing inside.

"The good thing", Mother Placid continued, "was that, for the first days at least, it was just mother and daughter, because with someone else it could get complicated."

Complicated is hardly the word. Harriett had called Esther on the day of Dolores' entrance, and two days later one irate grandmother was on the Regina Laudis doorstep. Esther plopped herself down on the ground directly in front of the Great Gate and vowed loudly and long, "I'm not leaving until you let her out."

—I was told that Granny had arrived but not that she was creating a commotion. I didn't need to be told that.

"I don't think Mrs. Kude was open to it", Mother Placid said in magnificent understatement. "She didn't exactly hold her tongue. She was strong-willed, strong-minded, strong-spoken. I had great sympathy for her. The real complication was clear, however. Both women claimed right of parentage." After four days, Esther gave up and went home, still deeply angry and resentful.

I knew Granny well enough to be pretty sure that once she stewed for a while, she would, as the realist she had always been, face the truth that there was nothing she could do to change things. A few days after Granny's retreat, I sent her a letter asking her if she could find a pair of plain sandals and enclosed a pattern I had made of my right foot. Granny wrote back immediately, saying simply that she was "sending a pair in A width because sandals in a larger width would be bound to make the foot spread."

216

From that time on, Granny set herself on a course of acceptance without ever announcing that was what she was doing. Whatever distress she continued to feel was never passed on in her letters, which still included the ten bucks—"just in case". Her eventual acceptance of the Community was also shown in practical ways—her forte—by sharing her special recipes or knitting night caps for each nun or sending books full of trading stamps for us to redeem.

Harriett returned to New York before going home. "She was in a state of shock", Maria recalled. "The word "loss" crept into her conversation frequently. I simply told her that Dolores couldn't walk the path she had chosen without her help. By the time she was ready to return to Los Angeles, I was able to report to Dolores that Harriett was in much better spirits.

"It helped", Maria said, smiling, "that we had received a well-timed letter from Dolores, addressed to the two of us, giving 'monastic instructions for mealtimes'. It served to lift Harriett out of her doldrums. Dolores' directives? '1. Have a big, juicy filet mignon. 2. Eat slowly and chatter like mad. 3. Rattle dishes and silverware. 4. Have seconds on everything and lots of ice cream for dessert. 5. Leave whatever you can't eat on your plate.' "

Maria stayed in close touch with Mom. I didn't want Maria to be burdened with my personal problems, but she took it upon herself to help Mom. I had a new awareness of Maria's importance in my life. In a sense, she helped prepare me as much as if she had been inside as a Community member. She is really a sister.

217

Twenty-Two

"Formation is from forever to forever."

This expression is not literal in the monastery but one that indicates that a person entering an enclosure of monastic formation needs to accept the bond of another kind of observance guiding her life. The bond, of course, is love, and if I had not been motivated by love I would not have come through the gate.

But after I was inside the monastery, I found myself in a terrifying experience of aloneness. I could not believe that God could let me face the journey that lay ahead alone, and I prayed persistently for the strength to see me over the bumps in that road.

The first big bump came sooner than I had expected. Within weeks, Mother Placid was transferred to the Abbey of Jouarre for an unspecified time. Although our relationship had changed abruptly after my entrance and existed now almost entirely on bits of paper, this left me despondent. I had become reliant upon covertly passing notes to her that usually began with "You never said it would be like this!" Now I was to be completely without her. That was a blow.

The two women I was now dependent upon were the zelatrix and the mistress of novices. They are the women most involved in the postulant's interior life and progress. Both women lived in the novitiate. Each guarded her realm. The first thing I learned was to be careful not to ask one for information that was the domain of the other.

—The second was discretion—or shut up.

The zelatrix interprets and teaches the monastic customs—the ropes, if you will, of how to navigate within the world of a monastery. She teaches the newcomer how to mark her books for the Divine Office and helps with material needs. Mother Miriam taught me the rubrics, which are literally the directions for a liturgical service but which have come to mean general procedures to follow, rules that establish protocol.

218

Mother Miriam also gradually initiated me into various Hours, and I quickly learned to memorize and to recite the Latin chants. It was like learning lines. But the meanings *of the chants escaped me. I had no idea what the prayers* meant*; consequently, I just sang along in the Latin I had learned by rote.*

As mistress of novices, Mother Anselm was in charge of Dolores' monastic formation and her work schedule. She was the one whose permission Dolores needed to meet everyday spiritual wants and requirements.

From the very first, the older—and French—Mother Anselm found it particularly unsettling having to deal with a twenty-four-year-old who had come from Hollywood. It wasn't long before she confided her prickly situation to Reverend Mother Benedict and requested some backup.

I think Mother Anselm was more comfortable teaching sisters how to sew numbers on clothes or "do" apples—"do" is just another word for various tasks: you "do" dishes, "do" numbers, "do" rocks. There was no official changeover in formation mothers, but I detected a collaboration because I was sometimes sent to Reverend Mother to unravel things that Mother Anselm didn't want to deal with.

When I was with Reverend Mother, I felt I was under a microscope. I suspected she was making sure I kept my place. But she did seem to understand me. One of the first things she said to me when I began to meet with her was "You will have a great deal of trouble because you're not always going to get the justice you feel is your due."

—I've always felt this direct access to Reverend Mother from the very beginning made it easier for me to stay. I figured that the fact that she had also been a professional woman deepened her sensitivity to me.

In fact, as she told me several years ago, that sensitivity came from the reality that she saw, in you, a great deal of her younger self.

She never told me that.

219

All the bumps would, I prayed, merely take time to tolerate. It was difficult—but not impossible—to adjust to schedules and meals at regular times and those incessant bells that seemed to proclaim everything. My embarrassment over the shiny tunic was short-lived; it soon got as dusty as everybody else's and wasn't noticed. I could learn to live without the convenience of my own bathroom, having mail and telephone calls monitored, not having money for incidentals such as paper and pencils and even postage stamps. As letters were sent by regular mail, I began to ask friends to enclose stamps—then all of five cents each—if they expected replies via first class.

Affecting everything was lack of time to do what was expected. The compulsory sewing of your number on every piece of your clothing had to be done in two weeks, and although the stitching wasn't a major chore—Granny had taught me to tat—finding time to do it was next to impossible. I sewed my number—47—over and over with white thread on black garments and black on white and found that Granny had been more lenient in judging my handiwork than Mother Anselm was. When my stitching didn't pass muster, I had to do it again.

There was the problem of sleeping. My life on the outside allowed me to stay up late if I wanted to and sleep late because I could. Now I had to go to bed at dusk and get up before dawn—which I thought was just crazy. I used to brush my hair thoroughly at bedtime, but now I had all of five minutes for that plus washing my face and brushing my teeth before I got into bed. Many times I completed my ablutions in the dark. It wasn't long before I needed sleep more than I needed to brush my hair, and eventually I didn't give a tinker's damn how I looked, but during those first months, I was overanxious to appear proper.

"I never talked to Miss Dolores at all when she came in", Mother Abbess David confided. "It must have seemed hostile. The Community was not encouraged to interrelate. I recall she asked me one morning if her collar was on straight. I replied, rather curtly, 'It doesn't matter. Nobody will be looking at you here.' "

—The very first thing the movie star says is "How do I look?"

220

It was difficult to leave all reference to my previous life outside the gate, although I wasn't that eager to answer questions about my career—not because I thought I shouldn't be speaking of it or that it was now inconsequential, but because I had so much to learn that I hadn't the need to talk about it.

—Still, you must have thought someone would ask what it was like to work with Montgomery Clift.

Yes, that is the second most-asked question.

And the first?

What it was like to kiss Elvis.

I was allowed to talk about career with Mother Anselm because it directly affected who I was. And many months later, I learned that Mother Mary Aline, though she did not introduce the subject, was quite curious about my movie background. She had long harbored an ambition to found a monastery in Hollywood!

Dolores was kept up-to-date on Hollywood news, courtesy of her friend Sonia Wolfson, who wrote regularly. The enclosed postulant was aware of the sale of the Twentieth Century-Fox back lot—the result of the *Cleopatra* fiasco—to make room for Century City skyscrapers. She knew of Joan Crawford's retreat from a second teaming with Bette Davis and when Stephen Boyd began shooting *Fantastic Voyage* with Raquel Welch. But she was increasingly conscious of her ignorance of what else was happening in the world.

Mother Ida's news of the day didn't cut it for me. How enlightening it could be, I thought, if what was happening in the world came to us through the consciousness of those nuns interested in particular issues. I was interested in films. When it was Oscar time, I could bring the Community a taste of what was happening. I wondered why no one had thought of this, and I had no way of knowing if any of the other women felt the same way.

Of course, I was keenly aware of being restricted. I used to love jumping into my car and zipping down to Malibu Beach to forget my

221

woes. But you can't run away from your woes in the enclosure. If you get angry at someone, there's no way to hang up on her. You may have to sit next to her in chapel or do dishes with her all week. Since you knew nothing of a person's life before she entered, there was no way to understand her behavior.

"In those days," Mother Placid said, "we usually knew very little about the backgrounds of our novices. Once in a while, you would find out that a novice was, say, a lawyer, like Lucille Matarese, who is now Mother Maria Immaculata, our subprioress. But she didn't generate the whispers Miss Dolores did. It was the 'actress' thing, the 'princess' thing."

Dolores found it hard to ignore the scarcely disguised hostility that fueled those whispers. No one actually said anything, but there was no mistaking the message: "We aren't impressed that you were an actress." The few Community women she had come in contact with prior to entering were considerate and nonjudgmental. The majority of the nuns making up this Community, she was dismayed to find, could be, for all their culture and education, petty.

—That's not to say they were not good women. But—they were women.

Mother Dorcas Rosenlund, in describing the pitfalls of monastic life, summed it up another way. A gastroenterologist before she entered Regina Laudis, she is now the Community's baker. Life in a monastery is "the new martyrdom", she said. "They used to throw Christians to the lions. Now they make us live together."

It was a help to be able to write letters to Maria, the one person with whom I could share my intimate thoughts, but there was barely five minutes a day that I could steal for that; so I wrote them without pondering whether they "sounded right", something I used to spend considerable time doing. And my already tiny script got even smaller and more cramped because I had to use whatever scraps of paper I could get my hands on.

But even with Maria, Dolores was careful not to go overboard with complaints about life in the monastery. She tempered criticism with agreeable commentary, such as sharing her surprise and pleasure when Mother Agnes, the mistress of ceremonies, asked her to serve as reader at suppertime. Usually only professed nuns were readers. On occasion novices read, but it was highly unusual for a postulant to read.

Dolores didn't mention the constant thoughts of leaving or the nightly tears, but she asked Maria to pray that she would have "the guts to continue". Maria's keen and sympathetic eye recognized Dolores' struggle, and her almost daily letters were full of encouragement. She was Dolores' first visitor, within weeks of entrance. And she came bearing a gift, a small cactus plant—fittingly called the Crown of Thorns.

Most of my friends and colleagues looked upon my move as if I had disappeared into a foreign country, and they didn't think they could visit. Visits were not really encouraged anyway, as the superiors felt it was difficult enough to get integrated, much less to try to introduce the monastery to others.

Visits by Valerie Imbleau didn't pose such a problem. The *Come Fly with Me* adviser had accompanied Dolores to the monastery in the past and needed no introduction. She had shared her own thoughts of vocation with Dolores and now, in the fall of 1963, was preparing to enter Regina Laudis herself. Val did just that the following year but later left the Community.

Among her other visitors during her first months were Fathers Mike Doody and Armando Salazar, and Gerry Brent, the Tuna Queen from her *Francis of Assisi* days.

— You know, there's a notation by Miss Brent's name in the monastery guest book identifying her as "a friend of Dolores Hart—a *real* one."

Father Mike tried to come at times when we didn't have a chaplain so that he could offer Mass for us. During his visits throughout my postulancy, he tried to talk me out of taking vows. He had not changed his position that I could do more good for the Church by returning to Hollywood than by writing letters or visiting in a parlor as a cloistered nun.

Winnie Allen, Dolores' New York roommate, was also an early visitor, one who came under a dark cloud. "After my divorce," Winnie reflected, "I anguished that, because of the Church's stand on divorce, my relationship with Dolores could be at stake because I had broken my vows. She insisted that her feelings for me would be unchanged but was unsure about what the official Church position might force upon her. She asked for a meeting with Reverend Mother Benedict. Mother Benedict acknowledged the stand against divorce but readily assured her that she would not dictate what Dolores' personal reaction should be and would back whatever she decided."

— In so doing, Reverend Mother gave me another early sign that, although formed in the strictest classical way, she could make space for the new generation to exist in comfort. My relationship with Winnie has only grown over the years, and, in fact, she and Mother Benedict became very close friends, too.

Our mutual friend Merv Kaufman, of the Kaufman and Hart Oscar party in New York, had one hell of a time arranging a visit. Whenever he called, Mother Mary Aline mistook him for a reporter who had been making annoying requests for an interview and put him off with her firm "Miss Hart is not available." His letters were likewise suspect, and it wasn't until Dolores confirmed his credentials as a friend that permission to visit was granted.

They had a parlor in Saint Anthony's, and Merv was surprised when Dolores announced she had just been assigned, for personal spiritual reading, the entertainment section of the Sunday *New York Times.* Reverend Mother Benedict had become convinced that the instrument for receiving the Word of God was tuned to past experiences.

"At the end of our visit," Merv recalled, "I asked her if I could send her anything. 'What do you mean?' she wondered. 'Well,' I said, 'is there anything you want, anything you *need?*' Dolores furtively peeked over each shoulder and then leaned in close to the grille and whispered softly, 'A vodka martini—very dry.' "

❦

224

A postulant is not a member of the professed Community. Although I came in daily contact with the mothers, sometimes worked alongside them, we didn't speak to one another, and that made me uneasy. We postulants and novices had our own common room, where we sat together and talked—but only about our work. If little or nothing happened to me on a particular day, I didn't contribute anything. I just listened.

My uneasiness was compounded by the fact that Reverend Mother, a Francophile of the first water, and the very French Mother Mary Aline tried to outdo each other in being monastic. The difference between them, or so it seemed to me, was that Mother Mary Aline was constantly trying to show *what being monastic meant while Reverend Mother was truly and effortlessly monastic whether she was leading a discussion of the Rule or arranging flowers in the chapel. I thought Mother Mary Aline was a bit of an act.*

Whenever we came into contact, there was something about her demeanor that I took as jealousy. She whipped me with caustic looks. I thought I understood the reason, since she had wanted to be an actress when she was younger.

—*She did remind me a little of Hermione Gingold.*

Mother Mary Aline once accused me of doing something improper. I had not done it, and I told her so. She said I was not to argue with her. "When I tell you that you did something wrong, you did it!"

I replied with all the cool resentment of Bette Davis, "And I am telling you that I did not do it, and you don't tell me I did it when I did not."

She pointed to the floor. "Get down on your knees right now, you impudent American."

I got down on my knees and glared. She said I was a worm. I said that made me the greatest thing according to the Rule, a true daughter of Saint Benedict! She swept out of the room.

—Was this resolved?

That night I found a piece of chocolate on my pillow with a note saying that no argument must ever go unresolved beyond

225

the setting of the sun. Many versions of this scene, however, were repeated over the years—right up to Mother Mary Aline's death.

Within a very short time my skin broke out badly. It was probably the change in diet—but I couldn't rule out all that chocolate Mother Mary Aline was leaving on my pillow. Before, I was careful not to eat chocolate, and I stayed away from all fat. Here I had no choice; I had to eat whatever was put in front of me. I wrote Mom to send Clearasil. She did, along with some moisturizing creams that I was permitted to use. Reverend Mother was sensible about anything one needed to main-tain a healthy body.

Mother Columba, however, was frantic and wanted a doctor to look at me. She was afraid that, should I not make it in the monastery and return to Hollywood, everyone there would think they had ruined me. Concern for my acne was now, surprisingly, the only personal focus of our rela-tionship. I thought we had grown very close. It was a mystery why she drifted away from me after I entered. She had been assigned to tutor me in Latin, but other than that, it was as if I had become invisible to her.

As fall approached I found there was no heat in the cells, only a single electric heater in the hallway. When I returned from Matins in the middle of the night, I had to sit on the thing to get warm before I got back into bed. It seemed I was always battling sore throats, and the sinus attacks that had started in New York raged at times.

I became very thin and drawn. As there was some concern that I was on the verge of anemia, I was permitted additional meat in my diet. The regular diet for the Benedictine Order is vegetarian, but postulants were allowed meat twice a week.

The garden obedience was often the toughest time. Some of the work, such as lifting and moving large rocks and boulders to prepare the ground for planting, was a major struggle for me. I think New England must grow rocks. I wasn't very strong, but I was stubborn. I vowed to keep up with the pace set by Mother Stephen if it killed me.

"Hard work", Mother Abbess David verified, "was the order of the day because we had to subsist. We were a foundation; food was short, and we existed on what we got out of the land or what someone gave us. If someone gave us a sack of potatoes it was cause for a big celebration.

"I remember when I worked in the garden doing rocks. All that lifting was backbreaking, and I was always thinking of ways to do the job with the least exertion. Once I rigged up a long plank and rolled the rocks and boulders rather than lift them. Mother Stephen said that was not work. I could maybe have argued about it, but I didn't usually. I just stood back. It wasn't building me up as an independent person; it was building me up as a slave.

"For Mother Stephen, the hardest way was the best way, the monastic way. The work should cost your body something. Women have certain limitations, but I don't think Mother Stephen ever experienced one herself. She was raised on a Minnesota farm, and she was trained as a child to work hard. In a day when there wasn't much consideration given to what a woman could do on the land, nothing was too much for her."

Often when I reported for garden duty at ten o'clock, there was no one to give me my assignment, and I would have to stand and wait. I didn't dare to presume to begin a job on my own. One morning as I stood and waited—and waited—it began to rain. At 11:15 I was still waiting—belligerently—with angry tears joining the raindrops rolling down my cheeks. I don't know how much of my hurt came from being treated like a nobody. It would be hard for anyone to take, but being someone who had been catered to, fawned over—to have to stand in the rain and wait to be given a grubby job that everyone knew full well I didn't want was more than just being ignored. My dignity was being peeled away.

I was repeatedly close to tears during the day, but the only time I cried was during the Office of Sext, which followed the garden obedience. I would be so aggravated that I couldn't hold back the tears. They splashed down onto my book at the same spot every day, and my antiphonal became unreadable on that page.

Mother Irene Boothroyd—the Helen Boothroyd whom Dolores had met when they were both guests in Saint Gregory's—entered a few months after Dolores and occupied the cell next to hers in the novitiate.

227

Mother Irene remembered hearing Dolores crying herself to sleep night after night. "I empathized, but there was no way to try to comfort her. You couldn't go into another's cell, and you didn't report it to the mistress of novices. The two of us never discussed personal problems even when we were alone waxing floors every Wednesday night."

Dolores held most of her tears until she was in her cell at night. With no one to share the personal agony she held within her, she began a journal into which she poured all the pain. This journal grew and occupies two large diaries of personal reflections. The entries are chronological, although she sometimes went days, even months, without adding a word. Each one recounts an experience that sounds like the one that would send her packing. The first words she scribbled railed against the loneliness she felt was caused by Mother Placid's unexpected desertion:

> Have I done a foolish and stupid thing? Have I exposed my heart to loving only to be left alone with the coldness of pain?

I felt betrayed by God's abandonment and by what I couldn't help but feel was Mother Placid's as well. A pattern was being formed—of mother figure and child. I heard her as a learner and was comforted by the awareness that she was listening to me; thus, her departure for Jouarre had been a slap in the face.

During the months before entering Regina Laudis, I lived in a solid interior way with the Lord. My mind and heart were joined with Him. Now all I felt was a loss of that interior place, and this new life within an enclosure of thirty-five women was not all that promising a stand-in. Monastic life was apparently not a matter of relationship.

But I made no move toward the door. It would be comforting to say that I recognized that pain numbs judgment and was smart enough to put off this decision until I was more in charge of my emotions. But it was simpler than that. I was stubborn. I believed that I was called to take on this place and to follow Christ in His Passion. To be part of that experience—to live through what that means—I held to as my mission. I couldn't leave because deep down I trusted that God had to be there and that was what mattered. I swore that I would wait as long as I had to.

In this, she was unknowingly following her confirmation saint, Thérèse of Lisieux, who had also become desolate by the loss of God's presence. Thérèse took this as grace and trusted that God would permit her one day "to be led out of darkness into light". She vowed "to eat the bread of sorrow for as long as the Lord wills it" and not to "rise from that table, so filled with bitterness, where poor sinners ate, until the day He appointed."

Twenty-Three

If I had entered the monastery in the fifties, when unfairness was accepted, not questioned, I probably could not have stayed. But the sixties offered a hint of a freer atmosphere in which the Community might take its first tentative steps toward change and growth.

"The 1960s", Mother Abbess David explained, "was a time of ferment in the Community as in all religious communities of that era. Pope John XXIII convened the Second Vatican Council with the intention to 'throw open the window of the Church so that we can see out and the people can see in'. The new allowances, of course, ushered in all kinds of changes in dress, language and customs, and all religious communities were affected.

"The pope's call to follow Divine Providence to 'a new order of human relations' was even more critical when it came to contemplatives. It was felt that these communities held to an institutional narrowness that was psychologically unbearable, and because reform was taking place at the same time we were thinking of a permanent monastery building on the hill, every aspect of our lives came under scrutiny."

I was not fully conscious of most of this when I entered in the midst of Vatican II, but perhaps I could be called a child of the Council—one who would come of age within the bonum *of her own natural call. Many things that were now spoken of and defended as* new *ideas were things I had long championed.*

Coincidentally, and very significantly, I also found a teacher and a friend in Father Francis Joseph Prokes.

In 1957, as a newly ordained Jesuit priest, Father Prokes had visited Regina Laudis. He was the brother of Mother Stephen and had been invited to say his first solemn High Mass in the chapel on Trinity

Sunday. About the time Dolores entered, Monsignor Lacy, the man who had conducted her interview for the archbishop of Hartford, was encouraging Reverend Mother Benedict to rebuild the makeshift quarters of the monastery.

"Providentially," Mother Abbess David said, "we were helped by Father Prokes, who was doing his doctoral work at Princeton on the theological dimension of architecture and very much wanted to work with us to develop and design the structures that would take our monastery into the future. This work would become the basis of his dissertation, the underlying principle of which is collaboration.

"Reverend Mother appointed Father Prokes as the Community's official architect. After obtaining his doctoral degree, he returned to Regina Laudis, and though, as a Jesuit, he couldn't be the Community's chaplain, authorization was granted from the Hartford Archdiocese for him to live on the monastery grounds."

Father Prokes met with the entire Community every Tuesday morning, and I was very taken with his homilies at Mass, which he celebrated for us whenever we did not have a chaplain. He was a pinch hitter, so to speak. None of our chaplains made the impact that Father Prokes did. They conducted Mass, performed other chaplain functions but did not really enter into our Community life the way he did. He was a robust, energetic and vital man whose relationship with us would last for more than twenty years.

Father Prokes called a meeting of the whole Community to discuss the proposed buildings that would comprise our future monastery, specifically the new sanctuary. He spoke about architecture on three levels—artistic, intellectual and spiritual—as if it were a living thing. He was working so hard to get his message across that he was sweating. I've never seen an actor work as hard on stage.

He asked for our ideas on how the sanctuary should be designed, stressing that to plan the buildings, he had to know who we were, not only as a community, but as individual persons. No one said a word. He showed us his drawing of the altar, which I didn't like at all. When he asked for comments, I was the only one who raised a hand. I said I thought it looked like a giant whistle.

Father asked if I had an idea of what the altar should look like. I said I would like to see a baldachin over the altar—a canopy with a decided feminine image, perhaps a mother and a child—but I wasn't sure exactly what it should look like. The immediate response from the women was that our church would be too small to incorporate a baldachin, but Father Prokes suggested I make a model to show what I had in mind. Two weeks later I presented a clay model of my baldachin, which contained a molded image of our Lady and the infant Jesus, and both were naked. Father Prokes found it "lovely but not practical" for the proposed sanctuary.

One of the older nuns, however, found it obscene. One night, she took the model from the studio and buried it in an uncultivated area in the enclosure known as Saint Mary's Woods. This was not done surreptitiously. Oh no, she told me she had buried it to "save" my soul. She also said something I have not forgotten to this day: "You say nothing because you know nothing. You know nothing because you are nothing."

Since childhood, I had lived very independently. When I got into films, I was always being interviewed, listened to, and I got fond of saying what I wanted to say. I didn't like to be told to shut up.

"When Dolores came in and also, for that matter, when I came in four years earlier," Mother Abbess said, "the Community was different from what it is now. You walked into an atmosphere that was *theirs*. There was a real separation, and nobody told you anything. It was tight, especially tight for someone who was used to communicating, talking about herself a lot, that sort of thing. All of a sudden, you could not communicate. Think about that."

"You are not asked to think; you are expected to obey", Mother Placid explained. "Obedience isn't easy, and you're not obeying just the major superior; there are so many people you have to obey along the way. It is more than culture shock. It's humanity shock."

I often wondered if I should just be grateful that everything was determined by superiors who knew God's will better than I, leaving me free to apply myself to loftier matters. "Obedience", I was told, "is practiced by observing all the rules, customs and practices of the Order

232

and by making the will of superiors my own." But my *purpose in coming to a monastery was to find* God's *will in* my *life.*

Beneath my feeling of separation was an unshakable sense that the soul of this Community could not be dry or dead, that it was moving timidly toward the spirit of relationship. I recognized undertones of longing to push away from the encrustations of the old ways and move toward the new forms that allowed a broader freedom to find that new spirit.

Father Prokes was instrumental in awakening that spirit when he said he needed to know us not only as a community but as persons. Father felt strongly that, because we were following an ancient monastic practice, all of us were in denial about our professional lives. And he insisted that for a woman to become a religious devoted entirely to God she needed to integrate everything about herself, including what she had done in the world before she entered an order.

"Don't cut it off," he told me, "assume it. You are going to have to maintain absolutely in this Community that you are what you are—an actress.*"*

—That was something a Jesuit taught a Benedictine.

Father Prokes managed to reignite many of the feelings that I was trying to put out of my feverish brain. Denial of my previous career would cause it to fade away from memory, and my professional gifts would never be utilized to the fullest. And this applied to all of us. We could not truly contribute to the Community if we buried our gifts.

"It wasn't so much restricting women from utilizing their gifts," Mother Abbess stressed, "as there was no venue to use them. There was no way to employ their talents. Then the women were assigned work according to the needs of the Community."

Down deep, I felt Reverend Mother Benedict was of like thought— indeed, hadn't she jumped to my defense on my entrance day with the opinion that the new generation must be listened to?

However, she was also faithful to her formation at Jouarre with its strict monastic structures going back over a thousand years. I found that it wasn't until she had the guidance of Father Prokes that she found

233

a way to explore the concept of women in the Community connecting to the professional background that each brought with her.

❧

Even without direct communication, I became sensitive to an undercurrent of unrest within the Community, and I perceived that this agitation was directed at Reverend Mother Benedict. I wasn't sure what the rumbling was all about, but I remember saying to myself, "I have to do something about this." What that could possibly be I hadn't the foggiest idea.

"At that time," Mother Abbess remembered, "Reverend Mother's desire for a land-based community began to cause resistance among some of the women. Regina Laudis, as the only enclosed Benedictine monastery in the United States, was rooted in the hierarchical model of French monastic life. Some of the older French nuns objected to Reverend Mother's plan. They were still groping to find a comfortable niche in America and preferred preserving and bookbinding to raising animals and baling hay. The newer members of the Community were not only Americans; they came from academic situations, from professions, and they simply were not prepared to become farmers."

However, an immediate land-based problem had to be faced by the entire Community, professed and novitiate. Burritt Hill Road bisected the monastery property. Once used by the neighboring towns of Bethlehem and Woodbury, it had been closed to resident travel when Robert Leather turned the land over to the nuns. But now the townspeople wanted the road reopened. This would cut the monastery enclosure in two and make it impossible for the nuns to cross the road without breaching the restrictions of a cloistered order.

I was invited to a meeting of the elders to discuss how we could negotiate a plan to ensure that Burritt Hill Road remained under the jurisdiction of Regina Laudis. The road was becoming a hot issue. Some members, however, did not think the land was important enough to cause this fuss. Their attitude was that we should live the monastic life

234

behind grilles and stop risking our health in the exhausting responsibility of caring for so much land.

One of the older nuns sat knitting like Madame Defarge throughout the meeting. The click, click, click of those knitting needles was annoying, but no one in the room made an effort to stop her. I didn't care if the woman wanted to knit, but she was plainly showing her disdain for the subject at hand, which irritated me. I took it as long as I could, then went to her, grabbed the needles from her hands, and slammed them to the floor, growling, "Shove these and see if they'll knit!" and left the room.

Dolores' action shocked the nuns into silence. Mother Abbess recalled, "This was the first time such a thing had happened. We were not used to giving personal opinions when not asked to do so and certainly not in such a violent manner. But most of us were secretly pleased. It was, I believe, a defining moment in our Community life."

For my part, I was immediately sorry for what I had done. Not for the action itself—she deserved it—but for what it might mean in terms of my not being able to adjust to monastic life. When I left the meeting, I took a walk in the field behind the house until I could go no farther. I glanced over my shoulder at the barn with the hills in the distance, and in that moment an image of the Wyeth painting I love flashed before me. I was bowled over by a single thought: Christina, I know you at last!

When I next saw Reverend Mother, she made no mention of my outburst. I spoke to her about my experiencing Wyeth's painting of Christina's World *on an intimate level. Christina, I was now sure, was not retreating from anything. She was going toward something.*

Reverend Mother gave me a very knowing smile and said, "Isn't it wonderful to receive signs?"

As Benedictines following the monastic way of life established in the fifth century, the Regina Laudis Community did not adopt all of the Vatican II allowances. Many orders experimented with modified habits or eventually chose secular clothing. We did not. Reverend Mother felt

that our traditional black habit effectively enabled our choir work just as it was—signing, sealing and enclosing us. We still wear the habit. Even when we work, we wear the blue denim habit she created, using as her inspiration the work clothes worn by local laborers.

The Latin Mass was replaced by Mass in English in most American churches but not at Regina Laudis. The chant, too, was discarded by others, but Reverend Mother held fast that Saint Benedict's edict "You will sing the Office" was at the heart of the foundation and must be kept. Regina Laudis remains one of the few religious communities in the United States that sings the whole of the Mass and Divine Office in Latin.

Reverend Mother taught us that the chant has the power to communicate the life of God as no other music does. "You are singing the Word of God. You are not the author, only the medium. You take in the Word and possess it in order to release it. You have to be really at peace in order to do that successfully, because each person will possess the chant in a different way. You have to be so acclimated to it that you don't stop to think about it anymore. You don't need to because it's in you. That's the indispensable condition for singing it."

The chant functions as a daily discipline and spiritual glue. Each day Gregorian chant gives our Community its spine. It is a form of labor that comes naturally to some; others of us have to sweat it out. I did not have a strong singing voice, but Reverend Mother told me I had a perfect voice for chant.

> *—But then, she was also fond of saying, "You can tell a nun anything except that she can't sing."*

A fourth nun soon joined the monastic cadre responsible for Miss Dolores. Mother Cecilia Eichelmann was assigned to teach her the basics of chant as well as exercises for singing and breathing. Mother Cecilia had been a music major in college. She had a beautiful voice with perfect pitch. She was the oldest nun and very stately, up on a pedestal in the Community.

> *—She was one of those people you went around very gingerly. She described herself as a porcupine.*

Chant is not "follow the bouncing ball". It takes constant practice, and finding the time to practice presented another challenge. Practice was discouraged during work periods, and as a result it cut into my private time. I searched out quiet places inside the enclosure, anywhere I could find an isolated spot, and stole a few minutes each day to go through the exercises. I had to. When you're off-key in choir, you can feel the body tension around you. Because the chants change every day, I was assigned to a class for an hour each Wednesday to help me keep up with the Community. Nothing gave me more stage fright than having to sing one of those lessons in front of the Community. I used to wonder how I could be so calm on a movie soundstage with maybe a hundred people watching and yet be frozen in front of twenty nuns.

Harriett, too, had been going through a stressful time. The divorce from Al Gordon had left her with very little money. She was now earning her keep as a manicurist and had moved into a little house with a studio that she put to use in various artistic pursuits to keep her balance. Harriett's almost daily letters to Dolores presented a happy adjustment, though in suspiciously flowery terms that were overly upbeat.

Mostly, what I was getting was a phony smile. Now and then, there would be a letter full of misgivings, offering sympathy for my own qualms and begging me to reexamine my decision. Her melodramatic ramblings and progressively unsteady hand, however, made it quite clear that Mom was again drinking heavily. I was doubly distressed because, at the time of my entrance, I had given her an open invitation to visit and she had chosen the upcoming November.

I went to Reverend Mother with my frustration that, with all her smarts, Mom was still making a mess of her life. Reverend Mother counseled me that finely tuned instruments are often the ones that need the most care. At her suggestion, I composed another tough-love letter— the strongest one I had ever written, one that I knew could hurt Mom deeply. Consequently, I was uncertain of what state she would be in when she came.

But it was a perfect reunion. She was in good spirits—and in good shape. I was simply stunned with reverence for the new person I saw in her after such a painful time.

Mom brought me a pair of boots I had requested. She also brought a cowboy hat—make of that what you will—and my old clarinet. I had mentioned in a letter that I thought it might be fun to play it in the woods. I did that from time to time; it took the edge off. I've never seriously played it for the Community though, and it has been years now since I've touched it.

—*But I bet I can still play it—if I could find it.*

Mom also brought a large album of photos and personal mementos I had asked for. I felt it could be a great help in reevaluating the past and trying to put things into perspective—not to discover if there were things that I could not live without, but to take an account of my life and balance out relationships before taking a major step. In a few months, I would be due for the traditional examination with Reverend Mother and the council to decide whether I should continue.

I knew full well I was there on a trial basis to decide whether I had a true calling. The important thing for me was to find out if I could learn to live with the restrictions. I felt in my heart that I could, but it would take an awful lot of time to curb my independent spirit and to quit locking up everything.

True love is completely open and free of self. It has only to give, even if the price is pain. How does one express the desire to give? I think that one gives completely when he can totally accept all that another person is, by basking in the incredible uniqueness of God's love expressed in His creation of another human being. We just have to accept Him and be grateful for the love He plants deep within our hearts. Accept it, live on its fruits, and share it.

—That sounds very much like what I imagine a formation lesson to be. Is it?

No. On the contrary, the formation of that day was exactly the opposite. The goal was to seek relationship with God, not my fellow man. But inside I could not let go of the need to

238

love others, and, oh, the fight this caused within me raged constantly.

❦

On November 22, 1963, the entire Community was sitting together in the common room listening to a treatise on hospitality when the portress entered and handed Reverend Mother a note. Reverend Mother rose and said quietly, "The president has been shot. We must pray it is not fatal if the Lord wants him to continue." Every one of us was on her knees.

Just two years before, I had cast my very first vote for John F. Kennedy, and the thought that he lay dying was almost too much for me to bear. I remember my obedience that day was painting Christmas ornaments, and for the first time I experienced a full understanding of work as prayer.

Later, Reverend Mother called us together again and announced that President Kennedy was dead. She was profoundly affected. She felt he was linked to the very existence of Regina Laudis because American strength and sacrifice had liberated Jouarre.

In the refectory, there was a sign beneath a photograph of President Kennedy: "No recreation tonight." We were free to spend this time as we wanted. I put on my cape and hood and walked alone to the peach grove. I stood there, in the cold darkness, for what seemed a very long time, growing more and more connected to the intense grief that was surely being felt by the president's widow and his mother.

Over the next days, like the rest of the country, the Community lived with the impact created by the solemnity of the burial rite, which we witnessed on the little television set we moved into the common room. Members of the Community would come and go throughout the day as their work permitted.

The manner in which the funeral was carried out had that recognizable discipline of ordered movement and seeming impersonality that is so thoroughly American in character. But I could feel each one of the participants putting his whole heart into what he was doing. The incredible maneuvers of the Irish drill corps, the dirge of the Air Force pipers, the volley of muskets, the final poignancy of the bugle playing

239

"Taps"—all this concerted energy surrounded this death with a tribute made unique by the desire of each participant to get it right.

There was personal love in what they did, in the manner they did it. There was love in the way they folded the flag, handing it down to one another, much as early Christians must have handed the Eucharist to one another in the catacombs.

Reverend Mother had written a beautiful statement about Jacqueline Kennedy as a woman who presented a new Eve to the world, and as the youngest postulant, I was asked to read it to the Community. She asked me to include my own thoughts and observations, which I found easy to do because I had concentrated so hard on the woman.

> *To the entire world, Mrs. John F. Kennedy reigned with contained majesty. In the beauty of her silence, she renewed the American woman's stature: we are the material of which history is made. In those moments, two sacraments sustained her: one God given—the Eucharist; one man-made—the flag. I was awed by the youthful first lady's unbelievable assurance. In what had to be the most painful time in her life, she did not shrink from duty.*
>
> *Nor did she forget she was teaching her children something about living. It was there in the expression of her little girl as she looked to her mother's face on the steps of Saint Matthew's Cathedral. Rare trust as little Caroline tried to read in her mother's eyes the meaning of the event, learning to become a woman by watching the woman her mother was. The little boy of three letting go of the maternal hand and, unaided, standing at attention—John-John saluting his father. This silent scene exemplified the sure motherly touch of a woman communicating womanhood to her daughter and letting her son free to assume his inborn place as a man.*

As I read these thoughts to the Community, something captured my heart. It was the electric bravery alive within the very room in which I stood. Here were nuns in silent admiration for one woman's triumph over grief because they existed in the core of her victory. Here were women with courage to follow an invisible love—in a coffin of seclusion from the world. They follow with no obvious support to the brink of the unknown, there to set fire to a perpetual lamp of love.

I suspect that was the first time that I thought of these women as my sisters.

Twenty-Four

The Clothing—or Investiture—is the second step toward professed life. It's as if you're not really a nun until you wear the habit. Up to that time, although you are living in a monastery, you are an observer— simply a guest in the house.

To be clothed in the garments of the Community allows you to feel physically that you are part of it. You will now have a white veil and a new name. You are obligated to take on additional duties in terms of helping to maintain the house.

It also meant I would be totally separated from the world for a full year. Following the Clothing, a canonical year of strict enclosure is imposed by the Church on every novice, whether active or enclosed. I would see no one from the outside during that year, which was set aside entirely for my studies, duties and formation, for, in essence, I would be asking if I am truly called, asking to grow in holiness.

As Dolores wrestled with the decision to make her request to be clothed, she was thrown a challenge in a letter from her friend Ethel Levin, the wife of director Henry Levin, who had been at the helm of Dolores' two most successful films, *Where the Boys Are* and *Come Fly with Me*. In her letter, Ethel asked Dolores her reasons for entering a monastery, and she pulled no punches, labeling the cloistered life "selfish and useless". Dolores' reply, which Ethel shared with us, is a heartfelt application of very personal apologetics.

I hadn't felt the need to explain the reasons for my choice to many people for I thought that, at best, their interest bordered merely on curiosity, but Ethel's letter reflected such sincerity that I couldn't help being drawn into a vital connection. I had to dig to the core of my heart to respond to her challenges, and, in so doing, I faced the truth of my beliefs.

I had not, as Ethel suggested, chosen to escape my responsibilities in life by secluding myself from reality. I believed that if there is to be an ultimate and real salvation for the whole of mankind, it must begin by very personal involvement.

As a monastic nun, I hoped I would be a witness to the truth that love is real, and I was finding that it is no easy trick to live in solitude in the company of nearly forty persons. I figured Ethel knew what it was like to have houseguests for longer than a weekend, and I was sure she was able to put up with them because they were friends and she loved them. I was trying to learn to accept this same charity in relation to others because I believed on faith that each one of us is a creature of God, who is love Himself.

Was my life to be one of selfishness and uselessness? If so, then isn't all poetry, all art, all music selfish and useless? They too are witnesses to a truth that lies deeply rooted in the heart of man that cannot be expressed in any other form.

I prayed I was learning to embrace an awareness of my real identity instead of marching in a parade of hysterical fantasy. I might have spent years thinking I exist only because I see my picture in a newspaper, because I am Mrs. So-and-So, because I have money, rather than knowing that I am because I am related in all my experiences with the forces of life by being obedient to the unifying force that informs them. God is that unifying force. And if I am united to God, then I am united in the totality of spirit to everything else that attempts to be united to Him.

"If, in the final analysis, I have made a mistake," I wrote Ethel, "if I have given up the real treasure of life, I will have at least the satisfaction of knowing that I was wholly committed to my choice. But if I am right, then my joy will be the fullness of a final communion of love with the same persons who question, tolerate, kid or condemn my choice. My only justification will be the living of it, and I don't know if I have what it takes to do that."

—That was so true. I had barely gotten through the first months by the skin of my teeth.

I didn't know how to explain the contemplative life. All I felt was my own conviction in the power of prayer and in the deep faith that

242

prompts that prayer, but the letter to Ethel kind of gathered up the bits and pieces swimming about in my brain concerning the decision I was facing. Composing the letter had been surprisingly comfortable. Then reading it over began to clarify what the essentials were. Would I ask to be clothed? Yes.

Two months are set aside to prepare for Clothing—for practical reasons such as the time needed to make the habit (there are multiple fittings) and because the bishop determines the date of the ceremony according to his availability (the date for Dolores' Clothing was changed three times). The Community also needed time to arrange accommodations for her guests. Dolores' thirty-eight invitees exceeded the available space at both guesthouses, which sent the nuns scurrying to arrange outside accommodations, including several private homes in the vicinity and the Curtis House in Woodbury, the oldest inn in Connecticut. Dolores also wrote personal notes to several members of the Hollywood press who had been particularly kind to her, advising them of her impending new status, which they published in their columns.

I just felt it was a good way to keep my fans aware of my progress.

There had been a great deal of media interest in the ceremony, and several magazines and newspapers requested access. *Look* magazine was given permission to cover the event by the Hartford Archdiocese. An agreement was drawn up listing the ground rules. The article had to be submitted to the archdiocese to check for accuracy, and there were severe restrictions as to what could be photographed. This boiled down to two shots: one of Dolores in a formal dress before the ceremony and one, post ceremony, in her habit—but only through the Communion window. *Look* bowed out. The *New York Post* agreed to abide by the rules and was the only publication allowed to cover the event. The *Post* article, however, was widely quoted in other publications.

It is customary in most orders for the candidate to take a new name at the time of Investiture: new name equals new life. The new name was decided upon by Reverend Mother Benedict and revealed to the novice at the end of the ceremony. In my case, the chances were good that I would retain my own given name. There was ample precedent; Thérèse of Lisieux, for example, kept her own name. However, there was an older nun in the Community who felt very strongly that I should have the name Judith; it became almost an obsession with her. Because Reverend Mother was convinced that a name change could help in distancing me from the media, she asked me if I could accept the name of Judith, making it clear that my acceptance could reach out to this nun and perhaps save her vocation. Did I want to be Judith?

—Well, there is an entry in your journal—May 7, 1964—that reads: God knows I do not—but I will.

I knew how much it would cost Mom to think of me no longer as Dolores. Indeed, she did not hide her displeasure with my new name even though I explained that the title of Judith is a complement *of Dolorosa and was one of the reasons Reverend Mother had approved that name. I think, at the time, I also hoped that Judith's courage would give me strength.*

Both Judith and Mary represent absolute faith in God. Both gave their lives totally in praise of Him. Judith, introduced in the Old Testament, was a wealthy widow who became a heroine to her people at the time the Assyrians, an enemy of Israel, were laying siege to her town. The elders felt sure all would die and were about to capitulate, but Judith insisted, "God will not let us be destroyed if we are faithful." This brave woman risked her own life by going to the Assyrian general's tent, getting him drunk and cutting off his head! When she returned to her people, she was praised as blessed above all women on earth for what she had done. In the Latin version of the Book of Judith, you will see the phrase "non recedat laus" *("May praise never cease"). It is the motto that appears on our abbey crest.*

❦

My Investiture took place on June 29, 1964. It was a perfect summer day. As was the custom then, postulants arrived at the Clothing wearing a wedding dress, symbolic of marriage to Christ, and usually it was a family heirloom. That was a convention with which I was quite ill at ease. It had less to do with the garment itself than a conviction that it was premature. I was not going to be a full member of the Community. All I was going to do was exchange my postulant tunic for the habit of a novice. The wedding dress did not fit the step I was taking.

My discomfort with this was yet another example of my finding fault with the system. I spoke about this to Reverend Mother, who listened patiently and then brought out photographs of her Clothing and said, "I wore a wedding dress."

—*I knew that I shouldn't press the point.*

I dressed in a simple white gown that I found in our closet of clothing that had been worn by previous postulants. With it, I wore a lovely lace mantilla that my friend Father Salazar brought me as a gift. But I remained embarrassed. I decided that I would work on changing that part of the ceremony someday.

—And have you?

> *Well, let's just say my Clothing was the last time the wedding dress was used. After that, clothes that represented a woman's own professional or personal life were worn, to show more what she was leaving behind. It broke with the traditional idea that the woman was now the bride of Christ. The reality at my Clothing was that I was a long way from that step.*

All of Dolores' families were represented at the Clothing. Harriett was there—with Emilio Mazza, her new companion and partner in a Hollywood talent agency they had recently opened. Among Dolores' relatives were both grandmothers, May Hicks and Esther Kude; her uncle John Hicks' wife, Mabel; her uncle James Pittman and Sister Dolores Marie. Her religious family included Fathers Doody, Salazar and White, and Ray Powers represented her professional family. Valerie Allen,

245

Gerry Brent, Ina Balin, and her benefactor from her New York days, Irving Sachs, made up the close-friends contingent. Maria Cooper and Jan Shepard served as her godmothers.

As was the tradition, I walked with Mom and the other guests up the hill to the chapel in procession. I was seated with my guests until Maria and Jan escorted me to the altar, where I knelt before the prelate—who was, happily, my good friend Monsignor Lacy. I divested myself of jewelry, actually just hair combs and a small gold pin—and Monsignor Lacy made one cut of my hair. Then Maria and Jan led me back to the cloister, where the cutting was completed.

The cutting of the hair is a deeply felt experience because this moment is the first physical step for the nun to receive the habit. It can be terrible too, as it was for me, because I was giving up a sign of my femininity. In actual fact, my hair was not cut short. Reverend Mother felt a symbolic cut was sufficient out of respect for the individual.

—It was a practical consideration. If the novice should leave prior to making vows, she wouldn't have to leave with a shaved head.

My mind flickered with minutiae as my appearance changed—flashes from the past: my grandmothers brushing and brushing my hair, hours spent in front of a studio mirror having my hair made special for a scene. Now it was being made special for a better part. I changed from the gown, symbolic of marriage, to the habit and white veil, symbolic of a life of devotion to God.

It's a fair observation that, as an actress, I was curious about my appearance. I wanted desperately to see how I looked, but with nary a mirror around, the only time I saw myself in the habit was when I caught my reflection in a window pane. I immediately recalled I had worn a habit before—a costume—but the headdress I wore when I played Clare had felt like a helmet. I had, frankly, feared wearing a helmet for the rest of my life, but my religious headdress felt much more comfortable. Somehow it seemed part of my body. I felt free.

Following the Rule of Saint Benedict, *I knocked three times at the cloister door. It was opened by Reverend Mother, and I took my place beside her. I could see there were tears in her eyes.*

—Never since have I put my veil on without remembering the look on her face.

"Are you ready?" she asked quietly. She opened an envelope, took out a piece of paper and said, "Tu vocaberis Soror Judith." I nearly died. I had forgotten that I would be receiving a new name. I was now Sister Judith.

At the end of the Investiture there was a brief reception in Saint Joseph's to give me a chance to say goodbye to family and friends before retreating inside the enclosure for the next year. I remember that Mom seemed totally happy and even at peace. The last thing she said to me was about Reverend Mother. They had met several times in the year between my entrance and Clothing, and Mom had been quite drawn to her. "I looked into those eyes", she told me that day. "Don't ever doubt her, Dolores. She knows."

However, in revisiting that day, Jan Shepard remembered, "Everyone attending was very supportive and happy for Dolores. Even her mother seemed contented. But that evening a very bitter Harriett said to me so forlornly, 'It's all my fault, isn't it?' "

Twenty-Five

It is harder than I ever dreamed. It is so real it hurts and yet anything less would be unbearable in its sham. It is the ineffable brought to terms.

—Journal entry, August 1964

For one year after my Clothing, I would not leave the enclosure except for medical needs. No visitors would be allowed, and this applied not only to people I knew but to any guests. No telephone calls could be made or received except in the most severe emergency. Letters could be received, but they would first be read and evaluated. Permission to reply would have to be granted and the letter appraised before it could be sent. All of this was to help me become so formed in the customs and practices of the Order that they would become second nature to me.

Such a total immersion in monastic life is harsh, but I looked upon that year as a time for reflection and integration. I had only a short while to find out whether I could live the life fully. Until First Vows, I could still abandon my course with no strings attached.

As a novice I was not yet a full-fledged member of the Community, but I began to participate in many more aspects of its life. I did the same things I did as a postulant, but I was now expected to do them with greater regularity and attention.

My obediences in the garden and laundry continued (I would ultimately work at both jobs for seven years), but I was now required to be at every Office. If I was working, say, in the garden on a project that couldn't be stopped and the bell rang for prayer, I would be sent to pray; whoever was supervising me would finish the project herself. I had to focus on this very difficult rhythm of obedience to the Horarium— the Hours of the day—by doing it repeatedly over a long period until it became part of me.

During that year, there were times when I felt special, as if I were doing something very difficult—more or less unheard of—and I began to feel changes in myself. As a novice I began to take my turn as an acolyte, which required me to sing alone and was therefore a big deal. As a novice I was assigned a rotating obedience as reader in the refectory and in choir. I could now be a choir servant, the person who assists the hebdomadarian (the singer who leads the Office) and carry the holy water as she blesses each place in the monastery at night. This was a custom Reverend Mother brought from Jouarre. It's a privilege to perform this service, and I took it very seriously. As a novice I was able to join a schola, the little group that stands with the foundress and helps center the singing of the Mass—again, a big deal.

There was something pure about the lack of outside contact. I really began to dig into my life within *the monastery and to answer my needs* within *the Community. The separation from the outside world forced issues as it anchored me, made me look into myself more.*

To enter the contemplative life truly, you have to go through a narrow, lonely place in your being, where you face all your fears and selfish patterns, even when you don't know what these are. I thought I was very grown up, very mature. You don't realize what a child you are until God tests your heart and you go through that deep place all of us have to go through.

—I felt like a fisherman, knee deep in a roaring current, balanced on one leg with a fish on the line—and my suspenders falling down.

When Mother Placid returned to Regina Laudis, she was quite concerned that the radiant young postulant she remembered from a year before now appeared tired and drawn. She suggested to Mother Benedict that a meaningful obedience for Sister Judith would be art work.

I was assigned two hours a week that would replace one garden obedience—an unexpected gift very early in my canonical year that allowed me some time to devote to a real interest. I began to work with Mother Placid in a small room in the basement of the monastery building she called the studio. I called it a haven for those two hours a week, an answer

249

to a long, sighing prayer. Being reunited with Mother Placid, whose depar-
ture had left me so angry, was a grace I accepted with great joy.

Never having plunged into serious study of art before, a new world
opened up. Mother Placid was passionate about art. "It is not", she
would repeat often, "merely self-expression; it expresses something. In
all primitive societies, the artist was the storyteller, there to express his
beliefs, his tribe. Art has a practical meaning. It has a spiritual mean-
ing. It has a communal meaning."

Together we studied anatomy, design and sculpting. I made clay
figures for miniature crèches that were sold in the monastery art shop.
Our first major endeavor, however, was the result of a visit by the
California mosaic artist Louisa Jenkins, who had been introduced to
Regina Laudis by Clare Boothe Luce. Originally Louisa had come to
meditate, but after she and Mother Placid became friends, she began
passing on her artistic expertise. We were taught enameling by a
master. I learned to fire the tiny medals of copper with enamel glazes in
the studio's small kiln. Louisa also taught us to make ecretions.

—Ecretions?

> *That was what Louisa called them. Rice-paper collages. We*
> *tore up a lot of multicolored rice paper, glued the pieces*
> *together in thin, thin, thin layers to create a collage of*
> *abstract design and put heavy boards over it and walked on*
> *it. "Voila!" as Louisa would say. "Ecretions!"*

Before long, we found we could sell our wares—the ecretions, the
enamels and, at Christmastime, the small crèches—through the Catholic
Contemporary Arts Gallery on Madison Avenue in New York City.
Using my knowledge of movie promotion, I sent postcards about our
work to everyone I knew in New York. The gallery manager couldn't
believe all the people who came in.

—What did the artwork sell for?

> *I think the ecretions were priced at $150. Our pieces were*
> *priced at less money than the owner thought they could*
> *bring. There's an instruction in the Rule that monks are to*

sell their crafts at something less than the going price in stores so that poor people would have access to goods.

More importantly at this critical time, Mother Placid talked things over with me while working, which helped me understand the inner mechanism of the monastery. She threw light on the dissension I had earlier perceived among that group of older nuns. It was growing. At Sunday recreation, when novices were with the professed, I picked up on whispered complaints. Often when I came into the laundry room, nuns fell suddenly quiet, and I knew the women hadn't been discussing how to fold linen. When Mother Placid would return from a meeting, I could tell she was rankled. I could just feel it in her.

Those women in the Community who were not with Reverend Mother questioned the blind acceptance of her as foundress. They were traditional in most ways, but the American way of voting for a superior appealed to them. They felt they should not just accept but elect. They wanted to establish a new foundation without Mother Benedict and Mother Mary Aline at its head. They were also increasingly resentful when Father Prokes reminded them of Reverend Mother's accomplishments.

Father Prokes was never shy about promoting her credentials. "Do you really know this woman?" he would challenge. "Do you know what she has gone through to make this foundation happen?" Now, Reverend Mother was a tough lady, but she didn't elevate herself because ultimately she felt whatever achievement she represented was not a result of her will but of God's. She believed that her Community should accept that.

I shared Father Prokes' view of Reverend Mother. I had long since rejected my first impression, made when I was a guest during her twenty-fifth Jubilee, that she was naïve. The quality I had observed was not naïveté; it was holiness. I recognized her as a godly woman.

At each phase of formation you have a different formation mother. My new novice mistress, as she is called, was by-the-book Mother Stephen. Any gift I was sent was immediately submitted to her discernment. She allowed me to keep only very expedient things such as socks or writing

251

paper. There was no judgmental connotation when she said I could not keep a particular item; it was just not proper. I could accept that.

But I had a problem with being told how I should respond to a specific experience—say, to a book that she had also read. I resented her projection of her own personal experience onto my experience. And I could not abide being told what to write in my letters. I revolted then, but a seed was planted at that time that would flower years later.

—Did you have a shoulder to cry on?

> *I did not have a Community member's shoulder to cry on, if that's what you mean. To pose an internal question to someone just didn't exist then. No, I held it in. But even if you cry on someone's shoulder, you can do that for just so long.*

Because of the lack of communication, you had to rely on what you sensed from a sister who may have wanted to help but was prohibited from doing so—maybe a smile or a whispered "Courage" as you passed in the hall. I couldn't get rid of the impression that the religious life should bring forth kinship persons. It brought forth heroic individuals, true, but it didn't include a relational base, which was the way the Church started, wasn't it?

I can't imagine that men and women are meant to give up their impetus for fruitful relationships. I think fertility is part of us, and if you don't become fruitful at one level of your being, your fertility is to be used in another dimension. A person is not meant to be isolated.

—Not meant to be isolated? Are you speaking about monastic life?

> *No, I don't think isolation works for a person anywhere.*

Would a postulant or novice at Regina Laudis today go through the periods of isolation that you went through?

> *I hope not. I really hope that she would knock at my door.*

❦

252

The separation during the canonical year was extremely hard on Harriett. Unable to talk with her daughter on the telephone, her letter output doubled, every letter beginning with "Hi, Honey" or "Hi, Kiddo", never "Sister Judith".

Harriett had taken to giving interviews to fan magazines. Writers who could not gain access to her daughter came to her for quotes, which she effusively provided. In one interview, she announced that she had begun Catholic instruction herself so that she could "fully share and relate to" what her "daughter is living."

—Oh yes, that sounded great. That was the response that made everybody happy. There was no way to try to go into any greater depth about it with her. Actually, she began instruction three times. She did always try. She wanted so much to have something work. But, as with her forays into AA, she didn't follow through.

Harriett's life was beginning to show signs of falling apart. The Mazza-Hart talent agency was a flop, and with increasing regularity her letters hinted at financial problems. Finally she wrote that the trust fund was gone and her landlord was threatening eviction.

I thought Mom had gotten herself into a pickle by pouring money down the drain for booze, and I did not offer to send money. First, I flat out didn't have the resources to do that. I had no money of my own. But it would have been a cruel thing had I been able to send a check.

Like her, I was involved in a day-to-day struggle to maintain stability. I was dealing with my problems; she had to deal with hers. I knew how tempting it is to cry out. My battle to find the peace and comfort of God's presence continued every night. But Reverend Mother kept faith in me. She let me cry over day-to-day disappointments and failures because she thought I could pick myself up. When I did pick myself up, I felt stronger, and then I was grateful for her confidence in my strength. What we often need is another's conviction that we can make it.

"Money is not what you need, Mom", I wrote her. "What you need is the courage to live in a sober state of mind. If you go back to the booze,

you will just be showing me that I was wrong to have confidence in you."

❦

On January 9, 1965, I was summoned from the studio to take a phone call from Liliana Hicks, Daddy's fourth wife. I was shocked by her message: Daddy had suffered a heart attack and died in his sleep. He was only forty-four years old. He had been, Liliana said, "in bad shape for many months". I didn't know. He hadn't kept his promise to visit the monastery, and the only correspondence I had received from him was a birthday note containing a photo of my new half-brother, Bert, who was then only nineteen months old. Liliana told me that Daddy's last months were spent poring over a scrapbook of his Hollywood days, showing her what he had looked like as a young man.

A requiem Mass for Daddy was held in Pacoima, California. I was not allowed to leave the monastery to attend—that was the rule then— but when a parent of a Regina Laudis nun dies, the entire Community participates in the Office of the Dead, and they did so for Daddy. This was a special privilege since that offering was for members of the professed Community. It was quite touching.

I had a great problem integrating what I was feeling about losing my father and what I thought I should feel. I couldn't help but think that he had not earned the right to come back into my life even in death. He was a first-class charlatan, but I did mourn the loss of him—and the loss of the little-girl faith I had in his manly profile. That faith was paper-thin, yes, but beautiful.

> *—You've sent me tapes of Daddy's movie appearances. There's one scene in the movie with Robert Montgomery where Montgomery knocks him out in a fistfight. I had to laugh when I saw it because next to Daddy, Robert Montgomery looked so puny.*

I remembered something Sister Dolores Marie said to me at the time of Grandpa's passing in 1962. She had referred to his conversion at death as final, something that had ended. I didn't want to believe that, and now Daddy's death had revived this dilemma in me.

254

Of course, I took my pain to Reverend Mother and immediately felt my relationship with her changing, growing stronger as we talked. She was very sensitive to the difficulty I was having in trying to integrate the experience of death.

She told me that Daddy did have the right to ask redemption of me. "Anyone can ask for redemptive love", she said. "As a Benedictine nun you must say, 'Here I am, I am available.' Your father must be having quite a struggle now, preparing for his encounter with God. You don't stop your conversion just because you die. Conversion goes on in many levels of process even after death. Death is the initial conversion in relation to the body, but change continues. You have to trust that your own love and forgiveness will somehow make the way easier for your father."

Years later, Liliana confided that, in fact, Daddy had not succumbed to a heart attack. The real details were sadder to hear. In the eighteen months after my entrance, he drank continuously. On Christmas Eve, just two weeks before his death, he had gotten into a fight at a neighborhood bar and landed in jail. Liliana bailed him out, and a doctor prescribed medication. He took a massive dose of the pills and washed them down with the booze. Suicide was listed as the cause of death on his death certificate. Mom was the one Liliana called when she found Daddy dead. Mom rushed to her side and, ever the caregiver, fixed breakfast at 5:00 A.M. for Liliana and little Bert. Mom hadn't told me any of this.

"Don't try to evaluate too soon what happened to your father," Reverend Mother cautioned me, "because he still has many levels of purgation to go through before his life is completed. Death is only the beginning of purgation. We have a paucity of understanding our souls leaving our bodies and moving into another state. The fact is, the soul leaving the body must be purified before it is ready to see God. What has to happen is a mystery—we can't say that all of a sudden you die, go to Purgatory, and it's over. So we pray for the souls in Purgatory who are in process of change."

My daddy was a man in search of a star, and I had to rely on the mercy of God and trust that my own love and forgiveness would somehow make the way easier for him.

❧

The adjoining towns of Bethlehem and Woodbury had accepted Reverend Mother Benedict's offer to end the standoff on Burritt Hill Road. She had proposed that a new road be built that would follow their northern property line and leave the land intact, thus keeping the monastery enclosure unbroken. Further, she had promised that the Community would pay half the costs and provide half of the physical labor that would go into building the two-mile thoroughfare connecting Flanders Road with Route 61, which would bear the name Robert Leather Road.

Eight months into my canonical year—and for the next two years— the Community took on the grueling work of turning a forest into a roadway. In fair weather or foul, we women cleared the land with clippers, shovels and our bare hands to make it ready for the heavy machinery to lay the asphalt.

All emotions—joy, sadness, fear—were present, as were most of the women, led by Mother Stephen and Father Prokes manning tractors and Reverend Mother swinging an axe. I remember mostly gray, damp days that drew the color out of everything. I remember callused hands, bleeding knees, scuffed toes. And mud. Not only earth and water mud. Mud of dust and sweat, too.

At the end of each workday, I would stand on the edge of the road that was not yet a road but, like an eager child, stretching into growth. Although it was the dirtiest, hardest, most exhausting slave labor I could ever imagine, it was also a very real experience in corporate collaboration. It offered a new analysis of contemplative life, and I found that exciting, but I knew instinctively that it cut deeper into where the basic issues of the discontent within the Community continued to ferment. It was almost the straw that broke the camel's back.

All during the work on the road, the group of nuns at odds on almost every issue became more vocal in their disagreements with Reverend Mother. "Why do we have to have all this land to take care of?" they would demand. "We are not meant to get involved with the world. We came here to pray, to meditate, to be good contemplatives. What does this road have to do with monastic life?"

Reverend Mother stood firm and insisted that land and monastic life do relate. She fervently believed that, from the very beginning, Saint

Benedict intended that each monastery would be a center of holiness where monks could live contained lives, built around the recitation throughout the day and night of the Divine Office, but which also could provide all the other necessities of daily life. Thus, throughout history, each monastery has been a self-contained entity. In chapter 48 of the Rule, Saint Benedict states, "Idleness is the enemy of the soul. The brethren, therefore, must be occupied at stated hours in manual labor ... for then are they truly monks when they live by the labor of their hands."

Envisioning that the monastery would become an abbey one day, Reverend Mother foresaw a place with land and animals, a place of green that by the mid-twenty-first century might be the only conservation land left in our area of Connecticut.

During the work on Robert Leather Road, on one of those mud-encrusted days when, dog-tired and hungry, I took my usual place in line for supper in the refectory, all at once my attention was taken by the water pitchers on the shelf. They were all lined up with handles facing the same direction and made a sparkling, beautiful tableau. A small thing, I suppose, but I hadn't noticed it before, and it made me realize that someone had made that effort to make our lives more pleasant.

I soon began to notice other small things that made our life together more comfortable, a little more serene. From time to time, notes appeared at my place at table—notes of encouragement, with bits of grasses or flowers glued to the paper—from sisters who recognized and perhaps shared what I was feeling and cared enough to offer support. Each time I was confronted with a new grace, I was reminded of my trip on the Dutch barge when I saw my first windmill: "There's one!"

During a chant lesson, Mother Columba presented me with a book she had made herself. It was a charming depiction of the chants wherein the notes resembled cartoon figures she named Dot and Po who danced up and down on the staff. It became my constant companion as an uncomplicated and painless guide—as well as a reminder that I had not become invisible, that my good friend still cared about me.

257

But no matter how hard I studied the psalms, I still could not master the Latin. I could not grasp the meaning. There were nuns in the Community who could translate the Offices in a snap. I was still relying on the translations printed in the book. I had come to the point of just accepting this because there is something in the music that calls you even if you do not understand the words. The beauty of the melodies and the élan of the rhythm make you peaceful and prayerful. "Singing", in the words of Saint Augustine, "is praying twice."

Then one morning in Prime while we were singing Psalm 17 and we came to the verse "et eduxit me in latitudinem: salvum me fecit, quoniam voluit me." *I suddenly knew that this was an important verse. I could feel in my heart that it had meaning for me.*

After the Office, I sought out Mother Columba and asked her what the verse meant. She slowly translated: " 'Et eduxit me in' means 'and the Lord has led me into'; 'latitudinem', an 'open space', a 'free space'; 'salvum me fecit', 'and He has given me this salvation'; 'quoniam voluit me', 'because He loved me'. It's simple, Sister. God sets you free because He loves you." That was exactly what I had felt when I was singing.

That was the key that opened the Office to me. I used to hear sisters say, "I love Lauds; if I can get to Lauds my whole day is better" or "Without Compline, I feel I have not ended the day well", and I would wonder what they meant by that. Now I thought of the scene in The Miracle Worker *when young Helen Keller realizes the connection between the word she had learned only by rote and the actual thing it represented— water. I could identify with that moment. I knew that if I could stay with it and truly pray the Office, the significance would come through.*

Chanting the Office finally allowed me to comprehend each Hour of the day in answer to the question: Why am I doing this? Why am I sweeping the floor? Why am I lifting rocks? When you come to the Office you have the opportunity to bring to consciousness the fact that you are doing this in praise of God.

"Run while ye have the light of life, lest the darkness overtake you" appears in the prologue of the Rule. Reverend Mother often stressed in

our meetings together that I should "seize that moment". It was a message I deeply valued. I remained uncomfortable with elements of monastic life that I found unreasonable, and she once said to me, "I think you should write those things down." Now seemed an apt time to do some moment-seizing. I sat down and wrote a letter to Reverend Mother, the one person with whom I sensed I was earning a place of respect.

The letter seemed to write itself. Thoughts I had kept pent up since entering came rushing out.

> *A real suffering we women share is a need to establish ourselves as* individuals, *yet everything is geared to some sort of demonical force that wants to stamp out our uniqueness. How can we, as women from the outside, be asked to leave our experiences, like so much baggage, at the gate? Each of us is matchless and should, for the good of the Church and this Community, be recognized as such and drawn upon to share our distinctiveness. We must be essentially what we are in the deepest calling of our natures and should be encouraged to express the gifts we have in order to contribute, share and participate in the growth of the Community. We shouldn't be just used as animals to obey.*
>
> *There is a false image of each woman that is presented when she is so restricted, and so is denied the opportunity not only to permit other people to know her but for her to know herself.*
>
> *If only a newcomer had someone to talk to, really talk to and unload the pain, someone who could share her own journey within the enclosure and help point the way.*

The next morning, Sister Judith brought her letter to Mother Benedict, who read it in her presence. "Before you change things here," the older nun told the novice, "let's see if you can submit to this outfit."

Then she folded the letter neatly and placed it in the drawer of her desk.

Twenty-Six

At the close of the canonical year, another ceremony marks a further step in monastic life. Ahead of me was First Vows, which would last for three years.

During this time I would still remain free to change my mind; not until the end of those three years—five years after entering the monastery— would I make vows for a lifetime.

But, binding or not, I was making a contract with God. They may be called First *Vows, but they are* vows. *I knew in the core of my being that I would be committing for the rest of my life.*

It was sobering to realize that every woman who had been with me in the novitiate had left. My dear friend Valerie Imbleau, who had just been clothed, would soon also leave. As I got closer to vows, the personal pressure was more immense than when I entered because I now knew the life I would be choosing would be forever.

I received a long letter from Mom acknowledging the upcoming vows. She insisted she was not writing to dissuade me, but the letter was, in fact, a last-ditch attempt to do just that. She credited me with "special gifts that could do God's work on the outside" and went on to plead, "Is it ridiculous to say that Billy Graham has reached more with his homilies than someone in complete seclusion?" Then she moved in for the kill: "It is an unnatural thing for a woman not to give herself in marriage and to the love of a child."

I didn't need Mom's reminder of something that I felt intensely. It was very clear to me that what I was giving over was the right to my own body, relinquishing the right to have a husband, my own children. This realization was on my mind constantly.

When I was finally summoned to Reverend Mother's office, I felt I was at least willing to make those vows from an intellectual standpoint, but I was not able to—nor did I even want to—hide my emotional and very human reluctance. I needed to make certain that my motives for continuing were solid and to know without a doubt that making First Vows was the will of God. I did feel that God wanted me here, but the struggle was still so acute that I didn't know if it would be possible to endure. If my fears reflected a basic worry that I was trying to fit my 8½ AA into Cinderella's slipper, then perhaps the time had come to change the wardrobe.

The customs were not a problem for me; I understood them. They were an honest representation of the Benedictine values that I was trying to incorporate into my life. I still perceived the discipline as a barrier, yet something deep inside me knew that discipline is a way of curbing weakness that would cause only distortion and unhappiness.

Religious life is often painted as something entirely different from what it is. To be obedient and humble should be simply to stand in truth, unhampered by one's ego. If we can escape the need for recognition that is so built into human nature, we can free ourselves from our inhibiting patterns. It can be a blessed freedom—also a terrible freedom.

—Was submission the most difficult thing you had to learn?

Submission to what I felt was wrong.

Reverend Mother had a great breadth of understanding that gave her the ability to relate, but if she expected something of you, she put the fear of the Lord into you. Mother Placid said she would rather tell Reverend Mother she had murdered someone than tell her she had picked one of her flowers. I think I could say the same.

Reverend Mother was understanding and not dismayed by my hesitance. "Such anxiety is normally part of our makeup, and it has a value", she said with a smile. "It allows us to know the limitations of our surrender."

Those gray-green eyes that struck me from the first moment I saw them as penetrating and wise now had a profoundly consoling effect on me. The lasting thing about this woman—the thing that made her unforgettable—was that the most important criterion for her was whether something brought her closer to God.

"You must relax more into the light before plunging into a new set of responsibilities that your culture and background, especially, hardly

261

prepared you for. This sense of panic is not as long-lived as it used to be, but a period of further growth would make the step much less a strain." She recognized I was not an oddity of the sixties. I'm sure she sensed that a whole new generation of women would enter religious life if only it corresponded to their own internal sensibilities.

    —Indeed, everyone who came after me also needed to find her own identity in the Community and to learn how to serve in specific ways. Obedience must be required, yes, but not mindless obedience. It should require full consent of the nun in accordance with her gifts brought by her genealogy and profession and given in love.

Reverend Mother hadn't encouraged my entrance, but she was very receptive now. I received several letters of encouragement from her. "Monastic vows", she wrote, "are the maximum indication that truly we have come to know and believe the love which God has for us. The step that you are taking establishes you in a state of permanent commitment beyond which you can do no more.

    "But no amount of effort to communicate the sense of inner communion with Christ on the part of those who live this can be truly successful unless God first grants the favor. God did grant you the favor."

    She sustained me in my vocation. I felt a oneness with her. I knew what she was saying as I know red in various shades of pink.

    At the end of our retreat, she asked how I felt about taking a six-month extension. I felt relief.

Support came from within the Community. Once again, notes of encouragement began to appear at my place in the refectory. And, as always, Maria offered solid reassurance for commitment. In fact, commitment was in the air for Maria. In April she came for a visit and brought someone she wanted me to meet—a pianist, she said, by the name of Byron Janis.

    —I admired her understatement. Byron Janis, a pianist?

262

It was obvious that Maria was in love with Byron, and she was deter-mined to marry him over her mother's objections. Well, if Rocky didn't like him, I was sure I would.

Byron wore a cream-colored suit and fairly glowed. I felt connected to him immediately on both a personal and a professional level. We both loved Maria, and we both knew the nightmare of performing—how tough it is to live up to your own expectation and to face the fear of not performing as well as you had previously. Before they left that day, Byron said he would like to give me a piece of music—the very first song he wrote. He said he wanted it to be mine.

As the days passed, I was less and less concerned about specific elements of the life that had troubled me. My concern was being replaced with a feeling that the monastic vocation could be truly mine. I worried more whether I would be able to carry out what was needed.

—You said *whether* you would be able to—not that there was any question about *wanting* to.

> *That's true. When you first enter a monastery, you feel that you are on the outside of something and that, though it is invisible, there is a perceptible pulsing heart—a center of truth and meaning that promises to be more real than any-thing you have ever known and draws you toward itself. That's your path in a sense—in toward that deeper truth. And it starts to dawn on you that all your worries, your nervous tension about what you don't understand or how you think things should be, are ultimately not going to get resolved in the ways that were once available to you. You have to let go and experience a free-fall. Otherwise you stay on the outside looking into a mystery that you sense others are caught up in but that you can't enter. It is very scary to let go of all your old defenses and yet necessary to do so. It is highly para-doxical, but I think that is the form most spiritual truth comes in.*

263

When I came to the gate, I came with the promise of a forever commit-ment. It was now that force that took over the apprehension, and if there was any thought then of turning back, I have no recollection of it now. I knew the evil spirit was gambling on my changing my mind. I could feel he had big money on that. When, in the first weeks of my entrance, the flood of letters arrived from all those people I didn't know, telling me how grateful they were that I made that decision, I had a difficult time recognizing the person they were talking about. But I now knew the one they had been betting on. That seems contrary to the doubt, the anxiety, the panic I lived with for so long. But in a sense I never really felt like a person until I came to Regina Laudis. Staying was not a compromise but, in fact, the real challenge of my life.

I made my First Vows on June 29, 1966. First and Final Vows are written out and signed—Saint Benedict's shrewdest rule is "put it in writing". One promises to be bound to stability, conversion of life (for us this vow includes poverty and chastity and literally means one will change) and obedience. A memento card marking each personal cer-emony is printed for the celebrant to hand out to family and friends. My choice for the text came from Psalm 17: "He set me free in the open and saved me because He loved me." It was beautifully illustrated by Mother Placid's block print of a small nun literally dancing in happiness.

First Vows are not necessarily private—family members and friends can be invited to the short ceremony—but often they are witnessed by only the Community. No one outside the Community came to my First Vows, not even Mom. This had far less to do with her deep-seated feelings than with the fact that she had not been in good health for some months and had recently been hospitalized in Los Angeles. I knew this from Don Robinson, who remained in touch with her, visiting the hospital every day. She had been experiencing headaches that incapac-itated her. Her condition had been recognized variously as a pinched nerve, a sacroiliac problem and whiplash but never definitely diag-nosed. At one point she was told the pain was all in her head and that she should see a psychiatrist.

264

—I thought she did have some medical problem that was not merely alcohol again. I remember telling Mom that pain is real and we each must come to grips with its mysterious capacity to penetrate our lives. Sometimes the best way to fight pain is to agree to live with it. That sounds absurd, but pain is not useless.

One also receives the Kiss of Peace at First Vows, a tradition that is observed by the Community on special occasions and at every Mass. I've always found comfort in this simple, lovely ritual. I was approached by each woman in the Community, one by one, and received her Kiss of Peace on my cheek. Usually "Peace be with you" are the only words that accompany the kiss. But, as one of the senior mothers kissed my cheek, she whispered in my ear, "Why don't you leave?" The words sent shivers through me. She might as well have slapped my face. She was the last person I would have expected to do this; she was someone I had offered to help, the one for whom I had accepted the name of Judith.

That night in my cell, her remark triggered the habitual tears. But on this night the tears, instead of lulling me to sleep, gave way to a calm that had been absent since the night of my entrance. When I entered, I had no concept of what monastic life meant. I felt alone. Now I felt as if I were beginning a long-distance run, and I was bouyed by the knowledge that I had other long-distance runners alongside me.

I reached for my journal and began writing:

If the price of loving Him is the pain of having to look for Him, then the price of finding Him is the pain of having to share His loneliness in the Garden of Gethsemane. Loneliness is the worst suffering, and if we can endure this in faith, we have won our way to Him.

Twenty-Seven

I thought my life would change markedly after vows, but at first it remained much the same. I sensed a slight cracking in the wall between the professed and the novitiate—the smiles got broader and the nods a bit more frequent—but the boundaries remained.

The only immediate change was a move into another cell, which was prompted by my noisy nemesis, the tree frog. Father Mike had offered to climb the tree and capture the frog, but I was afraid he would kill himself. A move seemed safer.

Since my entrance, many colleagues had written, asking me to reconsider my decision and return to my career. I understood, for I knew that without the perspective of prayer and meditation it was surely impossible for them to become reconciled to the idea of me as a nun. I often wished I could have expressed to those friends that I hadn't left Hollywood behind. I came in with the desire to return—but not in a way they would understand.

Maybe my making First Vows put the cap on any expectation that I would leave religious life. But, whatever the reason, people from my past began visiting.

In 1967 my brother Martin began what would become semiannual visits. When I entered religious life, our relationship continued through letters, and Martin's salutations would reflect the changes in my status, beginning after my entrance with the simple "Dear Sister". When I was clothed and received my religious name, he wrote, "Dear Sister Sister". After my Final Vows he would write, "Dear Mother Sister".

His letters allowed me to follow his impressive journey through academia, culminating with a PhD in American studies from George Washington University. Among many achievements, Dr. Gordon—my kid brother—established the historical research center of the National Geospatial-Intelligence Agency, taught US history at the Smithsonian and Johns Hopkins University and continues to teach at the University of Maryland.

In addition to teaching classes and authoring several books, Martin has found time to share his expertise with my Community in a number of seminars conducted with his wife, Diane, who also has a PhD.

—I am also very proud that Martin's daughter is my namesake.

Don Robinson began making annual visits. Thinking back, Don said, "I remember at first it was an odd way to see her, behind the grille, but the grille was different then—it had double bars, which created a separation—and the parlor had the most uncomfortable stools. But, all in all, I felt quite close to her—I mean not cut off.

"During that first visit, she asked if I would meet Mother Placid. I still wasn't favorably disposed to her, but I said okay. Though I had accepted Dolores' choice, I was still not at peace with it, and we got off to a bad start. I'll never forget her first remark. She said, 'You think I'm Dolores' Svengali.'

"I replied, 'You might say that', and there was a kind of standoff. Through the years, however, I grew to like her. I began to feel at peace after several visits. I realized that Dolores went to Regina Laudis, not somewhere else, for a particular reason. Yes, she gave her life to God, but she gave her life to God to become a *Benedictine*. It was the Rule. If the Rule were to change, she wouldn't accept that."

My true mentor in Hollywood, Paul Nathan, came several times over the next few years. He supported my decision but never failed to tell me that he always felt a pang of regret that he hadn't packed me away in his bag and brought me back with him. Lois Nettleton actually took part in our Community life. She worked in the dairy, with the animals, on her hands and knees in the garden—whatever needed doing.

I received a letter from Stephen Boyd, who was scheduled to be in New York and asked if he could come to the monastery. I looked forward to seeing him. His trip east coincided with our Lenten retreat, when we do not have guests, but Reverend Mother granted special permission for him to come and even to stay overnight in Saint Joseph's.

It was not a comfortable reunion. It was obvious that Stephen had a difficult time dealing with the grille. He later admitted it was like seeing me in prison. He told me that he had become interested in Scientology;

remembering his distaste for organized religion, I cautioned him to think twice before getting too involved.

He left the parlor quite abruptly, but instead of going to his quarters in the guesthouse, he drove right back to New York. He did not visit again, but we continued to correspond; his letters increasingly concerned his immersion in his study of Scientology. The last letter I received from Stephen came shortly before my Consecration in 1970. He announced his plans to become an active member of the organization and said that his life and mine could never find a crossing point, which saddened me. Stephen died of a heart attack in 1977.

On the feast of the Assumption of Mary in 1966, a shy, petite Japanese woman presented herself at our door. Nobuko Kobayashi looked like a girl, but she was, in fact, twenty years old. She had seen some of my films in Tokyo and was moved to write for permission to visit.

The visit, which lasted a month, was the first of several Nobuko would make over the next few years, each one bringing her closer to the Community and, through her artwork in the studio, creating a lasting bond with Sister Judith. In her journal entry on the day of Nobuko's departure, Sister Judith reveals a transformation that is as significant as it is touching.

> Today is one of the most momentous days in my life. It is the day on which I knew myself for the first time as a mother. Nobuko called me Mother. I could not help but see a reflection of myself and Mother Placid. It's a new role.

In the months after my vows, a peace existed between Mom and me. It seemed at that time to be a new level of bonding. She visited again in November of 1966. She was in pretty good spirits if somewhat lethargic, which was unusual for her. She outlined her medical problems and gave me a rundown on the doctors she had been seeing but, on the whole, presented an enthusiastic outlook health-wise. She seemed determined to make amends for what she termed her "audacity" to have opposed

my decision. "Now that you're really in here, Novice First Class, I realize it was pure selfishness on my part", she said. "I was wrong. This is right for you."

But, in early 1967, out of the blue I got a call from one of her doctors in LA. He told me that if I continued to stay in the monastery Mom would probably die. He emphasized that I was responsible for whatever might happen. I was appalled. This man was putting her life on my back. I told him he had no right to do that. I was mad as all get-out. I truly didn't believe that anything was going to happen to her.

—Is it possible that he made this call at Harriett's request?

Yes, possible. Why?

Around this time, Harriett called one night—after midnight— asking me to come over, said she needed someone to talk to. It was obvious when she opened the door that she had been drinking. We sat and talked—rather, I listened while she talked and continued to drink. She was very depressed and self-pitying and kept repeating, "It's my fault. It's all my fault." I sat with her until she was tired enough to sleep. Just before I left, she apologized and said her words just seemed to fall from her mouth "like coins from a slot machine", adding as she closed the door, "put in by despairing people".

Mom died on May 8, 1967. She was only forty-six years old. We had spoken on the Saturday before her death. It was a hard conversation. I could tell she was drinking heavily. She was in a dark, selfish, mean-spirited place. We both were angry. I hung up on her. It was the first time I ever did that, but I had never been so hopeless.

I was truly sorry but was sure she would call back, as she usually did after a spat. When she didn't call on Sunday, I sensed we were in deep trouble. On Monday evening during Vespers, I was acolyte, singing the versicle at the lectern, when I heard the phone ringing faintly in the nearby entry hall. I knew instantly it was about Mom.

The call was from the Los Angeles Police Department. Mom had been found dead in her apartment. I got in touch with Granny, who said she would leave immediately for LA. She said she would pay my way, too, but Reverend Mother suggested I not go. Granny agreed to be my eyes. She would handle everything for me.

Granny was incensed to learn that the coroner's report listed the cause of death as suicide. She did not believe that. She had gone through everything in Mom's apartment, including the medicine cabinet, where she found a just-filled prescription of sleeping medication. There was only one pill missing. To the day of her death, Granny never accepted that judgment.

Emilio Mazza, Mom's companion, made all the arrangements for the funeral. Later Emilio sent me a small box of Mom's stuff. There was little that held value for me, only a handkerchief reeking of her cologne, her scent, and suddenly she was in the room. I grieved for Mom for a long time. It was more difficult to integrate her death than Daddy's. How much did that have to do with guilt—the maybe, maybe, maybe if I hadn't hung up on her, this wouldn't have happened? I don't know.

Every evening after Vespers, I sought refuge by walking from the chapel to the Hermitage, a small structure in Saint Telchilde's field used for quiet time alone. I was surprised when Mother David joined me one evening and walked with me.

I had been aware of Mother David from the time of my visits to Regina Laudis. She was the nun who had asked me to leave the enclosure on the very same path we were walking now. I knew from the beginning of my time within the monastery that Mother David was a tremendous centering force in the Community even though she was not a major authority then. She did not have to be an official for her authority to be felt. Certain persons convey that authority just entering a room; it flows from the sense of majesty they create. I remember being aware of that back in New York when Cornelia Otis Skinner came into a room.

But once inside the monastery, I had virtually no contact with Mother David. There was such a division then, and she had been faithful to her formation. She had, upon passing me in the hallways, smiled and nodded support, and I had received a card from her after Daddy's death that read: "You are not alone in this." But I didn't really know her.

Mother Abbess David remembered, "The knitting-needles incident when she was still a postulant had served to alert me to a purity of spirit in her. I had searched her out that evening to offer what comfort I could give her for the loss of her mother.

"I don't remember all we spoke of that evening, but Sister mentioned that she didn't like reading, that she would lose concentration. She enjoyed reading scripts, but that's because she's visually oriented. Whenever she described something, she would come to creation through a visual. She would say, 'Gosh, that sunset is just like the one in—and then she would name some movie. Of course, I wouldn't have seen the movie, but it amazed me that she always came from the visual. I could see that for her just to sit and read in her cell could be a problem."

—Before she entered religious life, Mother David had been a social worker, and once a social worker, always a social worker. She was sensitive to my reading problem and asked if she could help. After that evening, she and I started reading together during the short period after Vespers. We started with the unicorn books, which were in our library. We would read them together, out loud.

Over time, I came to the point where I was no longer in deep pain over Mom. I could look back, and the ache wasn't following me. I wondered if that had anything to do with my own capacity to believe in the peaceful release of our souls after death. I didn't know where that place could be, but I knew she was free—and I was no longer locked in my grief.

She was a childlike person—such a searching, groping person. She suffered deeply in her hopes. I've never lost the feeling that Daddy's death contributed to Mom's. She died barely eighteen months after he died. She loved him and she hated him, but I believe that my mother didn't want to be on this earth without him.

I don't have any real sense of either of my parents holding my life. It was more that I was holding theirs. As I grew older, that unspecified burden became an early sense of mission. I feel no failure in that mission because I feel no responsibility for their choices in life. But I believe what I am doing with my life somehow fulfills what was missing in them.

❧

271

The undercurrent of discontent within the Community only intensified during the late sixties, and there was no longer any effort to hide the growing resentment. With my actor's sense, I could tell that there was mutiny in the air.

It seemed to me that those unhappy women were interpreting Vatican II in their own way, protesting that our religious habits, Gregorian chant, Latin Mass—and finally the enclosure itself—should go. Reverend Mother stood firm in her belief that, however contradictory it appeared, openness to the future and unity with the past were not only necessary for the continuity of Regina Laudis, but possible.

— Continuity—that's important to Benedictines.

I was picking up darker vibrations, too—a growing mind-set that Reverend Mother's tenure as superior should be ended and a new centering official installed. They also wanted to end Father Prokes' position at the monastery. Some of the women even wrote letters to the Vatican asking that Regina Laudis be designated as a new priory. That's what they really wanted to form, something that was very neat and could simply be tied up and put into the hands of the local bishop. Then we would be just another nice, sweet, predictable nunnery that belonged to him.

Most of the women in the Community accepted Reverend Mother as both foundress and superior, and they wanted that to be endorsed by the Holy See. To end the standoff, Reverend Mother decided she had no choice but to take her case to Rome. In 1968, with Mother Irene at her side, she traveled to Rome for a meeting with Pope Paul VI—the former Cardinal Giovanni Montini, the man who had supported her call to found the monastery. He stood firmly by Reverend Mother and confirmed her place as superior. He also urged her to have a constitution composed, tailor-made for Regina Laudis.

When she returned to the monastery, Reverend Mother left no possibility open for further opposition. "I have been validated by the pope as the foundress and superior of this monastery", she told us. "I am in charge, and if I want the door latches painted green, they will be painted green."

— This is true. They were green.

Drafting the monastery's constitution was now the main order of business. Reverend Mother Benedict assembled a nucleus of professed nuns who would work with her and Father Prokes on its composition. In a surprising move, she invited Sister Judith, although only in First Vows, to join with them. She knew that this particular youngster would add the voice of the future in a no-holds-barred way.

This was an advanced concept for the monastery because usually the young people were afraid to say anything. It was a great gift to be included, as it offered me the opportunity to immerse myself inside a corporate vision of our life. I approached the challenge eagerly because I fervently supported Reverend Mother's belief that a new constitution did not mean throwing out fifteen hundred years of Benedictine Rule but taking on those perennial values with a new dedication.

Working on our constitution was one of the most incredible learning phases of my life. Among the women with whom I worked was Mother Jerome von Nagel Mussayassul, one of the most learned and gifted persons I've ever known. She was an accomplished writer and poet, fluent in eight languages. At various times in her life, she called Germany, Egypt, Italy and the United States home. She had been married to a Muslim émigré, a highly regarded painter. Together they gave shelter to Russian refugees and concentration camp survivors during and after World War II.

When her husband died, she continued writing, under the name Muska Nagel, yet felt a pull toward monastic life that led her to Regina Laudis. At age fifty she entered the monastery in the same year that I, at nineteen, was entering the movie world.

Mother Jerome spoke to me of her friendship with Sister Judith. "I served as sacristan at her Clothing. In those days, there was no way really to know someone, but the one thing that struck me was her utter simplicity. You never got the impression of a star coming to the monastery—never, under no circumstances. And that is part of her innermost being. That she made that impression always gave me a good feeling about Hollywood.

"We began to know each other when we worked on the constitution together. She was very committed—articulate, outspoken and quite

273

funny. But the lasting impression that I carry is that she is a good listener. She looks at you as if she is investigating what you're really thinking."

> *—I shared a bond with Mother Jerome—one that we kept to ourselves. I once mentioned to her that I despised putting my hands in dirt. "My dear," she said smiling, "the earth was made for humans to walk upon, not to grovel in, like worms."*

It would take a year to complete the first draft of our constitution, which Reverend Mother herself presented to the Sacred Congregation for Religious in Rome. We would wait two years for a response. The draft was rejected but with suggestions to facilitate a favorable consideration in the future. I felt they had cut out the charity and compassion and mercy. A number of versions would be submitted before our constitution was finally accepted in 1974.

> *—I see new documents coming out of Rome today, and they contain the very things we had included in that first draft. The substance of what we wrote all those years ago is used now to "bring the Church into the new millennium".*

Twenty-Eight

Set me like a seal on your heart, like a seal on your arm;
for love is strong as death, jealousy relentless as sheol.
The flash of it is a flash of fire, a flame of Yahweh himself,
love no flood can quench, no torrents drown.

—Song of Songs 8:6–7

Formation at Regina Laudis follows the classical stages of postulancy,
novitiate, first profession, then final profession and the reception of the
Consecratio Virginis, *the ancient Rite of Consecration to a Life of*
Virginity, which seals the love between the contemplative and God as
described in the Song of Songs.

It seems that the journey to Consecration should be one of climbing
up a mountain when, in fact, it is like riding ripples on a pond. If I had
to illustrate that passage, I think I would need a motion-picture camera
to capture the constant movement: up, in and out, and for that matter,
sideways too, illuminating the periods of despondency as well as joy.

As I moved toward the time of Final Vows and Consecration, I grew
more and more aware of the immensity of the responsibility that I would
be assuming and was again troubled that I wouldn't be up to it. The
decision as to whether a novice will continue to Final Vows is made by the
Community as well as by the individual, and in the spring of 1970 the
Community and I were in agreement that I was suited to the spiritual life.

Final Vows and Consecration had been traditionally combined in a
single ceremony, but Reverend Mother informed me that I was to
proceed in two steps. It was the first time the ceremonies of Consecra-
tion and Final Vows were separated at Regina Laudis.

Separating Final Vows and Consecration allows for two accents to
emerge. Profession is thought of as masculine because it requires the
woman to put herself forward, daring to say: I will promise this, I will
give myself, I will identify with the sacrifice and mission of Christ on

275

the Cross. Consecration calls on the feminine side of the woman as she receives the blessing of the Church on the promises she has made. This ceremony requires the bishop or abbot because it is an affirmation from the Church. The nun's marriage to Christ is sealed by the bishop's blessing.

I was to make my Final Vows on the feast of Saint Benedict, July 11, and to be consecrated on September 15, on the feast of Our Lady of Sorrows. Separating the ceremonies further enhanced the complementary aspects of the liturgies of these two feast days. They really said Joseph and Mary to me in a full Benedictine way.

I had decided to illuminate my own memento cards for the ceremonies. For First Vows, I used an acrylic of a unicorn I had painted; for the Consecration I chose a free-form image of our Lady painted years before by Mother Placid (with a tooth brush!), which I had found by chance under boards in the studio. People said it put them in mind of Picasso, which pleased me.

—Mother Placid didn't mind too much either.

Final Vows are binding. The three vows are stability (you promise to stay in the cloister, and the Community promises to keep you); conversion (you promise to change your life, which includes accepting poverty and chastity); and obedience (you pledge fidelity to the authority of the abbess). Your title changes from Sister to Mother, and from then on you wear the black veil and cowl.

In addition to making these promises, at Final Vows I was given a new name, the first and only time that has occurred at Regina Laudis. Reverend Mother confided that she had been considering giving me back my own name because she felt it was more appropriate than Judith. I was overjoyed. Even though I had accepted it, I had never ever been at peace with Judith. The only sadness brought by this change was that Mom would not hear me called Dolores again and this would have made her so happy.

A move to another cell was called for now that I was a member of the Community, this one on the third floor of the monastery building. The first thing I learned was that the third floor had been condemned by the *local fire department as unsafe. Every year there was an inspection, and the same improvements were stipulated.*

> *—It appears that we simply ignored the stipulations. I'm relieved that we are now finally in the throes of making the needed improvements as part of our restoration of the lower monastery, an ongoing project we call New Horizons.*

Since her entrance seven years before, I had remained in contact with Dolores—Sister Judith—by letter, yet I was surprised when she invited me to participate in her Consecration, to present the veil during the ceremony. "You, more than anyone else, have veiled me", she explained. I wasn't sure exactly what that meant, but I accepted her invitation.

> *—Most strikingly, you made certain that I was veiled in the most intense ways in matters professional, mainly having to do with the press, but which expanded into personal nurturing. You made me feel protected.*

The morning of her Consecration was dark and rainy. I arrived at the monastery early, hours before the scheduled ceremonial Mass, because I thought there surely would be a rehearsal.

I think most civilians must deal with immense unease in anticipation of a first visit to a cloistered monastery. My sole impression of monasteries came from movies I had seen. They were thoroughly gloomy. Although the masterful movie villainess Gale Sondergaard never played a nun on the screen, in my mind she was what I expected to find at a monastery.

I rang at the door of the main building, a plain gray structure that beggared description—industrial gothic?—and crossed the threshold into a small entry where a stern-looking nun looked through a grille. She said something in Latin in a low, accented voice. I thought to myself, "Gale Sondergaard lives."

The nun directed me to a small chapel where I was to wait. The chapel itself was from another era, another place—a perfect set piece for a French movie. I waited for a very long time, and when guests started to arrive, I began to get anxious. All of a sudden, a tiny nun with a Southern accent that seemed to drip magnolia blossoms appeared before me. "Are you Mr. DeNeut? Well, where have you been?"

This was Mother Ruth Barry, who, I later learned, was in charge of the sheep. She led me smartly through a door that put me smack back in the entry where she outfitted me in a robe (called an alb) and tied a rope sash (called a cincture) around my waist so tightly I wondered if they were going to let me out afterward.

I had no idea what was expected of me during the ceremony. "Never mind," she said, "I'll be right at your side—just do what I do. I'll nudge you when it's time for you to present this"—she handed me a metal plate with a folded piece of black cloth on it—"then you'll go up the three steps to the altar. The veil will be taken from you and given to Sister Judith. Then you will back down the steps and return to your seat. It will be fine."

Back down the steps?

The chapel was packed long before the Mass began, strictly standing room only. Seated near me were Maria Cooper and Estelle Coniff, there as Dolores' godmothers, and a young Japanese woman who was to present the ring.

> —*I wanted Nobuko to be a significant part of the ceremony and the depth of her participation to be acknowledged. The symbol of the ring was strong enough to bear her sentiment of belonging to us in the "foreverness" of this moment. This would blossom in a way I couldn't have anticipated.*

At the beginning of the ceremony, Sister Judith was escorted in procession out of the enclosure to a seat in the front row of the congregation, in my direct line of vision. It had been a decade since I had laid eyes on her. She wore a very simple crown of white stephanotis on her head, and she was more beautiful than I had ever seen her—on-screen or off.

My seat also gave me the opportunity to get a close look at the women who made up the Community of Regina Laudis, all seated in the choir area behind the heavy wooden grille. One thing struck me immediately: the good-looks quotient at the monastery was very high.

The veil is presented first. I managed the steps up to the altar with no show of nerves, but when I began the backward maneuver, I could feel immediately that I had stepped on my alb. A flash of my going tail over teacup stopped me cold. Then it occurred to me to switch my weight, which released the robe from underfoot, and I was able to continue my descent without further impediment.

The three Scripture readings at the Consecration came together beautifully as a journey through life from first virginal awakening, to mature love expressed for others, to the ultimate moment when the soul is released in death.

The Song of Songs is the text that is usually associated with Consecration because of the bridal imagery—the crown of flowers, the bestowal of the ring and the veil, the sobriety of the vows. It can be read as a celebration of human love, but there is also the love of God for His people, of Christ for the Church and of Christ for the individual soul. This emphasis must be shared with the vertical line of authority of the Father, who will ask more of the bride of His Son and also promise her more—not only a love that "no torrents can drown" but one that is itself the water of Life.

The second reading, from John 17, quotes Christ at the Last Supper, when He is about to die. He is going to die for others, to consecrate them with His own blood, and they are not even going to understand or care. He is praying to the Father for all those in His keeping. For the consecranda, those in her keeping are her community. She is not giving her life to be alone in mystical rapture; she will be living for other people. This includes all those "in the world" who will depend on her and whom she will not abandon.

The last reading from Revelation—always a difficult, symbolic text— foreshadows the total union with Christ that happens only at death. All union in this life, no matter how sweet, is imperfect; thus, the nun is looking ahead to that moment when the soul is released completely to be with God, and she is praying that she lives in such a way that she is worthy of that grace when the time comes.

Each of the steps involved in the ceremony has within it an inference that becomes more intense. When I came to the time of Consecration and I was given a ring, that was very powerful. This moment is the closest a nun can come to the totality of a woman's heart. I was saying, "I do."

For seven years, I had listened to and kept notes on every homily Father Prokes had given at Mass. What I received from his words contributed immeasurably to my theological understanding of spiritual growth. He had accepted my invitation to give the homily at the Consecration Mass, and I couldn't wait to hear what he would say to me that blustery morning. His thesis, framed by the gray, wet day, seemed to be "Don't rain on my parade." My first thought was, "He's giving me Broadway?"

"Mother Dolores", Father Prokes expounded, "took the reality and truth of virginity to the world at large by way of AP and UPI. She couldn't care less if you are unwilling to take the risk involved in joining her parade because nothing and nobody can thwart her search for truth in God. Yet, she couldn't care more because she desires with all her heart that you join her parade in total trust to where it will lead you, where you shall come to know yourself as a person related to a person as a member of the Body of Christ, the Church."

The moment of prostration—lying stretched out, face downward, in a position of submission—was initially frightening. But as I listened to the Litany of the Saints sung over me, I could feel in the floorboards beneath me its rhythm amplified through my body like a drumbeat. When finally I stood, I felt sheer physical exhilaration.

Late in the Mass—when the congregation lined up to receive Communion—I left my seat and stood next to the archbishop, where I could watch as friends received the Eucharist. I suddenly heard myself breaking in with an invitation for my non-Catholic guests to come to the Communion rail to receive a blessing. It was an unusual moment, I grant you, and it got me some flack later from a few of the elders. But at that moment I was concerned that the non-Catholics might feel left out and trapped in our tiny chapel while the Communion line

moved slowly, slowly to the rail. I needed them to be a part of the
ceremony, too.

❦

There had been the usual requests to cover the ceremony from publications and photographers, but Reverend Mother Benedict insisted the ceremony be kept private. Valerie Imbleau, who had returned to secular life and her profession as a photographer, was asked to photograph the Consecration exclusively. Her photos appeared in *Ladies' Home Journal*, and one of them is on the cover of this book.

To maintain security, Mother Irene, by virtue of her military background, got the assignment to police the chapel entrance and refuse admittance to anyone with a camera. She repeated this task at the reception for guests at Saint Joseph's, where the freshly minted Mother Dolores made a brief appearance. Guests who wished for more than an embrace or a handshake were directed to Saint Benedict's parlor, where she stood behind the grille for several hours greeting them.

I dutifully joined a long line to take my turn and present my Consecration gift to her—an 8 mm movie camera, for which she had expressed a desire in a letter: "The only film record we have is maybe a half dozen reels of activities like barbeques, things like that", she had explained. "I can't help but feel I'm called to change that."

> *—I've always had a great concern that new entrants to the*
> *Community have, as their heritage, some reference to what*
> *Regina Laudis is in terms of human behavior. That has been the*
> *motivation for my zealous sponsorship of documenting every*
> *facet of monastic life, which began with the little 8 mm movie*
> *camera and has continued through the technical advancements*
> *of videotaping and, now, digital recording.*

More than thirty people close to me had come to my Consecration,
many from a great distance, including Suzanne Zada, who finally was at
peace with my decision. Sister Dolores Marie was so happy for me that
she removed her personal crucifix from her cincture and gave it to me

281

on the spot. Grandma Hicks brought a medal that had been blessed by Pope John XXIII.

I hadn't seen Helen Pittman, Grandpa Pittman's second wife, since I was a child. Helen and Grandpa had had a long and happy marriage, and I was so touched when she confided that she was beholden to Granny for making her life with Grandpa possible.

I was glad that Pop—Al Gordon—was there. In the parlor, he asked me if we drank good wine at the monastery, and I told him of course we had wine but, unfortunately, no one knew anything about good wine. From then on, Pop sent every year a case of very good wine with which we celebrated distinctive occasions, and when Pop died, his brother Bernie continued the gift.

Cyril Ritchard brought an exquisite seventeenth-century wooden crucifix from Spain. It hangs in a place of honor within the monastery, reminding me, whenever I pass it, of this elegant genius and his tender affection for a fledgling actress.

The most unusual gift—and perhaps my favorite—came from Granny. It was a bright, multicolored jacket that she made from silk neckties snipped from the necks of her husbands and lovers over many years. Granny had begun the jacket when my mother was a child and planned it as a wedding gift for her, but when Mom married in a way Granny didn't feel was appropriate, the jacket was laid away, to be presented instead to a future grandchild. I've always felt the jacket was an apt gift. To Granny it represented love. I wore it to the reception with the Community following the ceremony.

> *—It is a fabulous garment. Perhaps if I am lucky they will disavow the custom of being buried in black and put me in Granny's coat. Wouldn't that freak out some tomb raider in a thousand years?*

At the reception in the common room, Byron Janis kept his promise to give Mother Dolores a song. She stood facing him as he sat at the little spinet and played it for the Community. "It was my first musical child, so to speak", Byron recalled. "It was composed at the Château de Thoiry in France and had words by the French lyricist Eddy Marnay, who wrote lyrics for songs made famous by Édith Piaf. It is called

'J'aime Celui Qui M'aime' ('I Love the One Who Loves Me'). It was the most meaningful piece of music I could give her as she was embarking on a life of love and commitment to God."

—*The overriding emotion I will always carry with me from my Consecration is deep thankfulness for the happiness of my family, friends, sisters and so many people who wrote to me. I felt joy in their joy of having a place in my life.*

Twenty-Nine

In 1966, the year I made First Vows, the number of religious women in the United States reached a peak—estimated at over 180,000. But that number was being depleted by a mass exodus, and the number of recruits was likewise declining.

The decreasing number of consecrated women left many religious orders facing an unsure future—a thought that disturbed me then and one I continue to contemplate.

Over the months preceding my Consecration, all but one of the ten dissenting nuns left the Community, which created a considerable hole in our workforce. During this period, three young women came to visit Regina Laudis.

Dale Rushton, a teacher with a master's degree in religious education, came at the suggestion of her confessor at Catholic University. She had no special interest in the monastery; it was just to be a visit. "If there was anything I wanted not to be," she insisted, "it was a nun."

Her father, a newspaper editor in Worcester, Massachusetts, seconded the suggestion of a visit. He had been intrigued by the fact that Regina Laudis was now home to a film actress he admired (so much so that he once skipped the Easter Vigil in favor of viewing *Francis of Assisi* on television).

"That was kind of shocking," recalled his daughter, "but he was pulled like a magnet to her beauty and intelligence. He respected that she had been drawn to something more in her life and followed it."

The two other women, also there for a visit only, came—hitchhiked, in fact—from Newton College of the Sacred Heart in Boston. Adele Hinckley and Laura Giampietro arrived in tie-dye and love beads. It was the era of national strife that was erupting in violence over the war in Vietnam. Experiencing discontent with government, displeasure with schools and dissatisfaction with conventional approaches to religion, young people were looking for alternatives.

When I heard that Adele and Laura had hitchhiked to Regina Laudis, I told Reverend Mother how impressed I was and asked what she thought of them.

She replied, "I think they are our future."

At first, the visitors from this generation came singly or two or three at a time—on weekend breaks from college. But before long, there were thirty or forty young people visiting regularly, many seeking relief from the confusion they were feeling in the turbulent sixties. A few had preexisting bonds of friendship with the monastery, but most were curious strangers who had only heard about Regina Laudis. This first influx of lay interest in us was oriented not only toward individual spiritual growth but also toward a communal experience.

—With this infusion of long hair and love beads, were you criticized for taking in beatniks?

I think the townspeople must have had binoculars because the kids did not camp out on the lawn with their funny clothes and guitars. The young men stayed in Saint Joseph's and the girls in Saint Gregory's. When there were a lot of them, friends of the monastery would put them up in their homes. But, yes, there was talk.

Patricia Kuppens, a student at Connecticut College, was one of those early visitors. "It really was a natural, organic thing", she said. "Adele and Laura had been making regular visits, and one weekend, Laura's boyfriend, Tom Camm, joined them. Back home, people began noticing a change in Tom, who had a reputation for walking on the wild side, and word got around that the change was because he had found 'an amazing place with really cool nuns'.

"Out of the chaos of the times we were all searching for some meaning and direction, so we just decided to find out for ourselves. When we came to Regina Laudis, we saw a tremendous happiness in each woman, a sign that they had discovered real community that had lasted over time. Other young people we met here felt the same way.

"The community aspect was one thing that attracted us a lot. Numbers of people were then experimenting with communes and cooperatives. But usually, they didn't have a long life span. It would go sour somehow, and coming off this experience of disillusionment, we were cautious. But, while we were here, we went by the monastery ways—we absorbed the hospitality of the Community, the graciousness of Reverend Mother Benedict and the understanding of those who worked with her.

"I'm pretty sure that some of us were aware of Mother Dolores' Hollywood background. A few had come because of her. I had seen *Where the Boys Are*, and there was the article about her Consecration in *Ladies' Home Journal* that went through my circle like lightning. She was a great draw, I think, for the men but also for the women in terms of identifying with her."

A religious community does not generate life by itself. It needs the complement of laypeople. Oblates *is the Benedictine term given to those who have a response to monastic spirituality but don't feel called to religious life. Oblates have existed for centuries, and most, if not all, Benedictine monasteries have oblates who are primarily related one-on-one to a specific individual.*

An informal program existed at Regina Laudis that provided a place for young persons to work with Father Prokes and the Community on the land. It evolved from a practical need for help. As far back as I can remember, Mother Stephen always needed help, and there always seemed to be some young person who wanted an agricultural experience—or maybe just some time away from home. These local volunteers would help out in exchange for food and lodging.

The new visitors also wanted to do some service—manual work—and we gladly gave them that opportunity. However, they recognized that they needed something besides the work to channel their energies, get them grounded. Working together bonded them but didn't particularly focus their desire to participate more fully in Benedictine spirituality and serve the life of the monastery within their own circumstances. But how can laypeople relate to a cloistered *order? How could they be more engaged with the monastic life was the question.*

286

Under the guidance of Father Prokes, Regina Laudis embarked on some—I guess it could be called—experimentation to see if there was a way we could make that particular gift of oblation more expressive of the contemporary scene. He directed our first month-long retreat experience around the restoration of our blacksmith shop, which was the first step in a structured participation.

But you don't become an oblate because you've hammered a few nails or mowed the lawn for a month. There's a challenge to accept; the question became: Can you also experience community in your own right? And then, of course, a request must be made. "Can you teach us how to form a community of our own?" they finally asked, many months later. "What are the principles? We must know why it works for you because we would like to have something like that with men and women outside the walls of the monastery." We encouraged and helped them to form communities, each with its own unique mission according to the character and gifts of the people involved.

The Closed Community was the first lay community to begin at Regina Laudis. The name does not mean that the group was closed in the sense of being isolated, but en-closed. The members said if they were going to be Catholic, they were really going to live it and not just pretend it. Because many were gifted in art or worked in construction, much of their concrete contribution in service took the form of building projects.

Among the core group were young couples—Joseph Giampietro and Sharon McGourty, Joseph Moller and Regina Paliotta, George Zifcak and Isabelle Giampietro—who married and raised families. They became doctors, teachers, social workers, computer experts and musicians, and all, happily, have remained in relationship to Regina Laudis. Group member Tom Camm felt he had an artistic calling—in dance—and wanted to pursue it, which took him away from Regina Laudis for a spell.

The Closed Community really was a pilot venture that, as more people started coming, eventually inspired other women at Regina Laudis to support other groups in their own areas of expertise. Thus was born the Associate Community, oriented toward making the vision of Benedictine life visible beyond the enclosure. They speak of their call

287

as "bringing life into dead situations". The Organic Community, whose members include Joan and Jim Gilbert and Nancy and David Stein, is made up of people interested in living organically as fully as possible. For them, organic means "according to the holistic principles of Benedictine life".

Persons in the healing professions came together to form the Healing Community, a group that in time founded Promisek, Inc., a Catholic educational and environmental association fostering authentic lay spirituality. Healing Community members Richard and Phyllis Beauvais also founded the Wellspring Foundation, a therapeutic facility in Bethlehem. At Lady Abbess' request, Mother Dorcas Rosenlund, also a Healing Community member, founded the Contemplative Medical Center at the abbey, a place of retreat, prayer and communal support for physicians, residents and medical students.

The Advocate Community came into being as a result of the controversy surrounding the Supreme Court decision in Roe v. Wade. *It is primarily made up of lawyers and other legal professionals dedicated to being advocates for the sacredness of human life from conception to natural death who often donate their professional services as needed.*

"Young people are always in a crisis; they're emotional—crying all the time", Patricia Kuppens said. "Creating those communities took a lot of energy from the monastery. There were many hours of discussion in the parlor with Mother Placid and Mother Dolores. Mother Dolores was especially instrumental in seeing that the young people had a voice."

—I was the catalyst, so to speak. I was there to do everything I could to draw them out, get them to say what was in their hearts. Also, I had the capacity and the training to make the meetings come alive. I would just project whatever was the best role in each situation.

Ten single women, including Patricia, Dale and the two hippie hitchhikers—Laura and Adele—made regular visits, joined lay communities and, most

288

significantly, related ever more strongly to the Community. Throughout the seventies, all ten entered religious life at Regina Laudis, thus fulfilling Reverend Mother Benedict's hope for the continuation of the monastery. Each of these women has celebrated her twenty-fifth Jubilee.

In 1969, Dale Rushton was the first of the ten to enter Regina Laudis and is now Mother Anne Rushton, an expert in chant. When she entered, she had no formal musical training, but she was sent to study with Dr. Theodore Marier, one of the world's masters of Gregorian chant. For twenty-five years, Mother Anne taught chant to Community members one-on-one and went on to help Dr. Marier write *A Gregorian Chant Master Class*, the most respected text on the subject.

"Early in my postulancy," Mother Anne remembered, "Mother Dolores went out of her way to get to know me. I thought it was because I have an impaired arm, but since then I've seen that she does that with everyone who enters. When it came time for my Clothing, and I was faced with deciding what would be on my card, she gave me the insight that at that stage in my development I needed the hand of the consecrated person. There is an imprint of her hand on my Clothing cards. She made the cards herself in our print shop."

When Laura Giampietro began visiting the monastery, she showed strong artistic gifts, thanks partly to her father, Alexander Giampietro, a professor at Catholic University and a renowned sculptor and ceramist. As a student, Laura accompanied her father to Italy, where she learned from the expert Emmanuele Rondinone many methods of pottery, a craft she ultimately established at Regina Laudis as Sister Perpetua. Her name and her pottery—as well as that of her apprentices—are appreciated worldwide.

Laura's schoolmate Adele Hinckley was twenty-four and pursuing an academic major in art and literature. "I didn't have a professional goal at the time but was looking to be brought into development of who I was meant to be", she reminisced. "I had always thought I would like to work in some capacity with animals but had never been in an education situation where science and things of that nature were pushed. I remember that I was impressed that the monastery land program was then adding a complement of animals as well as its own dairy."

Adele is now Mother Telchilde Hinckley, the first nun to be in charge of the pig herd, although at the time of her assignment she was heard to say, only half-jokingly, that if the job area she was being considered for "started with *p* and ended with *g*," she was "outta here". She now also oversees the monastery dairy.

Martha Marcellino was a curly-haired, miniskirted student at Sarah Lawrence College whose older brother John "Jocko" Marcellino cofounded the rock group Sha Na Na. As her taste in music leaned decidedly toward rock and roll, she was surprised to find how responsive she was to the Gregorian chant at the monastery. "I was even more surprised to find that I was attracted to the communal lifestyle", recalled Mother Noëlla Marcellino. "I had the impression Mother Dolores thought I had a religious vocation, something that I was totally unaware of at the time."

—Absolutely, I did. I remember thinking, well, it's obvious her mother didn't dress her, but still she was quite striking in her femininity—a demand of sorts to be wanted. But the bravado of her exterior was overshadowed by the innocence in her eyes. There was a call in that innocence. The intensity was for Christ.

Nancy Collins was an energetic protester of the Vietnam War at Connecticut College. "It was a free, anything-goes era, and it seemed at college there were no rules whatsoever", she lamented. "There was a lot of experimentation with drugs and alcohol and sex. Male students stayed over in the dorms. I didn't want to follow that crowd.

"I just happened to be at Regina Laudis at the time of Mother Dolores' Consecration. I had been taken with the magazine article and asked for a parlor with her. I told her very frankly about the challenges I was facing. She was intense—by that I mean a very strong presence—but wasn't shy to address my concerns in very down-to-earth terminology. I wouldn't have believed a nun could be that modern. She absolutely saved my integrity."

In 1975, Nancy made her entrance into religious life and is now Mother Augusta Collins, responsible for the abbey's grass-fed beef herd and more than twenty pastures for grazing and haymaking. She can usually be seen atop a John Deere tractor.

—Mother Augusta holds the herd of Belted Galloway beef cattle, made possible by the gift of a heifer and a thousand-pound bull from Uncle Vance and Aunt Gladys Kincaid. Within a very few years a herd of mismatched cows was transformed into a gorgeous black and white, Benedictine masterpiece.

Arlene Morfesi, a legal secretary in Manhattan, had recently ended her engagement to a West Point cadet. The broken engagement inspired a makeover, which daringly included champagne highlights in her brunette locks, suggested by her hairdresser, who also introduced Arlene to the Bible group she had formed with a Catholic priest. The priest, in turn, led Arlene to her first visit to Regina Laudis. She became a member of the Advocate Community and in 1976 entered the monastery.

—As our Sister Rachel Morfesi, she became secretary to Reverend Mother Benedict and now is one of the computer whizzes settling Regina Laudis comfortably into the twenty-first century. She was indispensable in the making of this book.

Jean Marie Baxter was no stranger to Regina Laudis. When she was one year old her family began regular visits to the monastery to see her Aunt Trish—Mother Placid. She began visiting on her own upon graduation from the University of Denver, where she had earned a bachelor of fine arts degree. Since the age of three, Jean had been interested in art, a passion she shared with her aunt.

"After college," she recalled, "I went to Europe and, when I returned, found a job in Boston. I thought I had fallen in love and became engaged but eventually faced the fact that my heart was not truly in it. Life was not turning out at all what I had idealized it to be. Something was missing. I was a confused, distraught and angry young lady.

"My visits to Aunt Trish became more frequent, and I met a number of young people in the Associate Community who were also searching. I was deeply impressed with their capacity to articulate what they were looking for—commitment. I began to recognize this as my search too and became a member of that group.

"I met frequently with Mother Dolores. She is motivated to unlock—whether it comes as an encouragement or a challenge. She recognized that I was avoiding a decision and in a brutal parlor told me flat out to get off the fence. She restored my hope in the *possibilities* of my life. This, in turn, opened an understanding of Aunt Trish's new identity, and it was then I began calling her Mother Placid.

"In preparation for my entrance in 1976, I had a parlor with Mother Dolores, and I was eager to hear all the wonderful things she would tell me about monastic life. But she said only that she thought I should study life drawing—which sounded wonderful to me—and plumbing. *Plumbing?*

"'Of course,' she answered, 'so you can have a practical entrance point for the Community.'

"Yikes! When my family heard that, it brought down the house. My mother was relieved that Mother Dolores hadn't suggested electrician. 'You could easily get electrocuted,' she said, 'but it is highly unlikely that you might drown.'"

—When the abbey is dug up in A.D. 3000, Mother Praxedes Baxter's metal sculptures—made by using blowtorches on rusted bathroom sinks—could be all that is left of Regina Laudis, and people will speak well of the artist who made them and of us.

Patricia Kuppens, now Mother Lucia Kuppens, the Community's librarian and cellarer, the most important work in a Benedictine monastic community, thought back to 1970, the year she first visited Regina Laudis. "I had struggles with my religion in college, as did almost every Catholic of my generation. My goals then were so conventional really. I imagined I would be an English professor or have a book-related career, I would fall in love, get married and raise a family. And somehow I thought I could do all of the above and still make the world a better place.

"Regina Laudis helped me see that I should put that last goal first if it was going to be anything more than a dream, and I had to start changing the world by changing myself. Someone once asked me why I kept coming to the abbey, and I answered that I was being taught how to be happy. I really did feel that way. I just got happier and freer as a person the more I was here.

292

"It took me a long time to consider a vocation. It just didn't occur to me for many years, even after so many of my friends entered. I am happy to say I accomplished all my goals—I am married, and I do spend my life with literature—just in a different way from what I imagined!"

> *— Mother Lucia is a true synergist, keenly well-versed in every quarter she touches, yet she is one of the most genuinely humble women I have ever known. It's a wonder to watch her disrobe the splendor that she deserves and give it to another.*

Margaret Patton was eighteen, a Bennington College freshman and non-Catholic when she first visited Regina Laudis with a schoolmate. She came from a celebrated military family, her grandfather being General George S. Patton Jr., most noted for his command of the US Third Army in World War II. The Third Army liberated more than eighty thousand square miles of European territory, including the town of Jouarre and its abbey, thus bonding the Patton name to Regina Laudis forever, a fact that Margaret was unaware of. Her father, the also prominent Major General George S. Patton, likewise had a lengthy military career, which took him from West Germany to Korea and ultimately to Vietnam.

"I demonstrated against that war while my father was serving in Vietnam", Margaret said. "I totally dismissed my heritage and what I perceived as the self-aggrandizement of the military. I hated being known as General Patton's granddaughter."

> *— It was a very weighty chip on her shoulder. She wanted nothing to do with the Patton legacy and refused to speak about it at all. Of course I found that kind of conflict fascinating. Reverend Mother was equally impressed and invited Margaret to raise the American flag on the next August 27, annually commemorated here as the day Patton liberated Jouarre. At our first parlor, she made a comment on our shared "notoriety" that has remained a private joke through the years. "Your face is your fortune", she said. "Mine is my name."*

"I converted to Catholicism and entered the abbey at midnight, January 1, 1982", recalled Mother Margaret Georgina. "Only my father came. It was excruciating for him, but he felt it was his duty to be there. After Mass we trooped down in the snow to the Great Gate. When the prayers were over and I was just about to go in, we heard several gunshots, very close, which startled all of us, most especially my father. It was Mother Dolores!"

—There was a time when I received some threatening letters, and oblate Ed McGorry, a retired New York City policeman, thought I should learn to use a firearm. On Saturdays we would go out to a field, where he taught me how to shoot a Winchester .22 as well as his police handguns. After a few weeks of training, I could get ten bull's-eyes with ten shots. I merely thought it would be grand to welcome General Patton with a salute he would appreciate.

Mr. McGorry's generous gift of protection has continued through the years, with several state troopers in our area volunteering their own time to patrol the property. One of them actually appeared in one of our stage productions. Now that's bravery.

"Mother Dolores", recalled Mother Margaret Georgina, "was extremely significant to my father and helped his relationship to the abbey. He really cared for her, appreciated her straight talk—and, of course, admired her beauty!"

Mother Margaret Georgina is in charge of the vegetable gardens, is mistress of ceremonies at liturgical events, handles preparations for clergy and guests, makes cheese and creates the sanctuary flower arrangements with such grace that I sometimes come to Mass early to observe the performance.

—Over time, she accepted the military background of her family and came to terms with her controversial grandfather. She even took on marksmanship instruction from Mr. McGorry.

It was only a few days after my Consecration when the walks started. I asked Mother David if it was possible, during the scant twenty-five minute period between Vespers and supper, for us to take a walk together now that I was legal—that is, professed.

294

Mother Abbess explained, "This had always been a time for meditation, but usually we stayed in choir until the supper bell rang. After Vatican II, it was no longer necessary to stay in choir to meditate; you could meditate outside. Before Mother Dolores came into the Community, I already had the practice of taking a walk after Vespers, and I welcomed the opportunity finally, after seven years, to get to know her."

We walked to Saint Mary's Woods on the same route that I took the very first time I came to Regina Laudis and was shown out—not too cordially—by Mother David. This time it was a congenial and unhurried walk; the first time we were able to let our hair down and laugh about the long, hard silence both of us had felt.

Thus began a tradition of daily walks that remained pretty consistent—we walked even in the rain and snow—and continued until the neuropathy hit me in the late 1990s. The walks stopped then, but the time together has not. It has evolved into an unofficial part of the day's schedule. I still call them walks, but now they take place anywhere on the grounds or even in Corpus Christi.

At first, I had personal needs to talk over. Mother David has a way of allowing me to integrate what is needed to make the vow to change work in my life. She gives me perspective. To this day, when something is disturbing me, she will say, "Listen up. God does not want this something that is distressing you. God wants you to be happy. Don't you realize that?"

> *—She has never gotten over straightening my collar. Now she straightens out my head.*

Talk during the walks always turned to something that was critical in the Community at the moment, opening up new areas for inspiration regarding Community development. We have kept that half-hour commitment for over forty-two years. That stability is, for me, such a gift because no matter what is happening in our lives, the relationship allows me to trust in my own gift for instinctually sensing the truth. It is probably why we were eventually meant to take on roles of service for the Community, she as abbess and I as her support. Although this time was never an officially scheduled part of our daily program, it grew into just that and has become unofficially honored by the Community—respected and protected and not interrupted.

>—*Today the Community not only supports this but insists upon it. The women feel comforted that this conversation takes place. It is touching that the Community relies on our relationship rather than feeling any jealousy. They don't feel cut off but truly believe that their own lives will be supported through that strength. For my part, the walks have been my lifeline through my whole vocation—the rope that kept me from sinking.*

Thirty

It was always Reverend Mother's intent that one day Regina Laudis would be an abbey, and central to that goal was the Community's right to elect an abbess for life, which we had included in our constitution that was finally approved in 1974.

—That wasn't ever taken out?

> *Currently the abbess is elected for an indefinite time. She must offer her resignation at age seventy-five, and if it is accepted she becomes abbess emerita.*

Elevating a foundation from a monastery to an abbey is an organic progression. A monastery may start out with a small founding group. If it endures and grows, it goes through stages—dependent priory, independent priory, then abbey.

There are really no tangible benefits to being an abbey, and certainly there is no power involved. This advancement, therefore, is not about clout or advantage, but about being available for greater service, greater obligation and witness. Although the leader of an abbey is elected by her community, she receives a rite of blessing from the bishop, who consecrates her as an abbess, the highest level a woman can attain in the Church. An abbess is recognized by the whole Church as head of her community. From the Vatican to the state of Connecticut, she is given due respect, and that elevates the whole community.

The approval for the elevation of Regina Laudis was made in 1975 by Pope Paul VI. The date for the ceremony was set for the feast of Saint Scholastica—February 10, 1976—the year of the United States' bicentennial, which was fitting, since Regina Laudis was the first women's abbey founded on American soil.

Reverend Mother was elected abbess. Her attendants for the abbatial blessing were her brother John Duss and her good friend Ella Grasso, governor of Connecticut and coincidentally the first woman elected to the state's highest office. The celebrant was Archbishop John Whealon, who bestowed the crozier symbolizing the abbess' authority for life.

From that day forward Reverend Mother was called Lady Abbess. She named Mother David prioress, the official who would govern the abbey in her absence, and Mother Jerome became subprioress.

The jubilation that day was contagious. So many people attended that, although no one ever came into the cloister in those days, we had to open the common room to receive all of them. The Franciscan community from nearby Meriden walked into the cloister en masse. That also had never happened before. Previously, nuns of other orders came individually with a specific purpose. But this was the whole community walking in the gate. It was a sign of freedom.

My ever-faithful Maria spent the entire day on her feet, interviewing and photographing our guests—all two hundred of them. She told me later the day had been one of the most satisfying and transforming experiences she had ever had. The topper was Lady Abbess and Father Prokes leading the Community in a folk dance of celebration. Their presence together, guiding us, was a gift of total reverence.

After the festivities were over and nighttime fell, I was in my place in the choir and saw our Lady Abbess alone, kneeling. There was such joy radiating from her face. She was in her sixties at the time, but looked as though she were forty.

Elevation gave her a perfection of her call. She put our foundation into the mission of the modern Church. In days to come, when things got stuck and seemingly impossible to move, I would think, "The hell with it, Lady Abbess will always be here." As far as I was concerned, Lady Abbess was the Church.

The seventies began what would be a period of development at Regina Laudis. Reverend Mother Benedict had made our foundation in rural Connecticut, and now, as abbess, she remained resolute that dedication to the land and, more importantly, its development to full potential would be a prime commitment. "Our land", she said, "anticipates the

very purpose of a monastic community—identification with and fulfill-
ment of the Christian mystery in its own surroundings." We do live by
the labor of our hands.

Much of our four hundred acres is forest, which has allowed us to
harvest wood both for lumber and firewood and provides undisturbed
areas for meditation and reflection. This wooded acreage is traversed
by streams and wetlands, making its care and management challenging.

We women learned to work this land ourselves as an integral part of
our Benedictine spirituality. The soil was hard and rocky, but Lady
Abbess was determined that the Community would draw its sustenance
from the property.

Under the stewardship of Mother Stephen, about a quarter of the
land was now being cultivated for pastures and hayfields, orchards,
raised-bed vegetables, flower and herb gardens, berry bushes and grape
vineyards. There are also areas managed for Christmas tree production—
Mother Stephen's personal passion—which, over the years, has contrib-
uted to our revenue.

As the beef herd expanded its number, the land it grazed also expanded.
Peripheral fencing was installed to enclose large pasture areas. The hay
barn was enlarged to include a sizable feeding area, and a separate
paddock was created for the bull. Ways of managing calves were
introduced. It became necessary to plant and to harvest more and more
hay. We began to grow corn silage, which meant plowing up alternating
hay fields and planting corn each year to supplement the hay and
pasture available.

The addition of feeder pigs and the gift of several Cheviot ewes from
our benefactress Lauren Ford necessitated building additional barns
and rotational paddocks. Mother Ruth Barry, who had been a book-
keeper before she entered in 1968, took charge of the sheep.

Our dairy began with Holstein cows in 1975 and later switched to the
Dutch Belted breed. The Dutch Belts give less milk than other breeds,
but it has a greater percentage of milk solids, more suitable to our
cheese-making operation.

Many of our women operate tractors and other large machines
necessary to cultivate the land. For a long while, the monastery owned
only one tractor—now considered an antique but still in operation for

spraying fruit trees. Our fleet has grown to a dozen, and I think I'm safe in saying that Mother Augusta, who took over the management of the land from Mother Stephen, knows all of them.

Mother Augusta confirmed, "I think I've managed to use just about every machine we have. Subsequently I have taught other women here to drive tractors and to use the hay machinery as well as chain saws, lawn mowers and brush cutters.

"We now have various sizes of tractors, from the very small John Deere 320 to the largest, a JD 2950, used for its bucket loader and superstrong pulling power in the operation of our biggest machines— compost turner, Bush Hog rotary mower, corn and grass choppers. For haying we have a haybine that cuts the grass, a tedder and rake that toss it and form it into rows, and a baler that compacts it into small square bales.

"I love our machines because they enable us to care for our land well. They enable human beings in general, but they definitely allow us, as women, to do work that we never could even consider otherwise."

I think a woman approaches a machine differently—not pressing it as hard as a man might, but becoming sensitive to the machine, caring for it—reverencing it, if you will. In a way, machines and tools are extensions of the person. Perhaps women feel this more than men do because we are not as strong and need the machine's help more.

We try to practice responsible stewardship. We've learned to submit to and cooperate with the weather, the land and the animals. Whether we are clearing acres of brush or fields of stone, preparing a seedbed or building a road, milking a cow or managing a whole beef herd, we have had to enter into the rhythm of life itself.

We feel that respect for God's creation inevitably leads to respect for our fellow men and women. Pope Benedict XVI reminded us during his World Day of Peace message, "Disregard for the environment always harms human coexistence. It becomes more and more evident that there is an inseparable link between peace with creation and peace among men."

❦

300

Father Prokes told me bluntly one day that I didn't have a particular area of productivity for the benefit of the Community. He was right. I had been assigned to almost every existing area of work and found I wasn't a laundress or a cook or, heaven knows, a farmer—as my days of milking and haying attested. Frankly, there are very few monastic jobs I'm capable of doing. I would always try, but I was persistent rather than competent.

One morning, for my garden obedience, I was given a scythe to cut some high grass near the chapel. It was a simple task, but I attacked that patch of grass with such misguided vigor that I injured my neck and shoulder. I had always known I wasn't as strong as Mother Stephen, and I was constantly trying to match her stamina. It was: anything she can do, I can do. Anything.

> *—I remember once standing behind her in line at suppertime and watching her load her plate with food. I did the same. When I sat down at my place, I looked at the mountain on my plate and just then realized I had to eat all of it.*

I whacked away at the grass with a vengeance, using the scythe improperly—I would never ask how *to do something—and though I could feel a strain I stubbornly kept at it. All of a sudden, there was a sharp stab that all but knocked me off my feet. Next thing I knew I was in Saint Mary's Hospital in traction for two whole weeks! My rotator cuff had been severely injured, and I had to wear a collar off and on for five years.*

> *—That hospital visit was the first time I had been outside the monastery in eight years.*

This injury took me out of the garden for good. The recovery period cut down my work in the laundry, but that remained a daily obedience for another year. Instead, I was assigned to work in the kitchen. Even with Granny's training I had never been much of a cook, so I was not overjoyed, especially since even an interim obedience at Regina Laudis can last a long time.

301

—That job lasted only a few months. I never knew why; no one told me, and I was too relieved to ask.

I held out hope that I would find my niche in the artwork I continued doing in the studio. My studies there had expanded into portraiture under the guidance of my monastic godmother Estelle Coniff, an art teacher who came to the monastery to give group classes to the Community and remained to work one-on-one with me. But during her critique of a portrait I had sketched—coincidentally of her—Estelle sighed and said, "Sister, I'm sorry but you got caught in the nostril. I don't think you're ever going to make a portrait painter. Have you tried typing?"

No matter, I was now going to be the Community's baker. First thing I was asked to make was matzo, and since I hadn't a hint of how to begin, I called Pop in Los Angeles, who gave me his family's recipe. It wasn't long before I was told that I would bake just the regular bread for the Community.

—It was recognized as your spécialité?

No. I'm sure that concern about long-distance phone bills had more to do with the decision.

Even if it wasn't my true area of productivity, this obedience resonated comfortably with me. The Russian word for hospitality means "bread and salt". It stems from an old European custom of offering both to guests as a sign of respect. I liked the idea that this humble food is given as a gift between friends. I liked that bread is broken and shared, and that we are nourished by the food and the friendship.

Bread has always been the mainstay of our diet and continues to mean life to us, both physically and spiritually. "I am the bread of life", Jesus told us. Catholics celebrate this with every Eucharist. Bread is transformed into the Body of Christ.

While the making of bread adheres to rules of science, it is, in fact, more of an art. The correct amounts and the temperatures of flour and water are the same for each loaf, but the weather and even my mood could affect the look and texture of my bread. I came to accept that each loaf was unique, each one unrepeatable, and embraced the differences—

302

sometimes crusty on the outside and, more often than not, soft and fragrant on the inside. Like people.

In his mid-seventies, Mother David's father died. Mr. Serna was a darling man, an earthy, full-blooded Peruvian. Mother David was concerned that she would have to buy a commercial casket when she really wanted to lay him to rest in a coffin of his people. I heard myself volunteering, "I'll build it."

Mother Mary Aline was dubious that I would be any more competent in carpentry than I had been in farming. She set the bar high by insisting the coffin be identical to the ones she had known at Jouarre and supplied her own sketch as a guide. Using almost forgotten skills I had acquired from Grandpa and newly learned design knowledge from Brother Jerome Blackburn, a gentleman who had helped build our barns, we built Mr. Serna's coffin in three days. It was very simple and, I thought, quite beautiful. Mother Mary Aline gave me a good review. She said it was exactly like the coffins at Jouarre.

I had stumbled upon my area of productivity. When Granny came to visit, I was hesitant to tell her I was the Community coffin maker, but she reminded me that I had come by the job honestly—Great-Grandfather Bowen, remember?

I always looked at the making of coffins as a way of strengthening faith, because to build a coffin for someone who is close is very difficult. It is done with the realization that this person is going to eternal rest in the pine box being fashioned by your hands. That you are creating this sarcophagus, this cocoon, is very sobering.

—How many coffins have you made?

In the twenty years I was the Community's carpenter, I think fifteen. There are eleven sisters at rest in coffins I made.

There had never been a designated carpenter at Regina Laudis, and at first I worked in the blacksmith shop. I made most of the door latches in the monastery, many chairs and tables—I'm particularly proud of the television cabinet I designed and made for our common room. I helped Father Prokes build the sheep barn, which was a major undertaking. I remember the first thing he did was lean a tall ladder against the side of the building and send me to the very top to nail down siding. It was two stories! I thought I would die. But I did it. From then on, I proudly wore a tool kit on my belt.

—On occasion, I still do.

In time, I got an assistant, Sister Nika Schaumber, a very pretty young woman with the sunniest smile. The two of us were allowed to leave the enclosure to attend night classes in carpentry at Kaynor Tech in Waterbury. The course in basic carpentry skills lasted a year, and when we completed it the two of us had learned enough to finish the half-completed carpentry shop interior ourselves. Students in Kaynor's electrical course came to wire the shop as part of their training.

My formation mothers had repeated over and over that all work must be stopped at the first bell in order to be on time for the Office. That rule was supposed to be a part of me. But one day in the shop I was just about to finish cutting a board with the power saw when the bell rang. I was annoyed because with one quick push I would finish the job and wouldn't have to set up the whole thing the next day. But just before the last chime, I heard my formation mother's voice in my head. "Your core reason for being is to praise God." Immediately I stopped the machine and turned to leave.

But it didn't stop. I looked back to see that the center pin holding the saw in place was wobbling frantically. Suddenly the blade flew off into the space where I had been standing. I was shaken to the bone. If I hadn't listened to that bell, the blade would have struck me in the heart. I've never forgotten the impact of that moment.

I remained our carpenter for over twenty-five years. In that time, I taught others to make coffins—among them, oblate Richard Beauvais and two novices, Sister Ida Nobuko and Sister Alma Egger.

Sister Ida Nobuko was Nobuko Kobayashi, who carried the ring at my Consecration. Eleven years later, after earning a doctorate in clinical psychology at the University of Ottawa, Nobuko converted to Catholicism and entered Regina Laudis. It was a life change that caused her traditional Japanese family great pain. After a few years, her father became quite ill, and she made the decision to leave monastic life and return home.

Sister Alma Egger, who has a master's degree in fine art, was the director of art education at the Stamford Museum and Nature Center in Connecticut when she began to relate to Regina Laudis in 1995. When I was hit by the neuropathy in the late 1990s, I had to face the reality that I was no longer able to continue as carpenter, and Sister Alma took my place. It was devastating at first to give it up, but there is nothing greater than having your place taken on in continuity.

"Mother Dolores shared her carpentry expertise with me", said Sister Alma. "I ran for a lot of 'gozintas'. She can be quite formidable. I always have a sense that she's connected, that she knows about things instinctively"—she tapped her forehead—"up here. I mean about us, as well."

In the late seventies, Henry Ellis was introduced to Lady Abbess and Father Prokes and, subsequently, to the whole Community. Mr. Ellis was an engineer by profession, a conservationist by commitment and a Catholic by conversion. His home was on Shaw Island, one of the smaller San Juan Islands off the coast of Washington State—four thousand acres of unspoiled land with only a hundred or so residents.

One-quarter of Shaw was owned or controlled by the Ellis family, and Mr. Ellis had decided to donate three hundred acres to Regina Laudis for the purpose of establishing a Benedictine community there. He paid a visit to the abbey to make his generous offer, which came, he said, with "no strings attached".

The first thought that popped into my head was, "What's the catch?" I immediately chastised myself for being suspicious. Was it because I came from Hollywood that I thought there had to be another agenda? I kept those suspicions to myself.

Thirty-One

When I was a working actress I took on personal relationships with the characters I played. They became intimate friends who had a story to tell, and I was their medium for a while. I didn't know what I would do when the matter of vocation hit me because I didn't know what to do with the people who inhabited me and drove me so deliberately. If I had no part, I wondered, what would I do with myself?

—Letter to Dick, February 1973

One morning Lady Abbess called me into her office. She took a folder from her desk drawer and handed me an envelope. I recognized it instantly as that fiery letter I wrote as a novice.

"I want to talk to you about these things you had a problem with a few years ago", she said. "I think we are ready to look at them now. We have to see what can be done to integrate these considerations, or else I don't know how the monastery will continue. Four deaneries will be formed at Regina Laudis. I would like you to be dean of education."

The purpose of the deaneries, she pointed out, would be to make sure that all the levels of the human person—emotional, physical, psychological and spiritual—were expressed and developed in each candidate seeking to be a nun at Regina Laudis. Classical monastic formation as it existed prior to the Second Vatican Council did not address all these levels, only the spiritual. Religion then was not a way of achieving personhood; it was assumed that all personal needs were integrated prior to seeking entrance into a monastery.

Certainly those dimensions of monastic life must have been addressed from the beginning in some fashion. But it was an innovation to divide responsibility for these areas into deaneries—Formation, Liturgy and Choir—and, particularly, to add an Education Deanery that would underpin the others. What Lady Abbess and Father Prokes were proposing was unheard of in fifteen hundred years of Benedictine

306

monasticism and did not have a precedent in tradition. Education in classical formation had only to do with academic study, learning about Scripture, the Fathers of the Church and the Rule.

"But I have no degrees, only a high school diploma", I protested.

"You don't need a sheepskin", she tossed back. "The only degree I'm interested in is the degree in street smarts. You are more than qualified to deal with people on the instinctual level because of your training as an actress. An actress is able to identify with many personalities. An actress recognizes, she listens, she connects the dots. You have the additional gift of being analytical, and you must admit you have a strong commitment to push for the result.

"The classical approach is not going to be sufficient to educate modern women coming in to the virtues of monastic life. Nor is it going to educate me and the rest of us who were trained classically. We have to find the way to make that bridge between the experience of contemporary women and the classical line. You mark the point of a new era, a new generation of vocations, a new world entering the monastery. I feel you are the only person who can do it."

Well, I had to agree with her. A professional actress does have to be able to express the range of human experience, and I did have the training to know how to access those dimensions. I would find soon enough it would take a whole lot more.

Change was necessary, but it took me a while to face the fact that I was dealing with something that didn't yet exist. It remained in limbo for a long while, and I guess I was thought of as a dean of something. With no job description forthcoming, I wondered at times if Lady Abbess had made me a dean just to keep me from leaving.

The definition was to come out of the meetings we had with Father Prokes, but there was only one meeting a week that the entire Community could attend. The whole idea of living in a corporate community structure was an awfully big issue to try to cover in only two hours a week. We were encouraged from the beginning to talk about what kind of deanery we wanted, but mostly we listened to Father articulate the principles of this new methodology in relation to the principles of our constitution. I took reams of notes that I prayed

307

would enlighten me eventually, but the one thing I immediately grasped was Father's intensity.

With his guidance, I envisioned the Education Deanery as a forum for anything *that people wanted to discuss. Education in this context is drawing out of the persons who they are, what their gifts are, what they bring to monastic life, ensuring that they* know *themselves and—this was important—can* express *themselves.*

I envisioned an Education Deanery in which ideas would come from a broader base of the Community that would permit the thoughts and ideas to rise—like a leaven—from the bottom to the top. You didn't have to be professed; you could be a postulant and be heard.

In preparation, I asked each nun to write a short biographical account of her life for my reference. But, as helpful as this curriculum vitae was, it did not fully address what I knew firsthand to be the crucial ordeal of the life.

It's a shock being in here. Once you enter, you feel and think things you never did before. All your patterns of life change; your professional life goes, and you are under the pressure of living closely with a lot of people. You suffer things piercingly. And, with nowhere to go with them, you can feel trapped.

I did not want anyone in my care ever to hear the words I heard less than ten years before: "You say *nothing because you* know *nothing. You* know *nothing because you* are *nothing." A place needed to be provided where a woman could get things off her chest. I wasn't that far removed from the younger women in age, a decade perhaps, and could remember feeling trapped, having strong views and nowhere to go with them. My tear-stained antiphonal reminded me of that every day. Perhaps, at least, I could be their sounding board.*

I invited every person to write down at the end of each day what she was experiencing and to do that without any fear that it would be judged or that the information could affect her relationship with her formation mother. Everything would be kept absolutely confidential. I called the idea "instinctual charting", but it was simply giving the women an opportunity to say, "This is what's going on in me", and to trust that it was all right to feel whatever she was feeling.

308

These pages were left in a basket I mounted on the door of my cell. They trickled in at first, but soon there were seven or eight pages waiting for me each evening. I would read them at night after Compline while the Community slept.

I did not set up conversations with each novice to discuss her charting unless she asked to meet with me. The charting was not for me; it was for her. It could be enough just to write down the gripes. I would evaluate whether someone's charting revealed something that should be changed or if the issue was an essential one for the process of becoming genuinely capable of submitting. But if someone asked to meet, I was available.

I have a feathered friend in Corpus Christi. A nice lady named Debbie at the pet shop in Woodbury wanted to sell a six-week-old African gray parrot worth $2,500 but only to the right people since African grays can live seventy years and she wanted to guarantee that he would be looked after for his lifetime. She thought we seemed a good bet. She knocked the price down by well over half, but that was still way beyond our means.

At this same time—not coincidentally—Don Robinson was involved in a lawsuit with his neighbor in Los Angeles, the entertainer Madonna, and he requested prayers by the Community for a favorable decision. Don won the case and asked how he could show his appreciation, and I said we wouldn't turn him down if he wanted to give us the parrot.

> *—Mother David and Mother Maria Immaculata both thought the fact that the money came from someone named Madonna was fitting.*

I named the bird Tobiel, but the nickname Toby has stuck. Toby shares Corpus Christi with eight pairs of finches and a canary, and I admit all those cages create a kind of disorder. But, in a purer sense, there is more design than meets the eye. The birds give a context to the space where women come to share personal problems concerning their monastic life. They don't have to enter a room that is dead quiet. It's alive. I think it enables one to speak of intimate issues.

309

The birds are a handful, and when the neuropathy hit I needed help with them. I hesitated to approach Mother Olivia Frances because she has the enormous responsibility of our kitchen, but she agreed to feed and water the birds on days I was out of the enclosure for medical appointments. To my surprise she began coming every morning! Still does.

❦

Part of my job as dean of education was to aid each woman to find an identification with some concrete aspect of our life—making bread, milking a cow, bundling hay—and to open up communication so that she might relate to others who shared interest in the same elemental area.

The women and I thought this sharing could take the form of small groups to address specific issues in Community work. We started with a garden nucleus and then a dairy nucleus. Over time, a number of these groups were created, among them a presentation nucleus, which is concerned with taking our traditional rituals out of the shadows and making them more understandable and visible, and a body-development nucleus, which promotes programs to nurture the women physically.

These peer groups were responsible for bringing new ideas of value to the deanery, but my underlying drive in forming them was to phase out the strict separation that existed between the professed and the nonprofessed. By design, these groups created a shortcut in the bonding process that I felt to my core had to replace the isolation of monastic life.

From the very first, the meetings of the deanery were not mandatory— never would be—but they were well attended. The younger women responded to coming together in this way. A small core of older women in the Community did not participate. This was a big departure from the classical emphasis on a person's individual relationship to God, and it did put a stress on them. The ideal of religious life for them was that you went in and you obeyed. You did whatever you were told. It didn't matter whether you liked it or were good at it—you did it. The obedience was what made the action valuable, not your giftedness.

310

"These women were critical of Lady Abbess and, especially, Father Prokes", Mother Abbess David explained. "Letters of complaint would go to the Archdiocese of Hartford—and, sometimes, to the Holy See—with regularity. No attempt was made to silence these women and, in fact, I was often aware of one of them sitting on the stairs just outside the common room where the meetings were held, furiously making notes on what was going on inside. She didn't have to eavesdrop; deanery membership was open to anyone in the Community who wished to be there for whatever purpose and for whatever length of time she desired."

I began to recognize in the charting if a particular reaction was just a passing irritation or if it was significant and could have a positive impact on our lives. By listening for the meaning behind the words, I was able to see particulars becoming universals—that is, someone expressing something that everyone is suffering with or longing for. Out of these insights came proposals and initiatives for change.

Mother Lucia remembered, "Sometimes you would find Mother in the library until twelve or one o'clock in the morning. She was always available. It wasn't as if she were just hanging around waiting for someone to knock. But if you knocked on her door, crying, "I've got to talk to someone, or I'm out of here", she would hear you out.

"She is a person who always draws on her own experience. She told about times she pounded the trunks of the trees with her fists—not to show how angry she got but to show that it is all right to get angry. She related Mother Columba's concern over her broken-out skin to encourage us to ask if we needed something. It was all right to ask, and it's not vain to want to look good.

"It was hard to get it through my head that you didn't talk when you were working. I thought that time was a perfect opportunity to share. That became my petition. An announcement was never made that this custom was changing, but gradually, organically it just changed. The silence became artificial. Now it's so natural to communicate in a work situation. We don't chatter aimlessly about anything that comes into our heads, but there's always the good feeling of being able to share."

311

Once the Education Deanery felt that a proposal should be put forward, it was presented first to the Formation Deanery. If Formation agreed that the idea warranted consideration, it was sent on to the Liturgy Deanery for confirmation that it fit in with the Rule. Then, if all agreed, it would go to the Choir Deanery for verification that the idea was good and would bring life to the Community.

Thinking back to the beginning of the deaneries, Mother Abbess said, "Education and Formation were to take two distinct roles in guiding candidates into monastic personhood. As prioress then, I was acutely aware that we were establishing the continuity of the foundation. But as dean of formation, my part was to hold for the *classical* line. My own formation was rooted in classical structures; thus, this half of the complement was very natural to me.

"It was a revolution—the Education Deanery—because that dimension had never been honored. The rationale was that *all* the Community— whoever wanted to participate—was given a *nonjudgmental* place to express herself. Mother Dolores was supremely gifted for this because she gave the task vitality; she has the capacity to be open-minded, and she always wants everybody to get into the act. It is the training in her.

"I did my part to run interference and support the foundation of the deanery, trying to ease the tension this created with those time-honored ways in which older members had been formed. But the women resisted being awakened to another dimension and were suspicious of the young upstart.

"There was so much resentment, too, on the part of the formation mothers because they felt they were being circumvented. They believed they were not getting the first responses from the novices now, that Mother Dolores was the recipient of the instinctual response—which was really the whole point! But we are all *sisters* here. Remember— sisters? women? jealousies? I think the level of frustration was very great for Mother Dolores in those early days."

— Yes, I was aware that it was the main cause of conflict. The novices were telling me things they wouldn't even hint at with the formation mothers. "How do I have the right to be conse- crated as a virgin when I've slept with guys?" is not a question

312

to be asked of a judgmental nun. I was, and still am, convinced that the work of developing the whole person, including her sexual nature, is indispensable for the process of monastic formation in today's world, especially if we, as Benedictine religious women, are going to be capable of assuming a true and fulfilling marital response to Christ within the bonded relationships of the Community. Virginity is not only a physical state, but has to do with the fullness of a woman. A woman's virginity can be restored.

I was being chided for trying to bring in a program to destroy the pristine vision of classical monastic purity. Some in the Community felt that Lady Abbess and I had lost our minds by dealing in such an open fashion with the young postulants. It was hard for them to believe these "hippies" would ever become monastic persons. Lady Abbess let me do what she knew I could do. She did not interfere or lay down the law. She was humble and giving and was again becoming the target for a small contingent of restless women.

There is always a lag between the theory and the practice of new thoughts, but resistance by the elders was evident from the beginning; consequently, any change could take years to gel. In meetings with the other deans, discourse was denied. I felt an incapacity to move anything, to affect anything, and I was constantly frustrated because I wasn't changing anything. I had no sense of inadequacy but no sense of accomplishment either—like an ant nibbling at a fifteen-hundred-year-old granite mountain.

I would become so angry I couldn't express the anger in words. Once I ripped up the agenda booklet—addendums to what I was supposed to do—and slammed the pages on the floor before charging out of the room. They said I had an awful temper. I didn't care what they thought I had.

—Did you ever apologize?

I'll apologize if I know I'm wrong, but I felt I was justified in correcting something that was out of order and unfair to the Community. Saint Benedict addresses this when he says that "unruly boys should get a severe beating with the abbot's

313

permission". He didn't mention the girls, but I assumed they got the same.

"We were all aware of the opposition that Mother was facing daily", said Mother Augusta. "It wasn't anything under cover. There were complements among the four deans, but there was always conflict, too. Mother Stephen was the dean of choir and my land master. She recognized that Mother Dolores had the instinctual base of the Community with her. But Mother Stephen's tendency was to beat you into submission. Mother Dolores would help me find my direction through conflicts by way of education. I would never have gone to Mother Stephen with a problem in a million years."

Mother Telchilde added, "Interestingly, Mother Dolores can also be very strict in support of traditional ways. She does not reject the traditional. What she rejects is letting the exterior stuff—how to fold your napkin, how to hold your book—become the reality. She never settles for the exterior show being all there is."

"She does not tolerate laxity in attending the Divine Office, most particularly the middle-of-the-night Matins", said Mother Margaret Georgina. "I can still visualize a furious Mother Dolores striding down the hall between the cells at 2:00 A.M., banging loudly on every door and calling out at the top of her voice, 'You are expected at Matins! You are expected at Matins!'"

"I could tell she was in pain", said Mother Noëlla. "There was always that pain in Mother Dolores that this education dimension wasn't considered legitimate."

On the walks with Mother David, my frustrations boiled over and cued four words at frequent intervals: I have to leave. Once, in a rage, I broke away and headed back to my cell and locked my door. Mother David was fast on my heels and asked me to unlock it. I refused. I then heard a strange sound of metal against metal. She had pulled a screwdriver from her tool kit and removed the hinges from the door. "We do not lock our doors in the monastery", she stated simply.

"Does God have the right to ask this of me?" I implored.

314

"Yes", she answered. It was a yes echoing Reverend Mother and Mother Placid through the years. I accepted it—again—in faith. But, I wondered, "Where is my bridge to her yes?"

—Did you ever really come close to leaving?

I never actually packed my suitcases. I just needed to talk it out.

Have you, in your present capacity, talked it out with young nuns?

Oh yes, but I've never met one who was as tortured as I was. I often go back to moments I had with Reverend Mother late at night—she was a night person, too—when I was facing an impossible situation. She would talk with me for hours sometimes. And I held on. So when I talk with a young nun, I never give up on her because Reverend Mother never gave up on me.

Remembering this transitional period Mother Lucia said, "In terms of the Community, our world of European spirituality broke open, so to speak, when we saw that Mother Dolores and Mother David could work together as a *team* in Education and Formation. I think it was that relationship that formed our new generation in the monastery and made it possible for us to stay."

When I was a postulant, Father Prokes' words had made an indelible impression on me. He said that in order to design a new monastery building, he had to know us—individually—and we had to know ourselves as well. In the time that had elapsed, we hadn't scratched the surface of this challenge. Really, the only time you said what you thought was in chapter meetings. But there was no discussion; you just said what you thought. Then the abbess made a decision.

After the Second Vatican Council, a whole process of modernizing the Roman Catholic Church, and religious orders in particular, began,

315

which offered us space to explore self-awareness. Father Prokes intro-duced the idea that in order for us to be creative within the Community we should have more input, which, in turn, could enable the abbess to make better discernments. He stressed that we did not come to a contemplative order because we couldn't make it in the world. We came to a contemplative order because we had reached some manner of success in our fields and with that could have a true sense of place in monastic life.

He encouraged us to reach for a more mature way of living together. He proposed bringing to consciousness the various levels of a person's development, using as a model the study on creative process developed at the University of California at Berkeley, which recognized the four stages necessary for creative growth: preparation, incubation, illumina-tion and verification. Father believed that these stages corresponded to what was needed to grow in religious life and—this was especially important to him—that recognizing them could help the nun understand herself better as a spiritual person and how she might best serve the Community through her own capacity.

We gave the stages our own names: instinct, justice, love and union. The instinct—or preparation—level in the creative process of an actor is reading the script, feeling the story. The justice level—incubation—is letting his role in the narrative germinate, by studying the lines, going interior with it, trying things out. Illumination—our love level—is when the actor gets insight into the character and he begins to come alive. It is when the actor experiences the "Aha!" moment.

At the union or verification level, the actor's insight has to be vali-dated. He must see if what was clear and exciting when he had the illu-mination holds up in terms of gelling with the other actors and connecting with the audience. In other words, he has to get out there and do it.

In the monastery, going through the different stages results in the discovery of a nun's special authority, what we call her domain. The process of discovering the domain of each individual nun is a corporate effort of the Education Deanery. Everyone gets involved as the nun considers her genealogy and instinctual depth, or bona; *her essential background of professional excellence, or* dona; *her knowledge of self, or* cura. *Spiritual depth and capacity for care of the Community are*

316

informed by these fields and allow each woman to see how she can become a leader for the good of the Community.

Sister Anastasia Morgan, who was Kathryn Patrice Morgan and a student in the land program when I met her, spoke to me of Mother Dolores.

"I knew her from her movies on television", she said. "For me, the thing that attracted me to actors and actresses—more than what they looked like—was their voices. Even as a little kid, I loved her voice. She's quite small really, but her voice mirrors what a large person she is. If you were going to give Mother a size, she's much larger than I am." Sister Anastasia stands six feet two and weighs in the neighborhood of 250 pounds. Since her Consecration, she has been the Community's blacksmith.

"I met Mother Dolores through the Education Deanery, which had not been long in existence when I entered. I got to know myself more in the process through Mother and Father Prokes, who was the first man, outside my father, who saw a positive thing about being a giant.

"In those formative years, when I was desperately trying to figure out my footing, Mother saw me where nobody else ever saw me and, in so doing, helped me accept who I am and what I was struggling with and trying to ignore.

"She gave me a project—to build a table to be raffled off at our annual fair. She said to look around the blacksmith shop and see what materials were available. I looked and looked but didn't find anything suitable for a table that was meant to be special. All I found were pieces of scrap metal and discarded slabs of wood. Mother said, 'Let the scrap tell you.'

"The table was built of only leftover wood and iron. Lady Abbess said it was so gorgeous we couldn't raffle it off. It's in our monastic art shop, and every time I see it, I think back to my life before I came here. I always felt like I was scrap, a piece of useless trash. I look upon my mission now as monastic blacksmithing. In our shop, we use stuff that everybody else has gotten rid of because they think it's no longer useful."

—The continuing work of the deanery, you see, is to take the woman where she is in process and try to affirm her past experience as relevant and necessary to her mission as it develops through her monastic life. She has to learn to accept herself, her experience, as the preparation for her call.

The doorway that opens to full realization is not a psychological doorway, but it is at the deepest level of our personhood where we are receptive to the love that is always seeking us, bound in union with our love of God and God's love for us. It's when we begin to understand this mystery that we are capable of apprehending ourselves as a new person, able to act in ways that were beyond our own expectations.

If we are open to the love of God—a love that is revealed to us through the love we share with one another—then we will discover who we really are. This is what Saint Benedict, in the prologue to the Rule, calls the "expansion of the heart" that is the fruit of religious life.

I have kept every chart that has been given to me. My cell is bursting with boxes of charts. I've been told I should burn all of them. I can't. I have never thrown one away simply because I feel that anything that was written from that level of human experience is sacred. I've written on the boxes, "To be destroyed at my death".

Mother Lucia reminds us, "Out of all Mother Dolores hears and absorbs from the simple charting, she puts those desires into a dynamic pattern that brings the Community into greater coherence around its own mission. Do you know what her domain is? Choreographer of domains."

Thirty-Two

The Education Deanery has supported programs that I feel have allowed as much integration of and reflection on the monastic experience as hours and hours spent reading books on Saint Benedict. They have cut across the daily plodding rhythm of the abbey and have helped to open up the Community.

The isolating separation between the professed and nonprofessed is now gone. It is allowed that we are responsible for one another. The newcomer may have relationships within the Community, and the members are encouraged to interrelate to help her. In short, she trades the romance of contemplative life for the reality in all its seriousness.

At the time I entered, the ideal was to forget the past and give yourself fully to the life in the monastery. The unique gifts you brought with you into the enclosure, along with your instinctual responses, were ignored in favor of heroic obedience.

We now accept that the Community is served better when we help each woman take her place through recognizing her passion and claiming her particular giftedness. Using her gifts will not be the only thing she does within the cloister, but it will be the area through which she approaches everything else.

There have been times when a conflict simmering inside me threatened to boil over. I still face some of the same questions I faced when I took vows—whether I am capable of fully living the life of a cloistered nun, whether I am up to the task. The questions are always there. But because we are no longer without communication, I can talk about it with a sister.

—Traditionally, members of a monastic community always went to the abbot or abbess to discuss a problem. We're much less stringent than we were then. When Mother David became the abbess, her method became "You do what you need to do and

319

then report to me." Lady Abbess' approach was more "I'll tell you what to do." When the Education Deanery began, it became permissible to go to another member of the Community, but, personally, if I have a deep problem of the soul, I still go to the abbess. For me, this tradition has always been a workable way of getting through a crisis.

Between Clothing and First Vows, the canonical year remains true to the custom of complete separation from the outside world. But now, at the end of that year, we have the commitment step. The novice can petition for an informal pledge to vows. In my day, it was all canonically regulated. When you fulfilled the time, and the novice mistress and Reverend Mother felt that you were ready to go on, the chapter then voted. You were called in and told you were received—or told you were not received. If you were not received, you were gone within a very short time, and nobody knew. That's how things were done then. We are probably the only community now that has the commitment step.

—When you were a novice, did you know any of the women who left because they weren't accepted?

Yes.

Were any of them close friends?

I couldn't make close friends then.

Another concept now integrated into our monastic life is fraternal sponsorship. Younger women who relate to specific areas of creativity are taught skills by older nuns who have developed expertise in those areas, most notably the care of the land and the animals. A hallmark of Regina Laudis is the cultivation of flowers as an essential complement to the work of the farm, and this particular know-how was handed down by our master of gardens and flowers, Lady Abbess. Even though we have cautiously entered the computer age, many things are still done by hand, as they were centuries ago, bookbinding for instance, and these techniques are passed down from nun to nun.

Daily life in a Benedictine monastery has always consisted of three elements: prayer, manual labor and Lectio Divina, the practice of *scriptural reading intended to bring a deeper knowledge not only of the Bible, but of oneself, others and God. Saint Benedict in his Rule makes time for it every day. Recently, Pope Benedict XVI likened it to "feasting on the Word"—first taking a bite (*lectio*), chewing on it (*meditatio*), then savoring the essence of it (*oratio*). Finally, the Word is digested and made a part of the body (*contemplatio*).*

The traditional form of Christian Lectio Divina is a solitary or private practice. Now, however, different forms of group Lectio have been followed. At Regina Laudis we find the Sunday evening Lectio period an excellent time to explore subjects of particular interest to members of the Community. Often our aspirations and our concerns interconnect with our meditations on the Scriptures, thus making our day-to-day experiences apt matter for study.

I encourage all members of the deaneries with any ideas that concern the Community—be it renovation of the monastery or meal preparation—to go to Education and put it out there. Part of the work of Education is to get to what we call the love response—to feel united with everyone around you. That's the ideal.

The range of topics that the Education Deanery has been able to incorporate into our Lectios is surprising. We've had Lectios on Shakespeare thanks to Deborah Curren-Aquino, a scholar at the Folger Shakespeare Library in Washington, DC, who visits us annually. She is brilliant and leads us through a different play each year. We've had a Lectio featuring the music of the South African Zulu choral group Ladysmith Black Mambazo, which related to a specific experience then taking place within the Community—a renewal of our understanding of the psalms at Matins. Whatever the topic, Lectio can be one medium to help the Community grow on a human level.

Regarding the news of the day—which was one of my pet peeves—the Community now has much more access to media than we had before. In the past, only Lady Abbess and maybe a couple of other nuns had some awareness of what was going on in the outside world. Portions of newspapers were read every now and then, but there was nothing like a general presentation of current events.

The Community is far better informed today. Now there is no one person who brings news to the Community. News can come into the

321

monastery from various sources: radio, television and the Internet; our portress at the door, Mother Debbora Joseph; and Mother Catherine of Alexandria, who is in charge of the art shop. Both women are constantly speaking with visitors from the outside.

Mother Catherine was Kathleen Talbot Stief, a professional chemist and married with two children before her entrance in 1983. In addition to the responsibility of the art shop, she is the abbey herbalist who grows and creates the legendary teas sold there. My personal bond with Mother Catherine began years ago because of the herbal throat tea she invented that never fails to hasten the end of a Connecticut cold.

Before she became Mother Debbora Joseph, Josephine Buck had been a New York debutante whose affluent family had a summer home in Southampton, where as a teenager she played tennis with neighbor Maria Cooper at the Coopers' summer house. Their adult lives went in different directions, Josephine becoming a Wall Street investment manager, until they met again years later at, of all places, Regina Laudis.

—Mothers Catherine and Debbora Joseph represent the face of the monastery to our visitors and guests. They exemplify the Rule that instructs us to behave toward each one as if he were Christ.

A crisis happens in the life of a cloistered nun when she comes to a point in formation where she feels judged. In the past, this could make it impossible to continue. The old monastic stand was "If you don't like it, leave." During the years before the Education Deanery, you wouldn't know when someone left the monastery. You would wake up one morning and her cell would be empty. That no longer has to be the case. Moreover, a woman who leaves religious life doesn't need to face the cold shoulder, as did Sister Luke in Kathryn Hulme's The Nun's Story, *nor must she end the relationships she has formed with other sisters. Relationships can and do continue after a nun has left Regina Laudis.*

Mother Macrina is a case in point. She left this Community over forty years ago—but not surreptitiously. She knew she did not have a contemplative vocation and left to enter an active Franciscan order. She comes back from time to time to renew her spiritual life with us. Likewise, Mother Nika and Mother Bernadette went to other orders.

Some, like Valerie Imbleau and Nobuko Kobayashi, go back into the world. Valerie's departure was the first significant one for me personally, but the emotional impact of it diminished over time.

It was no secret that Nobuko left because she could not really do the life. All of her sisters here sensed the pull she felt to go back to Japan and take care of her father. Now a successful clinical psychologist in Tokyo, Nobuko engenders a far closer relationship between Regina Laudis and Japan than we would ever have had. She comes back to us often and was instrumental in our introduction to Hatsume Sato, a Catholic woman in Japan who for many years has been helping people in need—physically, emotionally and spiritually. When Hatsume's dream of building a place to lodge these suffering people came true, Nobuko learned that she had one remaining wish—a bell for this refuge named Ischia in the Woods. Nobuko asked for our help.

Nobuko remembered, "The abbey responded so quickly and kindly, offering as a gift to Hatsume the lovely old bell that was hanging in Mother Dolores' carpentry shop. There is a Japanese expression describing such a quick response: 'On stroking a bell, instantly comes a beautiful echo.' "

—This story is included in Jin Tatsumura's 1995 Gaia Symphony II, *his ecological documentary that features Hatsume Sato as one of the remarkable figures of the twentieth century. Our bell echoes on.*

There have always been notable visitors to our monastery. Clare Boothe Luce, the former Connecticut congresswoman and US ambassador to Italy, was an early and frequent visitor, as was the actress Celeste Holm, who starred in the film Come to the Stable.

Dorothy Day, the prominent American journalist and social activist, came a number of times at the invitation of Mother Prisca Dougherty, whom she knew from the Catholic Worker movement. The Austrian philosopher Ivan Illich was a close friend of Mother Jerome. Theologians Ewert Cousins, Henri de Lubac and Pierre Teilhard de Chardin, whose books I kept at my bedside as a teenager, were all friends of Lady Abbess. Opportunities for the study of Scripture and theology were afforded through the visits of priests and theologians who shared with us the wisdom of their experience, study and prayer.

Buckminster Fuller, the architect, inventor and philosopher, offered a seminar on the environment. Colonel Charles Lindbergh, who came with his wife, Anne Morrow, gave a seminar on, of all things, the earthworm.

The Education Deanery has no powers of decision in the matter of guests, but we can recommend a subject and then aid in finding a master in the field. Experts in archeology, medicine, ecology, engineering, business, geology, botany and even seismology have offered the abbey their skills and knowledge.

The guest list is rich and varied and has included my historian brother, Dr. Martin Gordon; environmentalist René Dubos of Rockefeller University; New York City mayor Ed Koch; Vice Admiral Jean Betermier, former commander of the French Atlantic Fleet; Rabbi Richard Israel, director of the Hillel Council of Greater Boston; Enzo Fano, a UN water-resources specialist; Sir George Christie of the Glyndebourne Festival Opera; the great twentieth-century theorist and founder of integral humanism, Jacques Maritain; head of ABC News Roone Arledge; and nutritionist Andrew Weil.

With Mother Dolores as the moving force, professional artists from the stage, film and concert worlds visit Regina Laudis regularly—on retreat, like Lois Nettleton; to give a talk, like Broadway manager Lew Wilson; or to entertain and teach, as Gloria DeHaven and Veronica Tyler have.

Gloria DeHaven, a musical star at MGM in the forties and fifties, performed her one-woman show, The Spirit of Vaudeville. *Veronica Tyler, whose career has taken her to opera stages all over the world, originally came to Regina Laudis to do some soul-searching. Lady*

324

Abbess invited her to give an informal concert for us, and Veronica decided to stay on and give us a seminar in polyphony. This generous artist has returned to the abbey often to participate in concerts and productions and to continue to educate us in workshops.

Vanessa Redgrave has visited at the invitation of Mother Dolores. Permission had been granted for Mother Dolores to accompany me to a Broadway matinee of Eugene O'Neill's autobiographical drama, *Long Day's Journey into Night*, featuring Redgrave as Mary Tyrone, the character based on O'Neill's mother. Miss Redgrave invited us backstage after the performance and thoughtfully offered a bit of information about the real-life Mary that she thought would interest Mother Dolores. In the last act of the play, Mary wanders through the house in a morphine haze, bemoaning the loss of something that she knows would finally bring her happiness if only she could find it. That something, said Vanessa, was her Catholic faith, which she did, indeed, regain.

Vanessa was extremely interested in the abbey and asked if she might visit sometime and perhaps read some poetry for the Community. Mother Dolores invited her on the spot. But it was not until a few years later, when Tim Ridge of the abbey's Act Association escorted Mother to the revival of *Driving Miss Daisy* with Vanessa Redgrave, that the friendship was renewed and a date for the visit was set. The Community was treated to an afternoon of Shakespeare sonnets read by Vanessa and the Redgrave clan. Vanessa brought sister, Lynn, and brother, Corin, for a rare ensemble performance.

Performance artists have also been welcomed at the abbey. Dzieci—the Polish word for "children" and almost impossible for an American to pronounce—is an experimental theater group in Brooklyn that is as engaged with personal transformation as it is with public presentation. Dzieci's director, Matt Mitler, explained, "Everyone in the group feels a calling to serve something higher. We really don't perform before audiences. We have groups we interact with—call them witnesses—that actually change the dynamic, and we create community. What we do is evolving always. Always reborn. Always renewed.

"The company combines work of performance with work of service. We've worked a lot in hospitals, detention centers, hospices. We believe that helping others generates a profound healing effect that not only serves the patient but also strengthens the ensemble's work. But we do perform in more traditional venues such as New York's well-known experimental theater, La MaMa, where Maria Janis saw our production of *Fool's Mass* and insisted upon introducing us to Mother Dolores.

"We felt such a compatible vibration with Mother Dolores that we spent four days at the abbey, working with the Community in the hay fields and attending the Offices."

—Including Matins!

"After many months of enjoying the abbey's nurturing," Matt Mitler continued, "I felt the need for Mother Dolores to know our work, and I asked her about doing *Fool's Mass* for the Community. She agreed.

"As soon as we had a committed date, everyone at Dzieci became terrified because this is a very daring piece, a disturbing piece in some ways, and we didn't want to risk the nuns telling us to get out. *Fool's Mass* is set in medieval Europe during the plague years. A group of village idiots are forced to enact their own Mass when their beloved pastor dies suddenly. Although there's a great deal of improvisation, the basic structure is the Mass itself, but a Mass full of wild buffoonery and comic audience participation.

"The actors, in full costume and makeup, were already in character as the nuns arrived at the Jubilee Barn and immediately began to improvise with them. Their responses were at once touchingly eloquent and of such depth of understanding that it brought us new insight that we had no inkling of. We actors felt more entwined with the piece than we had ever experienced before. Since then we've been invited by a number of churches to bring *Fool's Mass* to their parishes. It's become our signature piece."

In the forties, before the word itself was coined, Anita Colby was a supermodel. She was known as "The Face" for her beauty and had multiple careers as actress, author, advertising executive, even host on the *Today* show. In her later years, after her husband had died, she was introduced to Lady Abbess through a friend who felt she might find some solace at the abbey. Lady Abbess, in turn, suggested she meet with Mother Dolores.

Anita, who was going through a really bad time, made numerous visits. One day she mentioned that her good friend Douglas Fairbanks Jr. had played the leading role in the London production of The Pleasure of His Company *and was exactly the kind of person I would like.*

Anita urged me to drop Mr. Fairbanks a note, and she made him sound so fascinating that I did, mentioning that I hoped his experience with our play had been as happy as mine had been. He replied very quickly, and our correspondence continued until his death. He was always asking questions regarding religious life. He didn't even know what the habit is called.

Mother Dolores has kept his letters and notes—all predictably charming and, insofar as they never met, unpredictably intimate. Fairbanks even revealed his long-lasting affection for Joan Crawford, who was his first wife. "Joan forced me to stand up to my parents," he wrote, "and made a man out of a boy."

He never visited Regina Laudis, but I've included him among our visitors because there is an observation in spiritual life known as "consolation without cause". This refers to a feeling of warmth and comfort that comes for no apparent reason. You don't ask for it. But out of nowhere, you instinctively have this marvelous feeling of well-being that comes from—somewhere. That was Mr. Fairbanks.

Another "consolation without cause" was the movie actress June Haver. I hadn't known June in Hollywood, but her brief time as a nun was the reason for all the secrecy demanded of me before my entrance into Regina Laudis. She wrote to me because she had met Sister Theresa, who remembered me from Corvallis, my high school. God bless Sister Theresa, because knowing June Haver was a precious experience.

Initially I was surprised that she was so open about her life as a nun and her return to Hollywood—not to her career but ultimately to a happy marriage and family life with the screen actor Fred MacMurray.

June wrote to me often, and with such firmness of spirit, always urging me never to lose hope about anything—referring, of course, to the fact that, after years of longing and deep spiritual communion, she had been at last allowed to receive the sacraments again. "Never, my friend," she wrote, "never take the sacraments for granted."

When June first visited us she discovered our dairy was in need of a semen storage tank. Her highly unusual gift of this apparatus, as one can imagine, got some interesting reactions from our congregation.

—Her letters and visits and generosity continued through the years until her death in 2005. Her daughters, Laurie and Kate, remain good friends of the abbey. To this day, I treasure their personal gift of a crucifix that belonged to their beautiful mother.

By the late eighties, the Community was looking toward an educational involvement—in the sense of formal education. This coincided with the arrival of Iain Highet, a Canadian student who was pursuing a master's degree in environmental studies at York University in Toronto. He was motivated to come on the barest suggestion from someone in his philosophy seminar that an abbey in Connecticut needed help with the hay. He had never been to an abbey and was not Catholic or particularly interested in religion. But he was genuinely interested in the land and joined the land program, working hard that year, learning everything he could from Father Prokes and Mother Stephen.

Iain had a certain charisma. His presence drew other young people to come and explore. It was really with Iain's coming that we started to formalize the whole structure that evolved steadily into our present Monastic Internship Program.

We knew that we had a tremendous resource in the land program that could be a practical educational base for young persons if it could be set up in a more recognized way. Mother Lucia was indispensable in structuring an educational program in which college students can learn something and we can be accountable for what they learned. For example, each intern adheres to a unique program created to reflect his particular interests. Thus, interns might learn to weave the wool of the sheep they have raised, develop the theological implications of cheese-making or discover the meaning of a chant piece at the blacksmith's forge.

We have been able to give classes in Latin and what we call Ritual and Creation—monastic customs, history and the liturgy that we follow. If students are interested in art, weaving or pottery, the nun they work with gives them reading materials and assignments to help them develop the theoretical measure of what they are doing. Some interns, both American and French, have received academic credit for what they've done here in agriculture.

Mother Lucia added, "We ask them to stay for a year in order to experience a whole cycle on the land. One needs all four phases: preparing the soil, planting the seeds, tending the plants, harvesting. If the interns don't stay through the four seasons, we feel they don't experience the totality of the process or see the fruits of their labor. The program is surviving, and I would say now that at least forty young people have passed through it."

Through the internship program, we have even had a hand in pest control. Our fruit trees were hit by a massive invasion of gypsy moths. The larvae of the gypsy moth is one of the most notorious pests of hardwood trees in the Eastern United States. Because we raise our crops organically, we were opposed to using commercial pesticides to control the infestation. Philippe Mennesson, now an engineer in France, was then a young intern working with Mother Perpetua in the land program. They learned about a natural way to stop the plague: spraying the trees with the ground-up bodies of the larvae. All the Community was mobilized to collect the creatures, picking them up with—thanks to Sister Ida Nobuko—chopsticks.

"It was a challenge, but we really did well", Philippe Mennesson recalled years later. "There was only one unpleasantness. During the grinding operation, we perceived a very bad smell. Those caterpillars stank worse than the compost."

❦

329

The Education Deanery also helped to open the Community to the world of dance. Lady Abbess was always after us to stand up straight so that we wouldn't get what she called the "nun's hump". She thought that dance, specifically ballet, would make us all more able to move with grace and dignity during liturgical processions.

—I think it was mainly to keep us from "the hump".

She found Miss Evelyn Jantzer, a retired New York–based teacher, who agreed to conduct a class in dance movement one hour a week, and the Education Deanery set up her program. Dance was a springtime explosion in the Community. It had been germinating in the hearts of the younger members, and it blossomed like the brilliance of new life on our land in April. Even Mother Ida, who was in her eighties, insisted on being part of the corps de ballet. We all wore black leotards under a sheath of black cloth, like a scapular. We even built ourselves a barre!

Miss Jantzer taught us for five years, and when she finally had to stop coming, a lovely English lady, June Christian, came for a two-day visit and stayed for three weeks. June was a highly trained teacher on the staff of the Royal Academy of Dance in London for fifteen years, and in later life has been an examiner for the Royal Academy, traveling the world judging competitions. She picked up the dance program where Miss Jantzer left off, and it was a fruitful experience for us all. Mother Perpetua was particularly responsive to body movement and shone as our star ballerina; I supported her as her danseur.

June visits whenever she is near the United States and, in 1986, became a monastic scholar and was given the name Maria Salome.

—Monastic scholar?

> *Monastic scholarship is an honor granted by the Community in recognition of the professional gifts of persons relating to us. Father Prokes pointed out that when we receive an hour of a professional's time it is a considerable gift that should be acknowledged. We gave a lot of thought to how we could do that and set up the monastic scholarship.*

330

Is this something that pertains to the Benedictine Order?

It doesn't pertain to the Benedictine Order. It pertains to Regina Laudis.

As a postscript, June Christian and I shared a poignant moment a few years ago when we were visiting the abbey at the same time. She and Mother Dolores were reminiscing about the dances June had created for the nuns, when Mother Dolores sadly informed June that her prima ballerina, Mother Perpetua, was now an Alzheimer's victim.

On past visits, I had always found time to stop by Mother Perpetua's pottery studio. Watching her work with such precision and skill was fascinating and just looking at that face—she bore a strong resemblance to the film star Linda Darnell—was a pleasure.

Her studio then was a ramshackle section of the barn at Saint Martin's—it had, in fact, a prior life as a cow barn—so Mother Perpetua was overjoyed when a new studio was built for her in the year she was diagnosed with Alzheimer's. From then on, she spent every moment she could getting all her recipes for glazes written down while she still remembered them. In 2006, her work as a potter would be finished, but her special gifts were passed down.

I invited Mother Perpetua to a meeting with Maria Salome and Dick in Saint Benedict's parlor. Mother was by then much slower in speech but still agile, and I had the hope that we might repeat a pas de deux. I would have been so grateful if she could make just a movement or two.

That afternoon, the two partners recreated their dance—in its entirety. The performance was graceful, unhesitant, in sync.

Before 1972 no one left the monastery for higher education. Some women had entered Regina Laudis with college degrees—Mothers Columba, Agnes, Jerome, David, Catherine and Lucia all did—and Mother Hildegard George and Mother Phillip Kline earned doctorates in child psychology and anthropology, respectively, from Union Institute's self-directed program, which allowed them to do their work at the monastery.

Until the Education Deanery began, no member of our Community had ever been sent out of the enclosure to further her education. I don't think it was considered unacceptable; it was just not considered at all, certainly not for the contemplative woman who was thought of as wrapped up and tossed into a wastebasket called a monastery.

Mother Perpetua went to Washington, DC, to study further the art of pottery, and Mother Praxedes earned a master's degree in art at Michigan State University. She has since continued her education by working with the Tomassi master sculptors in Rome, where her mentor was the famous Giacomo Manzù, creator of the bronze Door of Death *at the entrance to Saint Peter's Basilica in Vatican City.*

Mother Margaret Georgina got her BS in horticulture, also at Michigan State, and Mother Rachel earned her bachelor's in theology at Holy Apostles Seminary in Cromwell, Connecticut.

> *—And Mother Anne learned piano tuning in Waterbury—she's really good at it.*

Over time, it became apparent to us that most women entering the Community were not land-based individuals; that is, they did not grow up on farms or have much experience with large animals. It was pretty obvious that future nuns would come from a similar background—suburban middle class. As all our knowledge of the land was coming from Mother Stephen and the agricultural experts who occasionally visited Regina Laudis, we decided to send some members of the Community to specialize in fields that would move our plans for the land forward. In recent years four women of the Community, Mothers Telchilde, Augusta, Jeanne-Yolaine, and Noëlla, have received advanced degrees from the University of Connecticut in animal science, plant science and microbiology.

"It was really hard", Mother Noëlla recalled. "We had to balance the educational workload with our community responsibilities. But the discipline and contemplative focus of our monastic life was good preparation for doctoral research."

Mother Telchilde's study focused on a hormone that is critical to maintaining pregnancy in livestock. She earned a PhD and uses that knowledge to oversee our livestock management as well as the abbey dairy.

332

Mother Jeanne-Yolaine Mallet, who came from Nantes, France, was one of nine children, five of whom entered religious life. She earned a master's degree in plant science and was somewhat notorious for having written the longest master's thesis on record. It was two volumes!

Mother Augusta developed a method to predict the amount of nitrogen needed to fertilize grassland for optimal growth with the least risk to the environment. In addition to earning her PhD, she has won awards from the Northeastern Society of Agronomy for her research papers; her doctoral thesis was published in the society's Agronomy Journal, *and her methodology has been adopted by others in the field.*

Mother Noëlla focused her doctoral research on the microbiology of cheese ripening. She won a Fulbright scholarship to France to gather indigenous fungi from traditional cheese caves, which allowed her to develop the abbey's famous Bethlehem Cheese. The French government has honored her with their Food Spirit Award, and she holds an International Academy of Gastronomy's Grand Prix de la Science de l'Alimentation. She's also the subject of the film documentary The Cheese Nun.

These studies have enabled us to continue to improve our professional approach to our farm and have opened up other avenues of practical awareness that benefit our lives. I don't think we are the only monastery that sends its nuns to school. Most communities take some role in the ongoing education of their members. But I think we might be unusual in sending our people into fields other than theology, monastic studies and Scripture.

—Do people move out of the Education Deanery?

No. The people who come into Education increasingly don't want to leave it. It's not just a phase—"Oh, now that I've made vows I don't need that anymore." What began in the seventies as a clearinghouse for ideas from the younger members now engages the entire Community. Having the opportunity to speak freely, having a place where creative ideas are thrown around and we can brainstorm together— that's something everybody wants all the time.

Thirty-Three

Right after my Consecration, Reverend Mother gave me permission to begin photographing and filming Community life—cultivating the land, caring for the animals and tending the bees, chopping wood and haying, baking and preserving, even celebrations such as Mardi Gras parties.

Almost a decade later, I had amassed hundreds of 8 mm movie reels that were impossible to screen individually. The footage ached to be edited and made into a documentary. But by whom? The answer came by way of Dick's unexpected telephone call in September 1979 asking to visit me. A coincidence? I don't think so.

In the spring of 1980, I arrived at Regina Laudis to fulfill my promise to turn Mother Dolores' movie reels into the Saint Benedict centennial film. As I parked the rental car near the main entrance, a huge tractor rolled to a stop beside me, and a lean, lithe nun leaped off and vigorously shook my hand. "You must be Mr. DeNeut", she said with a broad smile. "Welcome!" This, I later learned, was the fearsome Mother Stephen. Her welcome served to lessen my uneasiness about the unfamiliar neighborhood I was about to inhabit.

At the door, I was met by the same severe nun who again greeted me in Latin—"*Benedicamus Domino*." This was Mother Mary Aline, the portress and cofounder of the monastery, and she instructed me that my response to her greeting should be "*Deo Gratias*".

At our next encounter, I forgot this instruction and said simply, "I have a meeting with Mother Dolores." Mother Mary Aline stood waiting, a barely visible smile on her face. For several minutes we faced each other in silence, and I remember wishing I had encountered the new assistant portress instead: Mother Dolores would have let me pass without the magic words. "Oh," memory kicked in, "*Deo Gratias*." We were in business.

334

Awaiting me was a makeshift editing studio in a corner of the carpentry shop inside the enclosure. Our schedule included morning and afternoon periods of two hours plus an open-ended session in the evening, which frequently stretched past midnight.

The studio was equipped with two ancient Moviolas—the ones operated by hand—and boxes of 8 mm film covering a decade in the life of the Community. Mother Dolores had decided that the 1980 Film, as the project was now called, should also be a learning experience for a member of the Community. So, in my first-ever adventure into film editing, I was considered a master.

The term master *refers back to the ancient custom in the monasteries of relating to a holy man who traveled in the desert and gave homilies to the monks who lived as hermits. This master figure represented the person of Jesus, who taught the disciples. Early in the history of Benedictine monasteries, the term* master *was transferred to the abbot and then to anyone who was charged to carry on the nobility and sanctity of his work. As time went on, the image became malleable, and we now use* master *to express the courteous acknowledgement of a person's ability.*

—It has its truth, but I think it has taken the scotch out of the scotch and soda.

Since the establishment of the Education Deanery, when a nun comes in, her gift to the Community is to bring her professional complement from the outside and allow it to teach the Community. I quickly learned it would take time for some members of the Community to accept instruction from within, because the women resented it then. I reasoned that if I couldn't bring them alive from the inside, I would introduce new voices from the outside.

My assistant was Sister Augusta Collins, a bright, serious young woman in her twenties whose healthy good looks put me in mind of the film actress Phyllis Thaxter. Sister Augusta had been one of the youngsters visiting Regina Laudis during the influx of college students searching for new meaning in their lives a decade earlier. She had entered in 1975 and now wore Mother Dolores' mantle as abbey photographer.

"I was so uncomfortable," Sister Augusta admitted, "because the Community was not all that thrilled to have somebody sticking a camera in their faces at an intimate moment. Mother Dolores taught me that you have to put yourself in the way. 'If', she instructed, 'you believe you belong in a situation because it's important to be preserved, then there should be no self-consciousness, no embarrassment and no apology.'"

Throughout the several weeks it took to edit three hundred reels, this master managed to stay about a half hour ahead of his apprentice. But what an education I got! Fully expecting reel upon reel of nuns praying, nuns singing, nuns processing, nuns meditating under trees, what I got was nuns working like field hands, nuns tending cows and sheep and pigs, nuns constructing barns and raised beds for organic gardens, nuns painting buildings, repairing roofs, operating trucks and tractors, blacksmithing—even felling trees! This kind of introduction served to form an early personal vision of the Community as women first, nuns second. The reels introduced me to every member of Regina Laudis save one—I didn't find a single shot of Mother Dolores, who was always behind the lens.

We structured the film around the Hours of the Divine Office. I found some lovely, though under-exposed, footage of Lady Abbess and Mother David cutting branches of red leaves for an autumn chapel arrangement. The low-key exposure, I hoped, would give it an early-morning look, right for Lauds, in the opening section.

Cutting 8 mm is very much like cutting spaghetti. And, unlike 16 mm or 35 mm footage, you are not cutting a copy print; you are cutting original stock, which placed a menacing responsibility on us. Each splice, of necessity, destroys precious original frames; thus, the cut had to be the right one.

The work was occasionally given a little boost by the discovery of footage that could be assembled into a montage, as happened with the Kiss of Peace, which is an affectionate greeting between members of the Community and also part of the celebration of Mass at Regina Laudis.

I found a snippet of film—only fourteen frames—of two baby lambs bowing and nuzzling as if they were bestowing the Kiss of Peace, which gave us a cute tag to the montage. Unfortunately, Sister Augusta made errors in the cuts, and there went our tag. She was despondent, and no amount of my minimizing the situation would allay her anguish.

When I arrived at the carpentry shop the next morning, there was the Kiss of Peace montage in its entirety. In the wee small hours, Sister Augusta, with determination and tweezers, had resurrected the lamb frames, each one barely the size of a grain of rice, fully restoring the sequence.

Mother Dolores followed our work with eagle-eyed intensity. Whenever a piece of spaghetti hit the cutting-room floor, she would ask, "What's that?" I would identify the footage I judged unneeded and, as often as not, heard, "Oh dear, I think it's important." The discarded footage was put back. Our completed documentary has a running time of over three hours.

> —*The worst times for me came when Dick kept making cuts to keep the film within a "manageable" length. With each snip I was shorn too. Later, when he wasn't around, I would gather up all the scraps and put them away. Just in case.*

There were a lot of disappointments during our three-week marathon, but there was only one near-suicidal moment. During the first viewing of the completed documentary on the Moviola, I was devastated to see that some of the footage, having been run countless times through the machine, was irreparably stretched and torn, the tears plainly visible on the tiny screen. Mother David—then the prioress—witnessed my misery and left the room, returning a short time later with a bowl of just-picked blueberries and a glass—a very small glass—of wine, which she offered with a suggestion: "Perhaps the tears are visible on the Moviola but will disappear when the film is projected onto a large screen." Totally ridiculous.

But that is exactly what happened. When the film was projected there wasn't the slightest evidence of the mutilation. I looked at Mother David with disbelief, and she was smiling. If comfort could be bottled, Mother David's face would be on the label.

Collectively, these three women gave me on-the-job training in Benedictine devotion, friendship and determination.

Soon after this collaboration, I became involved in numerous projects Mother Dolores provided, up to and including this memoir. Early on, I directed and videotaped a reading of Helene Hanff's charming *84 Charing Cross Road* with several nuns playing men's roles. Part of Mother Dolores' scheme for this project was to give the women more self-confidence in their ability to read well at mealtimes and, in the process, unseat their innate timidity. Twenty some years later, it would give me pleasure to know that a number of the women considered our little reading a breakthrough.

Difficult to imagine, but I managed to stage a vigorous rendition of *A Chorus Line*'s signature number for the novitiate's annual presentation to the professed Community—complete with gold top hats over veils, scapulars over tights. Not all of my efforts were successful. Very quickly I found I was not the right person to translate the life of Saint Gertrude the Great into play form.

With each new mission it became clear that Mother Dolores was making me available to the Community. I remember Mother David telling me, "She throws out the line." Well, she was not stingy with me.

My home during these projects was Saint Joseph's, the men's guesthouse, which had been both chapel and living quarters for the original nuns from France. On the second floor there are eight small cells, which, unlike the cells in the then building, have running water. Each has a narrow cot—a three-inch mattress on a wood frame, no bedsprings. I've done time in most of them and have never slept as soundly anywhere else in the world.

The downstairs area—basically one huge room dominated by an impressive stone fireplace and a long table that can easily seat a dozen or more—reflects the original purpose of the building as a recreational facility for the factory workers. You can still see dart holes in the walls.

Three meals are served daily. Although the Benedictine Order is vegetarian, meat, fowl and fish are frequently on the guest menu, which always boasts homegrown vegetables, fruit, the best bread in the world and, if you've hit it right, Mother Scholastica's peach marmalade.

A basket containing the carte du jour must be picked up by a guest at the main entrance, but a nun is on hand to set up and serve. Guests are expected to do the dishes and tidy up after meals and, upon departing, to remake their beds for the next visitor. Wednesday is bag-lunch day. It gives the women who work in the kitchen a breather, and, because I worked inside the enclosure, it gave me an opportunity to get to know some of the Community by sharing this lunchtime, a custom that began with Mother Jerome and Mother Irene and continues to this day.

I came early to the thought that Regina Laudis is the crossroads of the world. The guests who have visited make up a varied as well as impressive list of men and women of achievement in all fields—religion, government and politics, journalism, literature, nutrition, broadcasting, the military and the arts. I have broken bread and done dishes with many of them in Saint Joseph's.

During the work on the 1980 film, I frequently did dishes with Stephen Concordia, a young student who was in the land program. Stephen was studying for his master's degree in music at the New England Conservatory of Music, and when he got wind of our film he eagerly offered his services to compose a score based upon Gregorian chant for the finished documentary.

Chapter 53 of the *Rule of Saint Benedict* states, "Let all guests that come be received like Christ." Thus, cordiality and generosity expand the Regina Laudis maxim of prayer and work to include the basic human act of hospitality.

I was alone in the guest house one evening when five priests arrived—four from New York and one from the Philippines. Mother Maria Immaculata, who has been in charge of Saint Joseph's for a number of years, wasn't available to meet them and later asked me how tall they were. I thought it was an odd question. Not so. She needed to know so that she could assign them to the right cells because some of the beds are longer than others. That is Benedictine hospitality.

—Maintaining all the diverse works here would never be possible without the participation of our guests and the assistance of many generous lay professionals. We do not give formal retreats, but guests are invited to reflect on the monastic experience and welcome to join us in manual work. Working together or meeting together provides a context for giving Saint Benedict's

spiritual principles a practical application, connecting the body
with the soul and one person with another.

The night we finished the film, Mother Dolores got permission for us to share supper in the carpentry shop. Our table was a plywood sheet atop two sawhorses, but there were flowers and candles on it. We dined on the famous chicken pies from Phillips Diner in Woodbury—baked for us in the monastery kitchen—and we were able to toast the completion of our film with a decent red. It had been over twenty years since we had had dinner together.

The 1980 film spoke to me while it was being assembled, and it has continued to put me immediately and emotionally back into the time it was made. It visually writes Community life, and two sequences have special meaning for me: the first firing of our kiln and the building of the dovecot.

The outdoor kiln was fashioned after an ancient Italian design by master potter Alexander Giampietro, Mother Perpetua's father. The first firing began at Matins, and Community members and guests took turns feeding wood into the furnace throughout the night and into the next day until the inside of the kiln reached the a temperature hot enough to bake clay.

The door to the kiln has the shape of a human form walking right into the oven, pot in hand, and the analogy to our development in monastic life made me gasp. Before it is fired, a pot can be remolded, but afterward the only way the clay can change shape is if it explodes. Consecration is the high fire of monastic life. We live the same process and in the same suspense.

The dovecot was the first big undertaking for the Closed Community. It was also an important moment in the life of our Community because it was the first structure on the hill that Lady Abbess had envisioned as the site for the future monastery.

The project represented years of commitment, from collecting the stones to building the archway. Completing the archway was exciting.

We placed in the center of a wooden form the arch stone, which is the one that all the other stones press against to stay suspended. We interlocked the rest of the stones on either side of the arch stone. But the wooden form supporting the arch would have to be removed, and we didn't know whether the stones would hold together or collapse.

The moment the form was taken away—and this is captured in the film—we heard a loud crack. We held our breath as the stones settled into place. The arch held! The nuns and the laypeople clasped hands and joyously danced back and forth through that proud arch.

For me, building the archway is a metaphor for much in monastic life, specifically the work of the Education Deanery. Just as the builders carefully placed stone upon stone over the wooden form, the deanery was fitting new sisters into the Community in relation to the needs they fulfilled. The builders didn't know if their archway would stand, and neither did I know if the deanery would prevail.

Thirty-Four

At the time of my First Vows, I awakened to a new sensitivity. I not only recognized the need for change but might now be in a position to influence changes.

The reading at mealtimes, for example, had always disturbed me because it is a daily obedience—all of us have to read—and I couldn't help but be aware that a lot of the women just didn't know how to present a reading. I thought I should try to do something about that, and the best way could be through plays. It would give my sisters access to a kind of experience I believed they needed. As far as I could tell, no demands beyond skits to entertain the Community on feast days had ever been made of them.

The skits were a time-honored slice of monastic life—as a novice, I took part in a number of them—and, though the amateur level of performance was endearing, I found myself itching to improve the presentations.

Mother Placid was the first to encourage her: "The skits were the way we let off steam. It was all fun, but not a real vehicle to take the instinctual stuff and hook it up where it could be useful for a person to grow into another level. I felt from the beginning that, even as a novice, she pushed for that. She understood the dynamic. She was living it, coming to grips with it, moving with it in a way that could start a reform."

The first collaborative venture was an allegorical playlet, Synergetic Myth, *which Mother David wrote and I directed as a puppet show. We presented the show over and over in a series of very short performances in the art studio, which was the only space available and could accommodate an audience of just four persons at a time.*

Other short exercises were presented until I found a little gem of a one-act play based on the Old Testament story of Sarah and Tobias. I thought this play offered us a challenge to begin to experience sacramental theater and hoped it might lift the women to a new self-

awareness. Reverend Mother gave me permission to proceed, and Miss Jantzer volunteered to add choreography.

I began to appreciate any possibility that gave me a step up. Inspiration came from my Broadway days. I sent for a Samuel French catalog and searched for plays that contained good scenes for readings. I also expanded my theatrical boundaries and wrote and directed a one-act comedy I called Mousepiller, *which would accommodate all of the novitiate in their annual presentation for the professed Community.*

Interest among the Community in these amateur theatricals swelled and affected what we chose to present at our traditional Mardi Gras evenings. By the eighties we were regularly presenting more ambitious offerings—scenes from Shakespeare with the whole Community participating.

"I guess you could say Shakespeare brought us together", recalled Mother Lucia Kuppens. In the mid-seventies, well before her entrance, she was Patricia Kuppens, a member of the Closed Community. "I was then doing my doctoral work on Shakespeare at Yale and some of us in the Closed Community had the idea to present a full production of *A Midsummer Night's Dream.* I was elected to speak to Mother Dolores about the project.

"I asked Mother Dolores if she would work with us on it. 'Do you want me to answer you as a mother or as a professional?' she asked.

"I bravely said, 'As a professional, of course.'

"'Well, then, there is no way you can do this as a conventional production. Why don't you try it as a puppet show? I think that's probably proportionate to what you're capable of.'

"It was a good moment, a characteristic one as I came to know Mother Dolores. She's always insisted, 'Start with something that's *real.*'

"You know, we did it—*A Midsummer Night's Dream* with puppets. We spent the whole summer working on it, with Mother Placid making the puppets and Mother Dolores helping me direct it. We did it for kids but mainly it was for us. It was for the pure joy of it."

The group got compliments and requests for more. Snow White *and* Beauty and the Beast *were presented, again for children, this time in a tent we called the Unicorn Theater. There was a natural, almost organic evolution from those little entertainments to presentations before adult audiences at our summer fairs. The fairs had started in August 1950 as a fundraiser organized by friends of Regina Laudis; we sold our jam and our cheese and took kids on hayrides. By the late seventies we were hosting thirty thousand people each summer.*

In 1978 Lady Abbess had an inspiration to do Alfred de Musset's play A Caprice. *She remembered this comedy of manners from her student days in France and felt that it would have significance for a modern audience. I seized this moment to enlist the professional participation of my Paramount friend James Douglas and his wife, Dawn.*

James and Dawn Douglas first visited the monastery in 1967. They visited again the following year. When James left the Hollywood TV series *Peyton Place* in the mid-seventies, he was offered a leading role in *As the World Turns*, produced in New York City. He packed up his family and moved to the East Coast. Jim and Dawn maintained a close relationship with Mother Dolores, becoming oblates when the transplanted Douglas family moved from Manhattan to Connecticut to be nearer to her.

"It was bound to be", Jim said with a smile and a shrug. "When Dolores left Hollywood, we gave her a farewell dinner on her last evening. After dinner, when Dawn and I were doing dishes, Dolores' wine glass and mine both fell to the floor. The stems of the broken glasses formed an unmistakable cross. Dawn looked at me and said, 'Well, I guess we're in for the long run.' "

— Dawn was right. The Douglases have been immensely important in our lives. Not only did they become oblates; they also were among our first named monastic scholars.

A Caprice *became the first full production performed at our fair. It was quite ambitious and was greeted with enthusiasm by a small but very supportive audience. With this acceptance, James and Dawn began thinking about forming a repertory company at Regina Laudis. It was just a germ of an idea, but over the next few summers we presented another comedy of manners, a medieval mystery play and three Shakespeare plays. Attendance steadily grew. There was no denying that the plays were becoming a centering force for the fairs.*

344

Thirty-Five

Maria Cooper Janis confided she would like to introduce someone to Regina Laudis—the actress Patricia Neal.

I knew who Patricia Neal was, of course, but had never met her or even seen the film for which she won her Oscar because I was already inside the monastery when it was released. Hud *has since been shown to the Community, and Patricia is perfection in it.*

In 1963 Patricia, four months pregnant with her fifth child, suffered a series of massive strokes that left her incapacitated for several years. She gave birth to the beautiful Lucy, known in the press as the "miracle baby", and over time recovered with the support and help of her husband, the writer Roald Dahl. She eventually returned to her career, which resulted in a second Oscar nomination.

Maria's request to introduce Patricia came as a shock. Many years earlier, Patricia had been romantically involved with Maria's father, and Maria once vented her anger at Patricia by spitting at her. Over the years, Maria never spoke of her.

But, while accompanying Byron on a European concert tour, she had literally bumped into Patricia. Patricia's straightforward desire to connect and Maria's intuitive sense that her former enemy was in deep emotional distress had fomented a close friendship. Maria was sincerely concerned about Patricia's well-being and felt that she would gain much comfort by visiting the abbey. I wrote a letter to Patricia at her Great Missenden home in England, inviting her to visit when she was next in the States.

That spring, Patricia came to America to receive an honorary doctorate from Rockford College in Illinois and accepted my invitation.

"I thought I was looking forward to the visit," Patricia remembered, "but on the drive up to the abbey from New York I suddenly panicked and wondered what the hell I was doing, going to a Catholic nunnery.

345

"Upon arrival, I was taken to meet the nun who had written to me. I remembered her face. I had gone to see *Lonelyhearts* because my good friend Maureen Stapleton was in it and was quite taken by the work of the young ingenue. Now, face-to-face, I looked into the most astonishing blue eyes I had ever seen.

"Over the next year, whenever I was back in America, I arranged the trip to have a few days at my nunnery. When my marriage to Roald ended, I was hit very hard. I left England for good and returned to the States. I wasn't sure what I was going to do with the rest of my life. The only professional work offered me was in commercials, one for a coffee company and the other, fittingly, for headache tablets. I was a real basket case. I called Mother Dolores to say I desperately needed to come for a long visit."

It wasn't difficult to see that this woman was in deep pain over her personal life, but she was also an actress chomping at the bit to get back on stage. I sensed she had to return to her profession if only in something presented to the Community before she could be open to rebuilding her life. I asked Dick to suggest something and perhaps come back and work with her.

I had long admired Patricia Neal, and although the possibility of working with her was daunting, it was too tempting to turn down. I recommended a reading rather than a more demanding full play and suggested a scene from *Anastasia*—the "recognition scene" between the woman who claims to be the only surviving heir of Czar Nicholas II, who was murdered along with his family during the Russian Revolution, and the dowager empress, whose recognition Anastasia desperately needs. Wonderful scene—and only two characters, both women. Mother Dolores asked me—a little too innocently, I thought—who I would want to play Anastasia. As if she didn't know.

With permission to break the Great Silence, the three of us met after Compline every evening for a week to rehearse in Cosmas and Damian, the small hut inside the enclosure used for chant classes. It would be a staged reading, Mother Dolores and Patricia carrying their scripts, but both memorized their lines quickly.

346

It was decided that the scene would be videotaped to show to the Community at a later date. To familiarize myself with the videotaping procedure, I had to begin taping our rehearsals. Since there was no tape-editing equipment at the abbey, I would have to edit the scene in the camera, stopping and starting to include close-ups within master shots as we went along. This is not a comfortable procedure for any actor, and it hobbled us all.

I was struck at how alike their techniques were—both instinctive actors through and through. It was fascinating to watch them playing with and against each other and yet somehow uncomfortably tense. The atmosphere became more like a Hollywood soundstage than a monastery hut. Patricia, for all her enthusiasm at the beginning, became aggressive and demanding, monopolizing my attention and all but snubbing her coplayer. Mother Dolores, reacting to Patricia's antagonism, became impatient, distant. Arguments sprang up between them.

I seemed to be the target of Patricia's discontent, and her edginess was rubbing off on me. Tension grew between us—really, to the boiling point. In rehearsal, Dick framed a close-up of Patricia, an over-the-shoulder shot, and although I would just be feeding lines and my face wouldn't be in the frame, I had been trained to give the same performance I would give when the camera was on me. When the reverse angle was shot for my close-up, Patricia dismissively read her lines in a dry monotone while she looked out the window. That got my inner diva's Irish up. I sharply reminded Patricia of her craft. She took exception to that, liberally sprinkling her remarks with one particular four-letter expletive. Over and over and over.

All of a sudden I heard Mother Dolores' voice in a surprisingly curse-laden tirade that ended with "I am sick and tired of *your* miserable attitude. Why don't you leave?" Patricia stomped out into the night. A few moments later, Mother Dolores also exited, leaving me frozen in the middle of the room.

I had the sickening feeling in my stomach that I had, in a stupid outburst, ruined further communication with Patricia. I had no idea

347

when she walked out after my flaying words that this confrontation between two actresses would be crucial to our ultimate connection.

I looked for Patricia, but she had obviously left the enclosure. An hour later, I was summoned to the abbey entrance. It was Patricia at our front door. "I am a dreadful woman", she began. "Please forgive me. I don't want to leave."

How did this happen? How had she found the key to come back? The answer is one you would expect. It was a person of Christ, someone who loved me and loved the abbey, who had intercepted Patricia. It was Dawn Douglas. Dawn was just leaving the abbey property when Patricia shot out of the enclosure gate. She intercepted Pat and calmed her down, ultimately urging her back. A coincidence? No. But what a mystery of friendship and love.

"Dawn helped me put my behavior into perspective", Patricia said. "Mother Dolores had welcomed me into their hospitality, and in exchange I brought anger and bitterness with me. I couldn't get the thought of the woman who broke up my marriage out of my mind. Like a venom, it poisoned everything I did."

Our rehearsals continued uninterrupted, and I became aware that I was witnessing not only a professional alliance of two actresses working in far less than ideal circumstances yet giving thoughtful—and generous—performances but also the birth of a remarkable relationship between two women. Over the thirty years since *Anastasia*, I've marveled at how loving their relationship is. It can get edgy at times, but the bantering is civil, firmly based in the respect of one formidable fighter for another. They are honest women who share one indispensable ingredient for enduring friendship: a sense of humor.

"It was Mother Dolores' scheme, I'm sure," Patricia continued, "but Lady Abbess invited me to spend an entire month at Regina Laudis, and not merely as a guest, she said. If I accepted, I would live in the monastery like a prepostulant.

"I traded my street clothes for the black dress of the postulant and moved into a bare cell. I followed a strict regimen of work and prayer, kept the Great Silence, helped bake bread and weed the garden, and every morning, after church, I met with Mother Dolores. There were times when I felt I never wanted to return to the outside world.

"She challenged me. 'You haven't lost yourself', she insisted. 'You haven't lost your talent. You cannot lose what you have given your body to bring into being—you haven't lost your children. You can give life forever—if you will stop trying to even out the score. You must remember everything, not just the bad parts.'

"To remember? I didn't think that was possible for me any longer. My strokes had robbed me of my past, and I had gotten used to not even trying to remember. She felt the stroke was the key, that I would never have come into the reflective dimension of an enclosure except for the stroke. I would be just another aging actress fighting other aging actresses for a guest spot on *The Love Boat*."

Since all postulants are asked to write about their lives in order to begin to understand who they are and what they are called to be in this life, I suggested that Patricia do that. Because she found writing difficult, we gave Patricia a recorder to speak her memories into. Whenever she visited, she would add to that memory bank.

It began to occur to me that Patricia's growing library of audiotapes might be the basis for an autobiography. A friend of the abbey took the idea to the publisher Simon and Schuster and got a firm and unusual commitment: Patricia would have five years to complete the memoir, and the publisher would not have the right to read any of the work in progress until the due date.

Over the next three years, Patricia made many visits to the abbey. We kept a room for her at Sheepfold, the small no-frills farmhouse that had been Lauren Ford's home. All the work was done at the abbey and, therefore, subject to Patricia's schedule and the restrictions on my availability when she was here.

As we approached the end of the third year of collaboration with little but an extraordinary cache of notes, I realized that we would never make our deadline. That's when I asked Dick to come aboard as our partner. For the next two years, he and Patricia would meet at Sheepfold, and drafts would fly by fax machines between Bethlehem and Los Angeles until the due date for the manuscript was upon us.

349

We three spent the last week going over the text word by word, huddled together in Corpus Christi. Three days before the manuscript had to be delivered, Patricia stumbled in the darkened basement hallway and fractured her wrist. She was taken to Saint Mary's Hospital in Waterbury, where the remainder of the last-minute corrections were made at her bedside.

I drove into New York City and presented the finished manuscript of *As I Am* to our editor—whom we had never met—on the exact date it was due. A week later, we received a letter from her that began, "I must be the happiest editor in New York City." Not one change in our draft was requested. *As I Am* was published in 1988.

Thirty-Six

The abbey theater did not come into existence because I had had some kind of plan. When I entered the monastery, I believed that I had put acting behind me forever and that I was going to live a life of quiet contemplation.

Our theater happened—as is often the case in Benedictine life— because other people had a vocation that came into relationship with my vocation. It was the synergy created by our mutual love for the theater that brought our theater into being.

Since our Anastasia *tape had not been shown to the Community (everything in its own time at the abbey), I asked Patricia Neal if she would perform her one-woman show about Helen Keller for us. Patricia was devoted to Helen Keller. She had played Helen's mother in the original Broadway production of* The Miracle Worker *and, following her recovery from the strokes, performed readings dedicated to Miss Keller's life that Roald Dahl had written for her.*

Patricia gave the performance several times in the Unicorn tent on a hill outside the enclosure, before an audience of not only the Community, which supplied singing interludes for the readings, but many outside guests who were very generous with donations after the show.

During the last performance, an electrical storm with heavy rain knocked out electricity in the area. But it did not stop Patricia's presentation. She moved, with her audience, inside the abbey chapel where, lit by candles, she completed the show to a packed house.

Following the performance, Patricia, exhausted but exhilarated, turned to me and said, "You can't let that happen again. You can't have performances rained out. You have to build a theater here, right on this hill."

Our theater was built the following year with the help of Patricia and several other benefactors. It is an open-air theater that can seat two hundred people. It was designed by Mother Placid to capture the

351

character of a country barn, and Father Prokes kept a watchful eye during construction to be sure her vision was honored. The stage opens at the rear to the woods on our property so that the trees and the birds—and sometimes the insects—are a part of the theatrical world we create. Patricia made it happen. It bears the name she gave it that day—The Gary-The Olivia—honoring Gary Cooper and her daughter who died so very young.

A full production of A Midsummer Night's Dream *was our new theater's first presentation, followed by two more plays by Shakespeare:* The Taming of the Shrew *and* Much Ado about Nothing. *In all, we have presented six plays by the Bard.*

In 1986, Lady Abbess came to me with a request for a production marking her fiftieth Jubilee, something that the Community had heard at Christmastime for years. She wanted a dramatic presentation of Pablo Casals' oratorio El Pessebre *(The Crib), based upon the poem written by his friend Joan Alavedra in 1945, when they both were under arrest during the Spanish Civil War.*

Casals had refused to premiere the work in Spain and, instead, presented it for the first time in Mexico in 1960. It had been performed only one other time, in 1967 in Geneva; consequently, our production would mark the first time the work would be performed in the United States.

Reenter Tom Camm. Tom is the young oblate who departed the Closed Community fifteen years earlier to seek a professional career as a dancer. He had been successful in his quest and was part of a professional company in which he had met his wife. Tom and Sally were living in Michigan and had started a family with the birth of daughter Michaela when Lady Abbess contacted them and asked them to stage *El Pessebre.*

"Choreographing the oratorio was an exciting thought," recalled Sally, "but Michaela was barely one month old, and I was afraid it wouldn't be possible. 'But that's perfect', Lady Abbess insisted. 'She can play the baby Jesus!'"

The Camms worked on El Pessebre *for many months, commuting from Michigan for most of them. Working with the music Casals had recorded, Sally based her choreography on Catalonian folk dancing, using, because this story of the birth of Christ is told through the eyes of children, the great stockpile of youngsters who were around the abbey then.*

Tom and Sally danced the roles of Joseph and Mary. Not only is Sally's dancing something to behold, but she is a genius when it comes to teaching children to dance. The most touching thing was that the children became so involved. Those kids were not intimidated or shy; they remained themselves but also responded to the discipline of performing. When ballet star Gelsey Kirkland visited Regina Laudis during the rehearsal period, she complimented Sally, "That's exactly how children should be taught to dance!"

Everything about the show was beautiful, really. A particularly poignant memory was having Pablo Casals' widow, Marta, who was now living in Washington, DC, come to Regina Laudis to see El Pessebre. *She watched a rehearsal and was so moved, she cried.*

Sally remembered, "Almost everyone connected to the abbey, including every nun, was somehow involved—constructing flats, making costumes, headpieces and masks for the donkeys and angels. Lady Abbess was very much the driving force behind this project."

—If she had had her way, the show would have had a cast of thousands. There was a lot of Cecil B. DeMille in Lady Abbess.

El Pessebre was enormously successful and prompted another epic production, not as part of the summer presentations but solely for an invited audience to continue the celebration of Lady Abbess' anniversary. *The Mystery of the Holy Innocents* was an adaptation of the medieval mystery play *The Slaughter of the Innocents*, specifically chosen by Lady Abbess as a contemplative response to the ongoing controversy over the Supreme Court ruling in *Roe v. Wade*. Sally Camm again staged and choreographed the piece, she and Tom danced, Veronica Tyler sang, Patricia Neal and Dawn Douglas acted in it. Stephen Concordia, the young man who was in the land program during the time of the 1980 film, composed original music for the production. Coincidentally, Stephen was now considering a religious vocation.

In 1990, James and Dawn Douglas' fervor for an acting company was fanned by the arrival on the scene of Helen Patton, a young professional actress who also had dreams of founding a theater company. Helen, who is the sister of our Mother Margaret Georgina, had written an ingenious play called Love's Labour's Won *and brought a number of her skilled friends to perform it. Helen brought prestige as well via her training at London's Royal Academy of Dramatic Art.*

The next year, Helen and her RADA colleague Richard Rivas returned and were joined by two young people working in our land program— Alistair Highet, Iain's brother, and Melora Mennesson—in a production of Shakespeare's As You Like It.

It was a big production, and there was a terrific spirit among the people. For the first time there was a real sense of an ensemble. Everyone was asking, "What's next? How do we keep this spirit alive? How can we keep this sense of community growing?" They did not want their relationships to fold just because the play was over. I recognized that need and empathized with the ache they felt. It was out of that desire that the Act Association was born.

Alistair Highet remembered, "The Act Association sprang from this need to have a core of people committed to each other and to the abbey from one play to the next, and it didn't mean they would necessarily be the ones to put the play on each year, but they would support whoever did. Our mission was to create a context for this kind of community experience. We embraced that mission."

I felt, as a contemplative, I must put complements—persons who are in my same profession but not called to religious life—into those positions that could build a genuine community theater. I envisioned my role as a supporting one. This has not always been an easy road for a person who likes to have things her own way. But I learned early on that only when one chooses to work with others does life really happen.

James and Dawn Douglas, Helen Patton, Alistair Highet, Richard Rivas and Melora Mennesson formed the nucleus of the Act Association. This core grew with the addition of Kelly and Michael Briney, a New York couple with theater aspirations; Tim Ridge, a young man who

354

petitioned for an additional year in our land program to join the group;
and a carpenter-cum-stage technician, Kevin McElroy, without whom
we would never have had a show each summer.

Helen Patton recalled, "At the beginning, Mother Dolores was very, very present. She used to come and do vocal warm-ups with us, and at one technical rehearsal I noticed her lugging a huge Fresnel lamp and asked her if she should really be carrying that heavy thing. Not breaking her step, she replied, 'No, my place is inside. I am called to be contemplative, but until you all get your act together and fill these jobs, someone's got to do it. When you step up to the plate, I can go back to praying for you.' "

"Mother Dolores doesn't suggest plays but approves or disapproves choices submitted by the association", said Melora Mennesson. "She does go to auditions and rehearsals now and then, but she resists making suggestions, and I don't think she takes notes. The company doesn't always run smoothly. Problems arise, but it is rare when she is asked to arbitrate. Nevertheless, everyone knows she is the final authority.

"The plays are meant to reflect a reality both inside and outside the enclosure. Although Benedictines offer hospitality to the laity, they remain very aware of the necessity for enclosure. So there were always times when she was not present."

—There is never the necessity to make a decision to be inside
the enclosure rather than at the theater or someplace else, and
it is not a holier-than-thou posture to stay within the call of the
Horarium. The depth of corporate prayer life keeps me within
the purpose of my vows. It's not an intellectual consideration.
It's not a matter of decision *at all.*

"Putting on a play is a long process", Melora continued. "Work on each August production begins in January with auditions and read-throughs. For the next few months, rehearsals are scheduled on weekends only because people have family lives and jobs. As we get closer to performance, we rehearse daily. The Act Association presents only six performances of each play, which includes one for the Community only, over two weekends. It's a lot of work for just that.

"Yet we began looking at several plays to do between our summer shows. Jean-Paul Sartre's *No Exit* was one of them, but we felt sure it wouldn't fly. Because the choice is at the abbey's discernment, we thought we would never be allowed to do a play that takes place in Hell. But Mother Dolores was intrigued with the idea. She is, happily, adventurous."

Helen added, "We presented *No Exit*, in a translation forged with the help of Mother Jerome, in repertory with an original musical revue, *No Man Is an Island*. The dynamic between the two productions was incredible. *No Exit* was clandestine and dark; *No Man Is an Island*, open and frothy. And yet the audience would be called to contemplate the message of futility in isolation in both."

Melora recalled, "*No Exit* was performed in Our Lady of Light, the New England–style house across Flanders Road from the abbey. In hellacious weather! It was more than one hundred degrees inside. Nobody could breathe."

—Perfect for Hell.

We always had a play going each summer, although we lost our customary venue for the August fair the very next year. The weekend attendance at our fair had risen to forty thousand guests. That's a lot of traffic for Flanders Road and a lot of work for the nuns, considering that all the bread, cheese, honey, pottery and metal sculpture available for purchase came from the labors of the nuns. The fair was getting too big. It paid our oil bill for the whole year, but we could not risk becoming a fairground with a chapel attached. I think everyone was relieved when we closed down the fair.

The last show performed at the fair was a musical revue, You Got to Move, *compiled and performed by Tom Pomposello. Tom came to Regina Laudis by way of his wife, the singer Patricia Lawrence, who knew Mother Placid. Tom was an entrepreneur in every sense of the word. He was also a great bear of a man.*

Tom fell in love with the blues at a young age, and he spent the rest of his life playing and collecting what he considered the American folk music. *He ran his own company, producing music, animation videos and advertising jingles. Lady Abbess and I thought Tom should meet with our guest mistress, Mother Noëlla, because her connection to Sha Na Na would easily enable her to relate to his profession.*

Mother Noëlla remembered their first parlor. "Right off the bat, Tom said he wanted his profession to be assumed by the Community, but he didn't know how. 'What does a blues man have to give to an abbey?' he wondered. 'Some people would say there's no place for blues there.' I recalled the many times Mother Dolores has said, 'There's a possibility of sacredness in whatever you do, depending on how you do it.'"

"At our next parlor, we came up with the idea of celebrating American music of the second half of the twentieth century. And, since the year would be marking the fiftieth anniversary of the invasion of Normandy, it would also honor the moment when Lady Abbess received the call to found Regina Laudis.

"The title of the show came from a song Tom's mentor, the great blues guitarist Fred McDowell, had written: 'You Got to Move'. His lyrics sang of finding your belongings out on the street because you haven't paid the rent—and you got to move. And, too, when the Lord calls you, you got to move. The Rolling Stones had a hit record with it."

Tom recruited professional musical colleagues from New York, and their performances were fabulous. He did a masterful job of editing actual D-Day movie footage, which was projected behind these artists. Most of the music had never been performed at the abbey—blues, soul, rock and roll, music Elvis sang.

I knew Tom was special when I heard his music while we were in the chapel singing Vespers and Tom and his musicians were just finishing the Saturday matinee at the theater. Because it was August, the windows were open, and it was amazing to hear that music in relation to the Vespers chant. There was something about it that was mysteriously complementary. And it was so much fun.

After You Got to Move, *Tom remained in close contact. He was concerned about the potential lack of donations we might suffer without the fair to provide a substantial audience. He said he would think of something to do about that.*

Our next play was one I was very familiar with: The Pleasure of His Company. *Almost forty years had passed since I recited its lines on the*

357

Longacre stage. This time Pogo Poole was a devilish James Douglas. Maria Agee, a nurse in residence in the land program, played Cornelia Otis Skinner's part. Not long after that performance, Maria entered Regina Laudis and is now Sister Esther, who keeps our gardens beautiful. Although the nuns do not appear in the productions, several of the women have done so as members of the Act Association prior to their entrance.

Pleasure *was followed by another Broadway comedy,* Light Up the Sky, *and three fine dramas:* The Glass Menagerie, The Miracle Worker *and* The Country Girl. *We did not suffer from lack of attendance. We never had a super-full house, but we were building a base; people came back year after year, including a professional contingent who lived nearby—Richard Widmark, Fay Wray, Christine Baranski, Mia Farrow and Jason Robards. Mr. Robards' daughter, Sarah, is a member of the Act Association.*

"The first year I was in the group," Sarah remembered, "I was very content to remain backstage. I did props and costumes and worked on sets. But the next year, James read me for *Light Up the Sky* and cast me as Irene, the actress. Acting was great fun; I really loved it and didn't know I would love it. During this whole time, I was in the process of converting to Catholicism. That was a big part of it as well.

"I was so happy my father came to see me in *The Miracle Worker* although he was very ill at the time. He died not long after. Mother Dolores spoke at his funeral."

Although the link between drama and monastic life goes back to the origins of the mystery plays, we've always sought to sponsor the cultural and spiritual values derived from the best of popular theater too. In 2005, we presented our first book musical, a revival of My Fair Lady, *directed by Richard and choreographed by Sally Camm. Alistair Highet was Henry Higgins; Kelly Briney played Eliza Doolittle and, since there were never enough bodies around, doubled on costumes as well.*

Our "orchestra" consisted of Patrick Smith on percussion and, on electronic keyboard, our new chaplain—Father Stephen Concordia. Benedictine continuity.

Thirty-Seven

It was a time of great highs and, as if God were balancing the reality in our lives, great lows.

—Journal entry, February 18, 1991

The birth of the Act Association occurred the same year as my twenty-fifth Jubilee, marking a quarter century since my vows. Many friends came to the abbey to celebrate with me and witness the planting of their gift, a white dogwood tree, near the theater.

The tree is quite large now and brings back memories of each of them, especially the actress Martha Hyer Wallis, Hal's widow, who had been instrumental in smoothing out his ruffled feathers at the time I left Hollywood and who has remained in my life to this day. Although Hal was gone, Martha felt that she was bringing him with her to the abbey because, as she told me for the first time, "he had always wanted to come."

Karl Malden, who was then president of the Academy of Motion Picture Arts and Sciences, sent a jacket with the AMPAS logo, which I still wear over my habit. Karl and his successor, Robert Rehme, invited me back into the Academy.

> *—I'm pleased that Oscar time in Hollywood is now of interest to the women at Regina Laudis, and they are able to see some of the films in competition, courtesy of the DVD screeners that are sent to me. (The only movie they have ever asked to see again is* The King's Speech.*)*

It seemed to me that the Jubilee day was without flaw. After twenty-five years, I could appreciate the happiness I felt from the coming together of people I loved—yet, at the same time, accept and embrace the sense of separation I was also feeling. That night, I wrote in the journal:

359

These pages draw to a close the cycle of this journal that has held open to me the consciousness of my own process. I can see in it the tools that have developed the one authentic goodness in myself—my own dear, stubborn longing which has always driven me. Perhaps the deepest gift of the day is finally to realize that I really want to be a contemplative. I could not bear the surface existence outside. I want to live and pray and plumb the depths <u>within the heart of this community</u>. I want to keep this truth of the Jubilee in my consciousness: that all things are held and destined, and <u>so am I</u>.

We had already begun our slow move to the hill in the late eighties with the building of two structures, Annunciation, housing the novitiate, and Saint John's Tower, providing an area for our infirmary as well as a residence for Lady Abbess and several of the older nuns. Once again, the nuns themselves cleared the land and felled the trees that provided the wood for the new buildings, both of which are quite simple—hexagon-shaped and not unlike log cabins.

In 1992 building commenced on the most ambitious addition to the hill, which fulfilled a long-held desire of Lady Abbess—our new church. Two years later, the Church of Jesu Fili Mariae—Jesus, Son of Mary— was completed and blessed.

It is the most beautiful church I have ever seen—and not simply because it's ours. I truly feel that it answered the problem I've always had with all the paraphernalia—the stuff—one finds in Catholic churches that hasn't much to do with genuine piety. Ostentatious statues of saints don't muster a sense of worship in me or make me want to pray to a particular one. It just makes me angry over the money that was poured into making those figures that could have done some real good.

I was among the forty-five women then in the Community who shared ideas of what we wanted our church to look like, but Mothers Praxedes, Telchilde, and Maria Immaculata were at the helm. They are the true designers of the church. Father Prokes, a master architect himself, served as our architectural and theological mediator and guided the work.

Our church is a wooden, barn-like structure laid out like a classic basilica. It was designed as it is because of what people had experienced

360

at The Gary-The Olivia. We heard what had awakened them to the peace, the joy, the involvement—all the good things they felt when they partici- pated. Why not have a church that captures the basics of our theater and takes people into another sphere?

We used the same elements—the pine wood, the arches, the stage that captures the forest as its background—and framed them with walls of glass windows looking out over the woods on one side and a garden on the other, giving the feeling of being indoors and outdoors at the same time, with the altar placed where the priest would offer Mass in a nature setting.

By having clear windows instead of the conventional stained glass, one can look out and allow the beauty of what God has created to be the backdrop for prayer in every season. True, windowpanes can become dirty, but our views stay crystal clear because members of the lay community Auscultatores (which means "the listeners"), led by David and Nancy Stein and Melora Mennesson, commit annually to the main- tenance of the windows.

The very first Mass in the new church was its consecration by Archbishop Daniel J. Cronin, and the main—the extraordinary—thing that we all felt when we sang there for the first time was relief.

The chants sung at Regina Laudis are more than one thousand years old, but they don't have to sound like it, and they did in the lower monastery chapel. The acoustics, therefore, had been a big worry. I remember my heart was in my throat when we processed into the new building singing the Kyrie. I could hardly believe it when I heard the glorious sound. The acoustics were divine. The new church gave reso- nance and life to our voices.

Paula Prentiss, who has visited Regina Laudis often—sometimes alone, sometimes with her family—remembered each visit as if it were a scene in a favorite play. Paula recalled, "On my most recent stay, Mother Dolores took me to see the new church. We sat quietly in the choir area, and I talked about returning to my faith. I had been away from Catholicism for many years, but God had given me a sign in Hollywood when Dolores said to me, 'God never leaves you.' She said it again at that moment and pointed to the wall of windows overlooking the woods. 'Now just look', she said, 'if you are determined to see God while you're here.' It was autumn, and the woods were bursting with color. I felt like a child looking into the secret garden. I did come back to the Church, and I look upon knowing Mother Dolores as part of that spiritual journey."

—*I've always thought it fitting that the word* hospitality *contains the word* hospital. *It gives a foundation to the concept of caring for others. I associate it with healing and restoring and maintaining bonds of friendship too.*

With the completion of the church, the Community now looked toward renovation of the lower monastery. We had long anguished about the tiny kitchen that had served us and our guests for over fifty years.

"The kitchen was, in a word, depressing", said Mother Olivia Frances, the econome (steward). "We were bursting at the seams. We cooked for fifty people a day—twice—in an eight-by-twelve space that was shaped like a railroad car. We were always waiting for someone to close the oven door so that we could get to the freezer."

I brought the problem to the Education Deanery and got overwhelming approval to take to Lady Abbess a proposal for a complete reconfiguring of the kitchen. What we needed was expressed through informal plans by Iain Highet, and we were shocked to find the estimate for construction was $100,000!

Since Granny Kude's bombastic display of opposition to my entrance, she had made repeated visits to Regina Laudis and came to love the women in the Community. In turn, they took her into their hearts. It was only at her death that I learned Granny had been baptized a Catholic. Shortly thereafter a surprise arrived—in the form of a check for $56,327.10, her bequest to me. It represented all the tips she had saved over the years. So, even in death, Granny was watching out for me—"just in case". I asked that the money be set aside for the new kitchen.

At roughly the same time, Joe Allegretti, one of the Can-do kids at Saint Francis de Sales, visited Regina Laudis. On his departure, he said to ask him if there was anything he could ever help me with. So I wrote Joe that we needed $50,000 for a new kitchen. I figured he would either give me some money or think, "What nerve." I put the letter in the mail before I had second thoughts. This arrived three days later:

> *Dear Mother Dolores,*
>
> *I am very happy to give you the $50,000. For tax purposes I need to know exactly what it will be used for. The money will be soon coming. No, I think I'll just put it in this letter.*
>
> *Love, Joe*

Work on the renovation began soon afterward. The new kitchen is named Chiara, and it has a commemorative plaque honoring Joe's mother, Mary Rowe Maher Allegretti, and Esther Opal Kude, my beloved Granny.

In 1990, the Community was hit with a monumental blow. Lady Abbess was diagnosed with breast cancer. From that moment I knew that she was no longer a face to be dealt with externally, but internally. Her mortality was now, for me, a reality.

God had me in mind for her, and she was tailor-made to take me on. It was only a few months after I entered that my poor postulant mother turned me over to her; she didn't know how to deal with me because she was French and I was American.

Lady Abbess dealt with me as a person of worth—even while she seemed utterly to dismiss me when we were in front of others. I didn't understand this until many years later. She loved me as a mother but taught me as a foundress.

I had assisted Mother Mary Aline in her portress duties for almost ten years (and she was an unyieldingly tough boss). In the nineties I inherited the responsibility and the title of portress upon her death.

For several weeks before she died, she was bedridden in her cell, but whenever I tried to visit her, she refused to talk to me, even when Father Tucker told her to do so. She just would not budge.

—She went out glaring at you?

Yes. I didn't go into her cell even when Mass was said there. I could not cross the line—or, I should say, I would not cross the line. We broke the reed, she and I. Saint Benedict urges bending—not breaking—the reed. We broke it, and I regret that.

Thoughts of mortality brought to mind the first time I had encountered death—the passing of Grandpa's brother George when I was six. I loved Uncle George and was told he was away on a trip. As I was too little to go to the cemetery, I was kept at home during the service. I remember hearing the sound of a train whistle in the distance and thinking, "Oh, that must be Uncle George."

Death has been described as an end, a disaster; also as a beginning, a door opening. But if death is a door opening, what lies beyond the door? Might it be just nothing?

The purpose of Christian faith is to believe in the Resurrection; the keystone is that Christ rose from the dead. I think whether or not a person can get through the mystery of death is the ultimate test of faith. I can only surmise that, as Dolores Marie, I was named into holding the dead Christ as Mary did—and the Gospels do imply that our Lady did not accept death as the last word for her Son.

—Is there a built-in comfort factor in believing that life continues beyond?

I am not sure it really works that way. Religious life doesn't give you a comfort zone as much as it puts you up against the reality in a far more severe context. "Keep death daily before your eyes" is one of the "tools for good works"—spiritual disciplines—that Saint Benedict asks us to use every day. The point of Christianity—certainly of monasticism—is to answer the question "How do I participate in—and, indeed, how am I myself—the work of God?" These tools permit us to be open to that participation—to experience in our lives the gifts and the grace of God.

Do you have a personal view of what you are heading for?

I believe the body at death ceases to be a boundary, a confinement—but its capacity for communion remains. That capacity for communion is truly the essence of resurrection, and that leads me to consider that resurrected life must take the shape of everything that one has done in one's life to be a communicative person. In other words, everything we have done in life is the architecture of the eternal body. I am building that body now.

It seems new life always comes into the community to balance the passings. This period saw the entrances of eight young women and the final profession of Mother Monica Nadzam, who had entered in 1983 at the age of sixty-two, joining in Community her niece Mother Scholastica Lenkner, who is in charge of all our preserving.

—When Mother Monica entered, her two hopes were to become our cookie baker and to use a power saw! Well, she is and she has! I remember the first time she cut down a tree. Instead of falling away from her, it crashed down exactly where she was standing. The two main branches of the tree were formed into a perfect V and, like a scene in a Buster Keaton movie, came to rest on either side of Sister Monica, who was unscathed and standing strong.

There was now in place a prepostulancy program for women asking to be considered as candidates. In this phase, the woman begins to regulate her life within the order as befits a postulant. She enters into a relationship with the dean of education, and she begins to chart. She learns to pray certain Hours by herself and the schedule of the early-to-bed life. She also learns what is not permitted—a smoker, for example, must give up smoking—and finds out whether she is capable of living and training under real conditions. It is still structured, but it's not as restrictive as it used to be.

365

The first of the new postulants was Susan Postel. With a master's degree in psychology, she had worked in community mental health with the Jesuit Volunteer Corps in Seattle, Washington. "I had been adopted as an infant", she said, "but had never tried to find my birth mother. I had a fabulous upbringing by wonderful people, so it was not a priority interest for me. But when it became obvious that I had a vocation, Lady Abbess said, 'Look, you haven't really started to figure out what *your* life is about, much less what *this* life is about. You really have to find your birth mother if you can.'

"Mother Dolores was the one to choreograph the search for my heritage, and over time we did locate my mother and stepfather, who became part of my life."

> — *Susan entered Regina Laudis in 1990 and is now Mother Lioba Postel, the founder of our candle studio. I am continually aware of the grace in Mother Lioba that made her able to receive the goodness in her two families and be a daughter to each.*

The second entrant was a local Bethlehem girl, Karen Makarewicz, who came with an art background from the University of Utah. Her area of expertise was weaving, which, after college, she fashioned as artwork that was shown in galleries throughout Connecticut.

"But something was missing", recalled Karen, who is now Mother Jadwiga Makarewicz. "I needed to have my art be useful to others, and this frustration led me to the abbey, where I made a commitment."

Spinning and weaving, an integral part of Benedictine monastic life that was brought to Regina Laudis by the first nuns, has been enhanced because of Mother Jadwiga. As steward of the sheep flock, she has become guardian of the entire process of our wool production, from lambing to the weaving of the garments and tapestries that we sell. She bases her designs on our land—the hills and the gardens—and, strikingly, on the feathers of the turkeys who live by the sheep barn. She is the one who introduced Shetland sheep to the flock because they are a better breed for wool. Just a few years ago, she added a caretaker for the sheep—a llama named Giselle, who takes her job very seriously.

—There is a large and beautiful tapestry hanging in our church that never fails to remind me of my Consecration. It is a faithful reproduction of the Madonna by Mother Placid that was on my Consecration card. The tapestry was woven by Mother Jadwiga over many years—a daunting endeavor for which I will be forever grateful.

Janel Schullo, a Minnesota girl, became curious about theology in college. "Theology credits were required, otherwise I never would have taken a course," she recalled, "but once I did, I was fascinated and decided to make it my major. As I got more into the study I realized that, as absorbing as it was, there was an abstract quality that disturbed me, and I was drawn to exploring the justice movements in Central America. I spent a semester in Guatemala working at an orphanage. It was life changing for me. I came to see that my own country was poorer spiritually than Guatemala.

"I returned home with a growing sense of mission, dropped the classes for my junior year at college and entered the internship program at Regina Laudis. It was in the spring, and I was conscious that most of my peers from college were on spring break in Cancun and here I was, a college party girl, in a monastery. It was a signal that my life was going in the other direction.

"I felt I fit right in. I was with persons who were radically different individuals, but who were also just like me. I entered in 1993 and consider myself blessed to have found this place."

—She is now Mother Cecilia Schullo, and her most precious gift to the Community is her skill in the practice of massage and yoga. On scholarship, she studied self-awakening yoga at Nosara Yoga Institute in Costa Rica. This school of yoga is based on the belief that we learn through our body and that our body can tell us what it needs if we acquire the habit of listening to it, which complements the principles and practice of monastic life at Regina Laudis. Mother Cecilia now holds a degree from Lesley University in Cambridge, Massachusetts—a master of education in interdisciplinary studies with a special-ization in monastic yoga education.

Frances Levi Cooke's childhood playground was within the celebrated mansions of Newport, Rhode Island. "My family genealogy celebrates both observant Jews and Catholics," she said, "so I was educated in the Roman Catholic Church while knowing myself as Jewish."

As an adult, Frances' surroundings were the halls of government, where she represented the interests of Fortune 500 clients to state and federal, national and international bodies. In other words, she was a lobbyist. She began visiting Regina Laudis in 1984, having been drawn there by the abbey's reputation for chant. She became an oblate in 1989 and served the abbey by working with the Act Association.

She would arrive in her shiny black Saab, dressed in an Armani suit, smoking up a storm, and, within minutes, be in work clothes, moving stage furniture at the theater or cleaning the toilets in Sheepfold. She related to Sheepfold right off and recently has organized its renovation. She is our professional planner, making the abbey green while working out cooperative (and financially beneficial) ventures with suppliers such as Connecticut Light and Power, AT&T, FedEx and Kmart.

—At one time I wondered if we could really have in our midst a Jewish person who wanted to hold the flame of Israel and light it in our chambers. As Mother Daniel Levi Cooke, she does. She is a true zaddik.

Elizabeth Schumann first visited Regina Laudis while a student at the University of Connecticut, studying for a degree in fine arts, her specialty being landscape photography.

She entered our land program and just fell in love with the land. During a storm, a cherry tree near the church was knocked down—it really looked like nothing more than a piece of junk and was marked to be cleared out. But Elizabeth responded to the injured tree and asked to tend to it. When it came time for the tree to be cut down, Father Prokes was able to give it a reprieve. She entered Regina Laudis in 1993, and by the time she became Sister Ozanne she was effecting major improvements in our orchards.

368

—In order to take care of the trees, she created a new kind of work habit. Mother Maria downsized a scapular, and with longer boots, a colorful hardhat and layers of rope draped around her waist, she looks like a character out of Robin Hood.

Marsha Hutchinson was a law student when she first visited Regina Laudis. "I had left the Church and was not a practicing Catholic at that time", she recalled. "I remember watching the television production of *In This House of Brede*. This story of a London businesswoman who gave up her career to enter a cloistered Benedictine monastery absolutely pierced my heart. I mentioned this to a friend who, coincidentally, was going to visit an abbey the following weekend and asked if I would like to go with her.

"The abbey was Regina Laudis. Well, I must have sobbed the whole weekend in parlors. It was like my whole life came up in front of me; it was that dramatic. I got my law degree and began a career as a land-use attorney, visiting Regina Laudis regularly. I was searching for a way to have a relationship to the abbey as a layperson so, through the eighties, I became part of a group called the Benedictine Elementaries, which served to cement a relationship with the Community. But I still yearned to hook into the intensity of their lives. It was a call that, after twenty years, I finally answered."

—Marsha entered in 1996, taking on the role of Community videographer almost from the first moment. She also took on the responsibility of tutoring in English young Bernard de la Brunetière, one of several French boys in our land program. She is now Mother Emmanuelle Hutchinson, our guest secretary.

Chant drew Monica Evans, a Wall Street lawyer and a law professor at Santa Clara University, to Regina Laudis. "When I was a student at Sarah Lawrence College," she said, "I heard a record of chant by the monks of Solesmes, and I went looking for that music. When I first visited Regina Laudis in 1978, I found it. I felt a place that can preserve the chant, even through the bitter cynicism of that era, well, that's a place to be trusted." Monica entered in 1997. She is now Mother Elizabeth Evans, the first African-American in the Community.

— When Mother Elizabeth saw the television documentary Which Way Home, *about Mexican children attempting to enter the United States illegally, she was shattered by the story of two young boys, Eloy and Rosario, who had survived the dangerous trip across the border riding atop railway cars, only to wind up in the Arizona desert, dead and unclaimed. The image of those boys drove her to search out a place on the abbey land where she could reclaim their lives. She found a piece of earth that had never been tilled or seeded and turned this barren patch into a garden in their names.*

Our relationship with Iain Highet was not only continuing; it was gathering strength during this period. In recognition of his dedication to the Community, he was named a monastic scholar and given the name Joseph because of his commitment to care for the life of the Community and its land. He is immensely creative and helped us in developing our ecological consciousness. He became a member of the Luce, a body devoted to the growth of the Community in terms of its energy needs. But, in every area where there was a need of him—be it a problem with an animal, a car, you name it—anywhere there was need for brotherly concern, he was the go-to person.

It was becoming clear to Iain that being a consultant to the abbey was not enough. What he really wanted was to give himself in religious dedication to the abbey. He left to take courses at Holy Apostles Seminary, earning a master's in divinity without really knowing how that degree would be put to use, and spent some time with the Benedictine monks of Weston Priory in Vermont. But his heart was with Regina Laudis.

He asked to return to the abbey as Brother Iain, a dedicated lay oblate who offered his service wherever it was needed.

—He has always been a brother in that sense.

Tom Pomposello, who had been so concerned over our loss of income when we closed the summer fairs, didn't fret about it long. I received a presentation from Tom that got my immediate attention because it was

written entirely in capital letters. Tom wrote that way when he was enthusiastic.

He wanted the Community to record our chants (he called them the "holy blues"). There were several recordings of chant available, but as they were sung by male choirs, his idea was appetizing. I processed Tom's plan within the Education Deanery, where it was met with great support. I had an intuition that Lady Abbess would also be enthusiastic because of her conviction that chant had the power to communicate the life of God as no other music does. We got her permission to go ahead with the project on New Year's Eve 1996.

—Did you also need approval from the Hartford Archdiocese for such an ambitious undertaking?

Oh, as always when something new is introduced, some women in the house thought so. They would write me letters of complaint, asking how I could do such a wicked thing. Those letters were usually very carefully written; I knew a copy would be going to the archbishop. We never asked for permission and never received any comment from the archdiocese.

The pieces chosen for our recording were taken from what was chanted in the monastery on the feast days for Saint Lucy, Saint Agnes and Saint Cecilia, three women who were martyred as Christians. We also included the music for the feast of Mater Dolorosa, Our Lady of Sorrows. This music, presented from a distinctly feminine perspective, was selected because it communicates the irresistible power of love to transform suffering.

We put Tom together with Dr. Theodore Marier, regarded as one of the world's experts in chant due to his long collaboration with the monks of the Abbey of Solesmes, as well as his recognition by Pope John Paul II as the official guardian of the chant tradition. For over thirty years, our Community had studied chant with Dr. Marier; he had been part of our lives for a long time. He reminded me of Leonard Bernstein. He and Tom got along famously; both were masters.

371

The album was recorded inside the new church in two sessions. Tom brought in the best recording people and paid for everything out of his own pocket. He would not take a penny for himself, although Lady Abbess tried many times to reimburse him.

Working on the recording was a learning experience for the Community. Although it was a hand-in-glove operation, it put them in a professional context since the church was transformed into a recording studio. Likewise, the professional people found themselves in the Community's arena.

—And I was back on a soundstage, so to speak. I found that exhilarating.

Did anyone in the Community have any qualms about performing?

You mean that they thought we weren't good enough? No. I don't think they felt the pressure of a professional situation. They were singing as they usually do.

Women in Chant: Gregorian Chants for the Festal Celebrations for the Virgin Martyrs and Our Lady of Sorrows marked the first full Gregorian chant album to be recorded by a choir of American Benedictine nuns. It began as mail order only, but the response by the public was immediate. They sold out the three-thousand-copy run in one month.

Billboard—the magazine devoted to the music industry—listed *Women in Chant*'s debut on its Hot 100 chart at number 18, with a bullet! In show-business parlance a bullet means that the record is moving up the chart rapidly—an almost impossible feat in the area of religious music. It caught the attention of Sounds True, a Colorado record label, which picked it up for wider distribution.

During this time, Mother Dolores was meeting with Joyce Arbib regarding the possibility that she had a call to enter religious life. Joyce was then a vice president of Columbia Artists Management in New York, in its division of singers, which boasted the names Frederica von Stade, Samuel Ramey and Elisabeth Soderstrom. In 1998 she would become the eighth postulant in that decade.

372

—Because of her professional expertise, we relied on Joyce for advice in this new world of contracts. But it would not be the only area in which she would come to my aid.

The moment you had the CD in your hands for the first time, how did you feel?

I don't think that any film I ever made gave me more joy. This was public witness of the Community. I suppose I was the only one who understood what that meant.

The album has generated orders from across the globe. I was so delighted that it was touching people's hearts and revealing a hunger in today's world for the ancient music of chant. With this surprising success, Tom wanted to generate some publicity, but he needed a hook to get it off the ground. He asked if I had any objections to his using me to generate interest. "Your name," he said, "with all that comes with it—'Elvis' leading lady forty years later back in show business'—can get the CD the attention it needs."

I thought I might find myself on the firing line again, but I felt it was an opportunity to do what I can do. I felt absolutely that the archbishop had no right to tell us we cannot support ourselves, and this was what we were trying to do. We were also making a real contribution to furthering people's knowledge of Gregorian chant, an effort that is appropriate to a Benedictine community. As long as I maintained my enclosure, we were sure there would be no interference from the arch-diocese. And there was not, although there is a back story that might help explain that.

Before the CD project, in 1994, I had received a letter from Mrs. Bob Hope. I had met Bob years earlier when I appeared on the Photoplay Awards segment of his television show but had never met his wife, Dolores.

The Hopes had funded the building of Our Lady of Hope Chapel at the National Shrine of the Immaculate Conception in Washington, DC, and the letter was an invitation to attend its dedication. It would be a great honor indeed, as well as the first time I would leave the enclosure of Regina Laudis for other than medical reasons since my entrance thirty-one years before.

But, and it was a big but, permission to attend had to be granted by the archbishop of Hartford. I had never before made such a request and was reasonably sure he would see the value in extending his consent. I wrote a personal letter to Archbishop Daniel Cronin.

Archbishop Cronin denied permission in a letter that was unnecessarily condescending, saying he would prefer she "refrain from any public appearances or involvement with the movie star community."

> *—That's exactly how he put it. He didn't say the motion picture community or the entertainment community. No, the "movie star" community. I felt just like Mom at Saint Francis de Sales.*

After she simmered down, her mind began ticking. How would this be handled in Hollywood? She wrote to Mrs. Hope with her apologies, carefully suggesting that Archbishop Cronin might have misread the invitation concerning her participation but that she herself was in no position to challenge his decision. However, she added, should Mrs. Hope want to contact the archbishop directly she was certainly within her rights to do so.

Mrs. Hope did one better. She called her friend Cardinal Roger Mahony, the archbishop of Los Angeles, and asked if he might intercede on their behalf. The cardinal also did one better. He contacted Archbishop Cronin and said that Mother Dolores Hart was to be *his* guest. Within days Mrs. Hope received a letter from Archbishop Cronin telling her that he was happy to grant the request. No such communiqué was forwarded to Mother Dolores.

Laywoman Frances Levi Cooke, then Lady Abbess' volunteer secretary, accompanied Mother Dolores to Washington for the dedication of the chapel and the reception at the Vatican embassy.

Frances in now Mother Daniel, and she remembered the evening as if it had taken place just yesterday. "The Hopes greeted Mother Dolores as if she were an old friend, embracing and kissing warmly. I even heard Mrs. Hope whisper, 'Don't muss the makeup, dear.' The first chance I had, I asked Mother Dolores how long she had known Mrs. Hope, and she said, 'We just met—Hollywood people.' "

Every year following, I received a musical Christmas card from the Hopes, and the Abbey very generous support from Dolores.

After the chapel dedication, which received a great deal of media attention, all of it positive, I got a call from a woman who said she was with the Archdiocese of Hartford and wanted to interview me. When I told her I had been instructed by the archbishop not to do that sort of thing, she said the archbishop had told her to call. This change in the atmosphere, unexpectedly promoted by Mrs. Bob Hope's Hollywood know-how, coincided with the upcoming release of our CD.

> *—I don't think there is a saint in charge of public relations, but if there were, it would be Dolores Hope.*

So, I was the news hook for the CD—a far cry from my early days, when I had to refuse every request from media people, some of them belligerently insistent that "it would be such good publicity for you".

> *—I would ask them why on earth a cloistered nun would need publicity. I had a reason now.*

Our first break came with a few lines in the New York Times Magazine, *and it was as if a bomb had exploded: after that we were absolutely inundated with orders for the CD, and I began getting all sorts of requests for interviews, not only from Catholic publications and programs but from National Public Radio and many US and foreign magazines and newspapers. The* Today *show featured Regina Laudis on its Christmas morning program.*

Whenever anyone asked for interviews, the answer was yes as long as it was done here. I could not leave the abbey, but the press could come here.

"When people came," Mother Abbess said with a smile, "they would also see other areas of the abbey such as the farm and the dairy, the church, the crèche. That was the wonder and the goodness of it. Mother certainly was in her element."

On the strength of this unexpected success, Dr. Marier asked us to collaborate on a second CD, but before this could be realized, we were all hit with the devastating news that our friend and mentor Tom

375

Pomposello had been killed in an automobile accident. His sudden death at age forty-nine left the Community bereft. Travis Pomposello stepped in to finish his father's work. Our second album, Recordare: Remembering the Mysteries in the Life of Jesus, Son of Mary, *is dedicated to Tom.*

Recordare was another success, bringing the combined CDs to over one hundred thousand sold. With appearances on *Good Morning America* and a featured article in Oprah Winfrey's magazine, *O,* the nuns of the Abbey of Regina Laudis surfaced as an unexpected musical phenomenon, and this prompted a third recording, *Women in Chant: The Announcement of Christmas*, giving listeners an opportunity to experience the original Christmas music of the monastic tradition.

The Announcement of Christmas *carries listeners through the different phases of the season: the four weeks of Advent, Christmas Eve with the recitation of the genealogy of Christ, Christmas Day and Epiphany. It was again produced by Travis Pomposello—who, like his father, declined any compensation—but this recording does not have Dr. Marier conducting. Sadly, our dear master had passed away before the recording sessions, and Mother Abbess, truly his disciple, replaced him as conductor.*

Lady Abbess, who was very ill during this period, was unable to attend the recording sessions but praised our performance, which was the supreme acknowledgment. This was the woman who stood firm during Vatican II and insisted that Regina Laudis would continue the spiritual and aesthetic value of the chant, even when other monasteries were turning to more contemporary musical expressions. I hear her voice even today: "You are singing the Word of God that originated in the Holy Spirit. You have to be really at peace in order to do that successfully.

"When I hear you chanting," she said to us, "I hear women at peace together." This was an extraordinary statement because, for the entire decade—when all this was taking place—the women in the Community were living under the darkest cloud conceivable—one that threatened the continuity of our foundation.

Thirty-Eight

Although the Shaw Island controversy and its aftermath reached its peak in the nineties, its dark cloud hung over us long before. What I have to say about it is from my experience and, therefore, from a limited understanding. Up to the time the issue was settled, I was not part of our governance.

In 1977 Lady Abbess, with the blessing of the Community, accepted Mr. Henry Ellis' gift of three hundred acres of land on Shaw Island, off the coast of Washington State. I had cast an affirmative vote, although I wasn't truly convinced that Mr. Ellis' offer came, as he announced, with "no strings attached".

Three nuns—Mothers Prisca and Miriam; and Mother Therese Critchley, a formation mother who had been instrumental in creating our dairy—were sent to Shaw Island to begin work to establish a daughter monastery. Starting this way, on virgin land with but a single building, a few shacks and one tractor, it could not help but bring back thoughts of our beginnings in Connecticut. As a child may look like a parent, the new foundation has a likeness to Regina Laudis but in many ways is unique.

Mother Therese, now the prioress, recalled those early days: "After World War II, the Ellis family started buying up land on Shaw Island that had been foreclosed on homesteaders; and at the time of Henry Ellis' gift of three hundred acres, the family owned or controlled at least a quarter of the island.

"When we arrived, the residents of Shaw were curious about us, but as they watched us begin to work the land, they came to appreciate that we were very serious about being farmers as well as stewards of the land we shared with them. They even helped us with the machinery and the animals (less than a month after we arrived we already had a gift of a flock of sheep and two Jersey cows).

"The one permanent building on the property—Japanese in design and built by Mr. Ellis himself—looked to the sea over a large rock formation that gave the monastery its name, Our Lady of the Rock. It was so perfect because Lady Abbess had envisioned a foundation that could open the Community to the Far East. That building became our residence and chapel.

"Mr. Ellis was with us for the enclosure ceremony in 1977, and he frequently came to Mass. He helped turn the temporary structures built by the homesteaders into our guesthouse, dairy and preserving shed. He worked shoulder to shoulder with Father Prokes building the shed where we milk; they did it in one day. Mr. Ellis became an oblate of the Community and even asked to be buried at Our Lady of the Rock.

"He was kept in our daily prayers, but we did not see him that often because we were busy keeping the foundation going. We were not aware of his growing displeasure. The only hint came when he mentioned that he wished Mother Miriam and I had not destroyed some wild rose bushes when we cleared the overgrowth for pasture."

In 1979 I had my first encounter with Shaw Island when I accompanied Lady Abbess for a seminar on chant, which would include members of the Franciscan Sisters of the Eucharist and the Mercy Sisters of Alma, who also had foundations on the island. I will forever remember my first ferryboat ride, which is the only transportation to the island from the mainland. It was late in the day, and there was a mist forming on the water that took on softer hues of the blazing sunset on the western horizon. I felt as if I were sailing into paradise.

The seminar lasted a week, long enough to confirm that Shaw Island was, indeed, God's own design. It's the most beautiful place on earth. Mothers Therese, Miriam and Prisca had been joined by Mother Hildegard and Mother Felicitas Curti—a former professor of musicology and a grandmother of three. From what I saw, these women were accomplishing a great beginning for the foundation.

But, over the next several years, Henry Ellis' dissatisfaction with how the land was being developed continued to grow, along with his complaints to Lady Abbess. Now, Lady Abbess had made it perfectly clear to him that he would have no say in the growth and development of the foundation, and although initially he had accepted that, he continued to believe that the gift of the land entitled him to a say in how the land would be used.

Ultimately, he announced that he was withholding 150 acres from the 300 he had promised and, in fact, was poised to transfer that land to another group. Lady Abbess had no recourse but to sue for injunctive relief. The court ruled that the 150 acres be transferred to us as promised.

During this period, Mother Maria Immaculata had been engaged in revising statutes within our constitution and, with the lawsuit now behind us, she and Lady Abbess traveled to Rome to present the con-stitution to the Sacred Congregation for Institutes of Consecrated Life. Both were surprised when it was not approved.

The Sacred Congregation, under the newly assigned secretary, Arch-bishop Errázuriz Ossa, insisted that it be rewritten to align with the new Code of Canon Law. The criticism pertained to our firm stand on retaining the ancient ceremony of the Consecration of a Virgin as well as the tradition of choosing an abbess for life.

Lady Abbess felt very strongly that both matters were essential to our foundation. The Consecration of a Virgin is the Church's blessing of a woman who has resolved to give herself to God. It is not, she stressed, the woman's asking for the blessing of the Church; it is the Church offering to consecrate her. Never before had the Sacred Congregation had to approve this ceremony. As for the selection of an abbess for life, this had been part of our approved constitution from the very beginning.

The Communities of Regina Laudis and Our Lady of the Rock, meanwhile, had little awareness of the controversy with Mr. Ellis and carried on our monastic obligations as usual—which still included the daily prayers for him.

Mr. Ellis, however, bitter after losing the lawsuit, vowed not to rest until he ended Lady Abbess' authority at Regina Laudis and destroyed Father Prokes. He searched out and courted a handful of disaffected people previously related to the abbey, including a former member of our own Community—one of the group who rigidly opposed Lady Abbess and Father Prokes and had finally left secretly in the middle of the night. This was the same nun who had sat on the stairs outside the

Education Deanery meetings, taking notes. She had entered a decade before me, but I did not know her well. She seemed deeply wounded and had built a definite enclosure around herself. I found no way of engaging her. At that time, of course, any overture would have been against the rules, but in her case I didn't even consider breaking them. She was uncomfortable with the Education Deanery and resisted any change within the Order. It was her prerogative, of course.

Mr. Ellis took his grievances to Rome. He testified before Archbishop Ossa that our community lived a bad hybridization of Benedictine life and that our presence on the island was causing the entire population of Shaw great misery.

Then he took his agenda to the media, beginning with local newspapers, getting their attention with allegations that the abbey was being taken in a "cult-like" direction by Lady Abbess and Father Prokes, pressuring people to turn over money and land and, further, accusing Father Prokes of having despotic control over us and lacing his homilies with sexual imagery that stressed the potency of female sexuality. There was no truth in this, but the sensational nature of the accusations got a lot of attention, eventually claiming the interest of several metropolitan papers, including the New York Times, *as well as the television show* 20/20.

A concerned Maria Janis contacted Roone Arledge, the chairman of the ABC news department, to dissuade him from airing the program. Mr. Arledge was personally acquainted with the Community from his visits to Regina Laudis and, therefore, did not feel it proper to exercise his professional authority in the matter. Instead, he offered Lady Abbess commensurate air time on the network. She did not take advantage of his offer because she was now under orders by the apostolic delegate, Bishop Pio Laghi, not to communicate with any of the media.

Mother Dolores asked me to watch the show and give her my opinion of it. I thought the program weakly supported Mr. Ellis' agenda by manipulative editing of stock footage of Community life, such as a group of nuns riding in a truck en route to work in the fields, identified as "nuns who have left Regina Laudis". A photograph of Mother Jerome wearing prescription dark glasses, taken years before at an abbey fair, was used in a way that made her appear as sinister as Gene Tierney had while watching young Darryl Hickman drown in a scene from *Leave Her to Heaven*. I did think the hosts of *20/20* provided a fit summary at the end of the report when Barbara Walters turned to Hugh Downs and asked, "So what was that all about?" and Downs replied, "Search me!"

Our days were filled with silent gloom. It seemed to me that everyone walked with a heaviness about her. Not many of the women were knowledgeable of the continuing attacks because, at Lady Abbess' request, there was no discussion of the situation. That was an edict I struggled with. Part of the depression concerned our sadness over the passing of Archbishop Whealon, who had always been a great support, but most of it, I think, was caused by being kept in the dark.

That changed when Archbishop Ossa informed Lady Abbess that he had decided to conduct an apostolic visitation, which is a formal meeting between members of a religious community and representatives of the Holy See. The visitation was announced by Lady Abbess to the entire Community.

Shortly thereafter, two Benedictines, Bishop Joseph Gerry and Dom Adelbert Buscher, arrived for a four-day visitation during which they spoke to every member of the Community. The priests were pleasant and respectful, but some of their questions were unsettling. They were, I'm sure, trying to find if there was any justification to the accusations that had been made about Father Prokes and the alleged sexual content of his homilies, but it was very difficult for all of us who live under vows of chastity to be put through this line of questioning. It was hard for me to hold my tongue through my interview, but I did.

This was fortunate because, at the end of the four days, both visitators found our spiritual life at Regina Laudis without fault and, further, commended the Community for the way we were fulfilling our monastic obligations. This did not, however, end the controversy.

Not willing to concede, Mr. Ellis continued attacking us in Rome. My personal opinion is that Mr. Ellis had expected to play a leading role in our foundation on Shaw Island and that he probably would not stop his badgering until he got his way—or until Lady Abbess was removed. Since Rome always will try to resolve unpleasant disagreements quietly, Archbishop Ossa's way to do this was to put pressure on Lady Abbess, who was approaching ninety, to retire voluntarily and to urge that Father Prokes, a Jesuit priest, not remain at a Benedictine foundation but be reassigned within his own order.

Father Prokes' reassignment did take place. In spite of the fact that he had never been invited to Rome to confront the accusations made against him, Father was obedient. Lady Abbess resisted retiring from her authority as abbess for life, conferred upon her at her abbatial blessing. In response, Archbishop Ossa sent her a letter containing questions he wished her to answer. Lady Abbess obeyed the request, but instead of sending her reply she made an appointment for Mother David and me to present it in person to the archbishop in Rome.

We made the trip, but when we arrived for the scheduled appointment, we were handed a note saying that Archbishop Ossa would not keep the appointment. The reason given was "non opportuno": it was "inopportune". There was nothing Mother David and I could do except leave the papers. We were staying with Franciscan nuns in Rome, and when we returned to their house, I was so angry I couldn't see straight.

Feeling our pain, our hostesses arranged for us to accompany them to Saint Peter's Basilica that evening to hear the Rosary said by Pope John Paul II. After the Rosary, we had the opportunity to exchange a few words with His Holiness. He asked where we were from, and when we told him Regina Laudis, he gave his blessing to the abbey. It was a comforting moment, one that I took to be God's sign that everything would turn out all right.

> *—I still carried, however, the sting of the archbishop's hostility, which always conjures up memories of that little boy who made the necklace out of poor, struggling ladybugs.*

The Community appealed the Sacred Congregation's decision that we hold an election for a new abbess. When that appeal failed, a letter from Archbishop Ossa informed Lady Abbess that she would be vacated and that he had appointed a delegate from the Holy See to come to Regina Laudis as administrator.

382

Lady Abbess agreed to step down. "Now you know what real obedi-ence is all about", she told the Community, and then added, "We must always believe that with crisis comes new birth."

> *—I think, for Lady Abbess, this was the devastation she endured until her death: she thought that the foundation was over. I know this was in her heart.*

>> Are you speaking of your own feelings as well? You and I had phone conversations during this period, and I have never known you to be devastated except then. "If this happens," you told me, "if Rome would put someone in permanent charge of the abbey, I will have to leave."

> *At that moment, yes, I feared for the same thing, that the loss of Lady Abbess and Father Prokes could have been the beginning of the end for the foundation.*

Though I did not know it, I was the person who carried the news of his reassignment to Father Prokes. I drove to Father's home, Saint Lucy's, carrying a letter from his Jesuit provincial in Milwaukee. He read the letter but did not share its contents; instead he took from a high shelf a very old bottle of brandy, containing barely a shot of the ugliest liquid I had ever seen. It had long since passed vinegar. He poured out the dregs into two glasses and raised a toast "to the future". I could hardly swallow the sip I took and turned away to rinse out the glass. When I turned back, Father Prokes was no longer in the room.

Back at the monastery, a letter from Archbishop Ossa was shared with me. Not only was Father's reassignment effective immediately, but he was to have no further contact of any kind with the Community. I realized then that he had submitted to this order as he was reading the letter and must be, at that very moment, packing up. He had that kind of obedience. Our toast had been his farewell. There would be no goodbyes.

I felt ravaged in my heart. Father was my teacher. He had given me the basis for the Education Deanery but was very pure and chaste and did not insert himself into the operation once it was established. His work was to make something happen and once that was done, allow another to do it. I thanked God then that I had kept all my notes from every one of his homilies—his education, his discourse, his truth. I thought back to his greatest lesson: "When the master goes, the disciple is born."

❧

Reverend Matthew Stark, abbot of Portsmouth Abbey in Rhode Island, was now administrator of Regina Laudis. Certainly there began an intense period of sorrow for the older members of the Community, and there seemed no way to explain that to any of the younger members who had entered after this rip in the heart of the Community had taken its toll.

As portress, one of my functions was to carry the keys to the house and admit appropriate visitors inside the enclosure. I arose well before the bell for Matins so that I could unlock the door to the house if Father Matthew arrived to attend the Office. But when I entered the darkened chapel, I was startled to find the priest inside.

I apologized that I had not been there to welcome him to Matins and asked how he gained entrance. "Oh," he said, "I have a key."

A key to our house! I felt a rush of anger and the shock of fear.

I have a temper, an ouburst of emotion that flashes and is soon spent. The fear, however, persisted and provoked questions. Were we to be under house arrest? How will this manifest the true spirit of all we write about, sing about, all we entrust our lives to? Might there be no consciousness, no sensitivity of who we are? Is this to be the continuity of Regina Laudis? If so, this isn't where I belong, I thought. I don't care what age I am; I will just go do something else, because God is everywhere.

Mother Abbess recalled, "Oh, at that time, we were all leaving. We weren't leaving, of course, but projecting a stand. We had formed relationships, the deepest relationships one can have, and depended on them. You don't just walk away from that."

Abbot Matthew did keep a low profile and, for all intents, took his role to be our retreat master. He did perform chaplain duties but also conducted conferences regarding Benedictine life rooted in reverence for God and the human person, respect for learning and order and responsibility for the shared experience of community life in an atmosphere informed by our fifteen-hundred-year-old heritage.

384

—He also had, I was pleased to discover, a deep affection for Pope John XXIII—he quoted him often—and this became a personal bridge between the two of us.

As I began to see that we were on the same page, the situation began to feel less demeaning. It was encouraging to learn that the college preparatory school run by the monks at Portsmouth shared our focus on scholarly and artistic work and hospitality. The Portsmouth school had produced three US senators—including Robert and Edward Kennedy—plus a composer, a newspaper columnist, a novelist and screenwriter, a college president, a political satirist, an FBI director and, yes, an actor, Charlie Day.

Abbot Matthew was to officiate at the Consecration of five nuns, but Archbishop Ossa insisted all Consecrations be suspended for the time being—by which he meant until we did a study of the ceremony and understood its place in monastic life.

The briefest way to describe this is that the archbishop felt that we put too much emphasis on Consecration as opposed to final profession, which is the ultimate ceremony for most religious communities of women. But there is a strong, ancient monastic tradition for Consecration that is not hard to prove—if one is willing to listen.

Consecration is a very powerful and specifically feminine rite celebrating the nun as the spouse of Christ. I think the archbishop was afraid of that and wanted to reduce its potency. I think he also was testing our submission. There existed a quiet standoff, during which the number of nuns awaiting Consecration grew to nine and depression within the Community turned to despair.

I would be remiss if I did not acknowledge here the support of Father Robert Tucker. The best part of him is that as our confessor he was the greatest consolation to the Community. We would not have gotten through one of the worst times of suffering except for Father Tucker's noble heart—and his sense of humor.

When Abbot Matthew ended his tenure, Abbot Mark Serna—also from Portsmouth and an equally caring man—completed the assignment. What I remember most about both of them is that neither gentleman ever came across as "the boss", as I had feared they would. They were put in charge but never insisted on relating to us because they were in *charge. The brotherly and fatherly concern they showed us was genuine. They gave to me personally a fresh witness to the authority of the Church and were instrumental in helping me to accept that authority in friendship. This was a most healing experience for me.*

As I look back, that period of our lives was one of incredible formation for us that we could not have anticipated. The Community remained beautiful, strong and clear, and the new and positive relationship with Rome that Lady Abbess had promised came to be.

—Father Matthew never forgets to send me a note on my feast day, which may seem inconsequential but it is a sign that he remembers us.

On February 27, 1997, the completed chapel at Our Lady of the Rock was dedicated, with Lady Abbess, Mother Irene and Mother Maria joining in celebration the seven nuns now making up the Community on Shaw Island. On the chapel altar stood the crucifix given to the Community by Henry Ellis.

Mother Therese remembered the day with tears in her eyes: "We rejoiced in the completion of this phase of development. We marveled at the beauty of our new place of worship alongside many local craftsmen who had worked in the construction of the chapel. They were part of the 150 residents who attended the dedication—almost the entire population of Shaw Island!"

In the summer of 1998, the nine nuns in Final Vows did participate in the ceremony for the Consecration of a Virgin, officiated by Abbot Mark Serna. I think once we agreed to elect a new abbess and showed we were not going to fight Rome, the powers relented about this ceremony. Ironically, by suppressing it they had made it all the more meaningful and important to us!

Thirty-Nine

Except for getting the flu each winter and suffering a brief bout of neuromas, which were successfully treated by wearing orthotics, I had a pretty good track record as far as medical problems went.

But in early 1997, I underwent a root canal. I was in the dentist's chair for several hours, and on the way home I was reeling. Mother Irene, our infirmarian, prescribed bed rest right away. I slept from Friday afternoon to the following Sunday morning.

When I awoke, I expected the pain in my jaw but, when I put my feet on the floor, I felt as if I were standing on a bed of needles. The stings shot up my legs like lightning bolts.

We thought it might be a spur and made an appointment with Dr. Richard Biondi, the Community's internist in Southbury. Dr. Biondi referred me to a neurologist, Dr. Kenneth Kaplove, who thought that the root canal might have upset the neuromas; he prescribed medication as well as water physiotherapy. I began swimming every day in the hydrotherapy pool at a center for orthopedic rehabilitation in Waterbury and found that this was the only time I was not in severe pain.

It was a stroke of luck that this facility was in the process of moving to Middlebury and had to replace the pool to fit the new quarters. Greg Wright, the owner, offered to give us the old pool, which we installed in a greenhouse-root cellar on our property so that the entire community could take advantage of it.

The medication, however, brought no relief. I was then treated with cortisone shots in both feet, but I continued to experience pain and difficulty standing and walking.

Thus began a two-year fruitless—and often counteractive—odyssey to find out what was plaguing me. Throughout the rest of 1997, all of 1998 and most of 1999, I saw a succession of doctors in the Waterbury and Southbury areas whose diagnoses widely varied. One doctor treated for arthritis. A rheumatologist diagnosed osteoporosis. An immunologist and an anti-inflammatory specialist both detected hypothyroidism.

An orthopedic surgeon, who strongly felt that the problem was the result of neuromas and metatarsalitis, had an ankle-foot brace made to ease the pain of walking, but after several months of wearing the bulky thing, I was no better. Another doctor said there was "a problem with anti-cardio lipin antibodies". I can't remember now what that meant, but he said it was very rare. Another simply told me I was losing the padding on the bottoms of my feet.

I think I had just about every known test in the world, including an MRI of my brain that revealed nothing abnormal. Yet I could barely stand or walk. On those occasions when I was taken to a doctor's appointment, I had to use a wheelchair. But that didn't work for maneuvering inside the monastery building. As the halls are too narrow, the wheelchair didn't work except in the large common room.

There was no time when the pain subsided. Even when lying down it was so sharp that I developed TMJ from clenching my teeth during fitful sleep. This caused difficulty in eating, which, in turn, resulted in continuing weight loss. The burning in my feet traveled up my legs into the pelvic area. It was depleting my strength, leaving me in a weakened state, susceptible to infection. Recurring mouth ulcers appeared as well as urinary tract infections.

Dr. Biondi felt that specially built shoes molded to my feet would help reduce the pain. Over the years a dozen or more were handmade, first by an old-fashioned shoemaker, Mr. Ron Pelletier in Monroe, and later by Jon Rood of Footprints in Newington, and they did have some short-term benefit.

> *—I was often so embarrassed to call these people and tell them the shoes were not helping that I finally wrote out an apology, memorized it so that I wouldn't forget anything and performed it on the telephone.*

With each doctor, each diagnosis, medications were prescribed and many interacted to cause other problems—cold sweats, hemolytic anemia and tinnitus that got so bad I could not bear the sound of the Community chanting in the church and even found the quiet of my cell

388

invaded by a cacophony of ringing inside my head. The minute the flu hit the East Coast, I was struck full force and developed pneumonia. Whatever was going on, my immune system was not doing its job.

I religiously followed through on the prescribed remedies while trying to maintain my work and prayer schedule. But there were days I would sit through a chapter meeting or a homily at Mass and the only thing I could think of was getting my feet into a hot bath—soaking in a tub relieved the pain a little. I fought giving up my job as portress. I was scared that it would take me out of association with the Community, but eventually I was forced to admit that I was unable to fulfill those duties.

I refused to give up my commitment as dean of education. The women had concerns that needed to be addressed, and they were unaware of the level of pain I was living with. Personal health problems were not spoken of or made common knowledge in the monastery. Certainly Mother Irene was kept informed, but she was involved then with our seriously ill Lady Abbess at the Tower.

Mother David and Mother Simonetta Morfesi were the only two who were living through it with me. Mother David visited my cell to bring me notes from the Community and massage my feet with a salve, and Mother Simonetta, who worked in our infirmary, took on the roles of nurse, counselor, friend and watchdog.

— Mother Simonetta did it all with such grace. She never made me feel like an invalid. With all her other duties, I know she did not get to bed until eleven or twelve each night. It was a tremendous service to me and a great hardship for her.

I did manage to meet with each sister in the Education Deanery, though the meetings were held in my cell, not in Corpus Christi. I was rarely out of my cell except for those Offices I was occasionally able to attend. I took all of my meals in my cell, and I had to be helped to the bathroom and in and out of the tub. I used to pray, "Oh, to have the liberty to take a shower again!"

— You know, the fact that the nuns were in the dark about the extent of my pain was the best thing in the world. I found that

389

by listening to their problems, I could turn off my own for a while. If they had known, their concern would have barred the door to the honest way of communicating we had established.

What about prayer?

I think common prayer, the Office, is very good for dealing with pain. It's where you know you are in union with others and with their prayers. But to be constantly praying by yourself when you feel pain, well, all you do is go back into yourself. You can do it for a while—two or three days—but, after that, all you can do is try to put your mind somewhere else. God did not create us to suffer. He made us for joy and goodness, and He made the body to be a container of beauty. I believe He wants our body to be a treasure. If not, why would God want His Son to be part of humanity? When we are in pain our only answer is to stay in that identification with God's Son, who transformed pain through love. You start to identify your pain as the prayer itself.

In the times when I was alone, one of the best friends I had was Toby. It was good to be with another creature that didn't care what pain was, didn't care at all. He wanted his head stroked or a peanut. And I was beholden to Bob Rehme for the Academy movies. I could watch them on the little DVD player in my cell. Movies are a good way to get into some other place.

"Mother Dolores continued to meet with me during this period," Joyce Arbib remembered, "so I became aware of her illness. I knew just from speaking to her that she was in hell, and yet she would see me each visit because she understood the importance of continuity in our meetings the closer it got to my decision to enter.

"I knew she was going from doctor to doctor close by the abbey. But being a New York girl and used to going straight to the top whenever I could, I consulted a neurologist friend who said, without hesitation, 'There's only one person Mother Dolores should see: Dr. Norman Latov, a neurologist at Columbia Presbyterian.'

"I called Dr. Latov and explained Mother's situation. He set up an appointment. Mother Dolores got permission to travel to New York, so

I picked her up and drove her into Manhattan and was with her when she met him. He seemed to know right away what she was going through. And from the beginning she trusted him."

Given my symptoms and all the proffered diagnoses, Dr. Latov had a strong feeling that I had a nerve disease called neuropathy—a new word for me. But New York City was two hours away; since I would need a driver, I could not see Dr. Latov regularly. I continued with the cadre of physicians nearer to home, following through with each one because I felt I couldn't drop a person in midstream.

The year 1999 began at the lowest point imaginable—the death of our friend Tom Pomposello. I felt the only way I could come to terms with Tom's passing would be to make his coffin, and that was now impossible. Brother Iain Highet offered to do it for me.

Brother Iain remembered, "I had never made a coffin before, but she guided me through it. It was a case of *being* Mother's body. Jeff Havill made some fine metal handles—sort of jazzy, with swirls—and Tom's wife, Pat, brought friends to stain the box a turquoise color. We did together what Mother Dolores had done alone before. It was a good example of how Mother's limitations called out the gifts of others, how the one centers the many, which is the general succession pattern of the continuity of life here."

At one point, two doctors agreed that Mother Dolores had tarsal tunnel syndrome and recommended immediate surgery. In fact, a date for the operation was scheduled. But Dr. Kaplove intervened, requesting that surgery be delayed until more information could be gained from a lumbar puncture, a spinal tap. This was performed without a problem and proved normal. But, in the days following this procedure, there can be a possibility of leakage of spinal fluid, causing severe headache. For

391

that reason patients are cautioned to be careful and rest for a day or so after the procedure.

I was not careful. I had a marathon of parlors, and as a result I felt as though I was hit over the head with a sledgehammer. I took a medication prescribed by a previous doctor, which interacted calamitously with other medications in my system. My body simply could not sustain whatever was going on. I collapsed and wound up in the emergency room at Saint Mary's Hospital.

A blood patch—injection of drawn blood into the spine to form a clot—was administered to stop the headache, and it was essential that Mother Dolores not lose consciousness during the procedure. She heard the doctor's voice ordering her to count backward from ten but couldn't seem to follow his directions. She was fading.

Then I heard Mother David's voice calling frantically, "Mother, don't go! Don't go!"

"Go where?" I thought, "I'm not going anywhere. Does she mean I'm going to die? I can't die. I don't feel well enough to meet all those people I haven't seen in so long."

"Count backward from ten", she ordered. "Count! Ten ..."

I repeated ten but couldn't remember what number came before ten. Eight? Seven? "Can I start with seven?" I asked.

The patch was successful. The doctors, however, were appalled that Mother Dolores was a walking pharmacy. She had to get off many medications. She sought refuge through alternative medicine at the Holistic Health Center in Southbury, where for the next several months she underwent acupuncture therapy, which did provide some relief from pain—but only during the sessions.

—With no positive results during this long period, did it ever occur to you that this could be what you were facing for the rest of your life?

I did have the feeling that it was forever, but I knew that was the evil spirit telling me it will never go away.

Did you believe it anyway?

Yes.

One evening at a social event in Manhattan, Maria Janis found herself seated next to Dr. Luc Montagnier, the French virologist who ten years hence would be a joint recipient of the 2008 Nobel Prize for his discovery of the Human Immunodeficiency Virus (HIV). Maria found a moment to introduce Mother Dolores' seemingly unsolvable medical mystery to Dr. Montagnier. He suggested she call him while he was in New York City.

Mother Dolores again got the help of Joyce Arbib, who was fluent in French, to make the arrangements with Montagnier. Joyce was now a postulant at Regina Laudis, having entered in November 1998, becoming the abbey's second Jewish woman to do so.

Dr. Montagnier proceeded to treat, by long distance, mycoplasma penetrans in Mother Dolores' blood, thinking that bacteria could have entered her system during the root canal and was wreaking havoc with her immune system. Under Montagnier's treatment, the persistent sores in her mouth completely cleared and did not return. But that had been the only positive result. The pain in her feet continued to flare up, and she began to experience new symptoms.

The passing months were now bringing frequent headaches, difficulties in speaking and shifting areas of pain, sometimes in my hips and bladder, sometimes in my hands. I had difficulty grasping and holding objects. I could not snap my fingers. Sometimes I felt as if I had menthol in my eyes. I was frequently nauseated and seemed to live in a fog, finding it hard to think.

Some days I would be hit in the face. It could be ninety degrees, but I felt as if I were wearing an icy mask. My face was cold—not to the touch but from the inside. The nerves in my cheek would twitch. I could feel them jumping, and I knew that freezer door would open and my face would go stone cold until nightfall. Every day it seemed as if I was

393

starting all over again. I've never felt so vulnerable. Was this going to be the pattern of the rest of my life?

— Sheila McGuire remembered your saying you were living a life of redemption. That was one of the reasons you had to accept this illness—because when you came into the monastery you offered yourself to God and said you would accept anything He sent you.

> *That's not entirely accurate. Believe me, I'm not that holy a person. The redemptive life, to me, is not asking for calamity, but asking for the ability to withstand whatever calamity is set in my way. I don't have to be brave all the time. I can ask the Lord to be brave in me.*

The very next doctor I saw listened to me sympathetically and then asked, "Mother, have you thought about seeing a psychiatrist?" That made me angry, but if I had wanted to give him a punch I wouldn't have been able to make a fist! I didn't want to admit I had something in my body that was advancing and could not be treated. And I couldn't face the possibility that it might all be in my mind!

I went home and wept over my total helplessness. Then I got really mad. I picked up the phone and dialed the number of the neurologist in New York City whom I had previously seen and had liked very much. I was surprised when Dr. Norman Latov answered the phone himself. He had not forgotten me.

"No, you are not crazy", he assured me. "All pain is real."

I got permission to put myself into Dr. Latov's care.

394

Forty

The term neuropathy *is used to describe disorders resulting from injury to peripheral nerves. It can be caused by a number of diseases or conditions that affect those nerves.*

Dr. Latov's early diagnosis of my illness was sensory peripheral neuropathy. He recognized the symptoms I was experiencing because of his research in the area and because he has personal knowledge of the disease. Dr. Latov is a victim of neuropathy himself, although his is in remission.

"In Mother's particular case," Dr. Latov told me, "she was diagnosed with other possible conditions because many of the physicians she saw weren't familiar with neuropathy. She had neuropathy all along because no other disease causes *all* of her symptoms. And her examination, which showed sensory loss, confirmed this diagnosis."

There are more than twenty known possible causes of neuropathy, Dr. Latov explained. Diabetes, rheumatological diseases and autoimmunity are major causes. Some infections can cause neuropathy and so can many toxins and drugs. "Neuropathy is, in itself, not always curable," he said, "however, if we can identify its cause, and treat it, the patient can improve."

Initially, Dr. Latov tested for causes. Mother Dolores underwent about twenty different tests, but these were inconclusive.

—Based on those tests, Dr. Latov redefined his diagnosis to idiopathic sensory inflammatory neuropathy. Having a true diagnosis at long last was a relief. It was also a disappointment. Idiopathic *means nobody knows why.*

"We call it idiopathic because we don't know what causes the inflammation", Dr. Latov said. "It is the diagnosis in about a third of all neuropathies. In some cases the neuropathy improves and stabilizes. My neuropathy did. I still have some residual symptoms; they're not all gone, but it stopped getting worse and is tolerable. In other cases, it continues to get worse. And in about 20 percent of idiopathic cases, the disease burns itself out. Again, we don't know why.

"Mother's symptoms fluctuate. She has good and bad days. In her case, on the bad days—when her disease flares up—she can experience a great deal of pain because her type of neuropathy attacks the nerves that carry pain sensations from the skin to the brain. It doesn't attack the motor nerves directly, so it is not crippling, but it can cause incoordination and severe fatigue. Motor neuropathy, on the other hand, which damages the nerves that control the muscles, causes weakness but not that much pain.

"Pain is an insidious thing", said Dr. Latov. "It follows you every-where. It affects everything you do. It wears you down. In some ways, it's harder to deal with than motor disability. When I met Mother Dolores, her level of pain was extreme." Thus pain management was an important part of Mother's treatment from the beginning.

"How people can accommodate living with pain is something that varies from person to person", Dr. Latov continued. "Whereas other people might be totally consumed with this, she's continuing to function at a pretty high level, being able to interact and to give guidance and reach out to other people. She's done that very well, which I think is a testament to her faith and inner strength."

Dr. Latov immediately began treating Mother Dolores with intra-venous immunoglobulins (IVIg) "It's a treatment that's widely used for inflammatory neuropathies as well as a number of other autoimmune conditions", he said. "It's also the only anti-inflammatory drug that, in addition to suppressing the autoimmune component of the immune system, actually enhances immunity. Most people taking IVIg report that they have fewer colds, because it protects them from infections."

—That's true. Since I've been receiving the IVIg, I have not had my usual bout with flu every winter, and I don't need to get a flu shot. In fact, I can't get a flu shot.

Twice a month, for the IVIg treatments in Manhattan, I have to miss Terce and Mass. I admit I found that just being in New York after more

396

than three decades was terrifically energizing. In Dr. Latov's office, I sit alongside other neuropathy patients for the two hours it takes for the contents of a plastic bag to drip into my vein. The treatment is meant to prevent the inflammation that assaults the nerves in my feet and legs and to keep it from spreading to other parts of my body. Basically it strengthens my immune system, and I have more energy.

The program is open-ended. One woman I spoke with stated she has been receiving these infusions for more than fifteen years. That was not encouraging news and served to remind me of something Lady Abbess often said to me, "You must remember, you have not written the script."

More often than not during the procedure, I'm able to visit with Maria, who lives only a couple of blocks away and arrives pulling a small carry-on case, which makes her look a lot like a pharmaceutical saleswoman. Tina Tockarshewsky, the president of the Neuropathy Association, also visits when she can. When Dick has been on this coast, Dr. Latov has turned his conference room over to us so that we can work.

At first the treatment left me wiped out. When I returned home I went straight to bed for at least a day. But over the years I have become more tolerant and have more vigor. Sometimes the alleviation of the pain is immediate. It's not like walking on needles; it's like I have sponges on the bottoms of my feet. When I arrive home I'm able to go right to Vespers.

I think that Dr. Latov has given me more hope than anyone that my condition will change. Each visit he asks how I am, and I say, "I'm the same." He says, "No, you are better." I didn't believe him at first. But when I look back to the beginning of the illness, even back to just a year ago, I have to acknowledge it. I am able to attend all the Offices again.

The tinnitus, for example, has scaled down to something that comes and goes. It no longer affects my pitch; I can sing again, not just silently mouth the words. With the medication, I can keep up with pretty amazing hours. I was able to turn in the wheelchair for a motorized scooter. It was liberating to travel around the abbey property on my own again. Inside, I graduated to a cane—one that Mother Anastasia made for me because she wanted it to be "classy".

There is real comfort in the vibrant sensation I feel that tells me the gamma globulin is helping. I remember the day I was accentuating that point with Dr. Latov and actually snapped my fingers. I had not been able to do that for four years!

I could not return to portress duties, but I was asked to take on Mother Mary Aline's work in hospitality. Her job was to coordinate all the guest relationships. Lady Abbess said it would not be my job permanently.

—But a short-term job at the monastery can last twenty years.

So I became guest secretary, the one who oversees the incoming requests for visits. Because I don't have the capacity to meet with all the guests, I share duties with Mother Noëlla and Mother Emmanuelle. Mother Emmanuelle and I read the mail and discern it. I make the "first wave" decision on who is invited; my task is to sniff out the crackpots. Mother Emmanuelle takes care of the replies and, with her taste, expertise and empathy, personalizes them according to what each writer is searching for.

—Really, I have been guest secretary in name only. Mother Emmanuelle does all the work. When she made her Final Vows, I asked her to take on the title because I felt it should be on the record. It is her place.

How many requests do you get?

I would say between fifteen and twenty a week.

Unless one of your old movies turns up on TV?

When Today *featured us on their Christmas morning show, we were flooded with requests. The same explosion occurred when the article in Oprah Winfrey's magazine was published, when* The Cheese Nun, *Mother Noëlla's documentary, and the HBO documentary on my life as prioress were aired. Lately, people have found us on the Internet. Our website has had a big impact too.*

Why do people come? What are they searching for?

Many working men and women are looking for peace, quiet, a place to think and pray as a counterbalance to the hectic pace of their lives. Some are seeking solace, guidance, in the face of a particular loss. Some, including young persons, are looking to deepen their faith; others express a sense of estrangement from their faith and are looking for renewal. The younger people are especially attracted to our sustainable agriculture and our emphasis on manual work and seek information about our internship programs. Then there are the women of different ages—but more and more, young women—who want to explore a possible vocation to contemplative life.

One of the things that we all learn in the day-by-day life of a religious community is how essential it is to be in relationship with others in order to discover our own true natures and to help us recognize what God is asking of us at each moment. On our own, our suffering can be an isolating experience, one that cuts us off from the flow of life. On our own, suffering can lead us to despair. I have been fortunate to have the support of my monastic community and my friends.

"To know that she suffers is a great grief because she is so loved by the Community", Sister Angèle reflected. "Given that so much energy goes to absorbing her physical pain, it's amazing that she continues to give energy to us. The Education Deanery meets every Wednesday morning for Lectio. The actress in her allows her to stand up, but the motivation, what's behind it all, is a love of this life and belief in our Community."

I can agree with Sister Angèle, having witnessed Mother Dolores at deanery meetings and the Lectios. At times I've found her physically exhausted at the end of our working day and thought there was no way she would be able to conduct a Lectio. But there she was, standing up at the blackboard, scribbling notes on the discussion at hand, keeping the meeting alive—getting her laughs. It's as if the pain doesn't exist when she's onstage.

"Mother is very much the conscience and consciousness of the Community", suggests Sister Elizabeth Evans. "I have no memory of Mother as other than with neuropathy, and, partly because I also have a neurological disorder, I've learned that her body is meant to incarnate a truth. It's difficult to witness her pain, but, as an actor, she is projecting her body out so that it can be seen.

"I entered just before Christmas. On Christmas Eve we have a long liturgy. Mother Dolores was one of the acolytes and noticed me wilting. She looked at me, and she winked. That wink—I've never forgotten it—was such a "yes, I see you, we're in this together and we're going to get through it."

Mother Dolores' assistant, Judith Pinco, spent forty years in the music business as a backup singer for several major entertainers and then was a primary school teacher in Los Angeles at the time she read the *O* magazine article on Regina Laudis and felt a pull to visit the abbey.

"At the abbey, I heard that Mother Dolores needed some help with her computer. Well, I'm a Mac freak, so I offered myself. We got along well. Eventually, I moved back to Connecticut and now accompany Mother Dolores to her commitments outside the enclosure. I drive, make arrangements, monitor her meds and nutrition and, on some occasions, become her bodyguard! Young people especially can get quite energetic.

"On a recent speaking engagement at Franciscan University of Steubenville in Ohio, we were heading for an eleven o'clock press conference when she had a fall and was taken on a stretcher to the hospital for observation. As she passed the group of waiting press people, she called out, 'Can you guys hang on until two o'clock? I'll be back!' She was back at two, had the press conference, then attended the dinner where she gave her speech. She went to Mass and chatted for another hour and a half with loads of young people who had waited to talk to her. I don't know where she gets the energy."

Perhaps the most succinct statement of support came from Harry Bernsen, her former agent—the guy who said when she left Hollywood,

"You've just committed suicide." After she was diagnosed with neuropathy, Harry dropped her a ten-word note: "If your feet bother you, I'll come and carry you."

❦

"The prognosis for her at this point", stated Dr. Latov, "is still in question. She is always feeling some level of pain, but even with flare ups, the pain is never as severe as it was initially. Her condition appears to have stabilized; it is somewhat improved and no longer getting worse. Going forward, hopefully her symptoms will recede and she'll be able to function without medication."

I had to learn the deepest law of spiritual life, which is common to all religions but key to Saint Benedict's Rule. I had to surrender. I had to turn over my very body to someone else and let go and watch another do what I thought was mine to do. The submission it takes to open ourselves is terrible, but ultimately the question must be faced: Will I just center on my own crisis or allow my life to be taken beyond that center of pain?

One of the greatest gifts has come through Ginny Ciochetti, a physical therapist who works with me three times a week in our enclosure. After a fall on the stairs one night, I could not walk or lift my foot. Doctors told me I would have to wear a brace on my leg for the rest of my life, but Ginny helped me to push back against that fate. "No," she said, "you need to walk freely, and we will get there." After six months of therapy, I regained the use of that leg. Now Ginny keeps me moving in different ways, giving me exercises to counter the neuropathy pain that would make me an invalid.

If you have a mission to accomplish, you need an openness to a spirit that can take on what you have to do and help you. It is a grace that comes from outside; you don't depend on yourself but on another to bring something through.

When we take the option to seek relationship—to reach out to others— our own sense of purpose is renewed. There is no doubt that suffering teaches us compassion if we let it, and compassion is the deepest source of strength we can possess.

Forty-One

The millennium began another great era of change. When the new archbishop of Hartford, Henry Mansell, introduced himself to the Community, he quoted from Saint Paul: "Trouble produces endurance, endurance produces character, character produces hope, and hope will not disappoint us."

This was an unmistakable message to us that peace was being made. Before he left that day, His Excellency said, "I am truly grateful that this Community is in my diocese, upholding the finest of the traditions of our Church."

We all have grown to love and respect Archbishop Mansell. But I am particularly indebted to him because of his understanding of my own mission as a contemplative with a call also to the people. He grasps the fact that my enclosure cannot be contained by artificial barriers, and I don't know how I could have sustained my many obligations without such a friend.

In January 2001, we in the Community elected Mother David Serna as our new abbess. For many years I had known deep down that Mother David would emerge as the successor to Lady Abbess, and as I reflected on our choice, it seemed to me as if we had just connected the dots on a pattern that had already been drawn. At her abbatial blessing in May, as a very frail Lady Abbess placed a golden cross of timeless Moche design around her neck, Mother David assumed the title of Mother Abbess.

I had been elected first counselor, and then Mother Abbess asked me to be her prioress. The prioress of a monastery has a lot of responsibility. I was very pleased with the title of prioress and had to admit to myself that I took pride in being thus specified as an authority. Maybe that self-satisfaction could be called a normal reaction. Wouldn't anyone admit to it if put to the wall? Okay, I admit it.

—And I don't feel any better for having done so.

With the appointment of Mother Maria Immaculata as subprioress, we moved into a new understanding of our spiritual authority—from monadic to triadic. The idea of the triad was introduced to me in the sixties, when, though only a novice, I worked on our constitution. The triad was the basis of the document we wrote for Rome that was not accepted, but it was out of this endeavor that my sense of what complement life should be—and what Regina Laudis spirituality could be—was born.

After the Education Deanery was formed, I proposed an examination of triadic authority to Lady Abbess, one that I felt could, in every level of monastic process, enable a nun's life to be richer and more fruitful. When there is just one who speaks, little progress happens, but when there are two in a complementary relationship who relate to a third, something creative will always come to pass. It's the basis for family. It's the Christian image of God's own life—Father, Son and Holy Spirit—the Trinity. It seemed to me that Saint Benedict, in his living Rule, gave us a triadic authority pattern—the abbot, the prior and the subprior. The abbot or the abbess need not be a monad who makes decisions in a unilateral way.

Of course, Lady Abbess was the foundress, and she had had a different experience. She recognized the wisdom of Saint Benedict's Rule, and she acknowledged the gift of Father Prokes' vision for the development of corporate life. But there was always a big gap between the conferences with Father and the daily life of the nuns. Our consciousness with Father was building toward another dimension—triadic authority. But in practice, our monastic life never advanced beyond the realm of monadic authority.

I wasn't countering Lady Abbess or who she was in making my suggestion. I was presenting what I thought should be a future orientation for us because we were Americans and because we were not going to be living with our foundress forever. We would be living with a new abbess, one whom we would be choosing.

❦

At 8:45 on the morning of September 11, 2001, the Community of Regina Laudis was in the midst of chanting the Eucharistic Prayer, the focus and the holiest part of the Mass. A half hour later, Mother Debbora Joseph, the portress, answered the phone in her office. Her sister was calling from New York City with the unbelievable news that the World Trade Center towers were on fire. Only a few moments later, that report was amended to disclose that both towers were deliberate targets struck by hijacked airplanes in a coordinated attack on the United States.

Calls poured into the abbey that day, most of them from people requesting prayers for loved ones who were missing. Mother Debbora Joseph began posting the requests on a small bulletin board for the attention of the Community. In a matter of hours, she had to replace that board with a four-foot cardboard substitute to accommodate all the requests. In less than twenty-four hours, over two hundred notes covered the cardboard.

There is always a constant stream of requests for prayers that come into Regina Laudis every day by phone, mail or word of mouth. Our job, if you will, is to be available through prayer, to give support through prayer, to absorb pain through prayer. Each nun can go at any time to pray privately in the chapel, but we see a continuum of work and prayer throughout the day as the ideal. Thus, we come together to pray at the Mass and every Office of the day and Matins at night.

To make sure everyone is informed of the requests, notices are posted and news is shared when the Community gathers in the evening after supper. This is our way of communally directing the intention of our prayer. We do not speak of a specific intention at each Office, but every one of us carries all those requests in her heart and mind. The requests focus and intensify the prayers of the Office.

We are always praying for people hit by disaster. Although we are shocked at a tragedy of such enormous consequence as the 9/11 attacks, in truth we cannot really know the experience. But when there are persons in the Community or people we know outside the monastery who are directly affected, they witness to that suffering in their own bodies. Their bodily presence is a tangible reference that both

404

intensifies our experience of the pain and gives us a personal focus for our prayers.

For over seven years, prior to her entering religious life, Mother Debbora Joseph worked as an investment officer on the ninety-seventh floor of the south tower of the World Trade Center. The second plane struck that tower at the ninety-seventh floor. All day Mother Debbora Joseph took the calls and posted the prayer requests but otherwise remained silent except for one little prayer from the psalms she repeated over and over: "Be still and know that I am God."

But everyone knew that she had once been present in that building. Everyone recognized that she had a commitment to the people lost, just as we knew that Mother Maria had a personal commitment to the victims of the Columbia *space shuttle disaster because of her work at the Center for Naval Analyses, and just as we suffered with Mother Telchilde during the Katrina cataclysm in New Orleans, her hometown.*

Our daily schedule is never interrupted. Work has to be done. Animals have to be fed. We have to stay here and pray and believe that we can help by doing so. It requires discipline and clarity about what your mission is and where your body needs to be, where it can do the most good.

For years, Mother Dolores and I wondered about three large film cases gathering dust in a Corpus Christi cupboard. In 2004 we discovered they contained kinescope reels of the live *Playhouse 90* production she did in 1960. James Douglas found a lab that transferred the kinescope to videotape. It is now part of the abbey library, and it may be the only existing copy of that live performance outside the Museum of Television and Radio in New York City. How she came by it is an absolute mystery to her.

The tape gave me the opportunity to screen To the Sound of Trumpets *for my Community. I was surprised that the intervening four decades hadn't dulled the memory of working with that extraordinary company in such a challenging undertaking. For my part, especially in my present situation of neuropathy, I was totally undone by the fact that I could remember that many lines. In live television, there are no retakes.*

In May of 2004, I accompanied Mother Dolores to Fairfield University in Connecticut, where she received an honorary doctor of law degree at their fifty-fourth commencement exercises.

She and the other honorees would be seated on the stage, but she hadn't been told that she would have to walk around a quad the size of a football field to get to there. She had been free from dependency on a wheelchair for only a few weeks, and I was concerned that she might not make it. But she did, with little sign of discomfort, even waving to the graduates who were calling out congratulations en route.

Her introduction that afternoon, extolling her accomplishments, went down in the Fairfield annals. She stood at the podium and heard a litany of her achievements that ended with these words: "She has the distinction of being the only nun in the world whose resume can be found on the website SwingingChicks.com." When the kids heard that, they burst into a roar. Mother Dolores stood and waited for the enthusiastic reaction to die down. When it finally did, she acknowledged it with a sheepish shrug of her shoulders which ignited another eruption of cheers.

> *—I have never been told what or who was responsible for the Fairfield honor, but it means a lot to me. I have the greatest reverence for education and had always envisaged myself a college graduate. I never will be—but, thanks to Fairfield, like the Scarecrow in* The Wizard of Oz, *I have a diploma.*
>
> *PS: The first letter I received from my bother Martin, after I had been honored, began with "Dear Doctor Mother Sister."*

I learned from my old friend Winnie that Anthony Quinn lay in a Boston hospital bed, close to death. I wanted so much to speak to Tony and to

let him know how much he meant to me, but the only way to contact him at that time was by letter. I wrote to tell him a Mass was being said for him. The letter, which was signed by the entire Community, did get to him in time, and his daughter Katy taped it to the hospital wall. She told us her father saw it and was comforted. I could only hope that it signified the same comfort that his note—the one I found pinned to my dressing room door so long ago—had given to me.

In 2005, we laid Lady Abbess Benedict Duss to rest from the Church of Jesu Fili Mariae. Archbishop Mansell celebrated the traditional monastic liturgy of burial as she lay in the cedar coffin that Sister Alma had made—with a replica of the Third Army star, which she had kept close to her heart in life, on its cover.

Throughout the day, a single thought recurred. During my entire formation, even when I was so outspoken and would challenge things that I did not think were correct, Lady Abbess had accepted my challenges. There had always been respect between us. She was the one who made it possible for me to stay.

On the day I visited the Neuropathy Association Bulletin Board on the Internet, I took another spiritual leap. There, I was stunned to see, were numberless accounts of fellow sufferers, many in far worse straits than I, which now called me personally into a new community, one that was almost unknown.

Although neuropathy had been around always, it needed to be better known. Most of what we know about diseases reaches us because somebody is trying to do something about them. Traditionally, that has come from hospitals and universities. But patients with neuropathy do not get hospitalized frequently; they are seen as outpatients. Universities are involved with research, but they had not done much research into neuropathy. The disease really had no constituency to spread the word.

That is, until the formation of the Neuropathy Association in 1995 by patients with the disease who met during their treatments in a doctor's office. Realizing how much they learned from listening to each other,

407

they decided to form an organization to provide patient support and education and to promote research.

What distinguishes the Neuropathy Association from other organizations of this sort is the fact that many of these were started by people who had the means to help them. The March of Dimes, for example, started with President Franklin Roosevelt, who put the US Post Office at its service. The Neuropathy Association started with a group of ordinary, not wealthy, people who put their time and skills together and made use of the Internet to promote the organization. It's truly a grassroots outfit.

Ten years after its founding, the association decided it was long past time to establish a neuropathy awareness program with a fund-raising dinner—albeit it a modest one—at Manhattan's Le Cirque restaurant, formerly the personal residence of New York's Cardinal Francis Spellman. It was a sold-out event for only 150 guests and appropriately named "An Intimate Evening".

Dr. Latov told Mother Dolores the association would honor key individuals who had supported the organization's efforts, and he wanted to add her name to the list of those recognized for helping to focus attention on this disease—of course, pending permission for her participation.

"At that time," Mother Abbess recalled, "we got only so many permissions a month to leave the enclosure, so this was something I had to weigh. The association didn't have a big funding operation, and if her participation could help, well, I thought she should go. If she had to go to one dinner a year, that wasn't so bad."

Permission to attend the benefit was granted. It was only the second time since her entrance forty-one years earlier that Mother Dolores was outside the enclosure for other than for medical reasons. Coincidentally, the benefit was held on her sixty-sixth birthday.

Maria Janis organized the program, pressing her husband, Byron, into dual-piano service with the entertainer Bobby Short, offering Patricia Neal in a dramatic reading and Tammy Grimes, the original Unsinkable Molly Brown, in a rousing reprise of that show's signature tune, "I Ain't Down Yet". The honorary chairperson for the event was another friend of Mother Dolores—Mrs. Bob Hope. "An Intimate Evening" raised over $180,000 for the association and achieved its goal of increasing awareness on behalf of its members.

Among the special guests that evening was a big surprise for Mother Dolores. During the pre-dinner reception, Brad Dillman, her costar in *Francis of Assisi*, walked into the room. Brad had secretly flown from Santa Barbara just to attend the event. He flew back home on the red-eye that same night.

The two friends had not seen each other since 1961. It was one of those movie-reunion moments: the leading man slowly making his way through the crowd, the leading lady rising, waiting—the embrace, the tears.

> —*I could hardly believe that Brad had come all that way just to see me. We had last been in touch when his wife, Suzy Parker, had died, just the year before. I knew Brad. Under his smiles and hugs, I saw a man who still felt the loss of the woman he greatly loved.*

Shortly after that evening, Dr. Latov spoke to me about his search for someone to represent the group—perhaps from the entertainment world who could do for neuropathy what Michael J. Fox was doing for Parkinson's disease. I told him I would investigate possibilities for him. I had been in casual contact with Gregory Peck, who also suffered from neuropathy, and Andy Griffith, because he had Guillain-Barré syndrome, another autoimmune condition. I checked with both, but neither was able to take on the commitment.

Dr. Latov then asked if it might be possible for me to undertake the role of spokesperson. It would be the first time a member of the Community would be allied with a secular group, and it would make demands on my time that were not centered within the enclosure. It could, in fact, take me out of the enclosure for personal appearances. The ultimate decision would be Mother Abbess'.

"The enclosure is what caused an obstacle, nothing else", Mother Abbess said. "Mother Dolores had given interviews for the *Women in Chant* CDs, but they were all conducted at the abbey; they didn't require going out of the enclosure. Initially, that problem was solved when Bobby Short, another neuropathy sufferer, agreed to partner with Mother, taking on the 'out' part. Mother, then, could do the 'in'."

I had long admired Bobby Short's talent but had gotten to know him as a friend because we often took our infusions at the same time and chatted during the procedure. Sharing the duty of speaking for the association with Bobby was an honor, albeit of short duration. Tragically, that marvel of a gentleman died just months later.

"Still, what Mother was asked to do", stressed Mother Abbess, "was a mission. She was being helped by the treatment, and there was a specific need. The thing is, I trust Dr. Latov. He really reverences Mother. If the mission takes her out of the enclosure, so be it. I gave my consent."

My appointment as spokesperson was announced during the first official Neuropathy Week, and I was immediately plunged into a media tour with seventeen reporters by way of back-to-back interviews via satellite feed from a studio in New York City. I began telephone and in-person interviews conducted at the abbey and made appearances on Catholic TV programs, on which questions from viewers often concerned neuropathy. Personal correspondence jumped in bulk with the announcement of my connection to the association.

Elaine Williams, Mother Dolores' secretary, took on the extra responsibility of writing the replies. "Questions regarding Mother Dolores' treatment", she said, "are predominant in the mail we receive because of shared pain and suffering. In the approximately 4,500 letters that have been given to me to date, there is a recurrent theme—expressed or implied—that Mother has become a source of hope and inspiration. Our responses are standard language, but there's a personal touch always."

I tell the people who write not to suffer alone with the illness, but to reach out to others, share personal experiences. There are many regional neuropathy groups forming across the country. These can serve as a source of strength and reassurance for all of us and are vital if we are to inform the vast public about this illness—as well as the medical community, which will lead to greater professional understanding and more effective treatments.

I do believe that, whatever the medium is, the connection to people has to come down to a living person. Some one *has to embody the realities, or it doesn't mean as much. I address what neuropathy sufferers experience not as a medical problem but as a spiritual reality of engagement with death. Because neuropathy cannot be cured, it goes with you to the end, and one has to come to grips with that struggle.*

Perhaps I, as a woman, can wrap the realities in a symbol of feminine truth, which has to do with what people think of when they think of our Lady or the meaning of motherhood. This community has given me a new purpose: a mission to be a spiritual mother; and in that experience I often feel another spirit moving me.

—Are you saying God is present?

Constantly.

In the spring of 2006, the Neuropathy Association was invited to testify before the House of Representatives' Labor, Health and Human Services Appropriations Subcommittee in Washington, DC, to address why there should be an increase in funding for research into the causes, treatments and cure of neuropathy. It was the first time the Neuropathy Association and its twenty million neuropathy sufferers were invited to give witness on Capitol Hill. Following on the heels of the testimony would be the third Neuropathy Association benefit, to be held in Los Angeles.

Because Mother's congressional appearance would be covered by the *CBS Sunday Morning* news show, we rehearsed her testimony in advance of the trip to Washington, which was made in the company of Sister Angèle and the association's Tina Tockarshewsky.

A luncheon meeting prior to her appearance on Capitol Hill was held at the offices of the association's lobbyist, where her eight-minute testimony was edited to conform to the enforced four-minute limit allotted the speakers.

It was interesting to watch her in this situation—a rehearsal for a professional appearance—and I was tickled to hear her say, when the final timing of the speech came down to a still-fat six minutes, "I could pick up the pace a bit." But no one seemed concerned, and I wondered out loud if anyone on the committee would really tell a nun to shut up.

Only then, as we packed up for our walk to the Rayburn Building, did a group of junior lobbyists come into the room to meet Mother Dolores and—I'm not kidding—get her autograph. She seemed genuinely surprised, then opened her briefcase and took out a handful of five-by-seven glossies—already signed and carefully packed. What an amazing coincidence!

— Well, you can take the girl out of Hollywood . . .

The committee room in the Rayburn Building looked like a movie set—cables on the floor, a Betacam set up and a sound man in the corner—not to mention the few dozen "extras", playing concerned citizens, seated in the audience. In that setting, all she needed was a canvas-backed chair with her name on it.

The hearing was delayed while the Appropriations Subcommittee members voted on legislation to support grants and loans to college students. This process taking place in the House of Representatives was televised in our room (the measure was approved). When the committee convened, the slightly harried chairwoman warned that the delay would cause strict adherence to the time limit. I worried that might throw Mother a bit and, in fact, the pages she held when she gave her testimony were fluttering.

But the lady was sensational. The picked-up pace added to the persuasive impact of her message; though she ran two and a half minutes over the limit, they didn't bump her.

— Our efforts did not result in an increase of government funding, which disappointed me. However, our allocation was not reduced either, as it was for many organizations at that time. Still, Washington gave me a breathtaking curtain call. The

412

"Miss Dolores" shortly after entrance into the monastery. I'm wearing the blue denim work habit Reverend Mother Benedict designed in the manner of the typical outfits of the local workers.

At my Clothing on June 29, 1964, when I received the name Sister Judith. Maria Cooper and Jan Shepard were my godmothers. My friend Father Salazar came from Los Angeles to lead the procession to the chapel. I was uncomfortable wearing a wedding dress, which was the custom then, because I felt it was not appropriate to the step I was taking; it was premature. It was the last time the traditional wedding dress was worn in the Clothing ceremony at Regina Laudis.

In 1980, walking with Lady Abbess on the hill that would become the site of our cemetery

With Father Mike Doody, whose counsel I sought often. Doesn't he look like he could be in a John Ford movie?

My brother Martin brought his daughter Dolores, who is my namesake, to meet me.

Maria Cooper visited frequently, wrote almost daily in the early years. She was a great help. I looked upon her as a true sister.

Sister Ozanne spends most days up in the tree tops. With her special work habit, she could easily be taken for Peter Pan.

We needed signs to mark the abbey property, and nobody wanted to put up something that said, "Keep Out". Our signs were designed to be beautiful, while at the same time a gentle deterrent to trespassing.

The number of ways Brother Iain Highet has served the Community would be difficult to enumerate. For starters, he worked on the ponds and streams, landscaped vulnerable places against erosion, took care of the beef herd and got the hay in twice a year. He led us on walks (here with Mother Jadwiga, Sister Maria Evangelista, Mother Dorcas and Mother Cecilia) to survey our land.

The Community working alongside Father Prokes preparing the land for building Robert Leather Road

Below Middle: The Community and oblates spent years digging rocks on our land to build the dovecot.

Lady Abbess (far right) and other members of the community take down a tree to clear the land for the building of our new church.

We raise our own food at Regina Laudis. Here the Community is planting our potato crop.

Above: Mother Stephen aboard her tractor

―――――

Left: Hard hats are as routine on our property as veils. Sisters Esther, Ozanne and Alma at the end of a day of chain sawing, chipping and brush cutting.

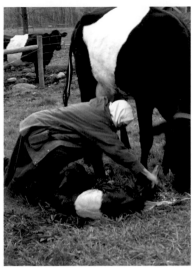

Mother Debbora Joseph gathering wood from trees the nuns have felled to load into the chipper— a machine that chops branches into mulch

Mother Telchilde has assisted in the calving process over seventy times; here she helped Maya in the birth of Angelique.

Mother Perpetua, our master studio potter, at her wheel

Mother Augusta and Brother David Aeschliman could be playing "Catch"!

Many visitors to the abbey join us in our work. Here Matt Mitler's theater group Dzieci works side by side with the Community on haying day.

The 1970 ceremony for my Consecration was held in the the chapel I saw on my first visit to Regina Laudis, and despite the cold, wet weather outside, it felt warm and even cheery due to the golden yellow panels of glass that dotted the window panes as a welcome. My friend Valerie Imbleau, who had returned to secular life following her departure from the monastery, was now a professional photographer and volunteered to photograph the ceremony. Her photos appeared in Ladies Home Journal *with an article written by Anne M. Wolf, who was the assistant to my Hollywood publicist, Frank Liberman. Continuity there, too.*

At the close of my day-long reunion with Dick in 1979, he asked to take a photo of me. We had only five minutes because the bell for Vespers was ringing, so I met him at the gate.

—The late afternoon was unbelievably gray and gloomy, available light almost nonexistent. Still, I began shooting a 36-exposure roll. I had clicked off a fast thirty five frames when Tarah, an abused runaway Weimaraner who had been adopted by the Community as a pup, came up and put her head in Mother Dolores' lap. I hit the button and our five minutes were up. Back in Los Angeles, the processed roll revealed thirty-five dull, dark and dingy frames. This is the thirty-sixth frame. I sent it to Mother Dolores with a note saying I couldn't believe how lucky we were.

God just came in and hit me with my key light.

The way we were. With Dick during the work on our 1980 film about Regina Laudis. We were sitting in front of the carpentry shop, which served as our editing studio. Mother Mary Aline took the picture. (She liked Dick.)

With Patricia Neal during a rehearsal of Anastasia.

To one master I said, "I'm going", and she said, "Wait." Lady Abbess
taught me the meaning of authority.

To another I said, "I can't stay", and she said, "Yes, you can."
I asked, "Oh I see, you win?" She replied, "No, you win!" Mother David
taught me the meaning of complementarity.

L'Osservatore Romano Photo Service

Lady Abbess had kept letters regarding the founding of Regina Laudis written to her by Pope Paul VI that she wanted to hand-deliver to his successor, John Paul II. I accompanied her to a group papal audience at the Vatican. I so looked forward to meeting this man I admired and with whom I shared the profession of acting.

When the pope entered, he passed slowly through the room, only stopping occasionally to greet someone. When he reached Lady Abbess, he paused for a moment and took the letters she offered, thanked her and gave them to his secretary, then moved on.

I was stunned that he did not give her more time. I thought Lady Abbess' heart would break at that moment. Without thinking, I grabbed her hand and forged ahead in the line and called out loudly, "But, Your Holiness, I am an actress!"

Pope John Paul II stopped in his tracks and turned back to us, allowing Lady Abbess to explain the value of the letters she had given over to his care. His Holiness was gracious and warm in his acceptance and once again turned to leave, giving me just a flash of a rather perplexed smile.

Pursuing a higher education

A trio of nuns found balance between a life of prayer and rigorous science to earn Ph.D.s from UConn

It was not easy for Mother Noëlla, Mother Augusta and Mother Telchilde to attend graduate school while keeping up with their responsibilities at the abbey. I was so pleased that UConn Traditions, *the University of Connecticut's alumni magazine, chose to report their story and make them cover girls as well.*

Bob and Dolores Hope funded the Our Lady of Hope Chapel at the National Shrine of the Immaculate Conception in Washington, DC. Mrs. Hope used some old-fashioned Hollywood PR to get me invited to the dedication.

The Story of Noah, *a medieval mystery play that traces its origins to a Benedictine abbey in Chester, England, was presented by oblates much the way it was performed in the Middle Ages, outside, in front of the sheep barn.*

Our first theater, a tent we named the Unicorn, was a step above the sheep barn but a long way from what I envisioned.

Our permanent theater, The Gary–The Olivia, was made possible and named by Patricia Neal. (A neighbor, Paul Newman, donated the roof.)

Dawn and James Douglas in
A Caprice, *the first full production
presented at our annual fair by
our fledgling theater group, the
Act Association*

A scene from The Miracle Worker.
*Melora Mennesson played Annie
Sullivan, and Helen Gilbert, the
daughter of core oblates Jim and
Joan Gilbert, played the youthful
Helen Keller. Jim and Joan had,
in fact, named their daughter after
Helen Keller.*

*With our 1999 presentation, we had our first blockbuster in terms of dona-
tions. It was* Love Letters, *the A. R. Gurney play that was a finalist for a
Pulitzer Prize. With only three performances, we made over ten thousand
dollars! We never made anywhere close to that on any other production.
The reasons it was standing room only were Patricia Neal and James
Douglas.*

Nine nuns who after their Final Vows had waited seven years to participate in the ceremony for the Consecration of a Virgin, were finally consecrated in the new Church of Jesu Fili Mariae in the summer of 1998.

Tom Pomposello's vision for our first Women in Chant *recording was fulfilled. Our new church was transformed into a recording studio, and the acoustics were wonderful. I've never heard our voices sound better.*

*Recording sessions were joyous. But tragi-
cally, we lost Tom before the second CD was
recorded and Dr. Theodore Marier before the
third. Blessed we are that Mother Abbess,
a true disciple of Dr. Marier, became our
conductor.*

I am recording a special contribution for the second Women in Chant, Recordare, *composed by our Mother Lucia.*

Mother Abbess and I listen to a playback with Travis Pomposello, who took over the producing chores for his late father.

L'Osservatore Romano Photo Service

During our disappointing trip to Rome in 1992, Mother David and I were taken to Saint Peter's Basilica to hear the Rosary led by Pope John Paul II. Afterward we had the opportunity to exchange a few words with His Holiness. He asked where we were from, and when we told him Regina Laudis, he gave his blessing to the abbey. It was a comforting moment.

The abbatial blessing of Mother Abbess David Serna was one of the happiest days of my life. She is standing on a Peruvian rug in tribute to her father.

Richard DeNeut

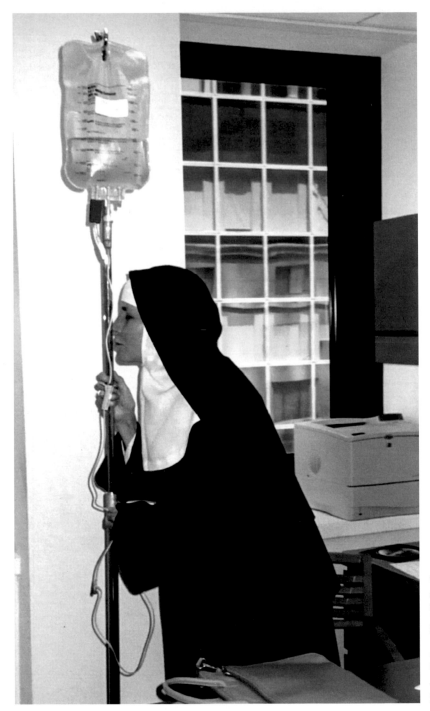

The dark night of the soul began its ebb when I met Dr. Norman Latov and started his intravenous treatments.

At the first Neuropathy Association benefit in New York with Brad Dillman, Maria Cooper Janis, Byron Janis and Bobby Short

In my new capacity as spokesperson for the Neuropathy Association I made what would be my first public appearance in forty years to testify before the House of Representatives' Labor, Health and Human Services Appropriations Subcommittee in Washington, DC. Sister Angèle, Tina Tockarshewsky and Dick made up my rooting section.

At the "Hollywood Homecoming" benefit I got a major surprise. Loyola Marymount University President Father Robert Lawton and Vice Chancellor Father Albert Koppes presented me with an honorary doctorate in fine arts.

As this was my first trip back to California since I left to enter Regina Laudis in 1963, the reunions were emotional. Here sharing time with Dolores Hope, my Malden family, and Don Robinson.

Fiddler on the Roof *with Tom Camm (who was a marvelous Tevya), Sarah Robards and Molly Shields*

Our theater's stability is what has allowed it to grow and change from a few wet actors in a tent to a repertory with a high level of professionalism. Since 2007, it has been under the supervision of Tom and Sally Camm, whose association with the abbey theater began over twenty years ago. The Gary-The Olivia Performing Arts Center has emerged with a mission to present and foster excellence in the performing arts through theatrical productions and workshops as an expression of Benedictine development of culture through the ages.

Rob Iulo and Adrienne Camm sing the "Tonight" duet in our production of West Side Story.

I usually can be coaxed up on stage on opening nights (or afternoons as the case may be.) It's the fire horse in me. Here Sally Camm and I hold our flowers while Tom Camm addresses the audience and cast of West Side Story.

We were fortunate to have Celeste Holm visit us for opening night of Oklahoma! *Celeste, a long-time friend of the abbey, played Ado Annie in the original Broadway production. The lady stayed long after the curtain call to talk with the cast.*

Patricia Neal, here with Mothers Lioba, Cecilia, Daniel and Jadwiga on their Consecration day, became an important part of our lives at Regina Laudis. She was the earth mother—strong, caring, honest, thoughtful, demanding—a friend for life.

Mezzo-soprano Frederica von Stade, a close friend and former client of Mother Angèle, sang a beautiful concert for the Community before the ceremony marking the final profession of Mother in April 2012.

Vanessa Redgrave had asked if she might visit the abbey one day and perhaps read a little poetry for the Community. When she came she was even more generous. She brought her sister, Lynn, and brother, Corin, who read with her.

In 2011, Home Box Office produced a documentary on my life that was nominated for an Academy Award in the Best Documentary, Short Subject category. I was invited to attend the Oscar presentations with the director and the producer of the film, Rebecca Cammisa and Julie Anderson. It was my third time on the red carpet but the first time I didn't worry about what to wear.

I wanted so much to share Granny's startling silk tie jacket, but the old photos had long since faded too badly to use. The Community set up a Hollywood-style photo op with novices Sister Judith, Sister Maria Evangelista and Sister John Mary so that Granny's gift can be seen in all its glory. (Maybe I should have worn it to the Oscars.)

In 2012, Mother Abbess celebrated her Golden Jubilee (fifty years since her First Vows). Archbishop Mansell was among the guests.

Hatsume Sato is a devoted Catholic woman who for many years has been helping people in need in the house she built in Aomori, Japan. She dreamed of hanging a bell in that place of refuge, and we gave her one that hung above our carpentry shop.

With my friend Toby in Corpus Christi

Corpus Christi is known as a "grandmother room"—a place where every-thing lost is found. And that's mostly true. I have a reputation for keeping everything. If something is misplaced, it usually turns up in Corpus Christi. It is a place that holds much of the history of Regina Laudis and many trea-sured memories for me.

With Dick working on the memoir

With Deacon Iain Highet at his Mass of Ordination to the Diaconate on December 4, 2010 at the Cathedral of St. Joseph in Hartford, CT. Priestly ordination followed in May 2011.

Mother Placid, my mentor and first friend at Regina Laudis, died on September 27, 2012. Her great gift was one of enabling a young person to make the leap from familial home to monastic home and hearth. She did this for every member of the Closed Community. People from far and wide, in their requests to visit, would ask to see Mother Placid. I knew why. She offered.

After years of projecting to build a new monastic complex on the hill, we have shifted our attention to renovating the original factory building where Mother Benedict and Mother Mary Aline had established the foundation in 1948. (Above, Mother Anselm with the contractor, Mr. Walter Duda.)

The New Horizons Renovation Project has unified the entire Community behind a fresh vision for the future, one that immediately addresses our needs for greater accessibility for the elderly, greater fire safety and more space for the new vocations we are so blessed to have. The new generation is helping us redesign the space without dramatically expanding the building's structural footprint. (Below, Mr. Chris Decaro, project manager for Verdi Construction, with left to right, Stephanie Cassidy, me, Mother Cecilia, Mother Lucia, and Sister Maria Evangelista.)

city presented the most spectacular burst of cherry blossoms in twenty years, and we were there on the peak day of its splendor.

❦

Early the next morning we departed Washington for the West Coast to attend the Neuropathy Association benefit, which was being touted as Mother Dolores' "Hollywood Homecoming".

Within my mission of service to the neuropathy community, I was reunited with my Hollywood life. As soon as we turned into the driveway of the Beverly Wilshire Hotel, I recognized the side street as one I used to ride my bicycle on.

I believe we are all meant to return to one another; to return in the center of truth that is God, who is Love. No one can ever leave behind what he loves, and I did love Hollywood, right down to Mr. Westmore's last powder puff and Nellie Manley's last hairpin. I found God in the Industry—as I have found the Industry in God.

It was a week of continuity of relationship. Maria kicked off the festivities with a tea at her former home in Bel Air, which the current owners graciously loaned us. Just being where I had spent so many happy times with the Cooper family brought tears to my eyes. My own family was represented by my cousin Ellisa Lanza Bregman, Mom's sister Dariel Pittman Carter, Uncle Bernie Gordon and Daddy's widow Liliana, who had become a good friend over the years. My ever-loyal Winnie came from Florida with her husband Carl. Paramount's A.C. Lyles reminded me of his nickname for me at the studio—Miss Ponytail—as he reaffirmed his support of my life decision. Sheila McGuire brought her daughter, Katie; she looked so much like my younger self that I could have been peering into a mirror of long ago.

For the first time since I had held her in my arms at her christening, I saw my goddaughter, Gigi Perreau's daughter Gina. I spoke with an old friend, Bob Thomas of Associated Press, just as I had at my last interview before I left Hollywood to enter religious life; at that moment, it didn't seem as if much time had passed.

413

Mother Dolores barely sat down for a minute during the entire afternoon, preferring to "work the room". She stood beside a piano with Hollywood friends for a lengthy sing-along of pop songs of the forties and fifties. If I hadn't physically sat her down on a sofa, she might be there yet.

"Sunday", Don Robinson said, "was reserved for me. We went to Mass at the Church of the Good Shepherd, which had been our parish, to lunch at the Polo Lounge at the Beverly Hills Hotel, as we had done so often, and then visited my sister, Kathi, and her husband, Don Koll, who had had a major stroke a year earlier that left him completely paralyzed, with no power of speech. Dolores had never met Don, but the connection between them was amazing. To watch him communicate with her with only his eyes made the day beautiful."

Sunday afternoon was spent at the Whitefire Theatre in Sherman Oaks, just blocks away from the house on Hazeltine Avenue. The occasion was a performance of a one-woman show that Mariette Hartley had written and was appearing in. Mariette, who forty-four years before was to have appeared in *Come Fly with Me*, had not seen Mother Dolores since 1992, when she visited Regina Laudis with a problem.

Many years before, her father had committed suicide, and the pain of keeping this hidden had traumatized her. When she appeared in a television drama that dealt with a suicide in a family, Mariette heard from many others who were trying to cope with this kind of loss, and she agreed to speak at a single meeting of people who had lost loved ones to suicide.

"But when I was asked to speak on a regular basis at meetings across the country," Mariette said, "I was afraid I couldn't face that journey back into hell over and over." She shared this fear with Mother Dolores, who told her, "There is an agony in going into those places, but I have learned in my years of contemplation that one's deepest wounds, integrated, become one's greatest power. You have to speak about it. It is your mission."

"I speak to groups all over the country now for the American Society for the Prevention of Suicide," Mariette said, "and there is much healing in those rooms."

The title of Mariette's one-woman play, written as a debt of gratitude, is *If You Get to Bethlehem, You've Gone Too Far*. The performance was also a gathering of old friends—a former college beau, Don Eitner, who directed the show; Marsha Hunt; Carol Soskin; Karen Cadle, producer of Mother Dolores' first interview as a nun, "Conversations with God"; and Judy Lewis.

Dolores Hart and Judy Lewis were both young actresses when they met in 1960. Judy had grown up believing she was adopted by Loretta Young but, in truth, was her biological daughter. In 1935, Loretta had starred with Clark Gable in the movie *Call of the Wild*. She and Gable had an affair, and, when she became pregnant, they could not marry because Gable was already married. Abortion, for the Catholic actress, was never a consideration. Instead, she went to Europe, and when she returned home with Judy, identified her as adopted. Loretta soon wed businessman/producer Tom Lewis, and Judy was given his name. She learned of her true parentage twenty years later.

In early 1990, rumors that Judy was writing a book that would reveal her parentage reached Loretta's ears and caused a long estrangement between the two. In a last-ditch effort to end the estrangement, Judy got in touch with Mother Dolores and was invited to the abbey.

"I had done all I could to reconnect with my mother and had given up hope", Judy said. "I needed Mother Dolores' prayers. Not long afterward, I received a letter from my mother that began 'Would you like to spend Christmas with me?'"

Unbeknown to Judy, Loretta Young had remained in contact with Mother Dolores through the years and had written during this same period asking prayers for the same thing. Judy first learned of this at the time of her interview for this book.

The "Hollywood Homecoming" banquet was a joyful experience, a time of reclaiming friends, among them two wonderful surprises: Sister Dorothy Bartels, who was, before Vatican II, Mother Anthony, my favorite teacher at Corvallis; and Ralph Leo, who was a member of the Paramount production crew on the movies I made there.

415

Brad Dillman and Mariette Hartley shared emcee duties, and among the kind people who spoke kind words were Lois Nettleton, Carol Burnett, Patricia Neal, Paula Prentiss and Richard Benjamin, Variety's *venerable Army Archerd, AJ Carothers, Sheila Hart McGuire, Jan Shepherd, Valerie Allen and Earl Holliman, who escorted me to the podium just as he had escorted Dolores Hart to the Deb Star Ball in 1957.*

I was at ease because I felt comfortably nourished by my three communities—my Hollywood comrades and colleagues, my monastic community in the person of Sister Angèle and the community of neuropathy sufferers represented by Dr. Latov and Tina Tockarshewsky—all together in that one room on that one night. In a movie, it would have been the "Carnegie Hall fadeout".

At the end of her speech, Mother Dolores had a really big surprise in store. Loyola Marymount University president Father Robert Lawton and vice chancellor Father Albert Koppes presented her with an honorary doctorate in fine arts, which she received with open, childlike happiness, sharing with the audience the time she skipped a final exam at Marymount to go to the audition at Paramount Studios, which ultimately launched her Hollywood film career and resulted in her failing the course. Mother slyly suggested that with the honorary degree "the Lord has the last laugh."

The next morning, Tina, Maria, Sister Angèle and I were taken to Palm Springs to visit Dolores Hope, who was certainly a force to be reckoned with. At that time, she was ninety-seven years old and thriving—beautiful, intelligent, aware, deeply Catholic. The house she had shared with Bob was fascinating architecturally, reminiscent, I thought, of our chapter house, but with a huge window in the middle of the roof. From all angles, the sky and mountains were visible inside the building; outside, there were secluded areas in which to rest, to dine and, for Mrs. Hope, to pray.

We had a wonderful lunch during which our hostess requested that Sister Angèle and I sing one of our prayers. We agreed that the Suscipe—I think it is Psalm 118—would be appropriate. It is short and sung three times as instructed by Saint Benedict in his Holy Rule. It is very moving and haunting because it is the prayer we say after we have signed our

416

vows. It is a shorthand way of referring to the moment of complete self-gift to God. "Receive me, O Lord, according to Your word, and I shall live; and I will not be disappointed in my expectations."

We drove back from sunny Palm Springs into rainy Los Angeles, the trip taking much longer than we had imagined. As Dick was at the hotel waiting, we left immediately for a high point of the trip: dinner with the Maldens—Karl and Mona and their daughter Mila.

That evening was, perhaps, the most emotional for me. I could see that Karl was noticeably moved, too. We sat with heads together the entire evening, and the years melted away.

Earlier in 2006, Karl had been presented with a medal from the government of Serbia, his native country (Karl's real name was Mladen Sekulovich). The medal—called the White Angel—was given in recognition of his years of artistic merit and for bringing honor to his birthplace. Karl had had a copy of the medal made, which he gave to me that night. I treasure it.

Faithful Brother Iain met our return flight at JFK. His broad smile not only refreshed two tired sisters but seemed to bring all of the Community there with him. Two hours later, we arrived just after Compline, at the lower monastery door and found the entire Community gathered to greet us. At that moment, I knew this was the true homecoming.

"We always do that when someone comes home", said Mother Abbess. "There's a tradition in Benedictine communities to greet the wayfarer by singing the Benedictus and offering the Kiss of Peace. It's not a big thing, and we don't linger. The travelers are usually very tired. Mother Dolores looked completely exhausted, so we hustled her off to bed."

The basket on the door of her cell was bursting with notes from individual sisters, each eager to meet with the prioress as soon as possible. She couldn't resist reaching in and taking one of them. She sat on her cot and read its contents, then placed it aside and brought the whole basket into her cell. For the next hour or so, light could be seen peeking from under her door.

Forty-Two

During my reunion with Mother Dolores in 1979, following my visit with a dying friend in Louisiana, Mother took my hand and said, "Your friend continues through our work—Benedictine continuity." It was a nice thought. I would come to know that it is much more than that to Mother Dolores.

In medieval times, when physical life itself was very uncertain, villages were prey to bandits, attacks by enemies, famines and numberless endangerments. Other Catholic orders moved about, but Benedictines stayed in one place. The stability of a monastery became a physical refuge for people. Thus, fear and anxiety gave way to trust in the continuity of monastic life.

That same gift of stability operates on another level. By staying in one place, we are a center for constancy. No matter who they are or where they come from, the people who are attracted to Regina Laudis can find a way to connect with us because we believe everything is related in God. We are all members of His Body.

Put very simply, we have the perspective of an old tree growing to great heights in one place for a long, long time. From the spread of its roots below, the Community knows what's under the soil, and in its sturdy branches it makes room for the many creatures that come and go.

At the center of our stability is the Eucharist. The sacrament I received as a child buried within me the comfort of continuity through the Body of Christ. God assured this little girl that the sacramental life of His Son would embrace the goodness in her and pass on through her the stability of His love. This daily Communion created in me a vision of purpose through all the situations and relationships of my life, and when this became relevant, I undertook to live as a loving person and to open my heart to those in need of me.

❦

The continuity of the Body of Christ reveals itself to me every time we face the death of an older member of the Community and wonder how we will possibly get along without her.

Throughout her life at Regina Laudis, Mother Jerome was sought out by many people for her wisdom and faith. With her worldly background, she was a magnet for the young and the old alike. For me, she was a kind of sorority soul sister. We spoke a language that few others understood because our lives had been opened to similar places and people, to adventures that were not common memories in the monastery. When I knew this aristocratic and cultured woman was going to die, I felt bereft for the monastery, losing its tie to her world.

Likewise, when my old nemesis Mother Stephen lay dying and Mother Abbess and I kept watch at her bedside, I wondered how this woman's boots could ever be filled.

"Suddenly," remembered Mother Abbess, "Mother Dolores took Mother Stephen's hand and, with such force and conviction, said, 'Mother, your mission is to help us keep our land. Send us women who will keep the land.' Mother Stephen did hear her words because she squeezed Mother Dolores' hand in accord."

> *—I figured I should seize the moment to give Mother Stephen a mission for her future life. If we don't stay devoted to the land, giving thought to its future, someone will covet it. I'm always asking young members of the Community how they picture the land thirty years from now. I need to know from those younger women how they will manage the property when we are not here.*

Over the years, I've felt not a little relief when a younger member of the Community begins to assume leadership in a region that appeared imperiled. Today there are two postulants and a novice, all products of our intern program, who seem cut from the same materials as Mother Stephen and Mother Jerome.

Laura Adshead, from New Zealand, holds an Oxford degree in classics and language. With this and her further study of international politics in Paris, she might have had a career in affairs of state. Instead she spent a good portion of her life in the fast lanes of advertising and marketing in London and New York. Her background, graceful bearing and sophistication immediately put me in mind of Mother Jerome.

—Laura is now Sister John Mary, and I'm still reminded of Mother Jerome whenever I see her in Lady Abbess' rose garden. She and Brother Anthony Castigliego have constructed a gazebo there as a place for meditation. Mother Jerome, whose cell overlooked that garden, would be pleased.

Two postulants—Stephanie Cassidy and Katie Healy—who entered in 2011 seem to be a continuation of Mother Stephen. Both women have strong faith. Stephanie is an artist, but she is discovering something here related to her Native American heritage: communication with the land and with the herd.

—She makes a stunning cowhand.

Katie Healy writes songs in the Irish tradition. Like Mother Stephen, she has a connection with the land, for her songs come out of what she hears when she listens to it.

—Have you found anyone to continue your nexus?

The hardest thing to access can be one's own continuity, and the closest I've come is to ask, "Do I have any continuity myself?"

I think so. I have a nominee.

Tell me.

Sister Maria Evangelista. I've covered several Education meetings, and from the first one when she fearlessly introduced the subject of poor attendance at Matins, I immediately thought of you charging down the third-floor hallway.

In 1995, when she was Kathy Fernandez—whose parents were immigrants from the Dominican Republic—she went with high school friends to hear Pope John Paul II say Mass at Aqueduct Racetrack in Brooklyn, and by chance she met Sister Cecilia, who invited her to visit Regina

Laudis "sometime". On the subway home that day, Kathy wrote a letter asking for permission to visit.

She revisited the abbey frequently throughout her high school and college years. After earning a BA in women's studies and religious studies from Hobart College in upstate New York, she took time out to study in India, and when she returned she resumed her trips to Regina Laudis, with her absorption of Indian culture prominently displayed by a nose pin. Kathy entered the land program. Shortly after, she became a prepostulant, the first one to chart with Mother Dolores by e-mail.

> *—When she entered in 2006, the nose pin was gone. But since Mother Abbess remarked that we didn't recognize her without it, she put it back. She finds real joy in serving the theater each summer, took responsibility as stage manager, even made it part of her vow of commitment. I'm honored that you think of her as my continuity.*

Another woman who entered around the same time as Sister Maria Evangelista also shares a link with me. Mary Grace Elsen, a divorced mother of two daughters, and, for many years, a financial reporting manager for British Petroleum in Houston, was introduced to Regina Laudis by one of her daughters who was in our intern program. Mary was drawn toward our contemplative life and entered at age 53. She is now Sister Judith, the name I accepted at my Clothing some forty years before.

Judith is the right name for this tiny woman. Like the biblical Judith, she is a fighter with enormous courage to face challenges and has emerged a strong and productive member of the Community, bringing her knowledge of the world of finance as well as an unanticipated talent for bookbinding.

> *—She repaired my antiphonal and made those tear-stained pages a thing of the past.*

A palpable illustration of Regina Laudis continuity began in the fall of 1988, when that young Canadian student, Iain Highet, arrived on our doorstep to join the land program. One year later he entered the Church. Iain went back to Toronto to get a master's in ecology from

York University and secured permission to make our waterways the focus of his thesis, which brought him back to Regina Laudis. After graduation, he again returned to the abbey, living here as an oblate, and, for the next several years, while relating to the Community as Brother Iain, he explored men's Benedictine monasteries to see if the Holy Spirit might open up some path of monastic formation that could lead him to us permanently. He has never given up the hope that a Benedictine brotherhood will exist at Regina Laudis, and last year Anthony Castigliego, a prince of a man who had been my driver for a period, and the Act Association's Kevin McElroy joined Brother Iain; thus, his hope is gathering strength.

When our chaplain of seven years, Father Stephen Concordia, left in 2008 to establish his stability as choirmaster at Saint Vincent College, a Benedictine liberal arts school in Pennsylvania, we entered a period of three years without a permanent chaplain. There were friends such as Father Tucker and Father Douglas Mosey and Father Stan Kennedy who took on responsibility for saying Mass for us as often as they could. Then a new friend, Father Dominic Anaeto from Nigeria, was assigned to us for a year. Mostly, our sacristan Mother Maria got on the telephone each night to beg, borrow or steal a priest willing to pinch-hit on a day-to-day basis. It was all in God's Providence.

In 2009 the most amazing turn of events occurred. Father Vito DeCarolis came to offer Mass one day and saw how badly we needed a priest and how badly Brother Iain wanted to be that priest but had no way to fulfill the call. Father Vito is a friend of Archbishop Mansell— they went to school in Rome together. He spoke to the archbishop, and, before the week was out, the archbishop called Brother Iain to ask him if he wanted to be a priest of the Archdiocese of Hartford. Of course, the answer was a whole-hearted yes—but only if it was possible to serve the diocese by serving Regina Laudis as well.

Thus something entirely new was born through Archbishop Mansell's farsightedness and Brother Iain's willingness to take the risk of giving himself for the life of the Community without knowing exactly where it would lead him. On May 14, 2011, Brother Iain Highet was ordained to the priesthood. On the following morning, Father Iain offered his first

422

Mass at the Church of Jesu Fili Mariae—as our chaplain—giving us once again the comfort of continuity.

Father Iain is a hybrid. As well as being chaplain at Regina Laudis, he has accepted the exhausting burden of two additional parishes within the diocese. Further, he has no guarantee that, when Archbishop Mansell retires, the next archbishop will honor his unique call to serve both the archdiocese and the abbey.

—I pray that it may always be so. It takes courage to live without a safety net.

"Regina Laudis could have remained a French monastery, but it became an American monastery due in no small part to Mother Dolores. She was instrumental in planting the seed of an American spirituality." So said Brother Iain to me a few years ago. I had no idea at the time what he was talking about.

"You have to look back at the old European monasteries," Father Iain explained, "when royalty and nobility came in and brought culture into the cloister. They also ran the monastery. America is not an aristocracy, and Mother Dolores, even as a nun quite young in monastic years, found pathways to change that cultural pattern and take tradition to another level. She had to submit to a European formation that was fifteen hundred years old, so I think it's safe to say that her feet are planted in European past—and Hollywood future.

"There is always a need for spiritual figures who can make a bridge between tradition and innovation. It's difficult for this country to accept a spiritual person who is not known for achievement. She knows what she's representing to people, and it's not the twenty-year-old. I don't know of any women in the American church who have made the crossover from public life to spiritual life as dramatically as Mother Dolores. Young people especially respond to her not only because of her movies but because of what she now represents as an American consecrated virgin.

"She helped to create a new spirituality at Regina Laudis. She is the one who made it possible for a whole other generation to relate to

423

monastic spirituality. I wouldn't be here either. But without the complement of Mother Dolores and Mother Abbess, this new form of spirituality would not have taken root. They have formed Americans into nuns in a way that Lady Abbess could not have done."

"She was the right choice for dean of education", said Mother Abbess. "Mother recognizes people's instinctual feelings—when they are free and when they are locked. I think that when emotions are locked Mother Dolores can't stand it. That's why she grabbed those knitting needles. She knew that nun was livid but her emotions were locked and she couldn't get them out.

"Mother pushed for us to risk revealing how we honestly felt, and this was frightening. We did it so very awkwardly at first."

> —*I was only taking steps to open a gate to human communication again, something that monastic life had somewhere forgotten or cut as a part of purification. At least that was my experience of the nuns who came from Jouarre. Their humanity was there but strangely separate from their religious life. It was Lady Abbess who made room for that humanity by introducing the dimension of education that allows a person who is seeking monastic life to quarrel with the past even while honoring its values. If I have helped bring only one thing to fruition, it is this capacity for, let us say, freedom of speech.*

My part now as the dean of education is to look toward the Community's future, and this takes me even more deeply into Benedictine life.

The younger women (in monastic years) began to feel hampered in the deanery meetings. They had reasonable concerns but not the interior freedom to express them. They did not share the history of the established members; they had had diverse experiences. They felt vulnerable if they happened to be seated next to their formation mother at a meeting, and this restricted their candid responses. There was no out-and-out animosity between the age groups. It was simply a matter of human nature that the older women were more set in their ways and the younger ones felt they would not be understood. Thus the younger women asked if they could form their own deanery, and I told them to go ahead. I meet with each deanery once a week, and my juices are flowing again.

424

"This is what Mother Dolores loves," explained Mother Abbess, "to take on new challenges. It's what she responds to. She has a real reverence and a real tenacity. She doesn't let go of something once she takes it on."

—I once asked Mother Abbess if the two of you ever lock horns, and she grinned. "Oh, much of the time", she said. "I want A-B-C-D. She hates A-B-C-D. Mother said something to me recently on which I have meditated: 'I'm not wrong! I'm different!'"

I am not easily persuaded by "religious" answers, in spite of the fact that I am a Roman Catholic convert and a member of a monastic community. I've found my answers step by step. The act of consecrating my life—body and soul—as a medium for God was a natural extension of my dedication to the media of theater and film as a professional actress. There was no time that I can remember when I didn't want to be an actress, and when I finally did start working in front of the camera, I had the absolute sense of being in a holy place. Holy *means belonging to God.*

It has been said that, through His Incarnation as Christ, God moved into the world as an actor. I believe that. He made things happen through dramatic action, by engaging with people and by forming relationships that became the foundation of the community of the Church.

I would suggest that the theater is the art form that most fully offers us an opportunity to reflect on the Incarnation because it is the presentation of one body to another. I've long believed actors are deeply contemplative by nature. Theirs is a true calling. The fervor that actors bring to the camera lens or to an audience to reveal the passion of a human being is the same intensity that a religious brings to God.

In an actor's life there is room for love for many people, those who surround him in his profession and those he portrays. The consecrated life also means loving many people in an intense and enduring way.

425

To a remarkable degree, our theater has been shaped by traditional Benedictine vows of stability, conversion of life and obedience. As Benedictines we take the vow of conversion of life so that we have the willingness to change and adapt to what God asks of us and the ability to see the operation of grace in the challenges we face. Conversion of life makes stability possible.

Our theater could never have come into being without having at its heart a commitment to stability—people committed to living side by side in one place, on one piece of land. Stability is what allows the theater to grow and change—from being a few wet actors in a tent to a repertory with a high level of professionalism.

The vow of obedience is the one that people seem to have the hardest time with, and yet obedience is basically a simple principle, however hard it may be to submit to at times. Anyone who has been in a play can tell you that to pull it off means that you have to submit to a lot of demands. When everyone working on a play submits to what is needed, something comes to life that is greater than the sum of its parts. What is born is a community of the play, for many of our people the first deep experience of communal life.

"Although enclosed," Mother Abbess said, "Mother Dolores was called to be a public person. In reality, she never stopped being a public person. She has always drawn people to Regina Laudis and opened them to the Community.

"Mother will always have the heart of an actress. That's a place where she is totally alive in spirit."

"Although she is still very much a presence," said Alistair Highet, one of the founding members of the Act Association, "Mother is not able to be around the theater so much now. Mother Angèle is more the foot soldier.

"Mother Dolores will come and watch some of the rehearsals, but her role is more symbolic now." He paused for a moment and smiled. "But she does symbolic very well."

The Benedictine rule that we "receive all visitors as Christ" is for us an obligation to provide hospitality to all who come to us. One of the ways in which we express our hospitality is through the plays that we

426

produce at the abbey. People from all over can come to our land for an afternoon or an evening, sit inside our theater—which is very beautiful on a summer night, with hanging baskets and lanterns lighting the way—and partake for a while of our world and share it with us.

Our theater is a reflection of our spirituality; each play is nurtured within the context of the monastery and informed by the principles that govern our life. There is something of our monastic spirit that goes out through the bodies of the actors and touches our audiences. The place and the time that we spend there—I do think that is holy.

PAX

Acknowledgments

Mother Dolores joins me in acknowledging the generous contributions of so many people. We are grateful to all of you, especially to Mother Abbess David Serna and the hardworking, accomplished women who are the Community of the Abbey of Regina Laudis.

Our deep thanks to Valerie Allen, Winnie Allen, Deborah Curren-Aquino, Phyllis Avery, Tom Ayre, Mother Ruth Barry, Sister Dorothy Bartels, Gail Lammersen Belt, Bill Bergin, Harry Bernsen, Deena Hicks Binon, Dr. Richard N. Biondi, Shirley Hicks Borregaarde, Antoinette Bosco, Jan Shepard Boyle, Ellisa Lanza Bregman, Kelly Briney, Anita Busch, Brother Anthony Castigliego, Karen Cadle, Tom and Sally Camm, Rebecca Cammisa, AJ Carothers, Archbishop William Aquin Carew, Elizabeth Carpenter, "Maria Salome" June Christian, John Clifford, Ned Comstock, Father Stephen Concordia, Mother Therese Critchley, Chris Davis, Bradford Dillman, Mila Malden Doerner, Cort Douglas, James Douglas, Amanda (Mrs. Phillip) Dunne, Bernie Ebbins, Don Eitner, Beverly and Bud Fallon, Anthony Franciosa, Andrew Grosman, Ree Howell, Arlene Howsley Gardner, Phil Gersh, Joan and Jim Gilbert, Globe Photos, Dan Goggin, Bernie Gordon, Martin Gordon, Bert Hicks Jr., John Hicks, Liliana Hicks, Joe Halloran of Caesar's Camera, Mariette Hartley, Earl Holliman, Marsha Hunt, Valerie Imbleau, Asako Ishii, Byron Janis.

Hal Kanter, Vance and Gladys Kincaid, John Spaulding King, Nobuko Kobayashi, Jack Larson, Dr. Norman Latov, Bill Lavelle, Jennifer Lea, Vicki Leaden, Judy Lewis, Frank Liberman, AC Lyles, Laurie and Kate MacMurray, Al Marsello, Brother Kevin McElroy, Sheila Hart McGuire, Melora Mennesson, Philippe Mennesson, Barbara Middleton, Matt Mitler, Patricia Neal, Lois Nettleton, Sheila Nevins, Hugh O'Brian, Dale Olson, Hiroko Onoyama, Helen Patton, Ron Pelletier, Gigi Perreau de Ruelle, Donald Peterson, Judith Pinco, Dariel Pittman, Cordula Polenek, Travis Pomposello, Paula Prentiss, Ray Powers, Robert Rehme, Timothy Ridge, Sarah Robards, Betsy Holton Robinson, Don Robinson, John Rood at

Footprints, Adele Russell, George Shapiro, Janne Shirley, Deanna Smith, Andre Soares, Carol Soskin, Jim Stevens, Bernadette Dolores Stewart, Larry Swindell, Tina Tockarshewsky, Nancy Boyden Talley, Pamela Tiffin, Father Robert Tucker, Allan Weiss, Stuart Whitman, Greg Wright, Suzanne Zada.

With appreciation, the letters of Ina Balin, Joan Crawford, George Cukor, Father Michael Doody, Irene Dunne, Lady Abbess Benedict Duss, Douglas Fairbanks Jr., Harriett Pittman Hicks Gordon, June Haver, Dolores Hope, Bill Knotts, Esther Kude, Ethel Levin, Myrna Loy, Paul Nathan, Tom Pomposello, Father Francis Prokes, SJ, Anthony Quinn, Father Armando Salazar, Gene Smith, Loretta Young.

This ten-year commitment frequently needed a cheerleader, and we had the best—the nonagenarian "It Girl". Thank you, Betty White.

There are several people who have gone the extra mile for us and attention must be paid. Thank you, Father Iain Highet, Mother Irene, Mother Telchilde, Mother Augusta, Mother Rachel, Mother Simonetta, Mother Margaret Georgina, Mother Noëlla, Mother Anastasia, Mother Jerome and Mother Placid. Thank you, John Allegretti, John Aquino, Alistair Highet, Maria Cooper Janis, Merv Kaufman, Karl Malden, Lawrence Schiller.

We are beholden to these ladies for their caring attention that was above and beyond any expectation. Thank you, Elaine Thérèse Williams, who transcribed our 225 tapes (in spite of Toby's recurrent and thoughtless squawking) while dreaming, I imagine, of parrot fricassee. Arms around you, Mother Lucia, my Benedictine interpreter, whose emails always began "I don't know if this will help . . ." It helped.

God bless Susie Grobstein.

Richard DeNeut

INDEX

431

441

446

450

315–16; Shaw Island conflict, 379–80, 382, 383–84
prostration, in Consecration ceremony, 280
Psalm 17, 258, 264
Psalm 47, 199
Psalms 118, 416–17
Psalter, 201
publicity activities, DH's: after *The Plunders* production, 123; after *Francis of Assisi* production, 123; after *Loving You* production, 55–56, photo section #1; for *Come Fly with Me*, 187–88; for *Joan of Lorraine*, photo section #1; for *King Creole*, photo section #1; photos for, xiii–xiv, 69, 96, photo section #1; reporter questions, 167–68; for *Sail a Crooked Ship*, 159
puppet shows, Regina Laudis, 342–43. *See also* theatrical productions, Regina Laudis
Purgatory, 255

Quinn, Anthony, 57–58, 60, 61–62, 64, 75, 213, 406–7, photo section #1
Quinn, Katy, 407

Rachel Morfesi, Mother (Arlene Morfesi), 291, 332, photo section #2
Rainbow Inn restaurant, 34
Randall, Tony, 64
reader duties, DH's, during post-Investiture year, 249
readings, mealtime, 201, 207, 208, 223, 338, 342
Recordare, 376
recreation, scheduled, 208–9
Redford, Robert, 101, 170
Redgrave, Corin, 325, photo section #2
Redgrave, Lynn, 325, photo section #2
Redgrave, Vanessa, 325, photo section #2

Redhead, 100
Rees, Alun, 153
Regina Laudis: abbey designation, 257, 297; chaplain position, 198, 231, 358, 422–23; DH's first visits, 98, 103–7, 109–15, 146–47, 160–61, 169, 174–75; donations to, 117, 142, 305, 328, 363, photo section #2; founding of, 107–9, 112–13; *Lisa* screening, 164–65; oblate experimentation, 286–88; reconstruction process, 231–32; renovations, photo section #2; road problem, 234–35, 256–57, photo section #2; Shaw Island controversy, 305, 377–86; signs for, photo section #2; Vatican II changes, 235–36 *See also specific topics, e.g.,* Benedict *entries*; canonical year, DH's; Education Deanery; Gregorian chant; land stewardship; Prokes, Father Francis Joseph
Regina Laudis, DH's entrance: announcement process, 195; application for, 180–82; archdiocese approval, 189, 191; arrival for, 197–98; ceremony for, 198–202; feelings about, x–xi, 191, 196–97, 201–2; pre-entrance retreats, 183, 191, 192–93; preparations for, 183, 193–95; responses to, 183–84, 197–98, 211–15, 242; secrecy approach, 179–80, 184–91, 193–94. *See also* postulant phase, DH's
Rehearsal Club, 104
Rehme, Robert, 359, 390
religious feelings/faith, DH's: in Boyd conversations, 155, 176; during Broadway production, 96, 98, 103–4; at Chartres Cathedral, 137–38; during childhood, 25–29; in M. Cooper friendship, 124–25; at G. Cooper's funeral, 149; during DeNeut romance, 70–71, 119–21;

451